Dear Norean

A stroll down
Memory lane.

Lorna & Eric

ISBN: 1-4196-4390-8

Editor's note:

I have tried to compile a realistic cross-section of the many contributions to this Memory Book. There is a high proportion of "war stories" which is understandable in view of the fact that many contributors who 'gave their all' during those turbulent years are now the men and women who have the time and technology to share those experiences with us.

There are some extracts from books that have been contributed to this project, which the authors will be publishing in the future, under their own titles, or which have already been published, and have had sections reprinted here, with the kind permission of their authors.

If you wish to 'take issue' with any contributions, please do so with the authors concerned.

If you have a 'counter point of view' on any subject, then you will have the opportunity to express yourself in the sequel.

This book has been produced in as modest a format as possible in order to reduce the publication costs to a minimum.

I would like to thank the contributors for the work they have done to get this project completed.

I also apologise to all those who contributed and who were not included due to lack of space or duplication. To choose which articles to use is rather like judging a baby competition in which there are many beautiful babies, but in the eyes of each mother there is only one winner. Please forgive?

The most important vote of thanks goes to Mr Bill McDonald, without whom this book would have never been realised.

For me it is a bit of "pay back time" to those who risked and lost their lives, or who still bear the scars of battle, so that we can be here today to enjoy these wry nostalgic moments.

We *do* and *will continue* to remember them and the ideals for which they fought.

Chris Higginson

RHODESIAN MEMORIES 1

Here is a collection of stories, poems, anecdotes, and cartoons all with a Rhodesian flavour.

These are stories about Rhodesians and are written by them in many cases.

Each one reflects a facet of life in a country that now no longer exists, except in the memory of those who made it.

They reflect Pride, Humour, Remorse and Melancholy.

Travel with them, back through time, and see who you can remember!

Front cover poem is an extract from "2nd Provocative Verse" by Chris Higginson.

Back cover is a copy of a high quality "Map of Rhodesia" available from Bill McDonald at   braai@shaw.com . Size 31x27 inches (80x70cms).

Information about the Contributing Authors of books, when they have agreed to divulge this information.

Dr. Bob Doy spent almost 15 years in Rhodesia as part of a lifetime in the practice of medicine around the world. His experiences are contained in his book :
A Doctor's Odyssey - Memories of a Guy's Man (ISBN 1-4137-4735-3).

Derek Partridge: International traveller, linguist, "shottist", actor, RAF Officer, MD, Author and Columnist are just a few of his activities. Rhodesians will remember his RTV show "Frankly Partridge". His autobiography will be published soon.

Charlie Warren joined the RLI in 1973. He lived and fought with the regiment until it was disbanded. His book **"At the Going Down of the Sun"** describes his life and those of the men with him through those difficult years. (ISBN 1-4196-4217-0)

Chris Higginson, pilot, ocean sailor, photographer, poet and general dogsbody. Author of **Ist Provocative Verse**, **Reluctant Assassin 1** (ISBN 1-4196-1975-6).

Steve Bailey was born in the UK and came to Rhodesia as a child, went to Courtney Selous and Churchill, then did his National Service in the Rhodesian Air Force. His magnificent wildlife photographs are distributed throughout this book and the link to his web site is **http://www.pbase.com/mashona/my_africa_2**

Ed Goldberg was born in Que Que in 1950 and moved to Canada in1980. He is a pharmacist in Vancouver and has two children – Alon and Talia. His late father, Dr. Isaac Goldberg, was Resident Geologist on the Globe and Phoenix gold mine from 1949 to 1956.

"Pedigree" of **Nigel Rittey**: Raised in the bush. Lived all over the place: joined the RLI at Brady. In 1968, having decided that as he and General Walls had both reached the very peak of their respective military careers, Sergeant Rittey headed for "Civvy Street". He now enjoys model planes, cartooning and doing pencil sketches of aircraft.

Robin Norton has contributed some aviation photographs taken during the early 1970'ies which marked the beginning of his life-long passion with aviation photography. His web site is at **www.a2oxford.info** where his pictures are on display.

Basil O'Connell-Jones goes from a hippie lifestyle into the RLI where he is seriously wounded. His book "Amazing Grace" follows his experiences up to his finding Jesus and a complete turnaround in his life. ISBN 0-9660886-5-4.

S E Aitken-Cade wrote the "Kitchen Kaffir Dictionary" which was published in 1953. He was a master linguist of several African languages and his publication was designed to help new arrivals to Southern Rhodesia learn the basics of KK as a basis for further study of other indigineous languages. (2/6d)

Richard Randall lived in Rhodesia from 1957 – 1982 educated at St. Georges College and University of Rhodesia then joined Internal Affrairs. Presently he lives in France.

Dedicated to all those people,
young and old, black and white,
of Rhodesian or of foreign origin
who "lived the life"
and "walked the walk".

RHODESIAN MEMORIES 1

BY

MANY CONTRIBUTORS

EDITED BY

CHRIS HIGGINSON

PUBLISHED BY ZANJ PRESS
IN ASSOCIATION WITH
BOOKSURGE

SALES ENQUIRIES TO:

BOOKSURGE
To order additional copies, please contact us.
BookSurge, LLC
www.booksurge.com
+ 1-866-308-6235
orders@booksurge.com

or
Bill McDonald at
braai@shaw.com

Extract from '**Last of the Rhodesians' by Karl Greenberg**

Learning Afrikaans

Allan Wilson Technical High School, Salisbury, Rhodesia 1971-72.

My Afrikaans teacher was called Mrs Smuts. Oh my, what a f**king terror! Almost as wide as tall, but built like a Russian kick boxer; grey haired and uglier than a bicycle beaten into the back of a bus, she had a voice like gravel and a hand of steel. 'Sunny boy' me, a sweet faced innocent and extremely unwilling lad of twelve and a half, was getting on her indeterminate mound of tits within seconds. Her acceptance speech for the task ahead would be the start of an eighteen month bitter, and sometimes bloody, campaign. There would be no medals for heroics, but both combatants would emerge psychologically scarred forever.

Her first words to the nervous class were, "I hate boys!"

She turned her ferocious gaze on to every one of us.

"I hate little boys the most!"

She had our full attention.

"If it weren't for the fact that my useless husband doesn't earn enough money, I would not be here at all. I would not be forced to teach little boys Afrikaans. But, that is my job, and if I have to beat it into you, I will."

This was heavy stuff. I began to entertain fears of a second Holocaust; maybe she knew I was a half-fake Jew! (The only half I ever found was my docked dick, but unfortunately that wasn't faked.)

"Time to lighten the scenario", I thought.

I put my hand up.

"Ma'am, why don't you teach at a girls' school then?"

Half the class, the dafter ones, sniggered. The smart ones knew I had signed my own death warrant. Fifteen seconds later I was hauled out of my chair by the hair growing in that excruciatingly tender area next to my left ear.

"And clever little boys like you, I hate most of all!"

The Game was on!

It was a long and tedious war. Every day we were given woordeskat (vocabulary) to learn at home, and every day I didn't bother. Lessons always began with the same routine: a five minute oral test of the previous day's assignment. At first, Ouma Smuts asked random boys for the answers, and beat them with the heavy cane she always carried if they were wrong. It didn't take her long to clock that I flatly refused to learn the shit.

We were given a choice of two foreign languages to learn: Afrikaans or French. French was for 'Morfs' (Gays), the rugby playing macho boys said. Plus 'Afriks' had the advantage it was supposed to be relatively easy to learn. Why didn't they teach us something useful, like Shona, the Black Rhodesian's most spoken language? Then I could tell the Garden-boy to stop taking the piss by pretending he didn't understand English just because I asked him to wash my bicycle. Not as if I would ever try it; my

Father would flay me alive if he caught me fobbing my chores onto our domestics. It would sure come in handy though. I had no intention of going to live in a land that hacks people's heads off with giant weighted triangle razor blades or of living 'Down South' where the Afrikaners still swore revenge against the 'Rooinekke' after losing the Boer war.

I started this war of attrition slowly, achieving sixth from bottom of the class and a result of 29% in my first end of term exam. Beatings were restricted to two cuts of the cane three times a week. I definitely needed to put in some extra effort to enter the bottom five.

I improved my tactics by looking out the window while the mad cow screeched Afrikaans at the front of the class. Six months later I managed fifth from bottom, with 21%.

Meanwhile I took to wearing extra underpants and also allowed my delighted Father to have my hair sheared till not even a koeksister (a sickly sweet delicacy designed to give Afrikaner women large behinds, judging from Mrs. Smuts), would have stuck to it. That would eliminate one of her favourite hair pulling tortures.

Not to be outdone, the Marquis de Sade's Boer counterpart switched tactics too. Beatings were increased to every lesson. I was no longer asked if I had learnt my woordeskat, I simply presented myself and complied with the only word that she had managed to beat into me: the word buig (which means bend)!

'Buig! Buig! Buig!' the mal (mad) thing would scream, then she let rip with the cane. And now, as an added treat, she twisted my ear every time she passed my table and saw me gazing at a blank piece of paper.

I fought back hard. I filled my exercise book with alien emblems, and scattered here and there a few real Afrikaner words I had somehow retained, like pen, which meant pen, or bobbejaan, which meant Mrs Smuts in her hairy wool skirt and jumper. Even she was f*cking shell-shocked when I finally cracked it. Bottom of the class, with 8%! A triumph of gentle mind over violent body.

That was the sign of her uselessness. I was only 10% lower than the class average of 18% and it was then that her crazed mind snapped. When the results came out, she decided on revenge. She couldn't beat me to death in front of the class on my own, so she thought up a very ingenious way to murder me.

"I have decided to call each one of you out to the front of the class in order of your exam results. Each boy's mistakes will be read out, and for every mistake you made you will receive one cut with my cane."

At that point an image leapt into my brain: one of her sporting a small black toothbrush moustache instead of the thin grey one she had cultivated above her sneering mouth. For a few seconds the Afrikaans class became the maths room. I wasn't that good at maths, but I soon added up my total, and I wasn't sure if I could survive 92 cuts.

This was it! The end was nigh. Would they take my dismembered corpse and parade it around on the end of a teacher's cane like pieces of drying biltong down Oom Paul Kruger Street in Bloemfontein to the chorus of 'We are marching to Pretoria'?

She started with her favourites, giving them a light smack on the arse. Full of bullshit this bit, but by the time she had reached those with less than 60% she was in full flow. Norman, my mate, and a big bloke, was wilting after 13 cuts. Then she went on to Johnson, a tough, wiry, farmer's kid. He was a school border and had won the under 14s arm-wrestling competition. At 20 lashes he was crying; she stopped at 26 lashes, when the bell went.

"I'll deal with jou liefde tomorrow," the red-faced, sweating cow hissed at me as I filed out with the rest of my physically and mentally tortured classmates. I wasn't sure what she meant, but I had the feeling there was scant love towards me.

Being of logical nature, I knew it wouldn't actually beat me the next day. There was still half the class to abuse, and even if she speeded up the beatings to 30 a minute she wasn't going to fit me in. Just as a precaution, I wore three pairs of underpants the next day. Afriks was first on the class agenda; if my time had really come, at least I would be shot at dawn under a glorious fresh morning Rhodesian sky, my last breath filling my nostrils with her perspiring odour.

I decided I would refuse to be blindfolded, and I would have my last cigarette. Forget the fact I didn't smoke. Stiff upper lip and squeezed buttocks. Don't fart. Remember the school was named after the leader of the brave pioneer members of the slaughtered Shangani Patrol. They were 'Men of Men'; we were 'Men of Men', and we had the remaining bits of them after the massacre in glass cabinets to prove it!

Actually, I was full of shit, and was about to have it beaten out of me. Sure beats laxative.

What followed was a total anti-climax!

Mrs Smuts stood meekly at the front of class and, as we took our places, and told us to open our textbooks. I wasn't even sure I had one!

"What's going on here?" I thought. "Have I been reprieved?"

Thoughts of switching from a phoney Jew to a phoney Christian entered my head.

Apparently the deranged woman had gone too far in her attempt to kill me. Not even Bruce Lee could systematically beat up half of our class without eventually meeting some serious resistance.

It was the borders that told us day boys what had happened. Johnson was too proud to say anything. It turned out he had phoned his folks at the end of lessons the previous day. In doing this, he broke the golden unspoken rule. 'You don't go crying to Mummy and Daddy', but this time he had the backing of the other boys.

His folks didn't mess around; they drove over 200 kilometres to the school, and threatened the Headmaster with a law suit if that lunatic Boer woman's head wasn't served on a plate and given to a pack of Rhodesian ridgebacks to eat.

Some nosy borders, with jack shit else to do but hang around the Head's office, eavesdropping, reported that the meeting later between the head and Ouma Smuts must have been a really dramatic session and as she stormed out the Head's office an angry voice followed her,

"Touch another pupil again, Mrs. Smuts, I will fire you."

And she knew he meant it.

Game over.

I won! With a little help from my friends.

One day, Johnson, I'll find you and buy you a beer.

REMEMBER by Sylvia Lee

The country we knew is finished
And how we all regret
The loss of our land by the flick of a hand
For the new route now is set.
We had our share of the fighting
There were many we knew who died
But our troops had fame and they knew the name
Would be carried on with pride.
We never lost sight of our reason
There was always the courage and will
To live day by day, keeping terrorists at bay
On the river, the plain and the hill.
But we knew we couldn't continue.
Suspected the end must be near.
We wondered and guessed, talked with much jest
But the voices were all tinged with fear.
The men were called up for elections.
They came in, young and old.
The results came out and beyond all doubt
We knew we had been sold.
In the end, the death of an era.
The new way had made it's start.
They can change the names, play political games
But **RHODESIA** lives on in the heart.

AN INTRODUCTORY VOCABULARY IN ZIMLISH
(Being the beginning of Simbabwean and the end of English)

AGENNEST : Against, as in aggenest the wall
ARIAS : Regions or districts as in ebon arias (see ebon)
BED : A feathered flying animal
BUCK : Noise of a dog: or as in "Buck to the Future" with Michael James Fox
BUTTER : To Bargain , to trade in commodities
CUT : A small donkey-drawn vehicle of Scottish Origin
CUM : Peaceful, untroubled - all is cum in the roo-rull arias
DENSE : To move rhythmically to music
DOE : A hinged device, often wooden, for closing a hole in the wall
EBON : Pertaining to built-up arias, not roo-rull
EHTYL : Earth will, as in this ethyl grow plenty millies
EWER PEONS : People of light complexion
FEATHER : A greater distance, as in "Swedden is feather noth than Spen"
FLOW : A base, an aria for densing, hence a dense flow (see dense)
FOCUS : A prediction, as in the "Weather Focus"
GET : A Hinged device for closing a hole in a fence or a hatch
GADDING : A place of flowers, lawns, bushes
HED : Having Heard
HEST : Impulsively, without due thought as in "Merry in hest"
ITCH : Every, separately, as in "to itch his own"
JOCK : A jest or funny story
KENNEL : A high ranking army officer
KIPPER : A warden or custodian, as in house-kipper
KETTLE : A bull, cow or ox in the mess (see mess)
LO : Legislation, rules of Govmint, as in " Police kip Lo and odour"
LOAD : British Nobleman, as in Load Herring Tonne, Forrin Seki Tee
MERRY : To join in matrimony
MICK : Humble, as in "the mick shall inherit the eth"
MESS : With quantity, e.g. in the mess..... more than ten of
MESSES : All those who dont pay income tax as in the toiling messes
A NAARTJIE : A state of chaos when lo and odour breaks down
ODOUR : The proper state of things - the police will kip odour, also commend or instruction - the Kennel gave me an odour
PARROT : Free booter or Buccaneer - unlawful as in Parrot Taxi

PENTING	: Applying oils to canvas, redecorating a house as in "Merry in hest, repent at lesha, have quickie wedding and you can pent the kia later"
PHLEGM	: Fire - the burning tip of kendle
PISS	: State of Lo and odour
PLESS	: Place
QUINS	: Two or more, female monarchs
RIP	: To harvest a crop
STACK	: Wholly, or completely stack nekkid in PlayboysCentrefold
SEKI TREE	: A stenographer - a girl who types
SHIT	: As in " A shit of pepper"
SIMBABWE	: Yes tiddy the Simbabwe ruins were just a little aria near Fot Victoria, but under Comrade Robert Gabriel Mugabe we are expanding the ruins to cover the hol country
STUV	: To Starve
SUTTON	: Definite - sure, as in : " I am sutton that you cannot tek money"
SO THEN	: Pertaining to the South
TEX	: As in "tex keb"
TOCK	: To communicate by speech
VEST	: Knowledgeable : learned as "well vest in the ut of painting
WASH	: Device for telling the time, often worn on the wrist
WED	: An item of vocabulary, as in "My wed, the kennel is kipping lo and odour in the ebon arias very well seence a few extry mists lent their lesson"
WELD	: Our Planet, the eth
WHIP	: To Cry
YES TIDDY	: The day before today

Extract from KK dictionary 1953

DYNAMITE, n.—makina **K.K. 'dammit'.** Very useful when the bait has been forgotten. " Get out of the well. I have just set the dynamite." "Puma lapa mugodi. Mena fagili dammit, dammit !"

Drifting by Mike Beresford

Let the wind blow my thoughts where it will,
Let them drift on the clouds in the sky.
Let me close my eyes and find calm in this world,
Serene as a river that quietly flows by.
Bring back to good times, the joy and the laughter,
When we sang for no reason but singing,
When tomorrow was just a new day coming after'
The good day in which we were living.
Give me the mountains I climbed in the sun,
And the rivers I rambled through forested glades,
The strength that was mine at the time I was young,
When promises given were promises made.
Let me sail once again on Kariba's blue waters,
With the honk of the hippo and fish eagle calls.
Let God find a place for His sons and his daughters,
Where they will find peace when the cloak of night falls.
Give me time with a loved one with whom I can share,
All hopes and the depths of my dreams.
And we shed our concerns with the ghost of despair
And discover what life really means.
I welcome my memories of those good times past,
For they tell me that life's not a lie,
That I'm here for a reason and as long as I last,
There's a promise as great as the African sky.

RHODESIAN SCHOOLDAYS

Umpteen years ago, before such things as television, CD players, computers and microwave ovens, two eleven year old girls, Denise and Lynda, shared a desk at school.

Denise had coppery brown hair that rested on her shoulders and eyes like melted chocolate. Freckles dusted her pixie nose, one front tooth crossed over the other. Denise's best friend was Lynda.

Lynda was awfully pretty. Her long, almost white hair was pushed back from her forehead by an Alice band, showing off her dazzling blue eyes. Everyday she wore a different Alice band and everyday she chose a different best friend. Lynda had an air about her, as if she knew something of colossal importance. She kept fascinating

16

things, like baby mice or white rats, spinning silkworm's or chameleons. Sometimes she'd sell them, using the money to buy a one shilling sized tin of condensed milk from the tuck shop. Whoever had been chosen as best friend that particular day would be allowed to have a suck of sticky, sweet liquid.

It was on a very boring day during school holidays, that Lynda arrived at Denise's house. She had been on her way to town that morning she said, and had passed the market place. (People gathered here to trade goats, chickens, ground nuts, and witchdoctor remedies.) A man was leading a donkey by a piece of rope.

"Are you selling that donkey?" Lynda had asked.

"Do you want to buy this donkey?" he replied.

"Depends how much you want"

"How much will you give me?"

"How much do you want?"

"Fifty dollars"

"No way!"

"Well how much have you got?"

It went like this for some time until they agreed on a price of ten dollars.

"I'll be back tomorrow with the money." she assured him.

"So you see, if give me five dollars, I'll let you ride my donkey whenever you want," Lynda offered generously.

Denise had dreamt of owning a horse ever since she saw the film Black Beauty. Her mom had laughed at her when she said she'd like one for her birthday.

"Not in a million years could we afford it."

Gosh! Denise could just picture her moms surprise when she arrived home from work to find a donkey in the back yard. She saw herself galloping down the road on her beautiful grey donkey, hair billowing out behind her, laughing with happiness. At night she would curl up against his soft white belly, while God kept watch from behind the stars.

She was truly honoured that Lynda had invited her, of all people, to be a part of this wonderful plan. Not wanting to seem ungrateful or anything and feeling somewhat nervous at losing Lynda's friendship, she took a deep breath, counted to five and blurted out,

"If I pay half, then half of him must belong to me."

"Don't be stupid! We can't cut him in half."

"What I mean is, I own him one week and you own him the next."

"Well…. alright, but I get first week and I choose his name!"

Now that it was all settled, it occurred to Denise that she didn't actually have five dollars.

"I know what we'll do. We'll sell our old clothes." Lynda said.

"Who would buy old clothes?"

"Nannies dummy! Nannies buy second hand stuff because they don't earn much money."

Denise rummaged through her wardrobe excitedly, throwing out things that did not fit her any more. She couldn't see how the small pile would fetch five dollars. Holding up her best dress she asked herself, "yes?.. no?" Her mom had made it, spending hours embroidering bright red cherries on the pockets. Right before her very eyes, the dress turned into a beautiful donkey. Mom will be mad but it'll get lots of money she argued with herself. Perhaps enough to buy two donkeys! Onto the pile it went, along with the striped jersey her grandmother had knitted. Stuffing the heap of clothes into her dads big leather suitcase, she sat on it, lay on it, jumped up and down on it, before it would close and then, because it was so heavy, she had to drag it all the way to Lyn's house. The lid kept bursting open, scattering the colourful garments across the tar. A few times she thought of giving up, but that donkey just kept appearing right in front of her. At last, there was Lynda, waiting at the gate.

They went into the lane behind the row of big houses. It was lunch time. Servants sat outside their quarters dipping thick crusts of white bread into steaming mugs of sweet tea. 'Off' time was precious, they were annoyed at being disturbed. "Humba" they shouted. From one house to the next it was the same. Lynda could not understand it.

"Why don't you want to buy these clothes? They are good quality. Look. No holes."

"Aiee! You two! You are trouble. Your mothers will come here and blame us. Go now!"

"I know who will buy these clothes Den. People from out of town. Lets go to the bus rank"

Between the two of them they lugged the suitcase all the way to town. There was a lot of activity at the rank, people everywhere, some coming, others going. One bus had so much stuff tied to the roof, it looked as though it may topple over.

"We are selling old clothes." Lynda shouted.

A woman offered to take the clothes and come back with the money next week, but they could not wait that long. People rummaged through the case dumping clothes on the ground, but none of them had money. A man who had been leaning against a tree watching, came towards them. He wore a black and white checked jacket, the brim of his hat rested on a pair of huge round pink rimmed sunglasses. Denise couldn't take her eyes off his feet. They were shaped like a ducks, the toes spread out wide - six toes on each foot. He handed Lynda a ten dollar note, shoved everything back into the case, put a distorted foot on the lid, snapped the locks and stepped onto the bus.

"You can't have the suitcase it's my dads!!" Denise cried as he disappeared.

'You know Den, everything in town is more expensive. If we go into the bush we will get a donkey for one dollar."

"Where can we buy a donkey" she asked a very fat mango seller. As if to advertise how juicy her mangoes were, she sat on her haunches sucking at the stringy flesh. Bright yellow juice ran down her chin, along her arm, dripping off her elbow into the golden sand beside the enamel dish of merchandise.

Wiping her lips and nose with the back of her hand, she lifted her shoulders in reply.

"Where is the place with munigy donkies?"

"The location near industrial."

Her eyebrows moved in the direction of Bulawayo.

Lynda knew exactly how to get there, she had past it with her dad on the way to Loretta Mission she remembered.

"Do you think we should ride there on our bikes?" Denise suggested.

"Ah dumb!" Lynda said, pulling a face. "How will we get the donkey home?"

"Well who is going to ride the donkey home?" asked Denise.

"Me! Of course!"

"That's not fair."

"Well the donkey was my idea after all."

"Well then I am going to take my bike."

"You can't."

"Why not?"

"I'm not going to walk all the way there while you ride your bike!"

"But I have to walk while you ride our donkey."

"MY donkey not OUR donkey."

"Give me back my money then!" Denise folded her arms across her chest.

"Fine! I will."

"Right now!"

Suddenly Lynda had a bright idea. "I know! Lets both walk and then we can take turns riding him home."

"Promise Lyn?"

"Promise."

It took forever to get to the outskirts of town and the dirt road that would lead them to the location. The tar bubbles had slowed them down (the heat caused the tar to blister). Hoppity hop, pop, pop. You had jump as hard as you could if you wanted a really good explosion. Their shoes were splattered with sticky black goo.

There were no houses now, only thorny bushes adorned with spider webs. Long brown pods dangled from the monkey bread trees and snake apple vines crept through the undergrowth. (Not to be confused with monkey apple trees) A shimmering haze rose off the surface in front of them. Denise's older brother called it a mirage. They screwed their eyes up against the harsh glare of the sun and the sweat that dripped from their forcheads. Dry dusty mouths, a reminder of the forgotten water bottle.

Dung beetles and blue headed lizards were of no interest today. The shrill song of crickets went unheard.

A large Camel Thorn cast dark pools of shade across the road. This was a good place to rest. Playing noughts and crosses in the sand, a flash of colour captured their attention. Snake! Longer than Denise's dads station-wagon, yellowish brown in colour. For a moment all they could do was stare, paralysed.

"Cobra?!" Denise hissed.

"Python?!" Lynda hissed back.

"PYTHON!!!" They screamed in unison, clinging to each other.

"RUN! RUN!!

Denise expected to be swallowed whole, like Jonah and the whale. She could feel the snake's breath on her neck, ready to pounce.

She couldn't run any further. She would just have to spend the rest of her life in darkness – living in a stomach. Clutching at the stitch in her side, she screamed at Lynda to stop. The two girls glanced back fearfully. There was nothing. No snake. It had disappeared into the bushes. They got the giggles. Giggles turned to hysterical laughter. They laughed so much that tears ran down their dusty cheeks, leaving long white streaks, and they had to cross their legs so as not to wet their brooks.

At last, the village. No one seemed to notice them standing at the entrance. The air smelt the way clothes smell when you have been standing too long next to a fire. The huts were all the same. Round, red, mud huts with straw roofs. As far as Denise could tell, the only way to know which was your hut would be by the colour of the cloth hanging over the doorway. Chubby little piccinins' with naked bottoms, protruding belly buttons and snot covered lips played happily without toys. Nannies stirred large black cooking pots with long wooden spoons. Scrawny dogs lay about looking dead, while chickens pecked at the ground around their heads. Next to a stone well in the centre of the village, a group of men were gambling with bottle tops. There were donkeys! Lots of them! Black ones, grey ones, brown ones.

Denise felt as though she were in the flicks. One of those flicks where people get into a strange machine and land up in a foreign country. Lynda walked up to the men.

"I am looking for the man who owns these donkeys."

It sounded rude. Denise wished Lynda would be more polite.

"These donkeys belong to lots of people" one of the men replied without looking at her.

"Well I want to buy one."

The man said something in his own language, causing the others to snort.

"Have you got money?" he asked.

"Yes." said Lynda.

"OK. Take this one. Only five hundred dollars."

"FIVE HUNDRED! You penga!"

She flicked at her temple with an index finger, "I can get one in town for ten."

"Do you have ten dollars?"

"Yes."

"Give me ten dollars now. I keep this one for you till you bring the rest of the money."

"Eikona! A man in town is selling donkeys for only ten dollars"

"Then why are you here?"

"I am looking for him."

"Do you see him?"

"No."

"Tsk tsk, no one will sell a donkey for ten dollars."

"Come on Lyn, let's go!" Denise begged, feeling terribly ashamed.

She could see Lynda was not about to give up the fight. People had started to gather around them. She was afraid.

"I am going. With or without you," she warned, forcing herself to walk away slowly even though her feet wanted to run.

Suddenly Lynda was beside her.

"Five hundred! I can't believe it. He is a crook."

"If you think how much horses cost, ten is really very cheap for a donkey."

"Nonsense. They get the donkeys out the bush for free. We look like rich kids. That's why he wants to charge us so much. We'll come back tomorrow wearing our old clothes. What's a bet we'll get one for ten dollars"

"We don't have any old clothes Lyn. We sold them all"

PEACE by Mike Slater　　London 21/12/79

The British Foreign Secretary he looked so smug and gay,
He said that after seven years, a Peace was signed this day.
But what is Peace? A sightless hag who favours but a few,
And lets the weak get weaker still, and always takes her due.
For Peace won't see the measled child, her face a running sore,
Who died because a Marxist boot had slammed the clinic door.
And Peace won't see the beggar-man who lies on city street,
The victim of his own sharp axe which hacked off his two feet.
And what about the widowed bride who's haunting vision sees,
The body of her loving groom, all pulped from head to knees?
And Peace won't see the Tribal Chief who lies without a head,
Who to his execution-place by his own son was led.
And Peace won't see the shanty towns, the refuse-pit old men,
The tiny kids in ragged clothes, no, Peace will not see them.
And what of those brave warriors who in their wheelchairs sit?
Peace won't make them see again, nor yet their limbs re-fit.
And now they've finished Lancaster, and had their bit of fun,
They think that Peace is what they've found?
No – the war has just begun.

RHODESIAN LIGHT INFANTRY: SNIPPETS FROM MEMORY

By 2037 Sergeant Rittey J N (Nigel).　Served 19/2/61 to 19/2/68

The recruiting office King George the V1 Barracks, Salisbury in February 1961.
　　　Having been far too clever to go to University, I found myself beetling along the Borrowdale road on my way to KG V1 to join this new Rhodesian Army thing my mates were all yakking about. When I reached the boom I asked politely where the Recruiting Office might be found. This bloke with a nose spread from East to West, right across his unlovely "mush", said something impolite, followed by a description of where this office was and a warning about where I would have to "park that piece of s**t motor bike OK?"
　　　The office turned out to be a room in a dingy building with a mixture of various types of battered chairs, a few overflowing ashtrays, stompies all over the floor and some very peculiar characters lolling around. I found a seat in the queue between a long, tall, fair- haired character, who had come from Jo'burg. His name was Bernie Hetem who eventually turned out to be an acceptable guitarist and would-be rock star.

His buddy, Brian Van Der Poel, was there too. The fellow on my left was a rugged character who looked like a soldier even before he had been attested. This was Roy Roelofse who had come from Umtali having left the furniture manufacturing business.

A couple of Ducktails, hidden by clouds of cigarette smoke, could be seen from time to time stamping their fag ends out on the floor and causing the eyes of the attending MP to resemble those of a Gaboon viper focusing on it's prey. I think one was "Cammie" Collins. The other, like so many, is a mere flash of static in a few old brain cells…perhaps the Gaboon viper got him….

Finally the moment arrived to join this military thing, see the world, enjoy free board and lodging, free medical care, free pension, learn a trade and enjoy a generous salary of £35 a month. (They only told us about all the deductions after our first payday came around.)

We were told, "Do come in Sir, sign here…here…here…here…here…there too…tick this…tick that…great! NOW YOUSE ARE A F*****G SOLDIER! Get your backside into that line there for youse medicals / train ticket to Bulawayo!"

The medicals, conducted by two medico types…Doctors Ainslie and Lambert-Porter, seemed to be a matter of seeing how tall and heavy you were, whether you were alive and breathing…and could we perhaps actually see and hear things. The worst crime was for any of us to have been found in possession of flat feet. (I thought it perfectly natural that we should all have flat feet…how would we stand up if they were anything else…?)

I am reminded of a popular legend at the time, which tells of the occasion where a recruiting officer had met with a fellow bearing a close resemblance to Quasimodo and had tried to sell the idea that this cretin could join the Army and actually get paid while learning a trade. The officer was dumbstruck by the response from this prospective soldier when he countered…

"But I don't wanna join the Army to learn a trade …I just wanna kill people!"

Brady Barracks

We were collected at Bulawayo station by a Private Walsh and found ourselves poured into the back of a WW11 vintage "QL" which bellowed, whined, rattled and creaked its way to the gates of Brady Barracks. My first thought was that any Hollywood producer, seeking a perfect location for movies titled, "Escape from Stalag Luft 3", or, "Breakout from Belsen" would only have to paint it all grey and sprinkle a little snow around to make it work!

From the moment of arrival, the shouting started. For some reason these noisy people insisted that everything should be done "at the double". When those morons were trying to teach us to march, we quickly learned that our arms had to swing at shoulder height…"parallel to the ground" they said. It was only after passing out of recruit training that we were allowed to swing them at a far less abnormal angle of about 45 degrees.

Kit issue was hilarious. We were all rushed to the QM Stores where we stood around until summoned by the Gods to go get our issue. Very little fitted. They told us that *if* it fitted, you were deformed in some way. Funnily enough their kit fitted OK so we deduced that they must have all been a little misshapen.

Their boots were smooth with a mirror shine, but the ones we got were rough and pimply as a rhino's backside.

Their Khaki Drill shorts and bush jackets were crisp with creases you could sharpen a pencil with. Ours were presented as piles of khaki material resembling the cleaning rags used for washing Bedford trucks.

Their belt brasses and buckles belonged in the window display of Tiffanys…all shiny and golden. They gave us brass objects that looked like they had been recovered from Delville Wood.

Their belts were snow white. They gave us gungy "Gang" green jobs and told us about "Blanco" and how we could purchase it "for a very modest cost from the canteen".

Their berets fitted. Ours looked like the kind of thing a ship's cook might wear. We never saw if their "Drawers Cellular, troops- for- the- use- of " fitted them…or whether these "Jam Stealers" actually attempted to wear the darned things. We found that it was anatomically more correct to wear the brutes back to front as the "Y front" had clearly been designed by someone who hated soldiers. They became known as "Shreddies". Thanks be, to the Good Lord that the regiment never wore kilts!

On getting to the canteen and asking about this "Blanco" stuff, we found that we also had to have a few other things. Brasso, Starch, Cobra floor polish, yellow dusters, Kiwi polish, sandpaper (for smoothing off the Delville Wood relics prior to using the Brasso), cotton wool for "boning" the boots, an electric iron (not only for clothes but to get those blasted pimples out of the boot leather), washing powder and of course, "Bed Boards" and safety pins, so that one could painstakingly display ones spare bedding in exact box-shaped piles at the foot of ones bed for morning inspections. Having blown the coming months' pay, you were now in a position to re-manufacture just about everything they had given you.

The boots had to be ironed to get the darn things smooth after which it was a matter of a sort of spit and polish technique using Kiwi polish…the only polish that really worked. Initially it was layered on thickly. This was followed by hours of circular applications using wet cotton wool. Private Alistair Platt, a pasty little fellow and a fine soldier, with lips that looked like Mick Jagger's, (we couldn't use this analogy at the time as "Tackie Lips" hadn't begun to make his millions yet!), was the master of boot boning and earned the coveted "Stick Man" title several times. His boots could have been hung from the ceiling at a barn dance to replace the mirrored ball. If those boots had been caught by the spotlight, the revellers would have been blinded.

A few of our colleagues recalled

At this time we got to know more about the motley collection of characters who were to be our companions. Many are forgotten in the mists of time, but a few notables are recalled with no difficulty.

Jock Martin, an ex Brit army type who annoyed the Hell out of us by slow marching around the barracks at all hours of the day or night, making a dreadful noise with his bagpipes.

Sergeant Henry Lourens, supposedly ex Long Range Desert Group, who was a rugged looking character famous for the remark "Getting shot is b****rall...I've been shot before".

Steve Jones, Johnny Le Bron and Eddie Etheridge who were all archery enthusiasts. Eddie was killed years later while serving as a mercenary in the Congo.

Ted Wilde, wise in the ways of the Rhodesian bush, he grew up on a farm near the small town of Plumtree.

Jumbo Greipel, a giant of a man with a gentle heart.

Chippy Ackerman and his mate Herbie Lordan. These two were like circus acrobats. They demonstrated their prowess by swinging like orang-utangs from the rafters of the barrack rooms. Herbie was a master of the Bedford RL and could make those bellowing monsters really fly with superb double de-clutching.

The diminutive Jimmy Smith-Belton, later to make a name for himself in rugby circles.

Tiny Clemo was first spotted by the lads when he came to sign up as a "D" Company "Boy-soldier". We all thought this gawky child had got lost on his way to his primary school. It was rumoured that Orderly Officers regularly instructed the cooks to ensure he got more "graze" and milk than the other troopies in an attempt to grow him a little faster. (He spent a lot of his career as a "Jamstealer" and now lives in Randburg SA having later specialised in Logistics...a sort of "civvy" version of "Jamstealing"?)

Tex Benzies was a fellow motorcyclist who owned a Matchless 500 twin, which ran rings around my ancient ex-police BSA 600 side-valve machine. The old runways of the Kumalo airfield next to Brady became a sort of raceway for amateur Jim Redmans and Ray Amms in the Battalion.

Pat Miller. A fine shottist, as I remember, who served with distinction in later years.

Colonel John Salt, our CO, the "Main Man Wot Counted". He was a tall, cadaverous character with a booming voice, who was revered by us all. On parades, dressed in his KD's, he resembled a schooner under full sail. His shorts were impressive and cascaded down to well below the knees while the bush jacket looked just as if he had crashed through a marquee and taken the whole thing with him after wrapping it up with his belt and Sam Browne. Under the cap was a weather beaten face dominated by a massive schnozzola that, if pointed North or South, made him vulnerable to any gusts of wind from the East or West. He never did get blown over. Perhaps it was the stabilising effect of the ears of elephantine proportions that stuck out on either side of that huge bonce that did it.

Harry Crampton was a barrel-chested ex stevedore from Sydney Docks with a face revealing many excesses and huge paws. He was reputed to have been able to pull the cap off a bottle of Castle Lager using only his fingers. Some years later an unfortunate crocodile tried to take him while we were happily splashing around in a dam at Buhera. The croc lost and Harry was rushed to Enkeldoorn Hospital for treatment where he was reported to have spent his time fascinating the nurses. When the croc attacked Harry, he was not the only one to get injured. Alistair Platt turned the water into a froth in his frenzy to get away from the commotion and failed to stop when he reached the shore. He sustained an injury when he crashed into some rocks.

Cammy Collins and Bruce Cromarty, who probably did more than most in the development of "RLI Speak". This may have originated from the jive talk of Joburg Duckies, the lingo of the Durban beachfront, Afrikaans, Funagalo, Rhodesian schoolboy dialects and a motley collection of bits of barracks communication from dozens of armies around the world. Even the most "frightfully frightful fellows" from Sandhurst and the like, quickly realised that they had to learn it and use it if they wished to get their points over to us and earn our respect.

"Bok" Wentzel. A quiet little guy who later sadly lost his life in action.

Jack Barratt who modelled himself on Nikita Kruschev and who spent most of his later career as the charismatic barman at the Cranborne Corporal's Club. He was, as a Brit, most knowledgeable on all things Russian and probably caused a lot of anxiety for our "cloak and dagger" types at a time when the Russians were our enemy. They were the providers of AK 47's to all sorts of funny buggers around the world and harbourers of the cocktail-quaffing terrorist masters in Moscow.

Bob Hope who described himself as "six feet and then some". He had a flash of silver hair on the front of his head. He also went the "Jamstealer" route.

Joe Conway. The life of most parties.

Barry Bougaard, another vertically challenged character.

Derek Taylor-Memmory, a corpse-like member of what we rudely referred to as the "Turd stranglers" (Medics). I worked with him as a medical rep in SA where he passed away from lung cancer (I think) a few years ago.

Mick (Paddy) Ryan, who was rumoured to have deserted from the navy and who consumed copious quantities of alcohol, which stimulated his passion for "a good foit". He was once found kicking the canteen jukebox to a pulp. As the new RP Sergeant, I had to go and talk him out of it. There was no argument. He fell into the Land Rover without protest and was locked in the Box until justice took its' course on CO's Orders the following day.

Not such a gentle and cheerful Irishman was the notorious Sam Cassidy, who really was nasty when pissed. He spent a large part of his career confined to the Box. I hope the years mellowed him. Maybe cirrhosis got him first.

Piet Myburgh, the raw Afrikaner who was all legs and surprised the country by winning the Sunday Mail 110 Mile March. He was a really nice fellow with limited powers of communication.

Bob Meacham. A fanatical runner, he was always at the front of any foot-powered events. I seem to remember that he held the record for the fastest time "running" down the cliffside at Kariba Heights. This started from the Sergeant's Mess, turned at the main road hundreds of feet below and then involved flying back up again. A drunken game at that time was to pitch Dumpy bottles over that precipice and to listen to hear if you had scored a direct hit on a pile of rock down below, he must therefore have risked life and limb to do it. He could easily have found himself singing an octave higher.

George Molder. If ever anyone fitted the description "eyes like pissholes in the snow", he was it. He was the guy who put his Bedford RL, AD 808, over the side of a cliff near Kariba.

Basil Rushforth was a really mad motorcyclist and scrambles enthusiast. He was the envy of all the lads because he owned a Lotus Cortina GT that went like the bats out of Hell.

There was Sam Maulgue, a quiet and simple soul who owned a massive American car and who was sadly killed when it left the road around the Holy Circle and hit a culvert in the ditch outside B Company.

One of the people who led me to hate gymnasiums was Len Monson. Built like a compact brick shithouse, with cauliflower ears from years of hitting the canvas as a wrestler, he really gave us the works. On one occasion he ordered:

"Tallest on the right, shortest on the left!… From the right…NUMBER!… Odd numbers one pace FORWARD MARCH!…Odd numbers ABOUT TURN!…PAIR OFF!!…now, put on your boxing gloves…you've got 10 minutes to knock the living daylights out of the oke in front of you!!"

He was a fan of the drill instructor's "Gwelo Screech" parade ground commands, which made him sound like a spaniel being kicked in the nuts.

Sergeant "Beaver" Fraser-Kirk, one of the Vehicle Maintenance guys at the MT yard who, when asked by Captain Keith Dyer the MTO, why he was looking a bit rougher than usual, explained:

"It was those okes last night Sir. We each bought a crate of 24 Chibulis and when they were finished, somebody bought me a meat pie. I think the thing was vrot!"

Interesting buck-teeth were to be found under the moustache of the Irishman, Sergeant Paddy Driver. Also ex British Army, he could have eaten an apple through the strings of a tennis racquet.

The Battalion loan shark was Tiny Sevenster, one of the more punch-drunk RP's. This resourceful character could always lend you five quid as long as you paid him ten at the end of the week. He was reputed to have amassed vast fortunes over the years.

Another financial whiz kid was Kenny Mills who became a professional investment guru back in Johannesburg in later years.

A notorious British Army surplus character was WO11 "Crash" Hannaway, whose nickname was derived from his love of blowing things to bits. He was very good at it and brought this skill to the attention of the authorities by flushing a stick of "808" down the toilet in the men's room of a well-known Gwelo hotel. Legend has it that the ceramic bowl was blown to smithereens whilst the water tank was found swaying about still doggedly attached to it's copper pipe, the sewage system was trashed and the whole place was plastered with delicate shades of dark brown. The perpetrator was reported to have retreated back to the bar after pulling the chain of the ancient "crapper" thus sending this lethal turd on it's mission of destruction. He was said to have sat there with a cherubic smile on his face, quaffing his beer and occasionally checking his watch, until the moment of eruption when he casually asked, "Wot's going on chaps?" Somehow he remained in the army where his reputation as a bit of a pisscat flourished.

While "Crash" Hannaway was our A Company CSM, he blotted his copybook a little more by riding my very rare motorcycle (a 1000cc,vintage V twin1937 Brough Superior SS100 and which weighed about 700 lbs) straight through the swing doors of the WO's and Sergeants Mess, while wearing a Davy Crockett hat and with a musket slung over his shoulder. Fortunately my bike survived with no damage. Having not yet attained the lofty heights of Sergeant, I could not witness the scene inside the Mess.

Jock Press and Tom Douglas who sang the duet "Walking my baby back home" with a professional touch and a lot of feeling. The latter was our platoon commander before going on with a distinguished career in the Life Insurance Industry.

The famous Sergeant Ernie Walters was a survivor of the Normandy landings who owned several mementos from that era including Nazi flags and pieces of German uniforms. He also had a set of very poor false teeth of similar vintage, which he sucked at, waggled and left lying on his bedside locker when kipping. He was a Staff Corps cook and went down in history on that fateful day at a camp kitchen in Buhera, when, in a moment of vocal excitement, the teeth fell into a pot of porridge destined for the troop's breakfast. He was seen frantically digging about in the pot with his ladle while turning the air blue with colourful language and spraying copious quantities of saliva from his naked gums.

Among the musically talented troopies was another great beer drinker and guitar twanging fellow, Terry Dempsey, who later made a hit in the music business by composing, among many others, "Love is a beautiful song". He was not often sober at that time. Castle Breweries shares would have taken a dive if he'd chosen to go on the wagon.

Always bickering with each other were the Lloyd-Evans brothers. Lyle and Llewellyn were twins while Denzil, the third brother, was either the principal peace-keeper or s**t-stirrer-in-chief between them. They were fine rugby players and very likeable. At one stage they chipped in to buy a very smart Ford Zephyr, which they shared and fought over regularly. At a camp in Kariba on one occasion the twins were having a "barney". Fists and epithets flew about but, when I tried to break it up, I was attacked by Denzil who seemed to want them to knock the stuffing out of each other and resented the intervention in their family feud.

Mike Boone was a fanatical motorcycle racer and scrambles enthusiast. On leaving the military he made a career in the motorcycle business.

Lofty Cawthorne was an ex-pugilist serving time as an RP. He was perhaps a little less intellectually challenged than most other Regimental Police and, when held up against the likes of "Punchy" Pretorius, Tiny Sevenster or Jimmy Thurling, could almost have been referred to as "gifted". I later served my stint as RP Sergeant and got to know him a little better.

Many troopies developed into ruggedly good looking fellows and broke a lot of hearts around Bulawayo, Salisbury, Gwelo and other places in the Federation where they stopped long enough to fascinate the "birds", "cookies", "gooses" or just generic "fluff". "crumpet" or "crutch". Some however were rather challenged in terms of appearance. There was a troopie called Warren who was once told by a Drill Sergeant on a parade that he had "a face bearing a close resemblance to the scrotum of an elephant". Another unfortunate was a Private Newman who was informed by the terrifying RSM Reid-Daly that his face "was like a bucket full of arseholes". To my mind, these two were positively good looking compared to the very likeable Private Gouws who was tall but whose height was made up of about 80 % legs, 8 % torso and 12% for the rest. "The rest" was dominantly neck on which could be found a head like an inverted pear, out of which peered a pair of cheerful eyes situated either side of a snotbox modelled (badly) from a statue found in Pompeii. The whole protuberance was clad in an unhealthy yellow skin. Nobody picked on Gouws because he was a true gentleman who would stop at nothing to help his colleagues. I saw him at a Riot Drill once. He looked exactly like a Hermit crab occupying a sort of khaki coloured "shell" (his steel helmet) below which trailed two legs, two long arms and an SLR rifle.

There were a few really handsome types in the Battalion included a well-known OC of D Company who once borrowed my boat at Kariba for a jaunt on the lake. This included a degree of "au naturel" sunbathing in the company of a couple of nurses. The sunbathing (and perhaps one or two other things) was over-done and treatment was required for sunburn on some unusual parts of their bodies.

2nd Lieutenant Harry Harvey is remembered for a time when, as a wet-behind-the-ears "subbie" commanding our platoon on a bloody awful conventional warfare exercise on the Somabula flats, continually stated that, "the book says this / says that / says the other". Sergeant Bob Meacham, and indeed all of us, were getting a bit bored with what this "book" had to say but our subaltern rattled on quoting this tome of great knowledge until Bob had a go at him by saying,...

"But Sir, we haven't read this f*****g book!"

Major "Digger" Essex-Clarke was our first A Company OC. He was every inch a soldier and was feared but admired by all us new recruits. He was the one who ultimately decided if we got weekend passes, following the dreaded Saturday morning inspections.

Stories From Memory...
Congo border.

As happens in Africa the Congo blew up in late 1961 when the Belgians, in their infinite wisdom, pulled out leaving the indigenous population to fight over the prize. They have been fighting ever since.

Katanga, under Moishe Tshombe, decided to break away from the rest of the hooligans, which resulted in chaos. They were fighting God knows who for God knows what reason. The remaining Belgians packed their belongings into their cars and ran for the Northern Rhodesia border to the south bringing with them tales of dreadful atrocities committed not only by the locals but by the oddball and trigger-happy assortment of United Nations forces dumped there to keep the peace.

The brand new RLI was sent to Ndola by land and air and then dispersed into positions at Kipushi, Kasumbalesa, Solwezi, Mwinilunga and a whole lot of other "backside of the universe" places.

The trip by air was made in two beat up old Rhodesian Air Force Canadairs...a sort of DC4 Skymaster with different engines...and a Dak or two. A few Vampires also came up to provide air support against whatever someone might have put in the air. (The Katangese at one stage actually had an aeroplane or two including a Fouga-Magister flown by a mercenary that evidently did wreak a bit havoc amongst it's enemies on the ground.)

Some blokes made their way by road from Bulawayo bringing much needed transport and supplies. Initial transport was rented from construction firms on the Copperbelt but, until that was secured, we found ourselves as inmates of a disused Prisoner of War camp alongside Ndola Airport, which had once housed Italians captured during the Second World War. The plumbing was shot and the toilets were little oval shaped holes in the floor of the shower rooms. Some had feet painted on either side to ensure that one's aim was mostly dead centre. The walls bore the forlorn etchings of those lonely men who had been locked up there nearly 20 years before. Their names, if put on a piece of paper, would have made a good menu selection in a Pizzeria!

The road trips to our destinations were hot, bumpy and very dusty. When we arrived we looked like the contents of a vacuum cleaner bag... sort of moving piles of dust with red-rimmed eyes. After that, the only washing facilities were provided by plunging into nearby rivers, bathing and washing clothes, without soap. There wasn't any. At this time a tragic accident involving a Bren took the life of Private De Haas who became the RLI's first operational casualty.

I ended up at the Kasumbalesa Customs post, where, being a Bren gunner, I had to dig my trench on top of one of the giant termite mounds found in the area because our subaltern, Lieutenant Bob Davey, had read in the good book that your platoon's Bren had to have a superior field of fire. The authors of this good book had not known that the termites of Northern Rhodesia had made their homes from concrete. I was still digging at the crack of dawn while the other okes had been kipping for hours.

At one point the Katangese had kindly sent us a truckload of their "Simba" beer as a goodwill gesture. Rumour also has it that an approach was made at the time to our top brass who were asked "if perhaps they would consider hiring the regiment out to go and sort out a few of their enemies?"

We patrolled the border by Landrover and often met with the Katangese in their Austin Gypsies. We traded smokes, beers and bits of uniform with them. All this was done in sign language as they spoke no English and we spoke no French.

Screening refugees was a heart-rending affair. We were told of drunken soldiers tearing around Elizabethville spraying machine gun fire at will, looting and raping at random. Some cars carried bullet holes as witness to the horror these unfortunates were leaving behind.

After a few weeks we were pulled back to Kitwe for a couple of weeks R and R. The mining townsfolk entertained us royally while we fascinated their daughters. Some clot caught a dose of the crabs which resulted in all of us having to endure a "short arm inspection"…why "short arm" I will never know! There were a lot of guys standing on that parade in the middle of the Kitwe show grounds with their "shreddies" around their ankles, who were well enough hung to put horses to shame. Fortunately only a few found their courting tackle shaved and painted blue by the "turdstranglers".

The regiment returned to Bulawayo at 30 miles per hour in the trucks and Landrovers that had been sent up to support us. We had all grown from the experience…so had our piles!

The move to Cranborne Barracks.
The brass had long before committed to the idea that we should move to "Bambazonke" (Salisbury) to a new barracks that had been thrown up by the contractors, Messrs Holland Africa Ltd, at Cranborne on the main road to New Sarum Airport. Fond farewells were said to the birds of Bulawayo and off we went to pastures new.

All of us who owned civvy vehicles were to drive or ride them (or in some cases push them or tow them!) the 300 miles to Salisbury. A mileage allowance would be paid to us after arrival. This turned out to be about twice what it actually cost me to ride my ancient BSA from Bulawayo to Salisbury. The profit was quickly converted to Castle laager. All those without cars or bikes went by road or rail.

The new "home" was a big improvement on Brady and they soon had us planting trees and strips of Kikuyu grass all over the place. The rules were simple…if it moved you saluted it. If it didn't move you picked it up. If it didn't move and you couldn't pick it up you painted it white. Passing the tatty remnants of Cranborne today, on the way to or from the airport, produces a twinge of sadness, when I reflect on all the blood, sweat and tears we put into it.

Sergeants Mess rituals…

A newly promoted Sergeant would be formally welcomed to the Mess by the RSM at the Friday night "prayer meeting" and with due ceremony would find himself given a large chamber-pot filled with Guinness laced with other noxious substances. The "piece de resistance" was the sausage, which was found floating around in it. As a token of the generosity of his hosts, the novice was presented with a huge Havana cigar and was invited to finish the lot off in a given 20 minutes. Very few walked out of the mess…

Warrant Officers, Sergeants and even the occasional invited guest, if accused of any form of s**tstirring, could find themselves invited to wear a spoon around their necks for the evening and buying drinks all round. This famous spoon was about 4 to 5 feet in length and had been carved from a fine indigenous wood.

Dining-in nights involved getting dressed up in green pants, "Bum Freezers", dress shirts and bow ties. There was a lot of "Bull" that came with this tradition and it was only towards the end of these evenings that we could go bananas. On one occasion Sergeant Pete Eldridge had had the temerity to whip his table napkin out with a flourish and wave it about before putting it on his lap. RSM Robin Tarr made us do another "dining-in practice night" as a punishment for this dreadful act which he considered to have been to the prejudice of good order and military discipline. He was a little short on humour at the best of times.

Smoke breaks…

A ritual at the time was the "smoke break" which was usually declared when the nicotine cravings of our superiors became too much for them to stand. This involved troopies hauling out a wide variety of fags, pipes and cheroots and puffing away happily until "Fall In" was barked at them. There were a few favourite brands at the time. Filter cigarettes in vogue were "Life" and "Peter Stuyvesant", which were smoked by the guys who could afford them at about five bob for 50. The "peasants" among us, coughed our way through countless "Texan", "Camel", "Flag", "Springbok", "C to C" and, if payday was far away, "Star", which could be bought at 3d for 8. I enjoyed the cork tipped variety but found that after a bit of running around the bush carrying those things, I was often left with a pocket full of cheap tobacco and a box of paper tubes.

Many joined the army as non-smokers but quickly found they needed something to do while seated in the shade of a tree, building or truck, while tolerating clouds of smoke from all sides.

Perhaps they were influenced by a particular NCO, who commanded, "Smoke Break!!…those without cigarettes, go through the motions!"

Barracks bathrooms…

Whilst these were kept clean most of the time, they were always very noisy and filled with steam coming from countless sweaty men running piping-hot showers, basins and baths. At times it was difficult to see anything in this murk and, as using the dripping wall mirrors to shave was out of the question, you quickly learned to use razors by Braille. I began shaving while seated in the bath, a habit that I have not broken after 43 years.

These bathrooms, "designer built" by people who knew they would never have to use them, contained baths, showers, basins, urinals and rows of "crappers", all of which contributed to an endless variety of noises and not so delightful aromas at peak hours.

Drill and "Toy Soldiers" display.
1963 Rand Easter Show in Johannesburg….

Choreographed under the pace-stick of RSM Ron Reid-Daly, this display was lauded by Press and spectators alike. It took weeks of practice and damned hard work both behind the scenes and on the parade ground.

There were two elements to it. The first was a precision display of drill without a word of command from start to finish. The troops in full Greens came in to the stadium straight after the show-jumping events, which was a bit dodgy because of the horse droppings and piles of sawdust. We marched in a single block and moved to a set series of manoeuvres timed to a double tap on the base drum. The block split in four different directions followed by further splitting off and the performing of intricate wheels and counter marches. Finally the whole thing got back together as the original "column of klompies" and then exited the stadium to loud cheering.

The Toy Soldiers thing was equally intricate, but here we were all dressed in ridiculous costumes and carrying wooden muskets. Some guys were cavalry, which meant wearing a sort of "horse" made of plywood and hessian as well as a uniform. They performed in fear of an attack from the rear by the randy stallions quartered around the arena but, fortunately, none were propositioned!

The highlight came with the firing of a cannon that meant we had to fall down onto the grass, flat on our faces one after the other like rows of dominos. A few were unlucky enough to plop straight into the mess left by the show jumpers so, by the time the last display night came round, the red, white and blue uniforms had camouflaged themselves and stank horribly.

Accommodation was provided at the Milner Park show grounds and we were allowed out between shows to wander around the exhibits and fascinate the dollies. Very early on, Reid-Daly declared the fleshpots of nearby Hillbrow were to be off-limits. There were enough fights with Joburg's "Duckies" in the show ground let alone out of it.

Bushcraft and survival training with Alan Savory...

There must have been about twenty of us who gathered together one early morning at Cranborne, boarded Landrovers and headed slowly for the Zambezi valley. It was slow simply because our mentor, Alan Savory, drove his own diesel powered vehicle and set the pace for the rest. A camp was scratched out of the riverine bush on the banks of the Sapi stream about thirty miles inland from the Zambezi. Within a few minutes of chucking down our kit, somebody yelled "snake!" The unfortunate reptile (a fat Puffadder) was quickly beaten to death. Savory, a really jungly type, said "Ah! Dinner!!...and then showed us the Cordon Bleau recipe for Flambe Puffadder a la Savory. It tasted like chicken and wasn't too bad.

There followed a programme of intensive training on unforgettable subjects. How to build fall traps, pit traps, fish traps and snares. How to make weapons, such as bows and arrows, knobkerries, spears and knives. Where to find water. How to poison pools of fish. Ground tracking and aerial tracking. Which plants, leaves or berries were edible. The behaviours of wildlife found around Rhodesia and many more. By the time the course was over, we began to trust in our ability to survive just about anything, without "jamstealers" or air drops by Dakotas.

The only people who I can remember were on this course were Teddy Wilde, Mike Dippenaar, the late Dave Parker and a fellow called Williams. Sadly the others are forgotten.

At one point our mentor allowed us to try to hit a can in the riverbed with both his double barrelled .470 and his .375. The butt-shaped bruises on my right shoulder are long gone, but my printer's tray on the wall still holds the two cartridge cases I fired on that day. I hit the can with one of them.

The training culminated in a 60 mile footslog without food or water. This began when the two groups we had been split into, set off from our base on the Sapi stream to reach the Zambezi where we had to turn around and make it back to the camp. Our group was fortunate enough to follow the vultures to a zebra freshly killed by lions.

We ran to the scene making fierce noises that put the unfortunate lions, hyenas and vultures right off their breakfast. This gave us a haunch of meat that, while welcome in our hungry bellies, became a cumbersome and heavy piece of deadweight that had to be carried for many miles in the heat of the Rhodesian bush.

The other group did not have it so easy. All they could come up with for the protein part of their diet was a water tortoise.

It was surprising to me to find that the well-built "rugger-bugger" types did not fare as well as the skinnier guys when the chips were down and all we wanted to do was lie down and die under any trec giving a patch of shade.

This initial Bushcraft and Survival course became the fore-runner of the many used later by the SAS and Selous Scouts to sort the men from the boys. From what I can understand these later ones made ours look like a walk in the park and I have nothing but admiration for those who survived them.

Ours was quite rugged enough, thank you...!

NORTH EAST by Sylvia Lee. Written at Rushinga and the hill is Firifiji.

The winter sun shines from winter sky.
In the distance a hill throws its head up high.
All is quiet, peaceful and calm
And one feels that here one is far from harm.
But the village is fenced and security lights
Do much to alleviate fear from the night.
Grenade screens cover all windows throughout
And the bomb shelter crouches with sand bags about.
A truck goes out and it hits a mine.
Of the terrs who laid it, there isn't a sign.
But the truck is protected and injuries slight
Though the occupants tremble with shock and with fright.
Here men of all races work outside the fence
You see in the faces that nerves are all tense.
Each time they drive out you can see they're on guard
With fingers on triggers, keen eyes looking hard.
They're always expecting an ambush or worse
For this is the hell of the terrorist curse.
Yet these men still go out and get the work done
And if they return, there is still time for fun.

Reminiscences by Bruce McGregor

Whilst based in Darwin as 3 commando Fireforce, we were sent out into the Mavuradona area by truck. We had new Mercedes trucks by that time, courtesy of the SADF. The truck I was driving started to lose power, to the point that we could not keep up with the rest of the convoy. The convoy stopped and I looked over the truck. My intuition told me that No Power = Fuel Starvation, so I checked the fuel bowl for air and discovered a residue. I cleaned it out and Bingo! We were on our way again – but only for a short time.

Again the convoy had to stop while I cleared the residue from the fuel bowl – again we could continue – and again we were forced to stop. It got so bad that the rest of the convoy continued and left me and an escort behind to resolve the issue, which we could not.

The residue was not ferrous in nature as it had a soft feel to it. Upon studying it closer, I discovered it to be tea leaves.

Somebody had put tea leaves in the diesel tank. This in any other situation may have been funny to some and irritating to others, but in war this is regarded as sabotage. I do not believe that the person who did this thought about the consequences of his actions, like being ambushed while broken down. I also do not think that it was done in spite, because anybody could have been given that vehicle to drive. When queried about the substance I deliberately explained that I did not rightly know but it looked like rust.

Yeah! Right! A new truck with a rusty tank. Had I told them it was tea leaves, I'm not too sure what Capt Kip Donald would have done. Maybe it's better that way.

While in convoy to Mukumbura, Rob "Buzzard" Doulgheris (Support Commando) was lead vehicle.

We were drawing closer to our destination and I was starting to think of the shower and the beer at journeys end when Buzzard's truck came to a very sudden and dusty halt. I saw him leap from his cab and skirmish into the bush. I heard no shots, so hesitated, then I heard shots from where he had disappeared into the bush.

In my haste to get out of the vehicle I missed the step and scraped my buttocks on the step instead. Funny thing though - when the adrenaline's pumping you don't think about that pain in your arse when you are running for cover.

We heard no more shots, just a lot of noise, half query, half cursing, as the rest of the guys were scrambling away from the trucks. I then saw Buzzard re-appear with a guinea fowl that he had shot.

Anti-climax! – But obviously Buzzard had more that a beer and shower on his mind. If an officer had been present, I am sure he would have been charged.

Being ex SADF transferred to the RLI, I guess I had a special empathy for the others who were like me.

For example, while during our training the 31st of May came along and we all gather to sing the South African National anthem – although this was the last time I did that because of my experiences with the attitude of the South African Police.

They thought that they were doing us [Rhodesia] a big favour. Anyway – there were many occasions where I would assist in carrying Terrs who had been shot from a helicopter and laying them out for inspection – and I guess one gets used to that – but one morning after a contact which had killed some of our troops (I seem to remember it was three guys) in a river bed (and the Terrs got away during the night) a helicopter landed at Darwin where I was stationed at the time. I assisted in carrying one of the guys to the hospital. It was Jannie De Beer, an ex SADF transferee. We never hung out and we only acquainted by virtue of the fact that we bought each other a beer at the Park Lane hotel once.

I looked at him and I could not believe that he could be so lifeless.

I have never forgotten that image.

There was this Landrover based in Darwin that seemed to be cursed.

For many moons this vehicle was accident prone and the left front mudguard always needed replacing. Let's face it – in a one main street town, what are you going to hit? Right? Wrong!. This vehicle had already had "new left mudguard number five" when I arrived from Chesa that morning. I was instructed to wash and refuel my truck and get ready for my trip to Rushinga the next day. We had a shindig going on in the area and chopper fuel would be needed there. I dutifully washed and refuelled my truck, picked up the chopper fuel for the Blue Jobs and drove back to my parking area.

As I prepared to park however, Henry Botha decided he was going to throw a bucket of ice cold winter water over me while I was still driving.

NOT A GOOD FEELING!

Knowing the compression of these trucks and the gear ratios would lock the wheel if I switched off the engine, I decided a hot shower was more desirable that a cold one, so before Henry could discharge his bucket at me, I selected 1st gear, switched off the engine and bailed out. I can still see Henry laughter turn to surprise and I can still remember my laughter turn to dread as the engine pre-ignition caused the truck to stop, lurch forward, stop and lurch forward again towards this brand new mudguard on Landrover 06BC69.

I started running for the truck again, watching the stop, go, motion of the truck thinking "Yes!", "No!", "Yes!", "No!", "Yes!" and finally "Nooo!" as the truck hit.

Henry and I were given many extra guard duties for that!

Rhodesian Dawns by Sue Halsey

As kids we used to "make a plan" to get up at four in the morning, on the weekends, to watch the sunrise. When we went to bed, we'd bang our heads down on the pillow four times, that was supposed to be like an inner alarm and would wake us up. Whether it worked or not, I'm not sure, but we did wake up, get dressed and have to sneak out of the house without waking the dogs. If they woke up and got out they would rush around barking checking what animals had passed through the yard during the night. (We lived in the bush). Then we'd take off through the boy's compound down the footpath, the grass was always wet with dew, and it would be really cool except the bottom part of our legs, for some reason the grass kept the ground temperature warmer than the upper temperature.

We would head off for a walk, breathing in the damp grass smell, and usually get scared out of our wits when Partridge or Guinea-Fowl got disturbed and took off in front of us.

The best place to watch the sunrise was from the top of the water tank on the borehole, or from the Mexican Apple tree.

It was magic to watch the spider webs turn golden lace and sparkly, and the heads of the grass sparkling with the dew. The Doves would be the first bird we'd hear, such a peaceful sound.

Then we would smell the bacon cooking and the fired bread, the old Houseboy thought we were nuts. We thought we had outsmarted everyone, but only found out later that Mum and Dad always heard us.

One night, during the war, when there was a fire-fight in the locations, we climbed up the water tank and could get a view of the tracers going backwards and forwards, it was like our own fireworks display.

Talking of fireworks, remember Guy Fawkes Night?

We would be rushing around all day, or straight after school getting things ready, the little step ladder to put the rockets on in a bottle, or tin of sand, a "Guy" to burn, this didn't happen often, because dad wouldn't give up his clothes. There was one year, in Kensington we had a community Guy Fawkes, with a HUGE hay stack with Guy on top, boxes and boxes of Crackers, and about fifty car loads of people. All was going well until one of the men dropped his cigar into one of the boxes of crackers, (rockets) well, the shot off in every direction, and started a massive bush fire.

I got hit in the back and it nearly knocked me out, I was about 9 and the time. The race was on then, to get the cars out of the bush where they had been parked and onto the road, pull up bits of Mchekesana bush to beat out the flames, a night to remember.

We had some really bad bush fires around our place, one day my brother and I were out on our bikes as was normal, following the game tracks and looking for wire snares to destroy, when we got surrounded by a bush fire. We had to get into the middle of one of the cattle dams bikes and all and wait it out. The bush was really thick, and the ground very hot afterwards, even through our tackies. The most spectacular thing though was to see the Somabula flats on fire from the window of our train compartment, or if we were lucky enough to be in one of the old carriages, from the little balcony at the end.

We spent a huge amount of time in the Matopos, Dad was best friends with Skipper Knapman from Gordon Park, and we'd go out every weekend. He sunk the wells there, and I can remember the smell of the water, it was different from any other water I have ever seen or tasted, filtered through the sand it would come out kind of milky with the minerals, there was a run off donga which we used to paddle in. It was on one of our camping trips in Gordon Park that a leopard was inspecting the tent right where our heads were. We found his tracks the next morning. That was one of the first things we always did in the morning no matter where in the Matopos we camped, wake up and look for what passed in the night.

I wrote this in 1981 shortly after my "Goodbye" visit to our campsite behind Rhodes Grave in Matopos...

It crept me out when I re-read it, a kind of foretelling?

What will Be?

By Sue Halsey in 1981 after visiting the family campsite behind Rhodes's grave in the Matopos, for the last time....

The grass, once short and neat,
Now overgrown,   uncared for and shaggy.
The shady tree once vibrant and strong,   now half dead,
The huge leaves lying broken on the ground.
The water tank, full once,   with clean, cool water,
Now cracked, hidden   with grass and weeds.
Is this how it is going to be?
Forgotten,   Uncared for,   Neglected.
Is this all we have to live for?
Peaceful once,   now deathly quiet.
Gone.
Is this an Omen for the future?
Breaking Down,
              Fallen,
                     Dead.

"And all you see is a trophy? For me it is my Life!"
Photograph from Steve Bailey.

Extract from KK dictionary 1953
EMBRACE, vb. tr.—gumbatira, mbundira. **K.K. bambana.** "He was embracing my wife so I stabbed him." "Yena bambana na lo umfaaz gamena, mena chaili yena na lo pfumo gamena."

'Night Raid' by Karl Greenberg Rhodesia, early 1970's

We knew they were back!

The grinding war of attrition went on, year after year. In the dry season we normally had the upper hand. Our base was relatively new and our designated area for patrols seemed relatively free of this menace, as daily our small unit pounded the now familiar routes, our ever weary eyes open.

The rainy season always changed the situation. It was almost as if both sides needed respite from the game of hide and seek, a status quo, an unspoken agreement between the antagonists. We hated to slog through soaked grass and increasingly foul mud. The incredible majestic force of tropical storms kept us at base. Few dared to go out when those bolts of lightning started.

The enemy were happy to take time out to reorganise their forces in the isolated oasis packed with dense foliage for them to hide in.

We used an observation point on the small hill overlooking their self- designated territory hoping to spot them, but had no luck. Team leader reckoned that we would succeed tonight. The Old man, as he was better known, was frustrated with the previous failures. The whole thing was getting on his nerves, and he was starting to take it personally.

Night was their weakness; their soft underbelly. They always seemed a bit chatty after dark, but now their incomprehensible mutterings would be loud enough to be heard at base whenever a storm started to approach. They had got away with it for so long that they were becoming arrogant. Surely it would give them away at last!

We set up the ambush brilliantly. The Old Man reckoned the two of us could handle the job. I felt honoured as I was still in my teens. We picked up our fully prepared weapons. They had all been checked over that day. The last thing we needed was a faulty weapon.

The timing had to be impeccable; there was still a hint of light from another stunning African sunset touching the edges of the gathering storm clouds with hues of orange, and in the distance bright flashes of lightning were followed by the soft growls of thunder. We needed to be in and out before the storm hit us. We moved quietly from tree to tree, freezing if we thought we had been spotted, crouching low and silent on aching knees, then breathing a sigh of relief as their short suspicious silence would again be broken as throwing caution to the rapidly picking up wind, they used the opportunity to call others before the heavens opened up, cutting communications dead for both sides.

The other three members of our team were back at camp. They would know sooner or later if we were successful or not. Team leader told them to leave a few lights on, and that way the enemy wouldn't expect our surprise attack. For the first time in ages, the Old Man allowed those back at base to play the radio softly. A clever distraction. As we moved off nervously, I could hear the soft melody of the Paper Lace hit 'Billy, Don't be a Hero'. Somehow it helped to settle my nerves.

There was a watering hole below the small hill, and we knew they were using it. That's where we headed.

Adrenaline pumped through my body, overcoming my fear. I had an overwhelming feeling that this time we would get them.

Just before we had reached our intended cover of a group of bulrushes, we heard a noise, about three feet to our right. In the gathering darkness, we had almost stumbled on top of them.

Shit, shit, shit! The Old Man, gave me the agreed sign, and I opened up with all I had; simultaneously, he armed his huge weapon in one smooth stroke and brought it, on instinct, into play. We were in trouble; our hearts were pumping, my hands shaking from the suppressed excitement; if the Old Man missed, we were f*cked.

I turned on my torch, and caught the surprised common toad croaking away on a lily pad. Before it could draw its next breath and start that damn raucous din all over again or escape into the deeps, the Old Man brought the massive spade down flat from way over his head, and big mouth was airborne.

It must have risen six feet into the air; the shock wave pounded through the fishpond, the force powerful enough to create a miniature tsunami that broke over the concrete walls, splashing our feet, and it bellied up a few unsuspecting goldfish. It's a hard knock life. A few innocent citizens, caught in the crossfire.

The exploded corpse, guts hanging out of a surprised mouth, came down and lay at the Old Man's feet, spasmodically kicking like a flattened avocado pear with legs. With a deft swish, he scooped up the terminated toady and flicked it neatly over the hedge into the next door neighbours' garden. They were a strange lot, didn't mix in, so it was 'no problemo' sending them a croaked croaker.

We went back to the house, celebrated our success, and were able to get a decent night's sleep for the first time in days. Until the next lot turned up of course.

Later on, during further attacks, I would be in charge of the spade, and with practise I was able to hit the corpse on its down trip, whacking it smoothly over the border. This technique meant they travelled a good deal further into next door's garden.

Toading season closed after the rains, but not before the fishpond was full of their offspring. Using a small net I would scoop them up and tip them onto the grass so David our garden-boy could hack them into tadpole porridge with the lawnmower. The sieved, dried, drawn and quartered bodies were scattered liberally as a deterrent to future reckless parents.

Extracted from
"Last of the Rhodesians: Chronicles of a Colonial Anarchist."

Petrol Queues by John Baldwin

I was working in town for David Whiteheads and the folks were farming 25ks out of town. I had a Mazda 1600 bakkie and a Honda 90 motor bike and of course most often used my bike to get to work to minimize petrol consumption, but on the occasions I needed to top up the bakkie to go out to the farm to visit the folks.

The procedure was to load the bike onto the bakkie with it's plank ramp, go to work with both and then at the end of the day (6pm) pass by the closed petrol station park my van first in the queue which had not started yet. I checked that the garage had the guard there for the night, explain to him that I was filling up in the morning, ask what time they opened (normally 8am) and offer him a bonsela for watching the car overnight and then off load my bike and head home.

In the morning I would go to work early so that I could have off 15 minutes or so at 8am (tea time) to go to the petrol pumps and get the fuel then load the bike back onto the bakkie and drive back to work. So I had no worries about waiting in the queues, and didn't have take excessive time off to do what comes as a natural past time now.

The sad thing is I'm sure today I would have no tyres or headlight left by morning and the guard would have disappeared pocketing the cash or beaten up for it.

Queue Blues by Mike Beresford,

I've seen the world from the mountain tops and the fish in the blue coral sea,
I've watched the eagle soar in the sky and the Falls on the Zambesi.
But I have to say at the end of the day, my favourite thing to do,
Is see life from a different perspective, in a Zimbo petrol queue.

I was taking some fudge to my mother when I joined a long petrol line,
The lady behind was hungry, so I offered her that which was mine.
Her husband called on her cell phone to ask when her bakkie would budge,
She said, "Honey, I haven't got fuel at all but I've eaten a kilo of fudge."

There's a new social world in those columns of cars that form part of the lifestyle in Zim,
Loaded with crosswords and biscuits and cards and with tonic to drink with your gin.
The hours pass slow as the queues quietly grow and snake all around and about,
One girl, who went in as a virgin, was a mother before she came out.

The dramas of life keep unfolding as you watch and you wait and you hope,
Your battery is flat from the starting and you can't push the car up the slope.
You are needing the loo but you can't leave the queue, your spirits are starting to slump,
You must stay there all day and watch people pray to the God of the Petrol Pump.

Rumours abound as the cell phones ring round; Gaddafi has shut down the flow,
He won't even take Heroes Acre, for a few thousand litres or so.
Our leader cries "Foul" and his blind henchmen howl that its all a colonialist plot,
He threatens to seize the oil companies and urges that Blair should be shot.

We braaied up some wors on the pavement and swallowed a few lukewarm beers,
We buried the guy who was three from the front and his widow shed copious tears,
But true to the spirit of those gathered there, she refused to surrender her spot.
"I started at four in the morning and I'll stay - whether he's here or not."

New friendships start and lovers must part and business is done on the curb,
Your queue-mates have fun as they sweat in the sun and swap all the scandal they've heard.
In the fullness of time at the head of the line, you at last get your litre or two,
Then you pack up your gear and you head for the rear of the bread or the cooking oil queue.

Life After Death

Farmer : "Jacob! Do you believe in life after Death?"
Jacob: "Ack-chewully , No Sir!"
Farmer : "Why not ?"
Jacob : "Well , basicully , there is no proof that it ack-chewully exists , Sir!"
Farmer: "Well there is proof now."
Jacob : "Hai-bo ! Seri-ass?"
Farmer : "Yes absolutely! After you left early yesterday to go to your brother's funeral, he came here looking for you."
Jacob: "Eeishh...!"

Simple Delights by anon

Life was full of simple delights. We loved going to the veggie garden and picking fresh raw veggies and eating them. My brother loved onions, he would eat a whole one like an apple.

Couldn't go near him for hours afterwards.

Even the dogs gapped it.

The best though was the Mealies. We had an old Rhodesian concrete brick boiler for our hot water, and the garden boy would keep it going, or if it was his days off us kids were in charge of it. We would grab a mealie and peel off most of the leaves and whack it in the coals, while it was cooking we would sit on an old 44 gallon drum leaning against the fire-warmed bricks and soak up the sun.

Mealies never tasted so good.

We would walk on those drums too, rolling them up and down the long driveway, walk for hours, and play dodgem cars on them. you could get a real bit of speed up on a slight downhill, but coming up it again was a killer. Used to make them into battle ships also till Dad got them and chopped them in half for braai drums. Then we turned them into canoes.

Riding our bikes through the bush was always a challenge, as fast as possible along the footpaths through the acacia thorn trees, you got to know where to jink and where to duck, until some African put a snare across the path to catch his dinner. That would start us off on another tangent and we would spend hours scouring the bush removing snares. We found some once made out of 8 gauge wire, they would have caught a Kudu and held him.

As we grew up and the war intensified, things changed, priorities changed. Got married and had to contend with Hubby going off to the army.

Twice after he had gone I had crank calls telling me that he had been killed. Common sense should have told me that I wouldn't get a phone call, that I would be visited. Lucky I had family in the army and would arrive at my sister's house in a state of total panic and she would get onto my cousin who was fairly high up and get to the truth.

That was horrible.

Of course as soon as your man left, the car would break down, the cat would die, everything would go wrong.

We learned to cope with these emergencies and fix things ourselves.

We had to……….. no alternative.

Sergeant Gora by Richard Randall Maun, Botswana. December 2004

They were waiting for me as usual outside the District Commissioner's office: two lines of African Messengers in starched khaki uniforms, their wide-brimmed hats set jauntily to one side, standing rigidly at attention next to the Rhodesian flag. It was 7.30 a.m. on an April day in 1974. Sgt. Gora, facing the men, turned round smartly, and saluted me.

"Messengers ready for inspection, Sir".

"Very good, sergeant", I examined the men, noticing that the sergeant had made sure they were immaculately turned out. For the sake of form, I would now and then point out some slight irregularity of dress or posture in one of the men, which Gora always took very seriously and sternly lectured the offender.

I walked through the arched doorway and into my high-ceilinged, spacious office. My duties, like those of all District Commissioners, were very varied – official correspondence, meetings with chiefs, headmen, other government officials, members of the public, and adjudicating cases of African Customary Law. There was a time when I used to enjoy my meetings with the chiefs as discussions with them were generally short and to the point: the need for better roads, new schools, a clinic; could the D.C. not shoot an elephant or two to provide them with meat?, and so on. Now the situation had changed. The north of the country, especially in the Zambezi Valley where I was stationed, was infested with anti-government guerrillas, called terrorists ("terrs") by our side and freedom fighters by theirs. Talks with the chiefs, still loyal to the white Government, now centred around methods of combating the menace, locating and infiltrating enemy ranks and keeping the villagers on our side. There were daily reports of terr atrocities and more and more of our soldiers, of both the regular and territorial army, were to be seen in this once peaceful area, trying to contain the onslaught. We were an anachronism and the world, having undergone a bewildering sea-change since the Second World War, hated us for it and could not forgive us. The word "colonial" had now taken on a pejorative meaning, whereas a few short years previously it had stood for something honourable, at least in the eyes of Western Europeans who founded the colonies.

These "Messengers" were the eyes and ears of the colonial government, technically civilians, but to all appearances para-military. They had been a vital part of the civil administration of colonies throughout the Empire. They kept D.C.s informed on tribal matters and would report suspicious activities in the bush. The terrs consequently saw them as enemies. We relied on the messengers for much of our intelligence and the sergeants in particular played a crucial role in providing us with information.

Sgt. Gora was the first person I met when I had been posted to the district of Sipolilo. It was my first station. He greeted me with the faintest of smiles and seemed to be appraising me. I instinctively felt I would have to earn his trust. He was of slightly above medium height, burly, very black in complexion with strong masculine, well-chiselled features. Gora (meaning vulture in English) came from the main tribe of the country, the Shona. He looked ten years younger than his fifty-one years. A man of few words, he accompanied me wherever I went on my rounds, never complaining, always there when I needed him. He was superbly fit and never seemed to tire, even when carrying a 30 kg. backpack and an FN .762mm rifle. I was twenty-two years younger than Gora and in those days could easily walk thirty kilometres in the hot Zambezi Valley, on foot-patrol visiting villages or hunting crop-destroying elephants; but it was I who called the rest stops, never Gora. He never drank whilst walking, even in 40° C + heat and only took a couple of sips from his water bottle when we stopped for a brief lunch; he invariably returned to base in the evening with his bottle nearly full, whereas mine was usually empty by midday and my mouth parched long before sunset.

"Drinking water makes you weak", he would say.

Presumably, he hadn't read modern medical journals.

I came to realise that Sgt Gora's heart was as stout as his physique and he proved to me his valour on many occasions. The first of these, in the days before the terr incursions had become frequent in our immediate vicinity, was when our car got stuck in mud in a very remote corner of the district in an area seething with big and dangerous game – rhinos, elephants, buffaloes and lions. Try as we could, using sticks and stones under the tyres, we could not get the Land Rover out: the mud was like soft cement and the wheels had no purchase. I was recovering from a recent bout of malaria and still in a weakened state, not up to a long walk. We were out of H.F. radio range. The sun was setting and the nearest village where we could get more manpower to pull us out was some 23 kilometres away. It was a moonless night.

"You stay here, Sir; I go get help", Gora said, more as a statement than a suggestion. I wanted to remonstrate, to say that it was crazy to walk at night in this place, but I had an appointment the next day at 2 p.m. with the Provincial Commissioner, my immediate superior, coming up on a tour of inspection from Salisbury, and I had to be there. Gora knew that, too. So I let him go, not without misgivings. It was just after sunset. I watched him head off through the bush until the night swallowed him up, and then tried to make myself comfortable in the Land Rover. Around midnight it started to rain. I spent a fitful night on the hard, narrow seats listening to the gruff grunts of a pair of Verreaux's Eagle Owls and the distant, rasping call of a territorial male leopard, and eventually fell asleep around 3.a.m.

I woke up three hours later just as the sun was breaking the horizon. It was drizzling. Was it my imagination? –no, I could hear singing with Gora's baritone notes recognisable amongst the other male voices. I stood in the mud by the vehicle as they emerged through the bush, Gora at the forefront: 13 men, drenched, carrying picks and shovels, ropes … and singing. He had taken off his soaked hat, so didn't salute. "Good morning, Sir. Now we can pull out the car'', he said, almost blithely.

I looked at him carefully. He showed little signs of the night's exertions.

"Well done, Sergeant", I replied softly.

He had walked nearly fifty kilometres in the dark, with no compass other than his natural in-built sense of direction, amongst unseen dangerous animals; for much of the night it had rained and there were no visible stars to guide him. Yet he had unerringly found the village and by the force of his personality, no doubt re-enforced by his considerable local reputation, had persuaded a dozen men to follow him back in the dark through the bush to the stranded vehicle. He had kept up morale by singing and making light of the hazards of the bush.

"If you talk loud or sing in the dark, the animals hear you a long way off and keep away", he told me later.

It took us less than an hour to extricate the Land Rover and I ferried the men in two loads, back to their village. I naturally wanted to reward them for their stalwart effort. There were lots of kudus in that area and I shot them a big bull within 400 metres of the village. Owing to the presence of tsetse flies in the Valley, they had no livestock, and rarely ate red meat; so game meat was particularly welcome.

I set off for the office in the vehicle, Gora next to me in high spirits. The station was four hours away, situated near the top of the Zambezi Escarpment. I arrived there in good time and was able to shower and change in time for my meeting with the P.C. - thanks to Gora.

Shortly afterwards terrorist incursions from neighbouring Zambia became more frequent and travelling around the district become hazardous. Landmines were a constant danger. Most of the official vehicles were mine-proofed with thick armour-plating on their undersides. Most, but not all. One day a road gang was sent to the Valley to repair a small bridge that had been partly washed away by recent heavy rain. A tractor towed a trailer carrying the gang of fifteen workers to the bridge. The tractor's narrowly-spaced front wheels just missed the landmine buried in the road before the bridge; so did the widely-spaced back wheels. The trailer's wheels, however, were spaced such that one of them went right over and detonated the boosted mine, with catastrophic results. The explosion was heard from a temporary Roads Department camp some ten kilometres away and one of the engineers immediately sent a radio message to me at the D.C.'s rest camp which was half an hour's drive from the bridge. I knew instinctively it was a landmine. I called Sgt. Gora and we jumped into the Land Rover and raced to the bridge, oblivious to the possibility of other mines or ambushes. We had all seen casualties of the terror war during the past couple of years, but the scene of carnage that we came across was particularly shocking. There were six survivors, all with massive injuries The other workers were literally blown to pieces as the trailer was shattered by the explosion. The stench of blood and death was overpowering. As we examined the bodies, and bits of bodies, and tried to extricate mangled survivors from the wreckage, I noticed Gora's grim expression turn to grief when he came across one corpse: it was his cousin. The word cousin does not exist in

African languages: all cousins are brothers within the extended family system. We gently moved those still breathing – six men - to the shade of nearby bushes, bandaged them as best we could with our inadequate first-aid equipment, covered the dead with leafy branches and then Gora went and lifted the dazed tractor driver from the seat of the tractor (still on its wheels, the trailer having been blown clean away from it) in which he had remained slumped since the explosion, with burst ear-drums, but otherwise unhurt.

Sometimes terrorists returned to the scene of a landmine detonation, to bayonet survivors, so I told Gora to be vigilant while I shot off to camp to radio for assistance – a helicopter, a medical team, soldiers, police. I didn't like leaving him alone, but had no option. If the terrs came back, I thought, he would sell his life dearly. There was no chopper available as these were all being used on anti-terrorist raids to the east, I was told, but two ambulances and an army lorry with soldiers were on their way. Five cruel hours away… I returned to the bridge and consulted with Gora who was seated by his cousin looking grimly into the clear blue April sky, all signs of rain clouds gone. We decided, contrary to conventional first aid "wisdom", not to leave the survivors in situ, but to pack them into the Land Rover and head towards the ambulances, to meet them half way. This would cut down on the time they could get morphine and drips. We dropped off the tractor driver, still speechless and dazed, at the road camp and continued towards the escarpment. Those Zambezi Valley roads were bumpy and I suppose I should have driven gently, but I reckoned that the injured were beyond feeling bumps and I drove as fast as I could. I'll never forget that drive, Gora beside me rock steady and silent, the gut-wrenching odours from the back of the station wagon, the moans. I was grateful for Gora's strong and loyal presence.

When we eventually met the ambulances, one worker, a youth of no more than eighteen or nineteen, had died en route, which was not surprising as his right leg was shattered and the frothy bright red blood issuing from his mouth clearly indicated serious lung injuries. In his breast pocket he had a tattered Post Office Savings Bank Book indicating that his name was Shadreck Mandengu and that his balance was twenty-nine Zimbabwe dollars and seventy-five cents, no doubt all the money he possessed. I made sure, later, through Gora, that his mother received this savings book and his full monthly wage for that month. I also gave her the blood-stained pack of Bicycle playing cards we found in the one trouser pocket that was still intact. All the others in the vehicle survived, but were, to a greater or lesser extent, permanently disabled.

Following this incident and other terrorist attacks, the army sent in more troops and, for a few months, the terrs left the area. We knew they would return, but profited from this time to enjoy the magnificent wilderness of the Valley. Life took on a lighter aspect. I was again able to hunt, with Gora as my tracker, a tracker whose skills I have never seen surpassed. I am a fair tracker myself, but Gora could follow spoor where others could see nothing – over hard ground, a carpet of leaves, even rocks. He had no equal when it came to spooring game. Many were the times when we lost the spoor and he would tell me to stay put while he cast around to see which way the animal had gone, sometimes disappearing for twenty minutes. He would always come back with a wry grin on his face and would lead me to the tracks. Animals often seem to walk with a progression that does not conform to any human logic, turning this way and that, changing course for no apparent reason. But Gora, I am convinced to this day, could think like an animal: he would stop, look at the lie of the land, and, leaving the spoor, would head off in a different direction, only to cut across the spoor again a considerable distance away, thus saving on the time one would have spent doggedly following each footstep. He intuitively knew when and why an animal would turn and take up another course, or the most likely route it would take. This is an ability all the best trackers have. Trackers either have it or they don't, much like the special talent of top musicians. Such gifts can't be developed.

One hunt will live long in my memory. We were following the tracks of three bull elephants that had been raiding some villagers' maize crops growing along the banks of the Angwa River. The huge bulks and appetites of the elephants wreaked havoc in the fields, and the unarmed villagers, whose crops enabled them to eke out a meagre existence, naturally sought redress from the authorities against the nocturnal raids of these animals. The elephants cannily always left a couple of hours before dawn, knowing from experience that in the light of day hunters might attack them in the crops. We had arrived at the maize fields at 5 a.m., waiting for enough dawn light to make an early start after them. Retreating elephants walk faster than a man and they were already well away when we took up their spoor: three bulls, all large, judging by their big footprints. Gora and I knew we had a long hunt ahead of us and would not catch up with them while they were walking in the cool of the morning and anxious to get as much distance as possible between them and the fields where danger lurked during the day; but we also knew that it would soon be hot and the elephants would rest up under shady trees around 11 o'clock. We followed them silently, taking it in turns to spoor. There was no need to talk: we knew the business at hand. We had done this before. The elephants had left an obvious trail – dung, footprints, bits of freshly chewed vegetation, bent shrubs – and spooring them was easy work as we followed the animals through thick stands of grey mopane trees, then jesse bush and on into acacia woodland.

Around 10 o'clock the tracks indicated that the elephants were slowing down and soon we could see that they were ambling around in the bush, looking for suitable shade. Gora pointed out some yellow-green dung, still wet.

"They're not far, now", he whispered.

I took out an ash-filled sock from my pocket and shook it. We noted with satisfaction that the fine leadwood ash drifted slowly back towards us. Elephants can smell a man fully a kilometre away if he is upwind of them, and at close quarters the hunter must be very careful not to give the elephants his wind. In the heat of the day wind is often fickle and one must be constantly testing it, changing course if necessary. When an elephant gets your scent, it generally decamps quickly … but it may also charge. We continued slowly and silently.

Twenty minutes later the vegetation became much thicker, with trees densely packed. Suddenly, Gora hissed and, grinning with anticipation, pointed to a large umbrella-thorn acacia forty metres away. Through its branches I could make out the rhythmic flapping of large grey ears. The bush was quiet, all nature resting silently in the heat, save for a couple of turtle-doves cooing in the distance. There are always turtle-doves in Africa and their sound is so omnipresent that one does not even notice it – unless one is approaching the world's largest land mammals on foot to within a few metres. Then one's keyed-up senses detect the slightest sound and movement.

Gora with the light .762 F.N. military rifle stayed back and I unshouldered my heavy .470 Nitro Express double-barrelled big game rifle. My time had come; it was up to me to finish this. But first I needed to examine all three bulls to select the biggest tusker as I wanted to secure good trophy ivory. I advanced with a dry mouth, my pulse up a notch or two, working my way around to the right-hand side of the tree. The elephants were standing a few metres apart and it took a couple of minutes (it felt like hours) to make out their tusks through the leaves. One bull, the nearest, as luck would have it, seemed to have the best ivory, but I couldn't see all the length of his tusks. (Many a hunter, after hastily shooting an elephant that appeared to carry good tusks, has been disappointed to find that the tip of one of them is broken, or even that he is a one-tusker.) I manoeuvred further to the right, then the elephant moved forward a couple of steps and I saw his splendid tusks. There was no doubt, now: this was the one. I was just taking stock of the position of the other two bulls when I felt the wind at the back of my neck.

Bad.

Any second now the elephants would get my scent. Using the tree trunk as cover I quickly advanced to within twenty metres of the bull standing sideways on to me, aimed between the eye and the ear-hole and fired. He dropped like a stone, shot through the brain. As was my custom, I went up to him and gave him another shot in the temple, just to make sure, as I knew that many a downed elephant has only been stunned and has suddenly got up again and killed the unsuspecting hunter. This one was well and truly dead. I estimated his tusks weighed about eighty pounds apiece, good for the late twentieth century when the average weight of elephant tusks was much less than it had been only a few decades previously. Just after the shot, out of the corner of my eye, I saw one of the other two elephants rush off, crashing through the undergrowth; I presumed the other had also gone.

Gora came up to me to congratulate me and then sat on the elephant's rough and hairy trunk. I propped my rifle against the side of the elephant and walked off to admire him from a distance. I heard a slight sound behind me and swung around. There he was: the third bull, thirty-odd metres away, head raised, eyes staring savagely at me, tail held stiffly up, ears outstretched – five-and-a-half tons of rage and menace. I had seen too many elephants not to know what was coming next. With an ear-shattering scream of rage, he folded his ears and came at me like a steam train. I turned and ran. A charging elephant can easily overhaul a running man, and, unlike a puny human, is not impeded by thorny bushes and scrub. It was hopeless: he was gaining on me fast. And then I tripped over a root with the elephant right behind me.

I remember thinking, "so this is it, then" and wondering if he would kneel on me, stamp on me, tusk me, or pick me up with his trunk and smash me into the ground. Such thoughts go through one's head in micro-seconds. I was just scrambling to my feet again with the grey, mountain-sized, crazed monster bearing down on me a few paces away when I heard the single-fire staccato cracks of the F.N. rifle. Gora! The elephant stumbled, but got up again almost immediately. That gave me a few precious seconds to try to make it to a large termite mound. The elephant, trumpeting continuously, took off again, but this time it was not towards me – it was towards Gora who was in an open space a few metres away with nowhere to hide. I watched rooted to the spot in fascination as the elephant bore down on him with homicidal intent. Gora never flinched, keeping the F.N. aimed at the head of the bull. The .762's bullets were light, and designed to deal with humans - not the biggest of the world's big game. Gora was evidently aware of this, too, as he held fire until the elephant was eight paces away (I measured the distance later) and opened up, this time on automatic. The elephant fell to its knees, but groggily started getting up again. Before it could regain its feet fully Gora had changed magazines, whipped round to the side of its head and fired a quick burst into the ear-hole where the F.N.'s bullets would be able to reach the brain. The bull toppled over on to its side sending up a cloud of red dust, its legs quivering. It was over.

I ran up to Gora, breathless. "Bloody hell, man, that was close".

Never one to be expansive, Gora merely shook his head: "Ah, this elephant too cheeky. Are you O.K., Sir?"

"I think so. Bit bruised."

Gora walked over to the elephant he had shot, cut off its tail and presented it to me. We walked slowly back to the first elephant and I picked up the .470, slipped in two 500 grain steel-jacketed solids, and went and sat in the shade. Gora fetched the small backpack he had been carrying and offered me water from his canteen. We were not hungry.

"By the way, Gora – thanks".

As we walked back to the village to inform the villagers of the bonanza of meat waiting for them and to ask them to chop out and bring in the tusks, I recalled the times when other trackers and messengers had simply vanished in the presence of aggressive elephants leaving me absolutely alone. Gora was contemptuous of them.

During our walks in the Valley Gora and I were charged several times by lions when we had to stand our ground and shout and wave our arms and even run towards the on-rushing lion, a decidedly counter-intuitive procedure. This disconcerted the lions which are used to their prey and lesser animals running away from them. Lions are good at "mock charging". They would come for us at great speed, growling horribly and break off the charge from ten to five metres away. We also had a couple of narrow escapes from Black Rhino, but, for some reason, were never bothered by the feared Cape Buffalo which occurred there in big herds. Buffaloes never "mock charge", and when they rush at you with sinister, bleary red eyes and you have no convenient tree to shin up, only two things will stop them: their death, or yours. Fortunately they don't often charge…But we always kept a close eye on them when we came across them in the bush….

Sometimes my administrative duties necessitated my remaining at the station for up to two weeks at a time, and as the days passed both Gora and I would become increasingly frustrated with this sedentary existence. Gora had received little formal education as a child and did not have a high regard for paper work. I think he regarded it as somehow unbefitting an active man. He would pass by my office and briefly peer at me with an expression that said it all.

"Come on, man, let's get out of here and go and do some real work!"

I pretended to ignore him, but he knew that sooner or later I would find some reason to go into the field. I would send one of the junior messengers to summon him to my office and took pleasure in watching the smile on his face when I said,

"Sergeant, we leave for the Valley this afternoon. Ten days. Get everything ready." Often he had anticipated me and replied "everything ready, Sir".

And, indeed, I would find the Land Rover fuelled and all camping equipment and tinned food packed neatly in the back of the vehicle; it only remained for him to pick up some fresh produce from the local supermarket and my bottle of Scotch from the bottle store.

I was in my office in December 1975, the day after a visit to the remote north-eastern part of the Valley where Gora and I had discussed the co-ordination of a polio vaccination programme with the local chief and headmen, when I received a 'phone call from the police Station Commander. I was watching a lightning storm of particular intensity, such as occurs several times during the summer in tropical southern Africa. The lightning bolts lit up the surrounding koppies and the acacia trees with a breathtaking brilliance and the rain lashed down in buckets. I always found such weather highly stimulating.

"We've got your Sgt. Gora here in custody. Seems he beat up someone rather badly last night; I think you had better come over," said the Station Commander.

"I'm on my way," I replied, not wanting to discuss this startling news over the telephone.

Thirty minutes later I had the story. When Gora and I got back to the station after our trip, Gora went home to his staff quarters where he lived with his young wife and four year old son. He saw his wife was unhappy and at first he couldn't get anything out of her, but eventually she reported that a certain Samuel, a Roads Department foreman also living in the Government compound, had come over to her in a drunken state one evening whilst we were away. He had made indecent proposals to her and became noisy and abusive when she told him to get away. She said she would report him to her husband, whereupon Samuel retorted that he was not afraid of an old man and that she would do much better to have a younger man like him. He eventually staggered off, shouting that Gora was merely an uneducated Messenger who could not get a decent job. Gora listened to his wife in stony silence. Several neighbours had gathered around Gora during his wife's recital of the incident and having heard much of the loud altercation between her and Samuel, they were able to corroborate the story.

Gora immediately went to Samuel's house and shouted to him to come out. Now, Samuel, who appeared on the doorstep insolently grinning at the Sergeant, was a large man, several inches taller than Gora, well-built and some twenty-five years younger. Gora said quietly that he, an uneducated old messenger, was going to educate Samuel. Samuel laughed and told Gora he should go home and retire at his village. Gora then rushed at him and a terrific fight ensued in which Gora's uncommon strength, enflamed by his fury, proved far too much for Samuel whom Gora left senseless with a broken nose and several cracked ribs. Apart from a cut above his eye, a swollen lip and several bruises on his legs, Gora did not appear the worse for wear. Meanwhile, someone had called the police and Gora was taken into custody. He spent the night in gaol. Samuel was taken by the police to the local clinic where he was given medical attention. He was reported to be most uncomfortable, but "stable".

These were the facts presented to me by the Station Commander.

"Even though Gora was provoked, he did assault and injure a man," he said. "I should charge him. You can't take the law into your own hands, you know. And he is unrepentant".

"Yes", I replied, but I could see the twinkle in the Station Commander's eye. He knew Gora's reputation and, like me, found it difficult to condemn him for the forceful and decisive defence of his and his wife's honour. In fact, we rather approved of what he had achieved: swift, effective justice, even if somewhat forceful.

"I'll release him and you can deal with him as you please," said the Station Commander. "And if Samuel, when he recovers, tries to press charges for assault and battery, I'll threaten him with charges of breaking the peace, public indecency and defamation of character. That should silence him."

I was not sure if such charges could be made to stick in a court of law, but readily concurred.

Gora was released and I left instructions that he should go home and report to me the next morning. I had decided not to humiliate him by going to visit him in his cell.

When he came into my office and stood to attention I affected to be engrossed in some official document on my desk. I let him stand for fully two minutes. That was all face looked almost serene. I knew he must have gone down fighting and abusing the enemy. A man came up to me as I was inspecting the corpse and announced that he was Gora's elder brother. I asked him where Gora's wife and child were and he replied that they were away on a visit to the wife's parents in Mtoko, the next district. So she and the child, thank God, were safe. I went to my car and took a blanket that I always kept in the vehicle and wrapped Gora in it, and his brother and I placed the bloodstained body on the back bench-seat. The lieutenant came across and asked me what I was doing.

"Taking my sergeant to Sipolilo clinic myself", I answered, in no mood for any official obstruction.

He saw the look on my face and then realising that I was, after all, the senior government representative in the district, said nothing and turned back to the shed.

It was a long drive back to the station, as I drove slowly, the two Messengers and I squashed up in the front and Gora's lifeless body in the foetal position in the back. I recalled his powerful, virile presence the last time he had ridden with me in the Land Rover, sitting bolt upright, keen and alert. And now…

The funeral was eight days later. The station Messengers and I formed a guard of honour around the open grave; Gora, in a simple pine-wood coffin had been dressed in his uniform, including his hat. His widow stood behind our circle, her eyes downcast, expressionless. She held his son by the hand while he shyly looked around him with wide eyes. The Chaplain read some verses from the Bible, then it was my turn to speak. I took out from my pocket the notes I had carefully put together the day before for a fitting eulogy to a man that I had shared so much with, despite our differences in position and culture, over the months and years, a man who had been such a loyal and brave servant of the Government. I looked at the coffin and then put the notes away. How could the essence of such a man be portrayed in a few, grossly insufficient words of praise? I looked round at the Messengers and then, acting on an impulse, told the men to wait while I dashed off in my car to the office. Once there I found in the storeroom what I needed, an old leopard skin and a small elephant tusk confiscated from a poacher long ago. I was back at the grave site within ten minutes. No-one had moved and all stood in silence. I could see the questioning in their eyes.

I held the leopard skin in my left hand and the tusk in the right and said "This man was an example to all of us. We are all privileged to have known him. We salute a great sergeant, a great warrior and a loyal friend. Fortunate are those who have half the qualities of such a man".

I wanted to say more, but I knew that in Africa symbolism is more important than words, so I placed the prime symbols of chiefdom, the elephant tusk and the leopard skin, on the coffin. This would be my peroration. I signalled for the coffin to be lowered. The Messengers, under the new sergeant who had replaced Gora, fired three volleys of blanks over the grave, then the army buglers sounded the "Last Post".

The Ballad of Jeremy Bell   by Mike Beresford

I met him one day when in army pay, where the Sambas river flows wide,
Where Mopani flies drink from your eyes on the blink and the sun leaves you no place to hide,
We lived those six days in that sweltering haze, but I can't tell you I knew him well,
He was quiet, almost grim, and he lived deep within the spirit of Jeremy Bell.

Called up together we went hell for leather to the end of that bitter fought war,
We kept our own space and we kept our own pace, there was no need for anything more.
With time in the end I became his near friend, or as close as a buddy could tell,
It's the end of his trail, I'll tell you his tale – the sad story of Jeremy Bell.

Like the miners of old his Dad dug for gold and sought the impossible dream,
Never mentioned his Ma when we drank in the bar, I guess she dropped out of the scheme.
They followed the ore yet searching for more 'til it pinched where they never could tell,
He was raised in the wild from his time as a child to the man they called Jeremy Bell.

Pa worked like beaver, caught blackwater fever, and he died where he wanted to be,
His son shed a tear then he buried him there, in the roots of a baobab tree.
He closed up the shaft, paid the boys for the graft he sold what there was left to sell,
He drove into town and the wheels drummed the sound of a new life for Jeremy Bell.

Took a mining degree which was as it should be, for mining flowed strong in his veins,
Took the town by the tail as would any true male though he yearned for his wilderness claims
Then he found a true pearl when he courted a girl who drew him clear out of his shell,
He fell deeply in love with Barbara Bain and she loved Jeremy Bell.

The girl from the town wore that dour bush man down and soon they were happily wed
They grew in the joy of sharing their lives, their hopes and their fears and their bed.
The testing time came when the lure of his claim took them back to the bush he knew well.
So new life now came to Barbara Bain, at the homestead of Jeremy Bell.

He taught her the ways of the valleys and vleis, the rhythms of season and time,
The molten blaze of the sunsets and dawn that flamed on Kariba's shoreline.
The creatures that teemed in the lowveld, the tracks and the sounds and the smell,
Were the fabric of life now she was the wife of a miner called Jeremy Bell.

They drove into town with a bakkie with a load of crude ore from the mine,
They bought a few spares and drank a few beers and returned in the late evening time,
The moon shone serene on the bushveld scene as the headlights bored bright into hell.
His truck left the track and the crash broke the back of the wife of Jeremy Bell.

She was quiet and calm as she died in his arms while the sun rose up over the trees,
His light was now gone so he reached for the gun that was clipped in a rack by his knees.
In the darkness of pain he barely took aim but his face was smashed by the shell.
And though he lived on, the spirit was gone from the body of Jeremy Bell.

He healed with time and returned to his mine where he went through the motions of living,
Where his hideous face mattered not in a place where the spirits are blind and forgiving.
Who knows of his thoughts, his cries and retorts as he dwelt like a monk in his cell
Who knows of the fears, the hot guilty tears, in the mind of Jeremy Bell?

For two years he lived on, but he did not belong in a world without Barbara Bain
One night he walked out of his camp with no doubt to the hills, which solaced his pain,
He never came back down that Jesse bush track and no one knew quite what befell,
That sad, empty man, that once I had known, as a miner called Jeremy Bell.

Perhaps he's just part of the valley, in the streams and the boulders and trees,
Or maybe he flies where the fish eagle cries on the lift of a hot summer breeze,
Some days he will roam through the ruins of his home, where hornbills and guinea fowl dwell,
And he walks hand in hand through the mine dump sand with the woman he loved - Barbara Bell.

Extract from KK dictionary 1953

CORRECT,vb. tr. – gadzira, ruramisa, K.K. Longisa. A word constantly to be used as something needs correcting most of the time on any farm but more so in Rhodesia. Most of the work already completed requires correcting. "That hoeing is bad, correct it." " Lapa wean rimili yena mubi sterek, longisa!"

More RLI Snippets from Nigel Rittey

Other characters...

In the early 60's the Duke of Edinburgh, or some other high-powered dignitary, found an excuse to visit Rhodesia and, while the Royal Flight aircraft was parked at New Sarum, some bright spark decided it's safety could not be entrusted to the "blue jobs". A guard was called for from the RLI. One of the carefully selected soldiers was a little fellow with a big chip on his shoulder. He was always moaning and blasphemed anything to do with the establishment. George Dearnley probably had trouble living with himself let alone with his peers. The night was long and he got bored, so he started to do the equivalent of what he probably idly did all the time to the tube trains in his native England...he lovingly carved his name into a panel of the aircraft's undercarriage doors with the point of a bayonet.

His feet never touched the ground.

Another Anglo- Saxon screwball who spent his career swearing and cursing was Andy Headridge. His language was so foul and so interspersed with swear words that even his colleagues asked him to belt up occasionally.

Mystery still surrounds the disappearance of Pete Egglestone who vanished while swimming in the Zambezi at Chirundu. One moment he was there, the next he was not. He was never found.

Early recruitment efforts by the Army often went very wrong. During 1961 a couple of the Air Force Canadairs loaded up a bunch (the only description other than "mob", "pile" or "heap" that would fit!) of fine upstanding fellows who had been carefully selected out of England's finest youth. After a short while very few were left. A lot of them went AWOL and headed for South Africa where they were rounded up by the SAP and the SA Military Police. A special expedition of RP's and MP's was dispatched southwards to collect these miscreants and return them by train to the "Box" that awaited them back in Rhodesia.

Some time later, three or four more of these characters were nailed by the cops having been caught robbing a Post Office in Pioneer Street.

Only a handful stayed on as soldiers...and fine ones they were too.

The BSAP were usually a very tolerant lot. On many occasions when the three most favoured Salisbury nightspots "Bretts", "La Boheme" ("La Bomb") and "Le Coq d'Or" ("The Fly Button"!), spewed inebriated soldiers onto the pavement in the wee hours of the night, the cops would often either escort them home to barracks or call the RP's to come and fetch them.

The story is told of one character who moved to the new SAS and was doing his parachute training. He was pulled over by the fuzz while weaving all over the road in his car. When they asked him to demonstrate his sobriety...or the lack of it...by walking along a white line painted on the road, he said:

"Nay my China...not without a blerry parachute!"

A boring time of the year was the annual audit, conducted by the Government Audit Department. These "civvys" who were quickly nicknamed "the tickbirds", would swoop on the barracks and have a wonderful time counting,

"Rifles one, S.L.R. Troops for the use of",

"Land Rovers one, LWB, model 1962, Series 2, Reg. No. AB697,"

and of course,

"Drawers Cellular, pattern '44, troops for the wearing of", etc, etc, etc.

A SHORTFALL in the counting resulted in tons of paper but a SURPLUS was the most heinous crime of all because it caused many square miles of rain forest to be sacrificed.

Down at the MT yard we would carefully collect all our "baksheesh" tyres, wheels, spanners, batteries, gearboxes, tarpaulins and other "spoils of war" and put them aboard a malodorous and battered Bedford that did the daily garbage rounds. The driver would be told not to return to the barracks until such time as these civil servant types had gone home for their gins and tonics.

Popular hangouts at the time included the well known Palace Bar in downtown Salisbury. Right next door to the cinema (Bioscope!), it was ruled by the iron fists of a lady called Phyllis who was wise in the ways of the world…and troopies.

If still alive, she would have many stories to tell of payday nights in her pub.

Bulawayo was a good hunting ground for the fairer sex where a good spot for bad girls was the "Bon Journais" café. It was also a dive populated by the greasier "Duckies" who rode up on Triumph Bonnevilles, Norton Dominators and chopped up BSA's. Somehow these guys found it hard to co-exist with troopies…and vice-versa. Punch ups were frequent and unfortunately the leather lumberjackets and stovepipe trousers worn by them, proved far better than our KD longs and bushjackets when it came down to hand to hand combat. Our heavy belts gave us a bit of an edge though.

After an evening of mirth, merriment and mayhem it was customary to call at the pie carts where good "graze", washed down with powerful coffee, could be found for a few bob.

Thereafter came the ride back to Brady in a 3 wheeled "Rixi" taxi. These noisy little brutes were sadly underpowered and horribly unstable, but they were cheap, plentiful and, most of the time, got us back before the Military "Cinderella Hour" at 23.59.

Most troops had no transport and had to rely on thumbing lifts around Rhodesia. The public at that time were very accommodating and often offered free board and lodging to us rather than dump us on deserted roads late at night.

Private vehicles consisted mostly of very tired "heaps" bought on the "Never Never" which resulted in frequent visits by the Sheriff of the Court, whose representatives usually pounced on paydays in the hope of extracting their dues before the cash was converted into Castle Lager.

The status symbol of the day was to be the owner of a Ford Zephyr or a Zodiac. Major Tom Davidson had a yellow one much admired and envied by all. Most other English cars were not rated too highly but 2nd Lieutenant Barrett-Hamilton caused a stir by rocking up in an Austin Mini, which no one had seen before. When one of the "okes" saw the thing, he was heard to say:

"I scheme that outjie should park that thing on the grass at night so it can graze a bit and grow bigger."

Co-operation with the air force was always good. The chopper pilots, despite very sketchy briefing, could usually be counted on to find hot, tired troopies waiting at obscure…and often very difficult LZ's. Later in the Rhodesian conflict these fellows proved themselves to have been made of stern stuff, flying their clattering contraptions into very dangerous situations providing close support for troops on the ground. Sadly there were many casualties.

In the early 60's the Air Force were flying on a shoestring. Aircraft were in short supply and many of those they had, looked as if they had escaped from a museum.

On one occasion I found myself in the company of Willy De Beer, Mike Dippenaar, the late Dave Parker and a few others, waiting patiently on a patch of open ground between Mana Pools and the Zambezi escarpment. Our patience was rewarded by the grinding drone of an ancient Dakota which spotted our primitive air markers and made its' approach with flaps down. We could see that a huge crate was in the doorway ready to be dropped. This contained our weeks' rations, newspapers and mail destined for us, so it was a welcome sight.

On final approach, at low level, the big box of goodies was pushed out. There was no parachute and when the thing hit the deck, it exploded littering the Zambezi valley with tin cans, boxes, mail, bog-roll, biscuits, potatoes and what was left of the other vegetables so thoughtfully provided by the "jamstealers".

Forty years later it is probable that some of the wreckage is still there

A signal from the Air Force later suggested that they wanted their crate back, but they did apologise for the lack of parachutes. (It was rumoured that due to sanctions and shortages, the "Blue Jobs" had later experimented with hessian parachutes for the dropping of supplies.)

They never got the matchwood back!

A highlight of my later posting to 2 (Indep.) Company at Kariba was doing the "Vomit Comet" trip as observer on the South African Police Cessna 185's. Take off from Kariba was followed by the mandatory "beat up" of the barracks at Kariba Heights. Then the pilots screamed down to lake level (plus a couple of feet), turned right and belted it over the Blondin Cable in front of the dam wall which was cleared by a small margin. Then it was flaps down and throttle back to plummet into the gorge which was rather like flying underground. A part of the way down the gorge was a rocky outcrop, which seemed to be a nuisance to these crazy aviators because they had to bank at a steep angle to get through the gap. Fortunately they were very aware of the cable crossing the river at the banana farm at the exit so they did open up the taps again to get over the top of it. (Popular legend at the time has it that, on one memorable occasion, an SAP pilot had been haring down the gorge and met a Hawker Hunter of the RRAF engaged in the same activity but flying in the other direction.)

The flight continued with games such as "Hippo Crash-dives", "Bait the Buffalo" and "Irritate the Elephant".

It usually turned for home after Chirundu but sometimes took in Mana and even went as far as Mpata Gorge. The scenery was unforgettable.

Craziest of these SA pilots was a character called "R S" Du Toit who was usually a bit miffed if his passengers had not used their sick bags by the time he landed back at base.

The concept of formal "Goal Setting" was almost unheard of in the early 60's. It was only later that motivational gurus put down on paper things which most of us had been doing naturally all our lives. Goal setting must get started with a dream, which must then become an all-consuming passion and finally an itch strong enough to need constant scratching…in other words action. When men were thrown together by circumstance as we were, there was lots of time to dream. When a fire died down and the beer ran out, we sometimes shared these dreams. There were those who seriously intended to be promoted to a point where General Peter Walls would, if told by them to "jump", not dare to ask the question "How high?" Mostly however, the musings of the troops focused on beer, women, cars or motorcycles, farm or pub ownership and of course the Rhodesian Sweep. Sadly few action plans were drawn up to bring these simple needs to fruition, but the sharing of them gave rise to a tangible sense of companionship and camaraderie. We were all after the same goals.

Pets

Whilst the keeping of pets was generally frowned upon…except by married personnel at their quarters…there were a few informal ones worthy of recall.

Private Rossouw was at one time, the custodian of a young baboon. This animal had been seriously influenced by the beer drinking capacity of his mentor and was usually found in an inebriated state having polished off the dregs of many bottles of Castle.

At 2 (Indep.) Company at Kariba someone brought in a small Warthog. This also became notorious for it's drinking habit. As it matured it became more and more aggressive (possibly because it was either pissed or suffering from "babelaas") When this became a problem, Brian Bowley and a couple of others, threatened to give it "the unkindest cut of all". I cannot recall this animal's ultimate fate.

Of the "formal" animals the most famous was Lance Corporal Cheetah, the RLI's mascot. There was, in fact, more than one cheetah, as they had a habit of kicking the bucket from cat flu. He / they lived in the fenced area surrounding the Regimental ammo store near the assault course. This may account for the lack of any attempts by naughty people to break into the store.

At the Freedom of the City ceremony in Salisbury where the RLI were granted the privilege of marching through the streets "with bayonets fixed and colours flying", Lance Corporal Cheetah was seated in the rear of an open SWB Landrover following a detachment of troops as they turned left from one of the streets into Kingsway. The crowds were densely packed right up to the barricades. Out of the corner of my eye I spotted an old African who, after watching the departing troops to his left, turned his head and found himself staring into the eyes of the cheetah at a range of about two feet. He let out a yell and bolted for it. The cheetah merely yawned.

Break up of the Federation

Politicians… whose morals I have always placed in a category not far removed from those of used car dealers, lawyers and purveyors of snake oil…decided that the best way they could wash their hands of the matter of dishing out Real Estate in Africa to appease their electoral constituencies, was to do it in bite-sized pieces. To us they appeared to be thinking…

"Let's divvy up this thing called "Nyasaland" back to those fellows the Nyasas…we've given old Hastings Banda a rough time in the past so this will be a nice gesture. Then, when it comes to the big bit on the left here called "Northern Rhodesia", we'll let Kenny K and his boys have it (might get a bit of a whinge from the farmers and the Colonialists working on the mines and in commerce). When it comes to "Southern Rhodesia", we will have to get a bit cute, 'cos there's lots of Europeans and they really will get "beady" if we try to hand it to the locals on a silver platter. But first, lets put that old locomotive driver / boxer fellow with the Yiddish ancestry…old Sir Whatsisname… out to pasture, put in a puppet and then persuade all the worthwhile troops the southerners have, to chuck up the military by promising them untold riches if they opt out. (Just to ensure their bulldog is really toothless you see…don't want any of them revolting you know!)

If they don't want out, we should, out of good old-fashioned British decency, let them stay, or join Kenny K, or Hastings, if they care to.

OK chaps, that's unanimous…sun's over the yardarm…see you in the club for some 'drinkies'… what?…what?…what?."

Exit the politicians pursued by Christine Keeler and Mandy Rice-Davies.

Sadly many good guys opted for the money. A few ended up in the other territories. The departure of these comrades left many of us wondering if we had done the right thing.

The break up of the Federation was marked by a huge parade at Glamis Stadium where music was provided by several military bands all playing "en masse". A very moving farewell to Sir Roy Welensky, the ex locomotive driver and champion boxer, formed part of the proceedings and, a short while later, we received a little piece of paper thanking us for our service in the Federal Army. These were complete with the printed signature of the great man himself.

Those who took the money and got out, had a second piece of paper…a fat cheque for hundreds of quid signed by the Paymaster.

Salisbury, for a while at least, shook, rattled and rolled from all the partying hosted by the "nouveaux riche"…I wonder how much of their new found wealth was ever invested.

Many were broke and, being "ripe for the picking", were quickly recruited by groups such as Mike Hoare's Congo mercenaries who offered amazing incomes and untold riches to those who knew how to handle guns and blow things to bits. Some paid dearly with lives, or broken minds and bodies, and never lived to enjoy the spoils of that rotten little war.

More than forty years later the Congo remains torn apart by strife in spite of the efforts and sacrifices of these men, now only remembered by yellowing photographs in dusty shoeboxes or in the fading memories of widows, parents, children, girlfriends and comrades.

Many are buried where they fell in that God-forsaken country in graves long forgotten. God rest them…

The Medics.

These were mostly a pleasant lot devoted to the cause of preservation of Military Property (us!). There was however, a downside to them. They were "syringe happy". The book said that we were all to be regularly inoculated against all sorts of horrible "lurgis", plagues and poxes, so they would get us to queue up outside the Camp Hospital with sleeves rolled up, ready to be assaulted by their deadly weapons.

These hypodermics appeared to us to have been salvaged from a veterinary surgery specialising in circus elephants.

After a hasty wipe with an alcohol swab, their needles would plunge into our arms seeking firm contact with bone before the various venoms were pumped in. As fate would have it, some clown would ensure that when the real agony had begun to take hold, usually an hour or two later, we would be scheduled for a circuit of the Assault Course.

To cap all this they would regularly lose the records of those they had jabbed. To rectify their problem they would then call us all back for another round of pain and humiliation rather than have some individual miss out on their not-so-tender ministrations.

"Sick parade" was at set times of the day and was actually attended by some who really were sick. Malingerers wishing to avoid unpleasant duties and the habitual "Swingus Plumbii" sufferers were often there. These were, with great understanding and passion, given dreadful tasting remedies, ferocious purgatives or a kick up the proverbial backside.

These Angels of Mercy did excellent work really and were a likeable lot.

Annual Qualification tests

So that the army could be guaranteed that we all remained fine soldiers and did not decay with time, the "Bright Sparks" Department at AHQ designed all sorts of annual qualification standards. The most enjoyable was the "Marksman" where, provided you managed to shoot the living daylights out of a whole lot of "Figure Eleven" targets at various distances, which involved a lot of running (puffing and panting!) on the shooting range, you could add a couple of quid to your measly pay package.

Not so much fun was the high-speed, long distance marches with full pack, tin hat and rifle.

Then, if you survived that, they made you prove you could carry a troopie of your own size, along with your packs, rifles and tin helmets, and run with that lot over a distance of 100 yards.

Toughest of all was to swim the length of the swimming pool with your fellow soldier dragged helplessly in your wake.

Ration packs

The military nutrition experts had a hand in the design of these little brown boxes filled with things that were supposed to be good for us.

There were three varieties, (A), (B) or (C) packs, but Heaven alone knows what the difference between them was. They looked exactly the same.

Inside these "Jamstealer Gift Boxes" there were all sorts of exciting things. Every one had a pack of "biscuits". These would have made a hyena stop laughing and, if you were to glue them to yourself, there would have been no cause for the invention of Kevlar body armour. If you soaked them in water or boiled the living daylights out of them, you got a sort of gooey target paste, which tasted exactly like…gooey target paste.

The Rhodesian bush, when archaeologists from the future start rummaging around, will yield up millions of these slightly pale, oversized dominoes. It will puzzle them too that they will be dug up in close proximity to the shattered remains of the teeth of powerfully jawed carnivores and hominids.

The tins of "Braised Liver" were of great interest. We had never seen green liver before and especially liver that smelled like the inside of a Sumo wrestler's jock strap. Few of us actually ate it, so it is not possible to describe the taste. I feel sure it would have been memorable.

In a little silver and gold foil sachet could be found the notorious "Curry Powder" packed by Messrs Khatri Brothers of Salisbury. I never did meet with one of these brothers so I was unable to ask how they had managed to discover a wrapping foil so robust that it could contain this "Universal Solvent"…it went straight through anything, turned everything yellow and yet somehow proved to be a very effective radiator sealant for Bedfords and Landrovers.

A favourite was the "Condensed Milk". This was Nestle's finest and came in small tins or, at one time, in plastic tubes. As tea was always welcome out in the bundu this was a very tradable commodity.

Some "ratpacks" very thoughtfully provided a few sheets of the famous "Bronco" toilet paper which was savage stuff, but still preferable to the use of large leaves for personal hygiene needs. There were a lot of stinging nettles in parts of Rhodesia...

"Baked Beans" were almost always included in the ration, so quiet nights were often punctuated by intermittent blasts of flatulence, which put even the elephant to flight.

The sustenance was always welcome, but the side effects were not.

Some contained little tins of jellied methylated spirits. The idea was that you opened this tin and found a way to perch your mess tin of graze an inch or two above the flame. I bought a very clever Swedish designed petrol primus from a camping store in Salisbury. This little gem came in it's own canister which doubled as two cooking pots and required no priming or pumping. As long as you could filch half a pint of army petrol you only had to warm the tank with your hands to send enough up the stem to set fire to it. In a minute or two the thing would be purring contentedly and a little later a brew could be enjoyed while your mates were still trying to coax their stoves into life. It was swiped shortly before I left the army and I have never found a replacement. To the thief I say, "May your chickens all choke and the fleas of a thousand camels infest your armpits!"

RSM's

The first encounter with one of these military maniacs was during Recruit Training at Brady Barracks. A few of us were sent to fetch some kit from Llewellyn Barracks and, while doing the "hurry up and wait" thing some of us, having the attitude common to soldiers all over the world...

"Why run when you can walk?...why walk if you can stand still?...why stand if you can sit?...why sit if you can lie down?...and if you are lying down why not be kipping?"

We were doing just that.

Our reveries were rudely interrupted by a fierce, khaki clad, apoplectic fellow with a shiny pace stick under his armpit, who screamed dreadful obscenities. His description of our collective parentage was frightful. This was the notorious RSM Erasmus who had terrified Territorial soldiers for years and became a legend in Rhodesian military history.

Later Ron Reid-Daly became RSM of the Regiment.

He was renowned for his skills in the use of his pace stick. Legend has it that in one lightning motion he was able to insert the lead tip precisely half an inch up the starboard nostril of anyone suicidal enough to cause him displeasure.

His parade commands could be heard from miles away.

Robin Tarr came on the scene after him, but Reid-Daly was a tough act to follow and it took this replacement a long time to step into his gleaming boots.

Military vehicles

In the early days at Brady Barracks there were old aircraft hangars going back to the days of Kumalo Air Base. These served to hold all sorts of equipment and vehicles. These museum pieces included a few ancient QL's, Chev Fifteen Hundredweight's, Series 1 Landrovers and even a sort of "moving greenhouse" which turned out to be the Morris Quad…terribly useful for hauling the gun carriages used at the funerals of any military type who happened to "kick the bucket".

Later the Federal Government cut loose with their cheque books and fleets of new stuff came on the scene. There were new LWB and SWB Landrovers, Bedford J3's and the big RL's. The CO's Staff car was a highly polished Rover 90 saloon…pitifully underpowered but still an impressive ride.

Signals, at one stage, got their paws on a few Steyr-Puch Haflingers. These tiny vehicles could climb the side of a "gomo" like mountain goats and could reach a downhill speed in favourable winds of about 40 mph. They were fun but very impractical as they had about enough space to carry a vertically challenged driver and a piccanin for a passenger.

The Government issue motorcycles were very primitive Matchless 350's which were issued with half a seat. I never found out who knocked off the pillions. These bikes kicked like mules on start up, peed oil everywhere and handled like a bull on the shite covered cobbles of an alley in Pamplona. I failed to see why the cops got really smooth twin BSA 650's and Matchless machines, while we got the rough end of the stick.

Tonsorial talents.

Whenever troopies found themselves idle they were inclined to burst into song. Of course their talents were greatly improved by flushing the tonsils with copious quantities of Castle Laager.

There were several favourites…

"When the Saints go marching in" probably led the field and was sung on most occasions. Later it became the official Regimental March.

" Cocky Lobin" provided scope for improvisation by those sober enough to create the "chilaplapa" verses that followed the principal lyrics, whilst the well-known " Ten Green Bottles" was more rigid. As long as you could remember the simple words and were compus mentus enough to count backwards, you could hardly mess it up.

Hairier compositions such as "'T'was on the good ship Venus", "The Ball of Kirriemuir", "Roll me over" and many more were...some of the time at least...performed away from the ears of polite company.

"Izaka zumba", "Daar kom die Alabama", "My Sarie Marais", "Bobbejaan klim die berg"and "We are marching to Pretoria", got the South Africans going at full throttle.

The Aussies came up with a few that were far more advanced than the usual, "Waltzing Matilda", "My boomerang won't come back" or "Tie me kangaroo down sport".

One of these went …

"We're a bunch of b------s, b-------s are we.

We're from Australia...the a---hole of the world (and all the universe!)....

We'd rather f--- than fight for Li-ber-teeee!"

There were a few who were gifted enough to recite "Abdul Abulbul Amir" in it's original verse. Of course, this simple rhyme lent itself to very primitive lyrics, which were attempted by the more "basic" among us. These will not be printed here.

Nat King Cole was a firm favourite among our troubadours who often belted out "Mona Lisa", "Too young" and "Smile" using voices ranging from "superb", through "dodgy" to "bloody awful".

We sang while marching, digging holes, bouncing about in RL's, showering, bathing, drinking and just about any time and any place. It did a lot for our spirits....but then again the spirits probably did a lot for our singing!

Initiative tests.

These were dreamed up by someone who wanted to "keep the troops happy". One notable initiative test took place shortly after the regiment settled into Cranborne and it involved splitting the participants into groups of three. A set of objectives was handed out at departure time to each group. Ours was to get to Plumtree School where we had to get a signature from the Headmaster, then get a signature from the owner of the Hot Springs Resort (at the other end of the country) and get back into the barracks in a given number of days. It was made a little tougher when we were told that the MP's, RP's and the BSAP would be trying to hunt us down and would lock us up if they found us. We were not allowed money either.

Some groups sneaked aboard trains and slowly chuffed and puffed their way to their assigned destinations. Troopies also made use of African buses, trucks and other assorted transport. It was rumoured that some had even tried to cadge flights with the "Blue Jobs"!

Others (as we did) "liberated" civilian clothes and thumbed our way along the highways and byways cadging accommodation from kind-hearted Rhodesians around the country. Back then, motorists made a habit of picking up hitch hikers.

We figured out that our "hunters" would tend to look for us either at our points of departure/arrival or, in the vicinity of each objective. We were dead right and managed to evade capture and returned home proudly clutching our trophies after a very enjoyable "swan" at Government expense.

Conventional warfare exercises

In the early 60's there were lots of these. We dug holes at Woolandale rifle range and a whole lot more in the Somabula flats. Then, when we moved to "Bambazonke" the Bright Sparks department got us to dig even more at Forrester Estates north of Salisbury.

In 1961, just for fun, we dug up half of Northern Rhodesia in our efforts to make sure the various characters running around Katanga stayed on their own turf. This was a bit pointless as our positions, when all put together, probably covered a mile or two of the thousands of miles making up the Congo border.

I loathed living underground. Sand got everywhere. In boots, socks, shreddies, denims, rifles, food, water, up your nose, in your eyes, in your ears and just about anywhere you didn't want it to be. To this day, I have a lingering hatred for gardening and even for beach sand as a result of the years of doing mole impersonations.

Things got even worse when it rained and the dust became mud.

The exercises also involved a lot of footslogging and plenty of "standing to" with patrols and sentry duty at all hours of the day or night. I thought to myself that if I were attacking an infantry position I would only hit it when the silly buggers "stood down" after first or last light and not when the blighters were expecting us to have a go.

On many of these junkets we would be "strafed" by Provosts, Vampires or Hunters whereupon we were supposed to dive into our trenches. We were trained to keep still and not look at the attackers who could detect movement and white faces, but on the Forrester Estates "battlefront" one day, I remember there being a flurry of furious R/T transmissions as a result of one of the lads "dropping his rods" as a token of disdain for a Provost that was diving on our positions. He was never charged. Possibly because he had no distinguishing features for the RRAF Photo Intelligence to latch onto….?

With the change to a Commando structure the meerkats, moles, antbears and spring hares of Rhodesia breathed a sigh of relief…so did we.

Haircuts

Recruits were pounced on very early and quickly learned that somehow the military had a thing about highly polished military equipment and that one's head and chin formed part of the equipment the Government now owned.

Highly skilled (?) barbers armed with clippers just "drove" them north, south, east and west over our skulls until they passed the "cotton wool test" indicating that not a bristle remained.

It was only later that a little would be allowed to grow under our berets and, much later, traces of that disgusting stuff called hair would be tolerated under the beret line. Officers on the other hand often had great fistfuls of hair in plain view and got away with it.

Beards were verboten but moustaches were permitted for certain superior beings but the side burns, so fashionable at the time, were a definite "no-no".

In later years it became possible to grow fungus while chasing bandits around the bush and thus emerged the new order of "armpits with eyeballs" depicted by Ron Reid-Daly in his book about the Selous Scouts.

"Graze"

Army cooks came in all shapes and sizes but very few were overfed. This was probably because by the time they hurled "graze" on your "varkpan" (Pig trough), there was no ways they could still be hungry ...or "skraal" as we called it in troopie speak.

Soup was presented as a sort of smelly "dish wash" sometimes with mysterious bits of solid matter lurking around in it....bone?... hide?...entrails? The colour varied somewhere between pale beige and bright orange but, if you closed your eyes (and nostrils) it was possible to begin to believe that it was food.

Porridge was interesting in that some cooks dished it up as a thin slurry of oats or mielie meal, while others threw great lumps of a grey, rubbery substance at your "dixie", "varkpan" ...or if you were really privileged, a plate, and, if it didn't bounce or roll off, then you sloshed it with milk and sugar and beat it to death with your gums. Yet others, inspired by butt duties at Woolandale or Cleveland rifle ranges, modelled their culinary creations on "Target Paste, shot-holes for the pasting of".

"Cabbage Militaire" was a popular production. This involved boiling vegetable matter, rumoured to have been cabbage, until it was bleached white and would flow uninterrupted off a ladle. The better cooks found that the original green colour could be partially revived by the addition of magic ingredients, amongst which was baking powder and copper sulphate.

Coffee was easy. Huge amounts of the ground beans were tied up in a mutton cloth bag...used again and again...and tossed into a pot or coffee urn. This bag was left in the water and stewed for hours and sometimes days. I remember once having a brew that had actually burned. The stench was horrible.

On Christmas Day it was traditional for the troops to be served laced coffee by the senior ranks. For those who liked the brew soused in rum this was a good thing. Personally I found it revolting.

Sometimes their tea was really good but there were some Catering Corps guys who did not get it right. If you poured plenty of sugar in it the taste was acceptable enough.

Rice was difficult to wreck. A lot depended on whether you were served from the top of the pot or the bottom where it often burned to a blackened mess.

Zambezi Mud (Chocolate pudding), and Frogs Eggs, (Semolina) and dreadful jellies in lurid colours were a popular offering eaten only by those with rugged palates, but occasionally they came up with acceptable Bread Puddings.

Curry was dangerous and unpredictable but, every now and then, they got the formula right and being hungry, we ate it.

Millions of "spuds" over the years were boiled and pulverised beyond recognition but sometimes "French Fries" or roast potato were served up.

Cooks remembered were Norman Collard, the infamous Ernie Walters and a wild- eyed Hollander whose name I have forgotten. It would have been better to have forgotten his cooking….

The duties of the Orderly Officer included a mandatory visit to the troops dining hall to inspect the kitchen and enquire how the men were enjoying the graze, which was a futile exercise that tended to trigger the age-old mutterings….

"Who called the cook a bastard?…(Who called the bastard a cook?), and… "This food is shite Sir…but beautifully cooked!"

We were always bitching about the food and tended to lose sight of the hours of hard labour on the part of the Catering Corps who slaved over hot stoves and sometimes fires in an effort to ensure we ungrateful wretches were fed in line with the Napoleonic conclusion that " an army marches on it's stomach."

Berets

The beret given to us in 1961 was a dark blue thing thrown across the counter at the QM Stores along with a brass badge that needed sandpapering before rubbing with Brasso for hours on end. These circular discs of felt either flopped over the wearer's bonce or sat on top like a sort of blue cherry on a cupcake and the secret was to negotiate with someone who got one too big if yours was too small…or vice versa.

They came with tassels at the back which were not supposed to be chopped off (Damaging Government property!) but had to be tied together and shoved back inside the leather rim of this useless piece of headgear. The badge had to be dead level with the band and a prescribed height above it and had to be pulled against the beret by putting bits of cardboard on the inside.

Shrinking of these things was common practice. The more British you were, the more you shrunk the brutes. Some dedicated ex-Poms ended up looking like they were wearing a tight skull cap. Others never shrank them and spent their days looking like a ship's cook in a cheap Hollywood movie. Some used the "pork pie" style and resembled the losing entrants in pancake tossing contests.

They were supposed to be worn with the brim parallel to the ground but over time much of this was ignored in favour of more rakish approaches. One character at Brady looked as though his had been designed to hang off his starboard ear…how it stayed put was the subject of a lot of idle debate.

The degree to which they could be tilted back or forward was also tested at times. Some had the brim so low that if they blinked they wouldn't be able to open their eyes again and some were so far back they were accused of being hatless if viewed from the front.

Later the green beret was issued and the whole business started all over again. At the same time the chromed silver RLI badge came on the scene and Brasso shares plummeted.

Jungle Hats

The jungle hat was a much more practical piece of kit in that it kept the sun from boiling your brains and shielded your eyes from the glare.

They were made by various manufactures and thus came in all shapes and sizes. We had the "Pisspot" which had absolutely no distinction between crown and brim…a sort of pyramid shape. Some got the ones that tried unsuccessfully to impersonate the WW2 Australian slouch hat. If these were not starched you could not see where you were going, and, even if starched, flopped at the first sign of rain.

A few were perfect and had brims just big enough to do the job and were highly prized by those lucky enough to get them.

There was another model which had a small brim which could either hang down or be turned up for that "Sammy at the Seaside" look.

Pomona Guard Duties

In their infinite wisdom, the Military kept a lot of their ammunition and explosives at Pomona where they were stored in a whole lot of small buildings each set in amongst blast-proof earthworks. Dotted around the perimeter were what we called "Goon Towers" in which we spent some of our "two hours on" time. The "four hours off" was spent trying to catch a bit of kip in the gungiest guard-house that ever was. It was grubby, the roof leaked and the beds were steel with broken wire web bases on which was laid a thing called a paliasse. We quickly nicknamed these flea ridden, one inch thick pieces of coarse felt, "Friendly Donkeys", for obvious reasons.

It was a cold place in winter and hot as Hell in summer and, when it rained, the whole place turned into a quagmire. Food was delivered three times a day in a sort of insulated box which really didn't work very well so the meal and the coffee was cold when you got it.

At some dreadful hour of the night, a Duty Officer from KG6 came snooping around to ensure we were all on our toes. Most of the time they never troubled to go from the guardroom down to the enclosure, but then there was always an "Eager Beaver" who actually did. On seeing the "intruder" we were supposed to do the age-old "'alt!! Who goes there…?" This was a little Shakespearian for most troopies who replaced it with a challenge something along the lines of, "Oo the f**k are you?"

Pomona does not fall into the list of my better memories of military service.

Sentry duties at Cranborne

Rather more formal than Pomona guard was sentry duty.

Some clown, perhaps inspired by a childhood visit to Buckingham Palace's "bull and brass" Changing of the Guard (…or perhaps "Christopher Robin who went down with Alice…?"), decided the new barracks just had to have sentry boxes. Some idiot in the "shiny bums" at Army HQ, decided there would be one on either side of the main gate and the Holland Africa architects humoured him and built the things into the perimeter wall.

Other "Big Brass" then set to work with slide rules, pace sticks and tons of paper to decide the drill movements for the parade ground Guard Changes, exactly (precisely!) how many paces back and forth were needed to be slow-marched before each man did an about turn, the synchronization of commands, the arms drill movements and stamping of feet that the poor mugs on duty had to perform.

When an officer was spotted haring into the camp from the Airport Road, we were supposed to give a salute. They were often well on their way to their quarters by the time the salute was done but there were some of them who kicked up a hell of a fuss if we didn't get it right.

It was a pointless exercise as far as we were concerned, as we never had any ammo in our SLR's, only a bayonet to defend the whole barracks from invaders.

The parade before going on duty involved an inspection by the Duty Officer who was looking for tiny specks of disgusting "kipp", "gunge" or "detritus" that might have lodged in our rifle barrels thus impeding the progress of the bullets we didn't have. He also was trying to find traces of hair below the beret line, substandard Blancoed belts or Brassoed brasses and, their all time favourite, boot studs showing signs of wear which lead to charges because you were wilfully causing damage to Government property to wit…bootleather.

Some of these Charlies even got down on hands and knees to check that puttees and hosetops were a) parallel to the parade ground and b) that puttees were wound correctly.

The smartest of us would then be awarded "Stick Man" which was a great honour and which privileged the fellow to strut around clutching a small silver tipped stick until the next guy won it.

Two hours in those sentry boxes went by agonizingly slowly and on cold nights, hot days or wet weather, they were not places any sane person would want to be.

On my last visit to Zimbabwe I noted that the new order of barracks guards had propped a battered, grubby, over-flowing rubbish bin inside one of them. The dreams of those "shiny bums" of long ago, have now been truly shattered. The mind boggles at the howls of indignation that would come from the British public if a sentry box at Buckingham Palace were to be used as a garbage tip.

In Zimbabwe nobody takes any notice…

Shooting and firearms

In 1961 the army had already replaced their old Lee Enfield 303's with the SLR semi-automatic, which had a calibre at NATO standard 7.62.

As rookies, we had hours of weapon training with these things. This took place in classrooms, out in the hot Rhodesian sun and at the shooting range at Woolandale where we discovered just how accurate these weapons could be…in the right hands. Some could knock a tick off a bull's backside at 500 yards while others could not be relied on to hit a barn at six paces.

The targets for the shorter range shoots were either "Figure 11" or "Figure12" pattern, which featured fearsome looking gooks in camouflage kit printed on them. Most of us were content to just whack the things but the purists always tried for a neat grouping of shots between the eyes.

At longer ranges massive targets were the usual and more pride was taken in the achievement of good grouping, which while they may not have been in the bulls eye, indicated that you were a darned good shot and, had your armourer zeroed the rifle properly, they would have all been dead centre. We were forbidden to zero our own sights but many of us did break the rules from time to time.

The Stirling SMG was about as reliable as a two bob watch and was prone to stoppages and even runaways. The latter were hilarious and dangerous at the same time. All the troopie could do was keep it roughly pointed down the range while the thing emptied the whole magazine. Some claimed the things were not very accurate but I managed to get most of my shots on target. They appeared very much as if they had been churned out by the mile and cut off by the yard in the kind of factory that might be contracted to produce jacks for cheap cars.

Pistols were the 9mm Browning automatics which were about as good as anything around. These were usually meant for Officers, but we got to shoot with them on occasions. This brings to mind a time when, on a Saturday afternoon, Denzil Lloyd-Evans and myself were nobbled by Lieutenants Douglas and Harvey to patch up targets down at the 30 yard range. These two distinguished gentlemen had been summarily appointed to represent our Company at a forthcoming Battalion Shooting competition and wished to sharpen their shooting skills. Their shooting was appalling to say the least and, at the end of a boring afternoon, they were kind enough to let

Denzil and I "have a few shots". Much to their chagrin, our handling of the two Brownings was impeccable and the two Figure 11's both had a lot of daylight showing through by the time our magazines were empty.

The Bren was a favourite of mine, even though I carried this bloody great piece of iron-mongery up many gomos and battled under its' weight on many marches.

If properly set up, a "double tap" could produce hits on the target that were only a couple of inches apart even over long ranges.

A 3.5 inch Rocket Launcher was our anti tank weapon. It was a lot of fun to fire but the price of the rockets meant we were lucky to have a shot with the thing at all. In my whole career I was lucky enough to squeeze the trigger twice. They misfired regularly.

The Energa grenade was fired using a ballastite cartridge from the SLR. It was not very accurate as it had a short range and a high trajectory…sort of a poor man's Howitzer. If you did hit something it really banged a hole in it. There was never enough practice with these either.

Occasionally we were allowed to lob hand grenades. These "Mills" bombs were fun too. The explosion was often characterised by the howling of the base plug, which was a deeper sounding version of the ricochet sound effect so beloved by the makers of cheap Westerns.

Playing with things that went "bang" was something to look forward to…especially 808 plastic explosive. This stuff looked and smelled just like marzipan icing and it had a thousand uses. You could blow a railway track, bring down a tree, flatten a building or become a highly successful fisherman with it.

On a weekend trip in my small boat near Charara at Kariba, a companion and I had, after "liberating" a small quantity of this "pyrotechnic plasticine" (along with the necessary detonators and fuses), tootled along dropping sticks of the stuff over the stern just like any serious fishermen would do. The Chessa, Nkupi, Bream, Barbel and Tiger who had, up to then, scoffed at our more conventional fishing methods, quickly succumbed to this "depth-charging"… and then the engine stalled. With no electric starter up in the driver's seat, there was a frantic scramble to dive aft and tug the starting cord to get the boat underway before its marine ply bottom turned to matchwood. I could see the morning headlines in the Rhodesia Herald…"Two RLI men die when boat hits Kariba mine! Zanu PF claims responsibility!"

"808" could blow a fair sized hole through a tree if it was stuffed into the bottom of a broken Champagne bottle. The dome in the bottom of the bottle served as a good model for demonstrations of the Hollow Charge Principle… as did certain aerosol cans, ploughshares and even car hubcaps. Viva la Alfred Nobel!

Battle simulation was greatly enhanced due to the use of the Thunderflash which was a bloody great "squib" with an igniter fixed along its side. You pulled this "doohickey" and it began to hiss and spurt flames whereupon you needed to get rid of it chop chop if you were fond of your fingers.

Quieter, but a lot more dangerous, were the White Phosphorous grenades. These were used in conventional warfare exercises to generate instant smoke screens. I never experienced them being used in anger and am grateful for this. To be slowly roasted to death from the outside would be a ghastly fate even for one's worst enemy.

Instructor's Driving and Maintenance Course

As a seasoned motorcyclist, the time came for the Army to switch me over to things with four or more wheels. I had never learned to drive a car so I duly reported to the MT yard for my first lessons with an instructor.

This courageous fellow was Corporal Roy Capener who began with a tour of a standard LWB Landrover. "This is a steering wheel. When you turn it, this vehicle either a) turns, or b), turns over…all depends on how fast you're going. Then there is this metal pedal on the floor. If you push it down the thing goes faster. If you take your foot off it, it usually slows down…unless you're going down a hill in which case it could carry on going. To make the thing stop you have to stand on this other thing. If you do it too hard you will "gooi" all the "okes" to the front. This can be rectified by taking your foot off it and stomping on the pedal I first told you about. There is also this waggley thing here called a gear lever. You start by putting it in this corner here, then this one then that one, then that one and finally over here…but don't waggle it unless you've pushed that other thing over there…which can only happen when you've taken your foot off the thing I first told you about.

There's another thing…don't even think about trying to hit the 5th position of that waggley thing 'cos, if you're stopped… or going very slow the thing starts going backwards. If you try this and you're going fast, the Government will have your guts for garters and this thing's gearbox is gonna need a dentist!"

We survived the first lesson and, after days of blood sweat and tears, I was declared fit to be let loose on Rhodesia's roads.

A while later someone told me to go and do this "D & M" Instructor's Course down at "Hooterville" (Gwelo) at the School of Infantry. I was not yet a great driver at the time so I wondered at the wisdom of the Army's decision to train me on how to do what Instructors and Examiners did, which was teaching greenhorns (like me) how to drive big expensive pieces of military equipment and then testing them at the end.

At Gwelo we met with the four characters whose task it was to train us. The D & M School was headed up by Captain "Classy" Lloyd ("Frightfully Public School type"), with WO2 Bob Preller, C/ Sgt Norman Dale and Sergeant Pete Arnold (an ex Metropolitan Police Driving Instructor from Hendon in the UK), as our mentors.

Several weeks of instruction followed. We were taught how to fix "veekles" (as "Doppies" Preller pronounced it), how to float them across rivers, how to drive a whole lot better and how the things worked.

The course culminated in a trip down to the Sabi / Lundi confluence in a variety of antique transport. The camp was fun and we had a chance to put theories about the floatation of Landrovers into practice. This was achieved either by the use of a truck canopy frame skinned with canvas, or by simply wrapping the whole vehicle up in a tarpaulin and committing it to the deep. Ours did not sink, but then it didn't float either. We just couldn't get it into the water. A previous group of trainees had apparently managed to sink theirs.

A snippet of memory from that time was the lecture by the frightfully posh "Classy" Lloyd who, citing Archimedes, declared that:

"When an object is totally or partially immersed in a fluid...the f......g thing sinks!"

I obtained a B+ Grading on the course, which I understand is something of a record. This qualified me as an Instructor / Examiner. In the next couple of years I trained and tested dozens of drivers, amazingly without dents, shunts or other mishaps.

Subalterns

We had our lots thrown in with a great variety of these over the years. Some were admired, some were tolerated and a few were endured. A few are easily recalled.

There was Bob Davey. Tall, a little pink and with a hint of a developing "British Politician's lisp" but a fine soldier who learned very quickly to relate to the polyglot lot he was tossed in with.

Dave Parker arrived at Brady wearing some strange uniform from another regiment and very quickly made his mark on the troops. He was destined to become the Regiments' "Main Man What Counted" only to die tragically in an air crash in later years.

A young Barney Robinson, stocky and a little vertically challenged, was quickly nicknamed "Barney Rubble"...the "Flintstones" being in vogue at the time.

Of the more hirsute gentlemen was one known as "Hairy Holgate". What became of him I know not.

There was a frightfully earnest British one, a Second Lieutenant Johnson, who dreamed of becoming some kind of rally or race driver. He spent a lot of his spare time throwing a rather tired Ford Taunus around the barracks on two wheels. As far as I can remember he never did manage to write himself off.

Peter Batty was probably the most laid-back of them. Nothing ever seemed to get him excited.

Perhaps one of the ones we did not relate quite so well to, was the rather morose Lionel Dyke, who seemed to delight in anything that would get a troopies' back up. There were a few of those, but most, in time, successfully earned the respect of their charges.

Batmen

In 1961, the services of batmen at Brady Barracks were supposedly "streng verboten" for all but the senior ranks and officers. It was amazing what a few shillings would get you however and it wasn't long before we managed to secure their expertise.

The Khaki Drill bush jackets, shorts and longs (KD's), needed to be washed and then starched. Merely immersing them in a starch solution was not good enough. The trick was to brush a sort of "goo", made by boiling the stuff in a pot, onto the clothes and then "cooking" it dry with a hot iron. This gave you the kind of kit that could stand on the floor by itself. The "Stick Man" contenders actually lowered themselves into their shorts and then waddled to the parade ground using funny little 3 inch steps so that there would be no cracks or wrinkles in the things until they came to attention on the command of the Orderly Officer.

Everyone at some time or other had a "Lovemore", "Sixpence" or "Phineas" who sneaked in and out of the lines fetching and carting kit at all hours of the night.

They worked in one of the old hangars bordering what was once Khumalo Aerodrome and were constantly raided by the RP's who searched in vain for our forbidden kit. I never lost any.

In later times when Internal Security problems came to the fore and we were put on "standby", which meant lounging around with vehicles loaded and ready to go somewhere or other around Rhodesia at a moments notice. We never knew where we might be sent but the barracks batmen could usually be relied upon to come up with a reliable prediction. A typical conversation might have gone something like this:

"Hey Lovemore!…Upi mina hamba manje?"

"Hau Baas,…kubani Karoi!"

Township cordons

In the early 60's urban unrest reared it's ugly head. Intimidation of the local population was rife as political "parties" inflicted their viewpoints in rather undemocratic ways.

We were dug out of bed at unholy hours of the morning and bundled into RL's, J5's and Landrovers to surround areas of Harare, Highfields and other townships. The idea was to try to close the net on agitators and thugs while they were still in their sacks, kipping it off after the long hard nights of murder and mayhem.

The CID, and the other "cloak and dagger types", would then interview all and sundry bundling the rotters into jail while leaving the innocent free to go and do their daily business.

It was boring work being dug-in at the side of a township street, but we found ways to amuse ourselves nonetheless. Soccer matches with the picannins was a popular pastime. Those little blighters were good players and they often ran rings around us.

As good Rhodesians we had mostly grown up in households where the family dogs hated cats and black skinned people and they would erupt into furious paroxysms of barking if these came near. In African townships the boot was on the other foot. Their scrawny mutts went bananas when fair skinned Mukiwas invaded their territory. We could tell roughly where any one of our foot patrols was simply by following the racket made by these watchdogs. The bad guys probably benefited from these mangy sentinels more than we did.

Riot Drills

In the early sixties, the "powers that be" and the military were becoming increasingly uncomfortable with the problem of how to deal with rioters. The old "let's-break-a-few-skulls" brigade had to be reined in and rioters had to then be dealt with by the book...no mowing the blighters down or climbing in with sjamboks or truncheons would be tolerated. No "Gunfight at the OK Corral" methods were allowed either.

The Department of Bright Sparks sat in committees and came up with a formal "drill" to deal with it.

The whole "circus" began where the civil authorities had to formally sign the mess over to the military...rather difficult when the bricks and Molotov cocktails were raining down. Then troops would ever-so-neatly, climb out of their vehicles and form up. On command they would march to an area in front of the screaming mob where they split into a perfect square. Each man faced outwards. Great stuff, but the boffins forgot that in so doing, only 25 per cent of us could see what was about to break our noses or bash our heads in. Of course we were not supposed to duck or avoid these missiles.

The Officer in charge was supposed to call out to the mob with a megaphone saying something akin to, "I say chaps...you really ought to stop this Neanderthal stuff and go home!"

If these "chaps", after being cautioned three times, still hadn't given up, a "sniper" would be given an order to go down on one knee and bump off a selected trouble maker. In all the practice drills the officer, having selected a ringleader, invariably instructed, "Man in red shirt...ready...aim...fire!"

Had I been a political agitator at that time, I would never have been stupid enough to wear a red shirt!

I don't recollect these riot drills ever being put into practise.

These drills came to mind recently when a friend reminded me that camels had come about as a result of Our Creator delegating the design for a horse to a committee!

As close to a contact as I ever got.

The first "Gooks" had been nailed at Sinoia , the Oberholzer attack was long gone, the Truck driver Edward Juze was cold in his grave when a bunch of them struck at Nevada Ranch, the home of the Viljoen family. Some perpetrators came to their well deserved sticky ends but one was some time later reported to be making his way back to Zambia by way of a well known path down the escarpment near Chirundu.

A team from 1 Commando, raced to New Sarum where we boarded a Dakota and headed for Centenary airfield. An Aloutte flown by John Barnes picked a team of us up and we were dropped off in a tiny LZ not far from where this terrorist would be expected to pass.

A good site was found for an ambush where a "killing ground" was chosen after which we lay for hours in our positions waiting for our quarry to come scrambling down the rocky trail. At some time during the chilly night we heard him coming. Adrenalin was pumping but one of our number, being a bit cold and who had covered himself with his rubberised "poncho", took it off, making a hell of a racket in the process. Our target bolted away up the escarpment before any of us could sort him out.

The murderer was later bumped off not far from there by another unit.

Our uplift from the LZ the following day was interesting to say the least. Our "stick" was heavy, the air was hot and the chopper's blades only just cleared the tall trees surrounding the tiny clearing. We thought the pilot would take half of us and return for the rest later but he gave us the "thumbs up" for all of us to board.

By some skilful "eggbeating" and walzing around, he persuaded the machine to break out of ground effect and get us back to Centenary where he landed it like a fixed wing aircraft on the runway.

The Dakota somehow, in spite of the combined weight of our group, a team of RAR troops, all our kit and a Steyr Puch Signals vehicle, got us off the ground and headed for Salisbury. The RAR troopies had to be dropped at Mount Hampden where the walrus moustached pilot dropped the thing a few feet short of the runway. When the wheels hit the step where the tarmac began, there was an almighty jolt that bounced us against the straps and sent the aircraft back into the air again. The landing a little while later at New Sarum was a real greaser however and "Biggles" was quickly forgiven.

Beer drinking

In 1961 the price of a bottle of Castle or Lion Lager in the Brady canteen was tenpence. As our pay, after all the deductions, was around £25 a month, we quickly measured our worth in beer bottles…24 bottles to the quid X £25 = 600 bottles a month or about 20 bottles a night! Some actually managed this sort of consumption but if they smoked cigarettes at 2s and 6d for 50… or 8 packets to the pound…then sadly sacrifices had to be made.

Drinking was a serious business. Troops liked to sit around a table and make long lines with the empties and it was not uncommon to see tables completely covered with bottles at the end of an evening.

There were competitions to "stack" the bottles into huge precariously balanced pyramids, which made the practice of rolling around on the floor rather dangerous.

The usual "Drink it down-down-down" challenges were part of life. This became even more of a challenge when someone introduced the "Yard of Ale" which was a great way to either take a bath in Castle or learn to drink beer through the nose.

It was not only the low cost that made canteen drinking so attractive. The close proximity to one's own "fartsack" was a boon as one could hardly get run over or prang while weaving one's way home after an evening of mirth and merriment.

"Dumpy" bottles…originally with caps that needed bottle openers, came later and it was not long before the lads discovered that during long journeys in Landrovers, the parcel tray in the front had an edge to it that had been designed by a dedicated beer drinker. All you had to do was hook it under the lip of the tray and shove the bottle forwards.

I learned that as long as I had another bottle with a cap on it, I could hook it under the lip of another bottle of beer and by squeezing gently in the left hand and levering with the right, the top would come off with a loud pop. The puzzle about what to do about opening your last one when all the other bottles had no caps to use as a lever, was quickly solved. All you had to do was jam a cap back onto an empty one.

The screw-off caps and the arrival of canned beer took some of the fun out of it.

There were of course, a few seasoned brandy drinkers who bought the stuff by the bottle and sloshed it into a variety of mixers. Brandy and Coke was a great favourite but the real hooligans wrapped their faces around Cane Spirits or Vodka. Wine was not popular with the troops and would really only be drunk when everything else was in short supply.

Assault courses

A part of our lives, these were actually enjoyed by the masochists among us. The assault course at Cranborne barracks was designed by someone who hated soldiers, had spent a lifetime studying berserk baboons and was the son of a trapeze artist.

It had all kinds of un-natural challenges made of concrete, bricks, barbed wire, mud and filthy water. The most frustrating of these was a wall about ten or twelve feet high. Getting over the thing required a team effort, unless you had been blessed with arms long enough to trail your knuckles in the dirt as you walked about doing Homo Sapiens impersonations…there were a few!

The key was to get all the big okes to run to the wall and slam their backs into it where their interlocking fingers acted as a step for the next guy's booted "beetle crushers". This brave fellow would be tossed skywards by the big lad in the hope he could get his mitts onto the top of the wall. If successful, he put a boot on the head of his mucker down below and shoved himself upwards to the point where he could get most of himself on top of the wall. He was then supposed to extend a paw downwards so the next troopie could wrench his arm out of its socket. Once the top of the wall became over-populated, it was time to allow gravity to take over and to plummet to earth on the other side. The tough part was trying to get the bloody great "caber tossers", who had hurled you skywards, over the wall. They had no interlocking fingers to put boots in and did not even have someone's "bonce" to tread on to help themselves up. They either had to be blessed with the arms of an Urang Utang…. or pray that a comrade on top had been so endowed.

All of this "fun" was complicated by unnecessary handicaps such as packs, webbing, rifles, water bottles and "Helmets-steel-troops-for-the-use-of"…and Heaven help you if you left it behind.

Low strung barbed wire obstacles were a curse. The kit a soldier carried on him made the concept of shoving of a frightened hedgehog up an angry rhino's rectum, like "a walk in the park" by comparison. It caught on everything. They also produced tears and rips in your denims which meant having to stitch the things up using the needle and cotton so thoughtfully supplied by Her Majesty's Government as the contents of each soldier's "Housewife" repair kit.

The designers of these courses also happily assumed that the troops had all been born with the sense of balance of a mountain goat. There were gum poles that you were supposed to do high wire acts on without falling off and a sort of "Tarzan of the apes" monkey rope with which you had to swing across pits filled with foul water. These Charlies had lost sight of the fact that we would have to use the thing while clutching onto a whole bunch of kit and rifles.

I hated assault courses with a passion and decided early in my career that, if the enemy were ever to set themselves up at the end of such a set of obstacles, I would either, find a way around them, call in an air strike or wait for the blighters to "croak" from old age.

The Barrack Rooms

At the end of a long hard day spent doing all the things soldiers had to do, the time would come for us to kip.

The Barrack rooms had space for about a dozen of us and a Lance Corporal had his own room near the entrance.

The Law of Averages unfortunately came into play when it was time for "beddy byes"…although there was supposed to be a formal "Lights Out", troopies had a habit of staggering in at all hours which led to noise and other disruptions to our well earned rest.

There were "snorers", "whistlers", "coughers" and those with flatulence and beer burps to contend with, as well as the insomniacs who sat up and engaged in long conversations with their mates.

A few of us dutifully leapt out of our "fartsacks" at sunrise, on the Lance Corporals command while others had to be bodily dragged from their beds and pushed into action.

The barrack rooms were freezing cold in winter and hot as Hell in summer when the mosquitoes added to your woes whilst you sweated, lightly clad, on top of the sheets.

Each man had a bed with a coir mattress on dubious springs, a "Lockers Airman 6 foot" and a "Lockers Airman 3 foot". These olive drab pieces of furniture were supposed to be enough to contain his worldly possessions. If he had any more than the Army allowed him, he would have to store the surplus in his car or somewhere else.

Everything had to be polished. At Brady the wooden floors were coated with Cobra and a pair of "slippers" made from an old blanket were kept near the door so when you came in you were supposed to stand on them and shuffle your way to your space, polishing the floor in the process.

A "Lockers Airman 3 foot" at Brady was once used as a part of a drunken and rather bizarre contest between some of the more macho soldiers. They placed a "Mug Tin Troops For The Use Of" on the top of one of these and proceeded to attempt to use their suitably erect "courting tackle" to whack the thing down the length of the barrack room. The winner actually succeeded with a single blow and managed to dent the mug in the process.

Saturday morning inspections were endured. It was quickly learned that the barracks designers had carefully engineered "gunge" traps everywhere. At Brady there were rafters and grooves in the floors that could hold enough filth to actually show up on the finger of an inspecting Officer's white glove. These people seemed to have been gifted with the ability to scrape microscopic particles of detritus, using a pin, from such places as the joint between a plughole and a basin, or to detect the droppings of a moth on a light bulb at a range of five paces. A fingerprint on a windowpane was almost a case for Capital Punishment and the lack of cotton in ones' carefully displayed "Housewife", would incur the wrath of the Gods. Any of these heinous offences could cost us our weekend passes, so most of us tried our best not to let the side down. There were, however a few "gungy" types, who not even the Army could change. We soon did.

The MT Yard

The boss was Captain Keith Dyer who had a pleasant disposition until some damn fool chose to cross his path. His rugged "Mush" would darken to a dreadful purple and the offender would then get put in his place with a blast of interesting expletives.

The mechanics I remember were C/Sergeant "Rumpy" Jones, Sergeant "Beaver" Frazer-Kirk, Sergeant Gordon "Bird" Parrott and a fellow from a planet all of his own called MacAllister.

Corporal Charlie Cole was the NCO who kept the wheels turning and doubled as the projectionist at the Regimental cinema at the Canteen. When he moved on, I was sent there as MT Sergeant and it became my task to do all the things needed to ensure that 100 or more vehicles were treated with the respect they deserved.

These vehicles had to undergo a regular inspection known as the "406". To do these things, an officer (layman) would be given a clipboard and had to run down the list of items inspected and tick them off or, enter a "X" and write details of the problem he might have found. Quite how a wet-behind-the-ears Second Lieutenants' diagnosis of what might be wrong with a Landrover's gearbox, was supposed to have been of great value to the Military, remains a mystery. It was rather akin to asking a cook to perform a heart transplant. We had to re-do the darned things anyway when the "subbies" had finished, so the "406" proved a futile exercise and wasted acres of trees used in the production of the forms…triplicate of course.

No vehicle was supposed to have left the yard without a "Work Ticket" signed by the MTO or other authorized person. If stopped by the RP's and the thing wasn't signed, it was a guarantee that some form of ghastly punishment would follow. Of course, once it left the barracks, there was little control on where it went to or how it got there.

When petrol rationing came about as a result of sanctions, the tank of a Bedford became a very attractive target for troopies needing to siphon a couple of gallons to put into their cars and motorbikes so they could continue to get themselves around to pubs, parents and girlfriends, without hindrance. The authorities decided to introduce petrol that contained a purple dye. This stuff worked just fine and left a purple residue around the carburettors of any vehicle using it. The "wide boys" consequently took great pains to keep their car and bike engines spotlessly clean using that old standby, Jeyes' Fluid, which could be "liberated" from Army Stores who dished it out as a toilet disinfectant. At some stage the Jamstealers substituted this superb engine cleaner with a cheaper, locally made equivalent that really didn't work as well.

For a while I found my two-stroke Yamaha motorbike ran very well on Cleaning Benzene which I could buy in four gallon cans. Experimentation at a later stage showed that my private Landrover functioned reasonably well on a 50 / 50 mix of paraffin and petrol. It knocked a bit but it still got me around.

In 1967 the military made the mistake of transferring me as Admin Sergeant to 2 (Indep.) Company at Kariba. This came about after I had committed the dreadful crime of being seen smoking a cigarette while riding a military motorcycle at Cranborne Barracks by the ever-so-serious RSM Robin Tarr. Unbeknown to him, I had just sold my ancient Austin Westminster and bought a very old long-wheelbase Landrover and had purchased a 13 foot boat and trailer with a 30 horse West Bend motor.

I smiled all the way to Kariba.

When I arrived I discovered they had made another mistake. They had put me in charge of the Military's purple petrol! As the "Statute of Limitations" has, forty years later, run out, I can confess to a certain amount of "liberation" of P.O.L. supplies…all for a good cause of course. Water skiing, tiger fishing, wild life observation, bird and bikini watching were all good causes. Also how could we be expected to maintain Law and Order on Kariba's islands or at Charara or Bumi Hills if we had no petrol for boats?

One very important marine patrol came about when we heard that some of our "Chinas" were camped at Chirundu. As communication was as important as serious beer drinking, four of us took my boat down the steep road to the tailraces of the dam, carried it over the rocks and launched it into a reasonably calm backwater at the start of the gorge. Dressed in "civvies" so the militant Zambians and their trigger-happy "Gook" friends on the other side would not see us as a threat, we pulled out into the rapids. Reaching the banana farm where the river calms on leaving the gorge, we all breathed a sigh of relief.

The relief did not last long however as sandbanks meant we had to take the deep water channels which was where the hippo could be disturbed from doing what hippos liked to do all day long, or worse yet, forced us uncomfortably close to the hostile Zambian side of the river. As some time before this the Zambians (or the "Gooks") had shot up a Police launch as it patrolled the river, we were rather relieved to make it to the comparative safety of the Chirundu military encampment.

There followed a couple of days of serious beer drinking and "bull" sessions after which we ran the gauntlet all over again and got back to Kariba tailraces in one piece but regretting not having been able to take time off for fishing.

One of our "marine patrols" very nearly ended in tragedy. Dave O'Connor, Trevor Marsberg and I, set off from Gordon Bunney's Cutty Sark Hotel one Saturday for some fishing and beer drinking at Charara. Whilst defending Rhodesia against a surplus of Bream, Chessa, Nkupe and Tigerfish we became acutely aware of a massive storm coming in from Sanyati Gorge direction and ran for home. Near Fothergill Island the storm hit us and the lake tried its' best to take us down to its version of "Davy Jones' Locker" ("Baas Jonas's Bokis" perhaps…?) throwing waves at us that would have made a Bondi Beach surfer cry out in ecstasy. It was while flying off the top of one of these brutes that Dave O'Connor fell overboard. I managed to turn my frail little thirteen footer at the bottom of a huge trough between waves and go back to find him. He got back in the boat helped by a wallop from a big wave that broke over the tiny craft.

Cold, wet, bruised, miserable and a little nervous we made it to the Cutty Sark. My two passengers leapt out and then had to reverse my old Landrover and boat trailer into the breaking waves so I could time it right and get the boat to land on the trailer without it getting smashed to matchwood. God was with us. On the first attempt, a burst of throttle landed the thing exactly where I wanted it to be. At the same moment Trevor let the jeep's clutch out and pulled it out of danger. It must have been one of the days when the Lake Safety Authority boss, Commander Bob Ellis, was not at his post peering through his telescopes as, if he had been, we would have found ourselves in "deep kak!" Naturally it wasn't licensed and had no spare engine.

That boat was great for water skiing and we did a lot of it…seeing as petrol was so "cheap"! Usually we skied from the Cutty Sark where we were not too bothered by "flatdogs" or "mobile handbags". Some time later from up in the air on a flight in the SAP Cessna, our pilot indicated a couple of these horrible brutes swimming around not far from where we had happily splashed around.

Kariba could get hot. One day I saw just how hot when, from my boat near what was called "Venture Cruises" where the "Seven Hills of Kariba" (as the Italians who built the dam had called it) came down to the water. I spotted a large troop of baboons sitting in the water, cooling off their feet and backsides. They then went back up into the hills for a while doing what baboons do but then, every few minutes, they left the hot rocks and immersed their rear ends once more. They transmitted images of pure joy on their faces as their steaming bottoms made contact with the cooling water!

A frequent companion on our afternoons of skiing was a young American, Dale Birkenmeyer, who headed up the Tsetse Fly Research side of the Agricultural Research Council. He was one hell of a skier who made the rest of us look like rank amateurs. He was also privileged to be in charge of the A.R.C. boat powered by a Volvo-Penta inboard engine which made it just fast enough for skiing, but what was most important of all, was it's capacity to carry many troops and a lot of beer over long distances across the waters. (Did we not have to help him catch Tsetse flies from all over Kariba Lake…?)

The "Crew" at 2 (Indep.) Company Kariba were a cheerful lot. Officers included "Buttons" Wells-West (a.k.a. "Worlds Worst"), Roy Gardener and some Territorials. The CSM was WOII Harry Springer. The other sergeants were myself, Trevor Marsberg, Dave O'Connor, Brian Bowley and various others from RRR. Names that come to mind were Brian Strang, Arthur Allison and Stan Lewin.

Working hours were from early morning until noon when it became too hot to do much else other than drink beer, go fishing or water ski. All of these pastimes were taken very seriously.

The troops canteen at Kariba boasted a jukebox that flogged the popular song "If you're going to San Francisco", to death. It was, of course, a thinly veiled "anti-war" protest and tended to irk us professional soldiers more than somewhat.

Harry Springer one day opened the machine and removed the offending record, making himself a little unpopular with some of the "weekend" soldiers who subscribed to the ideal that "flower power" could solve the problems of the world! We knew that very few of the "Gooks" around Rhodesia would have much faith in the religion of a bunch of long-haired, pot smoking wasters.

The Barracks at "Kariba Heights" were once the single quarters of the Italian workers who, in the early fifties, had laboured for years in appalling heat. When the Army first moved there we could not understand why many of the windows were covered with newspaper and the few airbricks that could be found in each room were plugged up with paper too. Our conclusion was that this was their way of darkening the sleeping quarters so they could kip it off after a hard night shift. They must have believed that plugging the airbricks would somehow prevent the fierce heat from getting in. There was no air-conditioning anywhere.

My Sergeant's Mess room was oppressively hot at times, so much so that on one particularly sweaty night, I filled my bath with cold water and, using an old Landrover seat as a pillow, I slept partly under water.

Brian Bowley the camp mechanic, and his family went on long leave and asked me to "kennel" their Dachshund / Terrier crossbred mutt named Monty while they were away. He proved to be a great companion who followed me wherever I went. He went fishing, boating and even water-skiing with me.

It was a sad day when his owners returned.

I had to learn to wake myself up in the mornings all over again.

Extract from the KK Dictionary (1953)

BROTHER, n. - hama. K. K broer, broeder, (fr. Afrikaaas). – "Lo broer gamena yena siki maningi. Mena funa brief." "Mv brother is very sick. I want leave,"

The term is not used as we use it. It can apply to any relative or person of the same tribe.

The Kapfunde Flight. By Robert Trueman

In between my first ('56 -'62) and second ('70 -'79) tours of duty with the Department of Lands I had obtained a pilot's licence in the UK and on returning to Rhodesia converted it to enable flying there too.

The Department was fortunate to share their own aircraft with Parks & Wildlife and I was mainly engaged piloting flights over various Intensive Conservation Areas and Tribal Trust Lands, carrying out aerial inspection of farms for illegal cultivation etc., throughout the whole country and so managed to accumulate some useful flying time. As a sort of fill-in job, in September '73, I was detailed to fly up to Karoi, thence to Kapfundi Mission to over fly parts of the Urungwe Tribal Trust Land area, by that time considered to be 'terr' country. (It was to be only five years later that Air Rhodesia Viscount VP-WAS 'Hunyani' was brought down in this very area by a terrorist surface to air missile shortly after take-off from Kariba.... 38 killed in the crash, of the 18 survivors a further 10 were murdered by so called freedom fighters. The rest of the world looked on and did…..nothing!) I digress.

Apparently the District Commissioner there had several villages he had been unable to visit because of the security situation and was anxious to see what was happening. The Native Department did have its own aircraft and pilot and I was puzzled at the time as to why they had forgone using their own unit; I perhaps eventually discovered the reason why! I lifted off from Charles Prince Airfield at Mount Hampden quite early in Cessna 182 VP-YVU for the forty-five minute flight on over the Great Dyke, to virtually overhead Banket, then to cross the Hunyani River and rising slightly, over the Hunyani hills and looking next for the Angwa River. Finally the Karoi strip came up on the horizon, dead ahead on rising ground.

I took off promptly again after picking up an Assistant DC, to land Kapfunde Mission strip after a low pass to look for goats or any other hoofed obstructions, at around 10.00 hrs; it was already hot, well over 96 degrees F. The considerably concaved and uneven dirt landing strip was just a shimmer in the heat haze; it looked to get even warmer.

The DC was what I soon mentally categorized as an extreme old Colonial government type, lofty and vaguely arrogant, bringing his family complete with dog to the airstrip to see the plane; obviously accustomed to being fully in charge. On my aircraft, he most certainly was not!

Before taking off again I ascertained precisely where he wanted to go and with that information was able to plot a circular return route. Emphasizing that seat belts were de rigueur and must be worn at all times, particularly at this hot time of year, we were soon airborne, DC apparently trying to see from both sides within the constraints of his seatbelt, observing the general state of things on the ground. The Assistant DC sat alongside me in front and was viewing the starboard side anyway.

Perhaps thirty minutes later and well out in the sticks the DC called that he wanted to look at a village almost below and asked me to circle round; I looked around to sight clear the area (no other aircraft) on either side and was ready to apply a banking turn.

Unbeknown to me he had now unfastened his seat belt in order, it later transpired, to be able to get really close to the window to see directly below. In the instant we hit a large air pocket (not unexpected at that time of year and hence the fastened seat belt requirement).

The aircraft dropped vertically maybe a hundred feet almost instantaneously, creating zero gravity. The next thing I knew was the DC floating gently up toward the roof of the rear of the cabin, with pen and pencils from his breast pocket also in free flight around the cockpit. Gravity was abruptly restored as we reached the base of the air pocket, the aircraft recovered and simultaneously he landed back into his lately vacated seat in an almost inverted position, no doubt inflicting some pain in the process, to say nothing of jeopardizing the safety of the aircraft.

He was absolutely livid, suggesting that I had deliberately made the aircraft perform in such fashion to ridicule him!

I wish!

We returned in icy silence, despite the rivulets of perspiration from the heat of the day dampening all on board. We touched down back at Kapfundi and rolling to a stop; I turned off the strip onto slightly undulating ground to the side and killed the magnetos. Just about to routinely raise the wing flaps back to their zero position when he shouted to his Assistant to get out immediately and so enable him to exit from, as he put it, 'this infernal contraption'.

His Assistant hastily climbed out, opening the door wide to turn and tip the rear of the seat he had just vacated into a forward position. With much muttering, obviously directed at me which in retrospect must have distracted me from lifting the flaps, he clambered out, sharply turning to face the open door as soon as his feet touched the ground, to finally deliver some sort of further comment and as he leant forward to better engage my attention, his forehead suddenly came into contact with the still lowered trailing edge of the flap.

The flap is composed of two sections of sheet aluminium riveted together with a strengthening small triangular contour ridge every six inches or so. Where the two sections come together at the trailing edge, the double triangles then form complete diamond shapes. As a consequence of this, the resulting confrontation left a livid red line across the DC's forehead with corresponding diamond impressions at intervals.

He was certainly not amused; his Assistant was having difficulty by now in keeping a straight face.

I made out a report on the incident, but he must have later thought better of making any comment himself.

Poetic justice?

I wonder!

Canberra Bomber

Further Reminiscences by L/Cpl Bruce McGregor

The Bad Luck Of The Sap Casualty

For a while until mid 1975 the South African Police (SAP) occupied the base at Rushinga. In fact I think they built it, so it was like an owner / occupier situation. The SAP had the best rations and it was always great to spend a night there because the food was great.

This fact did not mean the war was far away. I remember it was from this base that four unarmed members of the SAP were murdered by the terrs on Christmas day 1974 under the so called cease fire agreement. I think that the RLI troopie knew enough about the terrs to understand that the ceasefire was a farce.

One thing that the SAP in Rushinga was very good at was finding landmines. If there was a landmine in the road, the SAP would hit it. They would send out a clearing patrol and sure enough another vehicle for scrapheap.

It was another early day for a SAP clearance patrol when their vehicle hit a mine. The driver was not badly injured apart from a really sore back, but he was able to walk over to another vehicle. He was being driven back to Rushinga for examination when that truck too detonated a landmine. This time he was hurt. Now it was back to Darwin by Helicopter. Late that afternoon it was decided to send him back to Bright lights (Salisbury). There was an aircraft leaving that evening and the medics managed to get this unfortunate chap onto the transport before its departure.

At about 20:00 hours (8 pm) we heard the plane gun its engines and then three loud bangs. It sounded like the aircraft had just been ambushed by terrs. Within minutes we were all aboard a truck racing for the airstrip. It was already dark so we could not see anything easily until we had covered half the landing strip. Then we passed three dead mombies, their bodies carved surgically by the planes propellers and then the light picked up the aircraft with its tail in the air and nose firmly on the ground. Inside the poor SAP fella who had just added another notch to his bow of life. Two landmines and an aircraft accident in one day. He was complaining bitterly.

I wonder how he treated life after that?

The Darwin Restaurant by L/Cpl Bruce McGregor

Mount Darwin was the military heart of the Op Hurricane area. Everything going out into and back from Hurricane came through Darwin. It was the re-supply hub of the North Eastern district and it had most support infrastructures there. If I was stationed at Mukumbura or far beyond Rushinga there was always the supply run back to Darwin.

When it came to food, Darwin itself was not that famous for anything cordon bleu but its kitchen was a permanent feature. Even though the Darwin mess was run by the RLI, every day it catered for troops passing through. Therefore one can imagine the workload of the cook who started early in the morning and pressured through until night. It made sense then to concentrate on food recipes that were easy to prepare.

This requirement was made more necessary by the incident of the aircraft crash that killed three mombies (Cows / Cattle / Beef) on take off at the Darwin airstrip. The cook utilized his culinary skills to reduce much of the sudden protein surplus to mince and for the next while mince was on the menu.

Eventually the complaints began about the frequency of mince on the menu. To counter the objection a sign appeared at the kitchen saying "Licensed to serve mince"

The complaints stopped.

The Training Of The "Attack Goat" by L/Cpl Bruce McGregor

When Mount Darwin was first occupied by the RLI and turned into a forward base camp, the area behind the District commissioner's complex (such as it was) became dotted with tents.

I arrived to find that apart from tents spread around the place there was a kid goat that had attached itself to trooper Lourenz, a mechanic. He would probably deny this fact, especially if the kid goat left evidence of its presence in the tent – namely a pile of goat shit – but seeing that from day to day he was the only person who was in the tent while the other occupants were out in the bush, ownership of the goat defaulted to him. There is however one fact that is undeniable and that is this goat was liked by many and the goat likened itself to the people within the camp as if we were part of its extended family.

As the kid goat grew and matured we noticed the characteristics of adult goats develop, most particularly if we were messing around with the goat it would drop its head in a charge (defence/attack) attitude.

I am not too sure who brought the idea up or when it started but one morning I arrived back from a week in Rusambo to find some of the men holding a Sergeant Major's badge of rank and they were using it to tap the goat on the head.

"Howzit manne! What's with the teasing of the goat, ek se?"

The RLI had its own version of the English language. Its vernacular would make any self respecting English teacher curl up in the corner and vomit.

"We're teaching it to attack the Sergeant Major," was the reply.

Of course it was as funny as I thought it was ludicrous. Goats surely did not process information like a human and therefore it would not be able to discriminate against rank – besides the rank as I remember was "borrowed" and could not be used to the train the animal indefinitely.

The day went by and we all had our jobs to do – but every time we returned from the bush somebody would "continue the goats training". It was not too long before we noticed a response from the goat. Show it a fist and the head would drop into butting position. Irritate the goat further it would charge. It was working but it seemed to me that I was correct. It could not discriminate between a Sergeant Major or another NCO.

There were a couple of funny incidents where the goat would butt someone but there was one not so good incident when the goat had a full crack at a sergeant from engineers. The sergeant lost his beer and in anger he turned and tried to kick the goat. The goat was agile of course and got away. I think that is when the goats' future took a turn for the worse. There must have been a few complaints against the animal but I think that while it was regarded as some sort of mascot there were a few reprieves.

I returned from a bush trip once in the afternoon and I realized the goat was not around. I asked Lourenz where it was.

He replied that the training had finally worked – the Sergeant Major took a full on charge form the goat and the Sergeant Major retaliated.

"So what happened?" I asked.

He replied, "Don't ask what you're getting for supper tonight."

I did not ask and I did not eat either.

Since then I don't eat mutton or lamb. I like to think that I was being spun a story and that the goat died of old age some where.

Not likely.

Extract from the KK Dictionary (1953)

BORROW, vb. tr. — kwereta, posa, poshwa. KK sikwerit. This universally understood word is derived from the old English expression, "I'll square it at the end of the week when I get my pay."

Anyway your boys will always be after you for a cash advance or a loan.

"Mena azeko mali. Mena aikona asi nika wena sikwerit." "I have no money. I cannot give you the credit"

If you want to keep or obtain labour you'll have to give credit. Make a note of it or you will lose it. Boys are honest but will not volunteer the information that they owe you five bob. If you have forgotten then you have not missed it. Therefore you had too much anyway and they are equalising things.

Mukumbura 1973 by David Slater
(What did you do in the war, Daddy")

Camouflage, camouflage, everywhere camouflage,
Underpants, undervests, Tee-shirts and track-suits.
Rifles dun-painted, green-on-brown camouflage,
Caps and binoculars, even black hiking-boots.
Packing-up, packing-up, black-tin-trunk packing-up,
Stowing away what you'll need for your stint.
Towels and razors, everything packing-up,
Look at your wife and see her eyes glint.
Eyes crying, eyes crying, darkly brown eyes crying,
"I'll miss you, my darling," she says as she goes.
Kissing your daughters, manly eyes crying,
Pretending to wipe a drip from your nose.
Moving-out, moving-out, always we're moving-out,
Never a moment to rest your tired head.
Sergeants all screaming, 'Company's moving-out,'
Maybe they're right – if we don't we'll be dead.
Rolling, all rolling, black wheels all rolling,
Taking us all to Devil-knows-where.
First gear engaging, black wheels a' rolling,
Convoy is moving, a summertime fair.
An ambush, an ambush, bullets scream ambush,
Whipping the leaves of the trees where you lie.
Down in the donga* lie victims of ambush,
A smoking old truck, and your best mate who died.
Drums rolling, drums rolling, seven snare drums rolling,
Beating away for the death of your friend,
Coffin slow-sinking, drums keep on rolling,
When in the hell is this war going to end?

*Donga – a dried-up watercourse

95

Time, Ladies and Gentlemen ... Please! ....
What a Pity - They have already Gone!

The once much-loved **George Hotel** in Avondale closed on January 4 - sold to Multi-Choice as their new HQ. A planned valedictory meal in the grotesquely named Freckle and Phart pub, or the depressing dining room, which was reminiscent of railway architecture circa 1946, was aborted, as it was semi-gutted well before closure.

Next door was **Nick's Place** where you went to sober up after a night out and Mrs Nick had the biggest legs this side of the Sahara!

Further up George Road, some Greeks opened a nice restaurant, **the Acropolis**, and were doing so well that they decided to beat sanctions and hid their profits in the back of some copper fire screens, only to get caught. The business was then run by the flamboyant Spiros Blismas, who had recently enjoyed free bed and breakfast at Chikurubi, following his venture into importing second-hand cars from the Forces in Germany.

Later Terry Rossiters son ran the place!

Charleston Hotel (ex-Kamfinsa Park) is also shut: "Due to ever rising costs," I heard. Both the above places underwent major changes in clientele, facilities, and ambience, even cleanliness but are fondly remembered for special functions and The George, especially for wedding receptions, when the Cambitzis ran it.

Since independence Harare lost the popular **Windsor Hotel** on Baker (Nelson Mandela) Avenue. It housed the Colony, where Edwin and Rachelle played twin pianos to international cabaret standards to discerning diners in formal finery. The Lincoln Room had fantastic value for money food in luxurious surroundings. It closed late November 1980 when the set three-course lunch, featuring baron of beef, rolled to the table and carved to order was $1,50.

1890 was the cocktail bar. Popular with lunchtime philanderers, it shut at 2:30 sharp, when drinkers moved next door to Branch Office (ex-Blue Room) opening 10:30 t o 10:30. Some heroic boozers returned to 1890, which shut at 11:30.

The Egg and I was in the same building, as was Lion's Den: almost impossible to enter unless in the RLI.

The day the **Windsor** closed (earlier than announced to avoid vandalism seen at Meikles' Long Bar by "souvenir hunters") beer was 38c; bar lunch 35c.

Opposite was a complex housing the raucous **Round Bar** and **Le Coq d'Or** where little French was heard. The building was owned by an American religious sect, which left the country at UDI. The premises were banned from selling drink or tobacco; dancing was proscribed. For years they thought it was a library!

Picture the indignation when they found the country's most bawdy, boozy, bare-knuckled, bra-less nightlife had flourished there for years!

Playboy was nearby, as was **La Boheme**: nothing to do with opera, it offered strippers of often-venerable years and was a target of an inexpertly thrown grenade during the "bush war". The entrance fee for **Sunset Strip** was 2 shillings and sixpence. **"The Gentlemen"** were the popular Rock band that played at Saturday Lunchtimes and Sunday Evenings!

Three major Chinese outlets closed after 1980: **Golden Dragon,** a hangout of pre-independence Ministry of Information people, the bar a favourite with international journalists,

The Bamboo Inn with a dark, dingy but somehow appealing pub run by the Kee family and later by an Irishman called (of course) Paddy and **The Mandarin**, next to Meikles Store which had no bar, but hacks and hackettes gathered round a service hatch as if in a Fleet Street club.

Down the way the **Pink Panther** also had a grenade lobbed in during the hondo. Run by two aged sisters from the Caucasus, they served delicious kebabs at the original site, later Linquenda House.

One also owned the **Georgian Grill**. PP later became **Alfredo's** then **Front Page**: restaurants with lively pubs, gregarious regulars, and liberal hours. The "Page" owners: a blonde and a brunette belonged in international glamour magazines.

Pino's in Union Avenue (Kwame Nkrumah) was arguably the best seafood joint around, but gained notoriety when someone complained and the ebullient eponymous Portuguese proprietor whacked him over the pip with a flambe pan.

The Bombay Duck between Jameson (Samora Machel) and Central was run, improbably, by ex-BSAP troopie, Tug Wilson; it served iridescent curries all hours for next to nothing.

In Greendale Avenue was the Rhodies idea of an English Pub, **The Red Fox**!

At Msasa, **The Red Lantern**, run by S-W African (Namibian) Germans specialised in eisbein, knackwurst and bratwurst that I can still smell and taste.

Beverly Rocks was a hospitable hostel: good food, great music, lovely gardens, (now a government training centre.)

Going east, the old **Jamaica Inn** was run by various characters including cross eyed Ruby Strutt, who was married to Jimmy Shields, the racing Driver; an ex-Federal hangman and Commonwealth boxing gold medal winner. Good stop there on the way to or from **Three Monkeys** in Marandellas (Marondera) for lunch. (Now a religious institute.)

Glen Lorne's local was the festive **Highlands Park**, run first of all by the Nicholls family and then by ex-Kenya big game hunter Toby Royston. Great dinner dances, lovely Sunday lunches, cream teas in the garden.

Down the road at Chisipite Shopping Centre was **The Howf of Chisholm**, which was super

The Spaniards, Marlborough (ex-Quorn) served incredibly good food, except for the soup, which was: always watery, insipid and costly. . You queued and often cleared the table yourself. The food was delicious and you either brought your own wine or bought rotgut Barolo.

Guido was deaf and when you came to pay he asked what you had and worked it out in his head. When he retired to the mother country, a redhead Italian bombshell bought the business and never looked back, until the Aussie Tax Squad arrived.

By that time she had opened **Sandro's** in Kingsway. There's not been another Harare establishment like Sandro's. Starting as a private club, it retained club land ambience till the end. Five stars cooking or basic bar lunch often polished cabarets; journalists and businessmen rubbed shoulders with cabinet ministers.

Sardinian Sandro also ran **Eros**: fine Mediterranean food and friendly bar and Sandrock's, for back-packers.

Close by was **Taco's** with punters Chalet as a suitcase bomb exploded at Woolworth's nearby with many fatalities? Regulars helped survivors. (Barbours was the real target.)

On quieter **Chalet** days, great juicy joints were trundled in at lunch; patrons sliced their own for 50c with pickles, mustard, horseradish chips and rolls.

The city's best pies were served in a motor sport-theme cocktail bar. There was a civilized snooker room (not a crummy pool hall.) It became a motor parts store, then a Spar.

Park Lane (now GMB HQ) the **Kaya Nyama** steakhouse was its printed "Doggy bags" as the steaks were so enormous.

The Clovagalix, on Fife Avenue, caught fire once too often, becoming Cafe Med, Borrowdale.

Caruso's on 4th/Samora was a great Chips d'Oliviera club-cum Portuguese pub/restaurant.

As Vila Peri, it moved to 3rd/Baines where the usually grubby Pointe is now.

Next-door was **Fat Mama's**, previously Spago's. Now called Mama Mia's, it thrives at Newlands.

The Cellar, Marimba Park was tops with journos and thc printing trade, serving wonderful whisky prawns, real rosti; the upstairs bar often seemed the centre of the universe.

Kamfinsa's Bizarre Bar (later IT, previously Buster's, The Cockpit, etc) was hugely popular with yuppies, briefly with buppies; once a licence to print money. New owners cut corners. Now it's a swimming pool sundries shop.

Meikles closed The Mirabelle, The Causerie, Flagstaff and Captain's Cabin, Bagatelle and La Chandelle.

Monomotapa lost 1001 Horsemen and Bali Hai, but gained La Francais from Avondale.

When everywhere else closed, you could get ABFs at **Al's Place** near the Kopje. Probably unlicensed: whether you ordered whisky, brandy or rum it came from one bottle; gin, cane, vodka, white rum another.

High -Chaparral (ex-Nick's Bar), Avondale opened all hours: a good greasy spoon where coffee and steak rolls helped avoid the worst "mornings after", especially after **Le Matelot** (ex-Lighthouse), died a death.

Aphrodite, Strathaven, was a superb Greek restaurant;

Demi's near State Lotteries closed due to commuter omnibuses' anarchistic parking. The original owners set up **Tavern Bacchus**, near Reps, which then became the **Manchurian**.

Up the street, **Copacabana** served wonderful Portuguese food, having previously been a great Chinese (White Lotus?).

Himalaya, nearby, did colossal searing noon curries at minimal cost but was avoided after dusk.

Rosedale's/**Rose Bowl**/Rose & Crown in Hatfield was a superb Sunday lunch venue with live entertainment.

One of the best seafood platters you could ever eat was at the **Kentucky**, also in Hatfield. When a Muslim outfit bought the place, proposing to shut it, locals raised a widely supported petition in protest.

Courts ruled in favour of the petitioners but it's closed anyway.

Jameson's **Tiffany's** re-opened after many years On a positive note there's a flurry of recently opened ethnic restaurants, tea and sadza, coffee shops and lodges; but sadly, few seem to have the character or characters in which the closed establishments were so rich, but time will tell!

Green Mealie Pie by Audrey

*2 Cobs cooked Mealies (What I do is to cut them off the cob raw, and then boil them in milk – or you can use tinned sweetcorn).

1-Tablespoon Margarine

1 Cup grated Cheese

1-Tablespoon Flour

Salt and pepper to taste

½ teaspoon mustard powder

2 well-beaten Eggs

*(500ml Milk if using raw cobs)

Cut mealies off the cob into container.

Melt margarine and add flour, cheese, salt, pepper and mustard gradually add milk and stir until thick. Let mixture cool slightly and add the 2 beaten eggs and mealies.

Place in a fireproof dish and bake in moderate oven for 30minutes (until brown on top)   (Goes well with a beer! Ed.)

SANG FROID ? by   Robert Truman

There is always far too much junk at the back of the garage; it inevitably ends up as a navigational problem when trying to drive the car in and the final inability to even half close the doors at last provoked a session of sorting and scrapping, a chore then temporarily sabotaged by the unearthing of the long forgotten shoe bag.

No cue was needed to recall the contents.

A rather faded pair of running spikes, the two toned leather now stiff and unyielding from years of neglect, the contrasting colours pale and stained, each heel somewhat intriguingly mutilated by deep parallel gashes on either side, yet still managing to convey a suggestion of original quality. My mind instantly thrust back in time as I ran a nostalgic, exploratory finger over the scarring. Surroundings blurred and for a short while I was back in Africa again.

The northern boundary of what was Rhodesia, now known as Zimbabwe, follows the matrix of the great Zambezi river. Here, toward the close of the 1950's, the mighty Kariba dam project was approaching completion and at last began to hold back the great river, eventually forming the world's largest man made lake some hundred and fifty miles long, thirty five miles wide and in parts over three hundred feet deep; a virtual inland sea.

The now displaced Batonka people, tribal territory fast disappearing under the rising water, were convinced that those damming the river would themselves be damned and so displease Nyaminyami their revered Zambezi river god that all kind of retribution was sure to follow.... sometimes we did just wonder a little! The terrain lying in this Gwembe Trough is undulating in the extreme in parts and many of the hills were latterly turned into islands by the water carried down river from the expansive Barotseland plains in Zambia, far to the northwest, thence over the Victoria falls and eventually into the new lake, the level of which rose as much as six inches a day at some periods of the year to gradually surround and isolate many hills, Many of the lower peaks, sometimes of substantial acreage, were left only temporarily protruding from the water, the encroaching shore line shrouded by drowned and dying trees.

My task, as part of the team formed by the Department of Wild Life and Conservation to work on what became known worldwide as Operation Noah to rescue wild animals which had been marooned on these slowly vanishing islands, was the running of survey levels to ascertain which islands would be first to submerge, with a time scale to total submersion so that early rescue action could be organized in order of priority. One such island with a relatively flat crown was due to be totally inundated within a few days and urgent action would be required.

The customary routine after a preliminary 'recce' to ensure that none of the 'big five' animals, elephant, rhino, buffalo, lion or leopard remained to require individual rescue format, was to form a long line of beaters composed of up to two hundred

Africans, starting on one side of the island to slowly drive every living creature before them. Finally, animals eventually took to the water on the farther side where small lightweight power boats, each with versatile crew lay in wait, manoeuvring alongside to catch the swimming animals, manhandling them inboard to be then hobbled by tying the legs together with plaited nylon stockings, (collected incidentally, by worldwide appeal), or by placing smaller vertebrates, monkeys, snakes, etc., in sacks. Boats would then quickly shuttle back and forth to the mainland to release their captives at a suitable locale.

Head Game Ranger Lofty Stokes, six feet four, hence the nickname, was in charge of the beating line, and my survey work for the moment completed, he asked me for assistance in the line, flanking if required.

There was a standing safety order with so many personnel involved that no firearms would be carried on these drives and individuals were obliged to rely solely on fleetness of foot or climbing dexterity in the event of any potentially dangerous confrontation. It says much for the inherent ability of the participants in these two spheres that no one was directly lost in the five years of the operation.

This current rescue venue was probably around a hundred acres in extent, almost flat and by now about to be totally immersed within the next twenty four hours; speed was of the essence. We arranged the usual line with some five yard intervals between beaters and having heard the holloa indicating that the boats were in position, a wave of the arm from Lofty started the line forward through scrub composed of alternating thorn and elephant grass interspersed with stunted Mopane trees. After several minutes, numerous Impala and Reedbuck were seen racing forward, which in some defiance of the endemic heat of the valley still managed to generate good natured banter between the beaters. Despite verbal cautionary warnings, this temporary loss of concentration was all that was needed to cause several kinks and bends to appear in the by now very crooked line, such affliction not solely reserved, as might be thought, to an English shooting day.

A halt was called to accomplish realignment. After much altercation and with the line at last now straightened, we started forward once more, but a short time later a new loop suddenly appeared in the centre of the line, which then came to an abrupt halt.

Even at a distance we could overhear much high pitched, almost hysterical exchanges and Lofty and I both rushed across, concerned but also peeved at this latest hindering interruption.

"Eeeny lo indaba?" we asked anxiously, almost together.

"What is the matter?"

The line now rapidly disintegrating as we neared a group of Africans retreating some twenty yards back from a patch of dense grass.

"Eee baas", one stuttered, eyes rolling......"Mbada, lapa", pointing toward the grass.... Leopard!! in there!

My eyes met Lofty's as we drew a little closer to the cover; surely not?

Who made the original reconnaissance?

This was all we needed with time at a premium!

Simultaneously we both heard the distinct, the unmistakable angry cough of a leopard....my brain was already sending urgent signals to lower limbs....move you idiots, MOVE! A leopardess crouched low at the edge of the tussocks, ears laid back flat, then a loud hissing as she launched himself at the pair of us. Now Lofty was justly and exceeding proud of the pair of new, rather ostentatious imported and for my taste quite gaudy, blue and white but nevertheless expensive running spikes with which he had adorned his feet against any eventuality such as the one now before us, but his standing start was as naught against my spectacular take off, shod in conventional bush boots. In what I calculated later to be under two seconds, I was already two good yards in front, but despite concentrating on the manner of my departure, I still heard Lofty's loud involuntary grunt.

I turned, eyes wide with concern, adrenalin releasing in a great burst as I saw him pivoting forward on his flailing blue and whites, the leopard now high on his back, forepaws, one on each shoulder; rear claws already cutting into the soft leather heels of those spikes.

I skidded to a halt, Africans rushing in all directions for the nearest tree, I watched, mouth agape, in what seemed almost like slow motion as the long and expensive telephoto lens of the camera Lofty habitually wore on his chest terminally telescoped into the red soil of the island; saw him now spread-eagled, face uncompromisingly shoved into the dusty earth, pinned firmly down with the leopard looking to effect a neck bite; the coup de grace?

I glimpsed the malevolent yellow eyes through the burgeoning cloud of red dust raised by the impact that was now slowly enveloping the scene. I vaguely recall a horde of Mopane flies swarming irritatingly around my eyes, eager for moisture and blurring my vision.

Brushing a hand roughly across my face I spun round, half blinded and rushed back toward the two of them, screaming wildly and incoherently, legs and arms flailing as I leapt repeatedly into the air like some demented being. Tearing the Bolex cine camera from the loop on my belt and with a single impotent gesture I hurled it with all the strength I could muster at the cat's head, to strike her nothing less than absolutely quite fortuitously, squarely on the nose.

She sneezed, shook her head once and then, quite suddenly and surprisingly her nerve seemed to break and springing deftly to one side, she turned to slink away with that effortless springing lope, tail flicking irritably, to disappear rapidly through the trees. The few remaining Africans now perched in the surrounding scrub trees gasped as one, "Aheeeee...Maiiwee".

Arms sagging, panting heavily, heart still pumping wildly, utterly exhausted from the trauma of those moments, I silently offered up a prayer of thanks for our deliverance.

Lofty? ....Huh! He rolled over, so relaxed, so laid back; sitting for a moment.

Clearing his throat to spit dusty saliva, he casually lifted and inspected first one heel and then the other in turn, scrambled to his feet, the bloodstained shoulders of his shirt in ribbons, his bloodied socks shredded, to perfunctorily glance around.

Nonchalantly raising one leg to dust off his shorts with a completely steady hand and as if he had just fallen over in some Municipal Park, he enquired optimistically, "Did you get a picture?"

There was a moment's hiatus; a fleeting interval; the tensions of the moment totally and instantly dissipated by the sheer inanity of the enquiry.

"No! " I croaked, grinning weakly, "but I did use the camera!"

Later, back in camp and first aid applied, he picked up the newly discredited shoes and with a sigh, flung them across at me.

"No b...y good to me", he swore laughingly, "You're the same size as me, you have them, nothing can catch you then! "

Nor did it.

Several times over the next year I had cause to think of Lofty; those spikes were instrumental in aiding my escape from an exceedingly belligerent rhino, with no provocation other than our presence to initiate the thrust of his massive armament through the Landrover door with sufficient force to almost overturn the vehicle, then proceeding to dismantle the panel-work piecemeal, forcing eventual evacuation and a run for a convenient nearby tree line, reached with negligible yardage in hand and just enough time to dodge behind one of those lifesaving trees.

The shoes were again employed in a similar rather rapid evacuation from the middle of a herd of up until then unseen buffalo in thick cover, during which escapade I swear I ran vertically up the trunk of a totally unclimbable Acacia tree to find three of my African gang already up there!

There was the lone rogue single tusk bull elephant objecting to my line of survey pegs, squealing with rage as he wrenched them from the ground, ears outstretched, head shaking repeatedly, trunk intermittently waving to search the wind, straining to catch my scent.....he finds me; no false charge this.... but that's another story....No, I think I'll hang on to these battered shoes for a while longer, after all, they really take up hardly any space...... That ongoing threat of that Nyaminyami curse perchance, who can say?

Perhaps spike wearers are exempt!

A Record of the Animals saved in Operation Noah.

Ant Bear 48	Baboon 268	Badger 12	Buffalo 78
Bushbaby 1	Bushbuck 320	Bushpig 44	Civet 5
Dassie 21	Duiker 257	Elephant 23	Genet 21
Grysbok 345	Hare 43	Hyena 3	Impala 1866
Jackal 2	Klipspringer 28	Kudu 300	Mongoose 14
Monkey 172	Night Ape 10	Porcupine 47	Rhinocerous 44
Sable 105	Scaly Ant Eater 6	Squirrel 6	Waterbuck 120
Warthog 585	Wild Cat 5	Zebra 46	

Henry Hartley [1815-1876] by anon

Credit for opening up Rhodesia belongs not only to the missionaries but also to the early hunters and prospectors. One of the most famous of the hunters was Henry Hartley who as a child came out to South Africa with the 1820 Settlers. He was born in September 1815.

In 1841 he moved to the Transvaal and went hunting in Matabeleland in 1859. Thereafter he paid visits nearly every season to Rhodesia. Henry became a good friend of King Mzilikazi of The Ndebele. During 1865, while hunting in Mashonaland, Hartley accidentally discovered gold. Soon afterwards, he, Adam Renders and the geologist Carl Mauch, while exploring north of Great Zimbabwe, realized the extent of gold present around the old African mining villages along the Mfuli and Tati Rivers.

At Potchefstroom, in December 1867, Hartley and Mauch announced the extent of gold present in Mashonaland, thus beginning the first gold rush as prospectors and miners from Europe and Australia began the long trek northward up the missionaries' road. The Transvaal Government did its utmost to get hold of the Tati goldfields, but the ailing king, remembering old enmity with the Boers, steadily refused to allow them a   grant.
In 1869 Hartley was engaged by Thomas Baines, acting on behalf of the newly formed South African Goldfields Exploration Company, to guide him to the Mashonaland goldfields. Baines ranked only just below Livingstone, Stanley and Park in the hierarchy of Victorian explorers in Africa. Baines must also be considered one of the founders of modern Rhodesia.

Northlea Comments by Dave Dewar. 17.1.2005

I have been reading with a growing sense of incredulity the sanitized versions of happy days at Northlea High that have been flying through cyberspace. Indeed, I phoned my brother Neil the other day to check if it was the same school that I went to, but he assured me that it was. It is clearly, therefore, my unenviable role to set the truth free. Mainstream life at Northlea can best be described under two main heads: Institutional Violence, and Sexual Rejection and Humiliation. In this missive, I deal only with the former.

Institutional Violence
The Beginnings

For me, it began on the first day of school when my old man took me to see the headmaster, Mr. Broughton. He breezily told Broughton to treat me like his son and, if I needed a whack, feel free. Charming, I'm sure! Broughton obviously put a notice up in the staff room announcing that it was open season, for from then on, it never seemed to stop. It was like feeding raw meat to a shoal of piranhas.

Violence took many and often subtle forms. I briefly raise, seriatim, only the most common of these here: physical violence, rhetorical violence, violence through humiliation, psychological violence, the violence of hard labour, the violence of exclusion, and the violence of retribution.

Styles of Violence
Physical Violence

Physical violence was the most common form but even within this general rubric, there were considerable variations in style. Here I raise a few cases only, by way of illustration.

Broughton was a 'beat by numbers' man, without a real passion for the task. He was also a talker of the 'this is going to hurt me more than it will hurt you' type. I could never figure out why he didn't save us all a lot of pain by simply giving it up.

Ray Suttle, of course, was the star of the show. Who can forget it? Feet a neat nine inches apart, knees slightly bent with the weight evenly balanced on the balls of the feet, a slow back lift, a full rotation of the shoulders at the top of the swing, the forward thrust of the hips to gain cane-head speed, and the sharp break of the wrist immediately before impact. Lovely to watch – but not so lovely when you were watching it upside down with your head between your knees! His placement, too, was superb. He would lay the strokes in a neat evenly spaced parallel pattern, starting at the middle, and spaced so that the second stroke landed just before the numbness caused by the first took over. The most common sight at Northlea was groups of boys with their pants around their knees while their mates admiringly observed the changing kaleidoscope of colours on their butts.

At the heart of the problem, of course, was the vexatious question of Latin homework. If you didn't do your homework, you got beaten, no exception. It was not as if we did not want to play 'spot the main verb' in a nineteen line-long single sentence of Latin prose which invariably began with "Caesar, having conquered Gaul, ..." (Incidentally, did you ever notice how he had it in for those poor Gauls? Unnatural, really) - it was simply that we were too busy. The situation would have been entirely untenable if it was not for the Guardian Angels – the girls who let us copy their homework in the morning before school. In our case, the resident angel was usually the sweet Maria Tihanyi – I still light a candle to Mother Maria on sacred days. We used to cunningly disguise the deed by manufacturing the odd personalized mistake (which I am sure fooled Ray not at all, but he was perfectly prepared to turn a blind eye to it). The real problem arose on the (rare) occasions when Maria made a mistake, which was then identically repeated seventeen times. Then there could be no blind eye and the carnage began.

Bryan Haddon was not, by wont, a violent man but when he lost the plot he would grab any implement to hand with the firm intent to inflict grievous bodily harm. The best strategy, when faced with this, was to abandon all thoughts of dignity and flee.

Joan Suttle was primarily a purveyor of subtle pain (geddit?). She was a master at tweaking the hair at the back of your neck and at twisting ears. However, when she flew into a rage, she was ten times worse than Brian Haddon. Your only chance was to fall to the floor, cover your sensitive bits as best you could, and lie perfectly still – precisely the recommended behaviour, I am told, when attacked by an enraged ostrich.

Muller Rademeyer was one of the more creative generators of discomfort. He had fingers as thick as my arm and twice as strong. His favourite trick (particularly when you were talking to your mates in class) was to grab the fleshy part between your shoulder and collarbone, and squeeze until his fingers met in the middle, while at the same time having a conversation with you. "Do you want to share your thoughts with the rest of us, De Vaar?" (He used to call me De Vaar and Pat Dewil, De Vill, which is the way in which we still greet each other today). You could only carry out your part of the conversation through the side of your mouth, because your ear was flat on the desk in the inkwell. My face is still curiously twisted from this practice. His arms were equally strong. Who could forget the sight of his namesake, Squeaky Rademeyer, desperately trying to loosen Muller's arm lock on the throat of a poor local before his eyes popped out of his head, in one of those engaging 'town meets gown' encounters at the bottom of the hill. To the best of my knowledge, the poor chap's only sin was that he recognised the importance of Elvis Presley in contemporary culture long before the rest of us (and perhaps also that he wore luminous green socks).

Jim Annandale was arguably the least prone to violence. For the most part, he kept his cane firmly lodged down the front of his trousers – I never knew what was on the end of that cane, but it seemed to work for him. When he did fly into a rage (for instance, if you commented on how important the role of America was in winning the Second World War), he gave ample warning: his eyes would swell, his moustaches would quiver and a dull shade of red started rising upwards from his neck. Fortunately these tell-tale signs usually gave you time to remember a pressing engagement and to edge slowly but purposefully away.

Unsurprisingly, according to my psychiatrist, the cycle of violence spread to the student body. Who could forget the feeling of impending doom when, sweating and sans shirt under the African sun, the circle around you began to close and the tennis ball was tossed from person to person, seeking the strongest arm, in a game of sting?

Or being the last link in bok-bok, with the fattest bugger in the school lining up to land on your neck? Even worse was when he was too fat to jump and he simply ran into you. To any casual observer it must have looked like a gays' picnic. In reality, however, one or two potential consequences resulted. The one was that your neck got buggered anyway as your head crashed into the backside of the guy two places in front of you. The other, if you were lucky, was that you reduced the reproductive capacity of the fellow immediately in front of you by about 40%.

Rhetorical violence

Rhetorical violence was widespread. Undoubtedly the most memorable form of this resulted from our association with the Kings African Rifles in the guise of cadets. The Regimental Sergeant Major was an extraordinary talent. He could march the full length of the rugby field, cursing at the top of his voice and never repeating himself once. The staff sergeants too, while not being in the front of the queue when they handed out grey matter, had a marvellous turn of phrase and used to pepper their instruction with homilies such as "Brace up, brace up! Your dressing's like ball-hairs – all tangled and buggered!"

My personal favourite was the solemn warning about venereal disease given to us before a cadet camp (mind you, unless you could get it from holding hands – and I'm still not sure about this – there was absolutely no danger of any of us catching a dose). The sergeant was impressing on us the importance of reporting any cases, "and don't tell me you got it off the lavatory seat. Only officers get it off the lavatory seat." It has taken me a lifetime to realize the validity of this observation.

I remember once lending my swagger stick to Kiriakopoulos (sp?), a muscle-bound Greek recent immigrant (an action, incidentally, that earned me a few corrective blows from Jim Annandale), but it was well worth the memory of Kerri, with his already tiny shorts and shirtsleeves rolled up a further two turns, swagger stick under his arm and, in a dialect similar to the one my wife tells me I speak fluently every Friday night, abusing everyone in sight at the top of his voice.

These events came at a cost. The problem was that my mates, Paul Shepherd and Tich Robb, and I used to stand together at cadets and we used to get the uncontrollable giggles. If we so much as glanced at each other we were gone; sadly, however, the effort of trying to suppress it caused serious internal damage which was only diagnosed much later in life.

Violence through Humiliation

Attempts at humiliation were common but were seldom successful. The worst, which was successful, was the practice of beating you in front of the girls. You walked (or hopped) back to your seat with a mouth crinkled like Charlie Brown's, trying to look as if you had enjoyed it, when all you really wanted to do was blub and put your bum in a basin of cold water.

Another was having to take part in amateur dramatics. It was bad enough having to make an idiot of yourself in public but we had to do it in association with Bruce Millar, who actually could act, making you look an even bigger dickhead than was absolutely necessary. This was frequently exacerbated by equivalently idiotic directing. One year I was Colonel Pickering in Pygmalion, and his first word as he runs onstage out of the rain is "Whew!" The director said I should say it so that it could be heard at the back of the hall. You try it! It has become a life-long obsession with me. After decades of failed attempts, I have concluded that it cannot be done. The closest you can get is a sound not dissimilar to a cow in labour, and it probably isn't worth the strange looks you get at parties.

Quite the most unsuccessful attempt at violence through humiliation occurred with the arrival of two new young (pretty) teachers whose names escape me now. In their collective wisdom they decided that they would impose discipline by making offenders walk across the quad with them, holding hands. Bloody hell! Within three days anarchy had taken root, as the worst villains in the school competed to be 'punished', while their pals shouted ribald words of ill-informed advice across the quad.

A repetitive event of humiliation was the annual Queen's Birthday Parade. Every year, most of Bulawayo crowded as close as possible to the saluting podium with their six packs of beer and waited expectantly. Frissons of excitement would ripple through the crowd as the Northlea squad approached. The underlying cause of this was Jim Annandale. Great patriot and warrior that he undoubtedly was, he wasn't up there with the greats in the marching stakes. The problem was that his right arm and leg had a tendency to move in the same direction in unison, and vice versa. One unintended consequence of this was that he usually gave the 'eyes right' command on the wrong foot. As the Northlea squad approached the podium, therefore, it broke into a curious gait of jumps, shuffles and stumbles (a uniquely Rhodesian form of 'Lord of the Dance', if you like) as everyone tried to get back in step. It used to take us at least a quarter of the circumference of the ground before some sort of order prevailed, while most of Bulawayo, or so it seemed to us, howled with mirth – and Jim marched on, imperious, sword aloft, and impervious.

Psychological violence

To be fair, psychological violence was seldom deliberate. The worst case of this that I ever experienced was at the hands of Miss Leigh, the geography teacher. One day she caught me using a few helpful notes in a geography test. I thought that all that would happen is that I would inflict a bit more pain on Mr. Broughton, but it was not to be. She called me back after class and spent three-quarters of an hour telling me what fine people my folks were and how their lives would be irrevocably ruined if they knew their youngest was crooking in a test. She then told me that she would sleep on it for a week before deciding whether or not to tell them. The worst thing about it was that she was right. I spent one of the worst weeks of my life waiting it out. In the end, she didn't, but it worked – that was the last time I ever crooked in a test.

The Violence of Hard Labour

Hard labour was commonplace: the only difference between Northlea and the prison system was that at Northlea you got it even if you had done nothing wrong. One form of this was compulsory cross-country training. Actually, once we learnt the ropes, this wasn't too bad. A group of us used to stop for a smoke under a tree and then take a shortcut home. Every year our housemasters had high expectations of us winning, based on our practice times, and every year we unfortunately and (to them, inexplicably) had a bad race day.

The worst, however, was league swimming. Every Friday, Sherro and I would skulk around the school trying to avoid the swimming master. Week after week we failed and Friday night would see us in the 100 metres butterfly (or freestyle or whatever), lagging some 25 metres behind, arms barely breaking the surface of the water, only to puke in the gutter at the end of it.

The Violence of Exclusion

Perhaps the greatest hurt of all was that of exclusion. Art was a case in point. Art was a compulsory subject but Sherro and I were only allowed to wash the palettes. Similar practices occurred with woodwork. We carry the scars with us still.

The Violence of Retribution

To explore this we have to advance many years. In 2003 I was travelling from UCT towards home in Wynberg on my motorbike. Dusk was falling and it was drizzling lightly. Ahead of me and coming from the other direction, a car stopped and waited to cross my lane in order to enter a service station. I immediately slowed down, sensing trouble, to ensure that the driver had seen me. Sure enough, the car remained stationary. Just before I reached it, I started to accelerate, confident that the driver had noticed me – and then it moved straight into my line of fire. My bike flew one way, I flew the other, and there we lay in the road, both battered. The driver's door slowly opened and who should emerge but Ray Suttle. (I am fairly certain I heard him say "Got you, you little bastard!", but I can't swear to it and he denies it). When he took me home (for his car was still going and my bike wasn't), bleeding and bruised, with my clothes shredded, and told the story to my wife, she said "Poor Ray! Are you all

109

right?" After bravely assuring her that he was fine, he proceeded to flatten my only bottle of single malt whisky.

Was it coincidence? Perhaps. However, when I later questioned the service station attendant, he told me that that the same car had been standing in the same place every night for four years without once turning in for petrol. Makes you think, doesn't it? In my own mind, and with the benefit of hindsight, I have realized one thing: I should at least have negotiated a sunset clause that first morning in Broughton's office.

Still, it doesn't do to complain. I can honestly say that Northlea played a major part in making me what I am today – an overweight cross-dresser with a phobia about exercise, a distorted visage, and a buggered neck, who still wets his bed at night.

To be born at UDI......... by Gwen Raikes

I was born in Rhodesia in 1965, so the war was always 'on' for me.

My parents were both in the Police Reserve, so they were not at home in the afternoons and at weekends, because they had 'duties'. My Dad used to do night duty on 'Baobab Hill', and Mom used to be either busy with the PR or with the troopies canteen out near the airport at Buffalo Range, or on duty as an auxiliary nurse.

The first time my Mom had to use the radio, she thought they were all talking 'Donald Duck' language, but by the time I was ten, she had taught me the "Alpha, Bravo, Charlie" alphabet.

She also made sure that I knew how to use a pistol in anger, when I was eight, in case something happened at home or on a convoy. Now I am in the UK, people think that was weird, but it was normal to us.

The war became very real for me when I was eleven, when one of the children in 'Standard 5' in the Chiredzi school was wounded in a convoy attack. Then we had bunkers and sandbags installed all around the school, and had to do 'drills', to take cover. I hated that, because the bunkers were dark and had spiders!

I remember how excited we were when the Salisbury show came around. We all were involved with projects and competitions, and we saw all the fascinating ideas, like what you could do with icing sugar, by using it for modelling instead of just eating it!

I always gave the beerhall a wide berth on my way to Luna Park, where they had those high chain swings, but you had to have someone to push you, to make it all worth while.

'Frankly Partridge in Rhodesia' by Derek Partridge.

"Howzit! Would you consider coming up to Rhodesia and coaching my son and other Rhodesian shottists?"

Paul and May Meyer, farmers from Makwiro, had heard I was in SA, coaching international trap shottists.

In 1976 I was chairman of the British International Shooting Board and a member of the British Team. The Clay Pigeon Shooting Association of South Africa had invited me on a tour of SA, to coach their shottists and to run a course for shooting instructors. I was very uncomfortable with apartheid (correctly pronounced it comes out symbolically as: "apart" and "hate") and was reluctant to go to Rhodesia, where—by all press accounts—that situation was even worse.

Based on that information, my first answer was a firm "No!", but Paul was persuasive... so, with considerable misgivings, I landed at Salisbury. As I stepped onto Rhodesian soil, I was overcome by an extraordinary feeling of peace, contentment and, most strangely, of belonging! I'd traveled in some 75 countries and never before experienced a similar feeling. Press stories had told me blacks were oppressed and resentful of whites, so I was astonished to be greeted by a friendly, young black Customs Officer! And so began the most treasured time of my life... in Rhodesia.

Apologies for having to use "I"... a lot but, when recounting memories, it's difficult to avoid! Included are some excerpts from press stories and letters written about me... but, no apology for including them and I'm most grateful to editor/publisher Bill McDonald for allowing me to relive—and share with you--my personal Rhodesian Memories. They will illustrate the depth of my feelings—not equaled before nor since--for Rhodesians and Rhodesia. It was the best time of my life, when I was able to achieve everything I had ever dreamed of doing: becoming a TV presenter, conveying information to viewers in an entertaining manner and—thanks to becoming known on TV—being able to help in some small way, to improve the lives and morale of Rhodesians, both black and white. None of this would have been possible without you, my Rhodesian friends, the finest people--of all ethnicities--I've ever met in my extensive travels... those I know and those of you who knew me from RTV. Even now—some 30 years later—whenever I start talking about Rhodesia... my voice quavers and the tears well up!

My first evening at the Monomatapa happened to be the Jacaranda Ball... I persuaded Jaycee organiser Celia Sparrow to get me a ticket and she put me at a table next to Bill and June Soutter, who—on hearing of my interest in TV--invited me to their home to meet Anne McCormack, who had been PA to Mike Hart-Jones, the Head of Programmes and Production at RTV. Anne is now re-married to Alan Shaw and has been living in her native Scotland for some years. She recently sent me an e-mail addressed to RPC... following my puzzled enquiry, she graciously explained that the initials stood for Rhodesia's Premier Celebrity!

Anne set a meeting with the British born Mike, who was brought up in SA, where his father managed a gold mine. He had been a stage manager at London's Royal Opera House (where he met his first wife Gwen), a cameraman and Assistant Director for MGM and a Floor Manager and A.D. for BBC TV before joining RTV in 1968. He was also a black belt at Judo and an accomplished cook. It had long been my ambition to be a TV presenter, but no one in the UK would ever give me a chance. So, following an instant rapport with Mike, when he said: "Would you consider working in our war-torn country..." no hesitation delayed my simple: "Yes". Mike had created over 300 TV series and produced and/or directed some 4,000 TV programmes and 200 documentaries in his 10 years at RTV... so I figured I'd be in good hands.

Mike Hart-Jones, Head of RTV Programmes and Productions

This meeting with Mike was probably the most significant event in my life, as he enabled me to finally start doing what I had wanted to do--more than anything--for the previous 23, frustrating years!

Twelve days later I returned to the UK, packed and flew back to Rhodesia to join RTV on November 9th, 1976... to become another "victim" of the UN sanctions imposed at the request of the slimy British Prime Minister, Harold Wilson... who was piqued at being outmaneuvered by a "simple" farmer, our much-admired and respected PM, Ian Smith!

I bought a used BMW 2002, as it was about the nippiest car for getting out of ambushes... that is, when you had enough petrol coupons to be able to drive into a potential ambush situation! I stayed with shottist parents Mike and Adelai Hodgson (now down South), until finding a delightful cottage to rent at 8 Midvale Road in Chisipite.

My cottage in Chisipite

At night the chorus of the frogs at the nearby dam was amazing; equally amazing was when the swarms of flying ants emerged from the ground and took flight, totally obscuring sight of everything else. With the rental came Alfred the cook and James the gardener, both older fellows from Malawi. I was very fond of them, but found the local custom of calling them "cook boy" and "garden boy" was demeaning and unacceptable to me. When I left, I decided to give them each a watch, engraved with my inscription of thanks. After much discussion about shape and size, they finally chose their watches from a catalog... then Alfred made a final request: he was very adamant that his watch should be made of "strainless" steel! Which reminds me of a note left for Anne McCormack (who spoke with a fairly strong Scottish brogue) by her maid: "Madam, I could not finish the ironing, because the iron is not walking." The watches were sent from England and later I heard reports of them proudly showing their friends in the village.

Although I had experience as an actor--in addition to my business interests--I had no previous experience as a TV Presenter. Mike started me off as RTV's first male continuity announcer, doing programme promos. This meant arriving at the studio an hour before the 5.0PM start of broadcasting, being allocated between 30 seconds and 4 minutes, to write and memorise a script about the evening's programs, changes and delays. Our standing joke was: "Here is a special announcement: tonight's programmes will run as scheduled!" Next was narrating the documentary series Windows from VisNews, produced by Tim Akins. Then I "graduated" to news... well, that's what it was called, but in reality it was only what government and military censors allowed—security precautions necessary in any war situation... but somewhat undermined, as we could get all the news on BBC overseas radio! Early on, when doing a weather forecast, I referred to "your" weather... Mike corrected me to say "our" weather... the start of my adoption as a Rhodie!

Mike then devised the live magazine show "Frankly Partridge", which I eventually co-produced and co-wrote. The first two guests he gave me were two friendly, but argumentative priests (Father John Gough and Dean John da Costa)... so I

113

didn't have to do much! In contrast to the large production teams on Brit and US TV series, our whole team

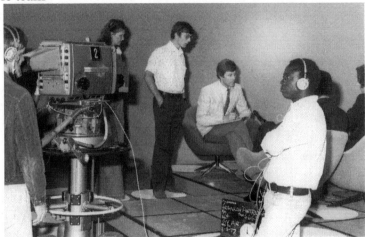

On the set of "Frankly Partridge", with director Harmon Cusack

consisted of Mike, his assistant Helen Gibson (after Madeleine Squair left) and director Harmon Cusack, with whom I have always maintained contact. Harmon was a decorated Rhodesian Army cameraman and is now a top film cameraman in SA, married to ballerina Lynne Holland.

Later, while on a trip to London, there was a photo on the front page of the Daily Telegraph of a Security Forces raid into Mozambique, one of the Front-Line States backed by that unholy alliance of Russia, China and Cuba. Among the various troopies amid the smoking battlefield ruins, one could discern a movie camera on top of a pair of legs... human legs that is! Harmon was astonished to receive the picture from me and... that I had correctly identified those legs as belonging to him! Harmon—carrying this large camera—went about his duties without an armed escort and, as a result of this and other similar ops, he was awarded the MLM (Member of the Legion of Merit). His reaction today to his then-cavalier attitude: "I must have been insane!"

That raid, code-named "Operation Dingo", was carried out by the SAS and RLI against Mugabe's ZANLA at Chimoio on November 23rd, 1977. I'm indebted to Dick Gledhill of RLI's One Commando for this passage from his book "One Commando": After being softened up by RRAF Canberras and Hunters... "It was on these 'externals' that the Selous Scouts, SAS, and the RLI secured their acclaim as probably the best special force units in history. Tens of thousands of communist terrorists, plus Mozambican and Zambian regular soldiers, and an unknown number of Cuban and

114

Russian 'advisers', were eliminated. The Rhodesians lost a few dozen men and, crucially importantly at the time, several irreplaceable aircraft."

RTV's photographer Plinio Battigelli, created the great Frankly Partridge logo, a montage depicting Rhodesia's war and peace activities. German-born Karl Dorn generously provided my FP wardrobe. Our cameramen were often Toni Fairfield's brother, Geoff and the talented Job Jonhera, who went on to become a producer/director for ZBC, then Head of African TV and, I believe, he subsequently rose higher at ZBC. All my shows had black floor managers and multi-racial crews. FP became something of a milestone, when Mike and I decided to invite the first-ever, black Rhodesian guests onto Rhodesia's "white" TV. When Harmon was on active duty, Graham Keightley directed the shows, with his assistant, Cathi Wilson. Chris Everson, Andy Rex, Nick Critchlow and his assistant Bev Freeman were also involved. Between TV and radio, I worked 7 days a week and RBC paid me the princely sums of $35 for Frankly Partridge, $30 for news and $5 for Continuity... at a time when—even back then--news anchors and talk show hosts in the US had multi-million dollar contracts!

Keith Simpson—who rarely praised anything at RTV--wrote a reasonably favorable critique in The Sunday Mail, headlined "Fast-moving new show by Partridge", "Three months in the newscaster's chair and it's top billing for Derek Partridge. Not only a show of his own, but his name up there in the title too: a pretty rare event on Rhodesian TV."

ILLUSTRATED LIFE RHODESIA

Publisher & Managing Director
GORDON M. GRAHAM
Acting Editor
BEVERLEY WHYTE
Editorial Assistant
GLENDA BRERETON

Feb. 3rd. 1977   Vol. 9, No. 23

Radio and TV star Derek Partridge once squired Rita Hayworth — page 16

In her February 1977 Illustrated Life Rhodesia article "Rhodesian birds' favourite Partridge", Jill Steed wrote: "If you were watching TV as 1976 became 1977, you'll have shared an experience which moved and inspired many people. DP, the 'new boy' of RBC TV, in a simple and sincere manner, offered his life's guidelines: 'Prayer for Peace' by St. Francis of Assisi, the 'Desiderata' and Rudyard Kipling's 'If'. "The resultant mail which Derek received is an indication of the impact, not only of those stirring words, but of the man himself upon Rhodesians. The speed with which he has established himself as a fully rounded character in a purely two-dimensional medium is nothing short of remarkable." One letter came from Samson Kwezani: "On New Year's Eve, Derek Partridge read us a very moving and to me, words of wisdom. So, with your kindness, can you please supply me with them. I think they are forthright and character building." Phillipa Berlyn—a Shona language expert, who often went out into the sticks on missions with our tough, "Special Forces" units-- told me that some members of Lt. Col. Ron Reid-Daly's elite Selous Scouts were openly weeping as they listened...

Our troopies were truly fantastic and I believe that even the highly-trained, battle-hardened Israelis acknowledged that our boys were the best in the world. A slightly exaggerated example is pertinent: a possible terr sighting in Vietnam: the Americans send over B52s to flatten the area, followed by fighter-bombers with Napalm to incinerate anything left standing... only then would large numbers of troops venture in. And, in Rhodesia, for a confirmed sighting: Alouette "G-Car" choppers would drop in a few 4-man, RLI sticks, who would take care of the situation and only call for reinforcements if they found they were outnumbered by more than say 20 to 1! In such cases, Dakotas would bring in more sticks for very low-level parachute drops, reducing the chance of being shot during their descent, compared to more normal, greater drop heights.

Memories of "Frankly Partridge": Of the 350 studio, location and street interviews for FP, the most vividly remembered one was at the Tsanga Lodge Forces Recuperation Centre for injured troopies, where the wonderful Lt. Dick Paget and his wife helped re-build their damaged bodies and minds. My pathetic attempt to play wheelchair basketball was laughable... while the guys who had lost limbs, wheeled circles around me! Their evocative coat of arms was a crutch crossed by an assault rifle... I still have the plaque. Also involved with Tsanaga Lodge were Claude Bower, chairman of the Rhodesian Memorial Fund and Col. Forbes Ainsley, Director of Medical Services.

Tsanga Lodge Insignia

a live studio interview about the Forces Welfare Club became a
st Sqn. Ldr. Alan Cockle finally rushed into the studio... after I'd
yself for a couple of minutes... hey, it's <u>live</u> TV, you can't just ask
eir thumbs and wait till the guest arrives!

able program segments include: Battered Wives and... to my
lusbands, with Brian Beecroft and Dr. Elizabeth Metcalf; The
unism, with Senator Father Arthur Lewis, covering the support
World Council of Churches. The City Rubbish Dump Scavengers,
uncil's Ronnie James was incredible... interviewing people who
und eked out a precarious living by recycling discarded items. The
scribe the appalling smell is this: after we left the dump, we pulled
n... the moment the attendant came out, he grimaced and asked what
was... he was yards away and the smell was just the small residue on
iicle... and people "lived" in that!

lloons, with Captain Terry Adams, was fun, as I did the interview in
newhere above Salisbury! Then there was our beautiful and world-
sculpture, with artist John Takawira. Two Scientologists came up
iote their "religion", in which you very expensively purchase your
iotion" ladder. I asked them about their organisation's break-in at the
nue Service... no comment and, as they claimed the ability to levitate
ugh solid objects... I invited them to demonstrate... no comment!!
Police Specials from Chief Inspector Dave Le Guern and Chief
oves was of particular interest to me, as my father had been a Police
l Palestine and I'd been a Special Constable in the City of London
ol. Don Granger and Tim Fourie described to our viewers the world of
which the terrs had created all too many. On a lighter note was
g's "The Jungle Book", for which—to the kids delight—I coiled
ge python costume and did all my interviews from within it!

nctions, we had very little film stock, so didn't have the luxury of
akes, as is common in TV and film. So, when doing street interviews
cation, it had to be done right first time... which served as wonderful

training for the rest of my career in TV and earned me the nickname from many companies of "one-take Derek"... well, not always!

Mike occasionally took us down south to do FP segments and one night we got caught in one of Durban's famous storms, which knocked out electricity all along the eerily, lightning-illuminated coast and obliged me to hump camera equipment up 15 flights of fire escape stairs to our rooms... in the dark! The evening before, some instinct had made me to look under my bed... where Mike had mischievously placed a tape recorder to eavesdrop on my nocturnal activities with a delectable SA beauty!

As Mike served with PSYAC, the psychological warfare branch of the army, he was often away from RTV, However, if it was really necessary to consult with him about program matters... he could generally be found at the Borrowdale Race Track, usually with other PSYAC members, Tom Nevin and Stuart Ingram!

Apart from doing FP programs with troopies at the "Sharp End", I went out to meet troopies and visit Protected Villages, sometimes flying in two-seater planes, which were occasionally shot at! On another occasion, our armoured vehicle broke down in an exposed area near the Mozambique border and—as we waited for help—it was a somewhat eerie feeling, wondering if we were in some terr's telescopic sights. I also toured Operational Areas with the ladies of the Border Patrol Welfare Fund (to which all my shooting coaching fees were donated), they were: Judy Garnett, Jeanette Mussett, Lady Graham, Ethelwyn Passaportis and Betty Smith.

RIDING in military style with the Border Patrol Welfare Fund — from left, Lady Graham, Mrs Judy Garnett, Mrs Jeanette Mussett, Mrs Ethelwyn Passaportis, Mrs Betty Smith and Mr Derek Partridge.

The Border Patrol Welfare Fund   15.5.77

There was a lovely story, revealing the wonderful Rhodesian sense of humour in the midst of a serious crisis... a war! Army personnel naturally had shoulder flashes indicating "Army". At one Combined Ops HQ meeting of senior Army and Air Force officers, the Air Force uniforms were adorned with little badges, indicating: chesty, tummy, leggy etc!

My worst memories are having to start each evening's news with the dreaded words: "Combined Operations Headquarters regrets to announce the death in action of..." and you could feel the whole country holding its breath, waiting for the names. I had to announce the death of my friend, RTV producer Rob Brewer, who was killed in a contact by an RPG. Rob's wife, Terry Brewer, was Look & Listen's editor. After Rob's military funeral, she told me that she'd noticed me crying "behind my shades". Sadly, other friends had to be read out too, including Dave Cordell (Sgt., Rhodesian Intelligence Corps) from the news room, killed by a grenade and, Lord Richard Cecil (from Britain's ITN), killed by a terr with an AK47.

A girlfriend (Ruth Rainey) died in the destruction of Air Rhodesia Viscount Hunyani. Years later, in Hollywood, there was an audition to play the lead in "Kariba", a film about the airliner brought down "by a terrorist bomb on board". The producers were not very amused when I politely told them it wasn't a bomb, but a ZIPRA Sam 7, ground-to-air, heat-seeking missile that downed RH 825. "What the hell do you know about our story?" was their understandable reaction... "Because I was the newsreader at RTV who had to read the story that evening...!" There was an equally understandable stunned silence at this extraordinary coincidence! I told them that 10 of the 18 survivors were killed with AK47s and that hostess Dulcie Esterhuizen had been gang-raped and then, while her assailants laughed, they bayoneted her to death. Most readers will undoubtedly recall the Very Rev. Dean John da Costa's reference to the reaction of the world's media as "... the silence is deafening."

"The Kwhizz Kids" was produced by Martin Norris (who recently contacted me from Australia) and his assistant, Margie Eatherley, with Martin Stubbins also involved. The contestants were 11-14 year old brothers and sisters... including blacks, coloreds and Indians. It was a sheer delight for me and I was often surprised at what they did... and didn't know! One of many amusing moments came in the final, when the question for twins Amanda and Melanie Wright was: "In what age group would you find a quinquagenarian?" After much whispered consultation, they ventured: "In the stone age?"! Unfortunately the answer was between 50 and 60 years old, so the winners were Dale and Charleen Hefer.

The Kwhizz Kids Crew

At RBC Radio, we worked in small, self-engineering cubicles where—as well as introing records and news reading—the duty announcer coordinated mic level VU meters, two record players and an audio reel tape deck. All the music had to be back-timed, so that it would end exactly on time for news bulletins and weather. The formality—including (I seem to recall) a minute of silence between each news item-- was quite stressful and not as satisfying as TV, as I prefer to look someone in the eye, when communicating. Showing me how to be a radio newscaster and DJ was the dedicated Roy Brassington, whose ambition was to become the epitome of a BBC newscaster. However, the formality wasn't quite as bad as at the BBC, where Lord Reith used to insist that his newsreaders delivered broadcasts, dressed in formal evening wear, including shirts with high wing collars (which stuck into the throat)... for radio!

In very informal contrast... I once announced that the next number would be played by Enoch Powell and his orchestra, instead of Enoch Light... not very tactful in a racially sensitive country, as Conservative Minister Enoch Powell had advocated repatriation of all the blacks from England! Later, in a weather forecast, I solemnly informed listeners to expect "thattered scunderstorms"! And, a classic blooper was when one of the girls—equally solemnly—read out from her doctored script: "Good evening ladies and gentlemen, this is the Rhodesian Broadcorping Castration...!"

Toni Fairfield was often to be found in the record library, preparing for her music programmes and, of course, there was the forces sweetheart, the lovely Sally Donaldson. Jill Baker now runs a company helping Rhodesians find work in Australia. At RTV, Geoffrey Atkins' (possibly also in Australia) show featured somewhat serious interviews, while Allan Riddell's programs were more light-hearted. Allan went on to become a successful, globe-trotting director of the Zimsun Leisure Group (including my first roost in Rhodesia, the Monomatapa) and a property developer, who eventually felt the ever-deteriorating political situation obliged him to move down south. We've stayed in touch over the years.

Other RTV and RBC colleagues remembered are: Gail Adams, Eileen Bailey, Norman Bisby, Joy Cameron-Dow, Johnny Clingen, Jeremy Dawes, Jack Day, Dave Emberton, Toni Fairfield, Tony Gaynor, Sonia Hattin, Lale Heathcote, Trish Johns, Allan Jones, Rick Larkins, Leslie McKenzie, Annie Nicholas, David Paterson, Margaret Patrick, Jenny Rickard, Malcolm Russell, Ian Salmon (director of TV Services), Eleanor Tapson (Terry Brewer's L&L colleague), Wrex Tarr, Caroline Thorneycroft, Annabel Tillbury, Jenny Stevens and Adrienne Verney. From the Film Unit: Tony Liddell, Ralph Stutchbury and Lynn Frewin. RTV receptionists Joan Ross-Brown and Pat Groenewald. Although no longer with RTV, also remembered is Lynn Mehmel and her "Crippled Eagles" partner, Robin Moore.

To me, SA had the worst black/white relations (followed by the US and UK) I'd observed in my world travels and it was easy to see—and understand—the black's resentment of whites in SA. But—to my astonishment—Rhodesia had the best... blacks and whites lived and worked together, socialized at home and in public places; there were mixed marriages and black millionaires. Although outnumbered about 26 to 1 (at that time: 7 million blacks and 250,000 whites), apprehension was unknown to me, even when alone with hundreds of blacks... in marked contrast to my guarded caution in Jo'burg, London and New York. All this, despite the lies propagated by the world's media! Lies like pictures of blacks lying on the grass--taking their mid-day siesta—captioned as having been "massacred" by whites and, journalists throwing sweets into rubbish bins, so they could publish pictures of "starving" black children scavenging for food. In marked contrast to all these lies, I remember having frequent discussions about international affairs with black waiters in the RTV canteen... discussions I would have been hard put to have had with many American black college graduates.

My relatively inexperienced view of Rhodesia was confirmed by Willy Lutzenkirchen, a broadcaster for West German radio and a journalist for Die Welt. He had worked in 25 African countries over 9 years, including 4 in Rhodesia. He considered Rhodesia had the highest standard of living for blacks in Africa and was also the finest example of racial harmony in the world. I was glad to find that my relatively brief observation of Rhodesian life concurred with that of a trained observer, with many years of experience here.

Wanting to redress this deliberate campaign of misinformation, I became the Executive Vice-Chairman Responsible for National Projects of Co-Ord-A-Nation, with chairman Brigadier Theo Passaportis and RBC's Jill Baker, who wrote me a very nice letter, welcoming my participation. They were doing a great job to help the troopies. My task was to implement Senator Father Arthur Lewis' idea of the women's weapon being the pen and that they should "Write for Rhodesia". But it seemed to me it was asking a lot to expect women to incorporate a mass of facts into personal letters. My proposal was that it would be more effective to produce a leaflet containing many facts and pictures of life in Rhodesia, specifically showing blacks and whites working and playing together. However, the committee (except Janet Kaschula) decided that my proposed leaflet was not something they should be doing, in case there was anything "wrong" in it which could reflect badly on Rhodesia. Obviously, no matter what I wrote, there would be people who would disagree with parts of it!

The transcript of an interview conducted by John Launder on Gail Adams' "Sunday Magazine" reminded me that I had drafts vetted and corrected by, eg: Professor Richard Christie (for legal matters), Bishop Paul Burrough (religious aspects) and by a number of black Rhodesians. It was also approved by PSYAC team members Ben Kaschula and Mike Hart-Jones, Security Forces Liaison Officer Col. Terry Hopkins, Major General Andy Rawlins, the Director of Psychological Warfare and, Provincial Commissioner Lionel Leach, who wrote to Co-Ord-A-Nation, recommending their working with me, saying: "He is obviously a man of action and someone who gets things done...".

Just one fact alone amazed me: 82% of the Security Forces were volunteer black Rhodesians... including officers. There was no draft or conscription for blacks... call-ups were only for 17-60 year old whites and coloureds! I—and obviously many millions of people around the world--had been conditioned by the world's lying media to believe that the Rhodesian conflict was a vicious race war between oppressed blacks and their white oppressors. To the contrary, black soldiers featured conspicuously amongst the most highly decorated members of the Security Forces, displaying extraordinary courage under fire and often risking their lives to save their white comrades-in-arms. Incidentally, there were also several hundred, weapon-trained women of all ages serving with the Army and Air Force.

So, given all that official backing and my feeling that--with their men fighting the terror war--the women wanted to contribute more, I resigned and formed the Welfare Organisation, Women For Rhodesia. Our logo, designed by Cyril Hartley (Janet Kaschula's father) of Mardon Printers, featured black, white and colored ladies holding hands. Philippa Berlyn, a wonderful lady and dedicated wildlife conservationist, married to University of Rhodesia Law Professor Richard Christie), became President of Women For Rhodesia.

As chairman, I asked WFR to collect more info on every different aspect of black/white relationships in Rhodesian life. Our team was: Margaret Clark, Maria Crampton, Janet and Derek Gordon-Farleigh, Judy Harper, Joyce and Cyril Hartley, Janet Kaschula, Irene Moss, Jean Orsmond, Sue Pichanik, June Soutter, Marjorie and David Samidzimu. I believe David was the son of a chief and President of the Organisation of Anti-Terrorist Groups, a very brave black man. The final result was the 4-page leaflet "Rhodesia As It Really Is", designed to tell the truth and combat the insidious propaganda war being waged against us. One of my black RBC broadcaster colleagues authorised me to include his statement: "Blacks are the worst exploiters and oppressors of blacks... far worse than whites ever were." With his permission (but not his agreement!), I modified "are" to "can be". I closed the leaflet with: "People's skins may be black and white... but the blood being spilled is the same colour."

Our slogan was: "A dollar a dame!", for which contribution they received 50 copies of the leaflet. One Salisbury civil service secretary sent out 650 copies... at her own expense! An American took 1,600 for his personal distribution and a British Peer took 500 to circulate among Britain's decision makers. Thanks to Rodney Pinder of Reuters in Jo'burg, we received worldwide press coverage, resulting in many press and radio interviews, which further increased distribution of the leaflet. Around this time, the SA Save Rhodesia Campaign sent a telegram to President Carter, offering congratulations on the 201st anniversary of America's unilateral declaration of independence from Great Britain... shades of 1965, sound familiar?!

Of course, not everyone agreed with the contents and there was criticism from whites, as well as blacks! Diana Mitchell and her political party, the National Unifying Force was particularly strident in its criticism and was clearly politically motivated... despite their extraordinary claim to be non-political! The NUF claimed to represent the interests of black Rhodesians. However I attended an NUF meeting, where 5 black Rhodesians came in with my group... but there were only 3 other blacks at this well-attended, NUF function! I was told that some of these so-called black supporters were among the first to send their money and families out of Rhodesia. Then there was an article in The Herald headlined: "Peace women fall out": a statement had been issued, dissociating themselves from the leaflet... causing Women for Peace chairman, Mrs. Pat Cooper, to have to refute it as untrue! All the criticism served to bring the leaflet to many more people's attention, thus ensuring that thousands more copies were distributed worldwide!

My response, published in The Herald stated: "Let the critics do something better!" and asked if any of them had ever done anything to correct the countless lies told about us by the world's media... and answer came there none! I pointed out that no one was obliged to send out leaflets and that people would only do so, if they believed it would help Rhodesia. So, how did they explain that hundreds of thousands of leaflets had been sent out by—according to the Herald—"thousands of Rhodesian women"! I closed by inviting the critics to read some of the letters of thanks we received from women who had lost their husbands or sons in the war.

An editorial in The Herald summed it up beautifully: "Better than bleating" and went on to comment that "thousands of Rhodesian women" were sending copies overseas, wanting to do anything "to counter a never-ending stream of propaganda and vilification against Rhodesia." It then singled out our most vociferous critic: "The National Unifying Force, which never seems to unify anything but spends its time issuing almost countless statements criticising others..." The editorial closed with: "The pamphlet urges those who read it to come and see for themselves. Those who do will find more good than evil in Rhodesia—of that we are sure."

While it's undoubtedly true that Rhodesia could have moved faster to remove certain aspects of racial discrimination, "Smithy" had set out to rectify the remaining shortcomings.

Nkomo's paper the Zimbabwe Times ran several days of tirades against me and the leaflet in "Hew to the Line" by Tsanga Shanga and C.G. Msipa's "I write as I please". To their editor's credit, when I sent my response, he published it under the heading I requested: Partridge also "Writes as he pleases". Apart from refuting their criticisms, I thanked them for giving the pamphlet such great publicity among the black population!

There was also personal criticism and I was even accused of working for the Rhodesian Government and—in an amusing, total contradiction—of being a spy for the British Government!

Despite the few dissenting voices, the RAIRI leaflet was considered a huge success at promoting the Rhodesian cause around the world. Apart from the many congratulatory letters from Rhodesians and our supporters overseas, letters of thanks and congratulations were received from President John Wrathall, Prime Minister Ian Smith... actually from John Snell, his Principal Private Secretary, as the PM almost never signed letters! John wrote: "He has asked me to thank you most sincerely for all that you are doing to help put across the Rhodesian cause. With the Prime Minister's best wishes." Also from Deputy PM D.C. Smith and these ministers: Jack Mussett (Internal Affairs), Mark Partridge (Defence – no relation), Roger Hawkins (Combined Ops), Elly Broomberg (Information), Rowan Cronje (Manpower & Health), W. Walker (Education), H.G. Squires (Justice), Air Marshall Archie Wilson (Transport & Power), Deputy Minister Andre Holland (Information), as well as Major General Andy Rawlins (Director, Psychological Warfare), Mark Oxley (Secretary for Foreign Affairs), Bill Ferris (Director of Information), Lionel Leach (Provincial Commissioner, Mashonaland East), Ian Campbell and Mrs. Millward at Immigration Promotion. Most were addressed to Derek, not Mr. Partridge... just as I was just Derek to every Rhodesian.

One of the most surprising supporters of the leaflet was my friend David Mukome, who became the UANCZ Foreign Minister. He then sent out—on behalf of the new black majority government--13,000 copies of a leaflet... written by a white man!

One evening, over dinner with Lt. General Peter Walls and his wife, Eunice, I volunteered to serve in the military, but Peter decided that, due to the morale-boosting effect of my work at RTV and the PR work I was already doing for Rhodesia around the world, it was better to leave me doing that. I recall my disappointment when his two beautiful daughters, swimming champion, 2nd Lieutenant Valerie married Lt. Keith Harvey and Mary married Col. Pat Armstrong!

After several meetings with Senator Chief Jeremiah Chirau, President of ZUPO and the Council of Chiefs, I placed ads and articles in The Herald asking for money, school books and toys for black kids whose schools had been burned down by their fellow countrymen, the so-called "Freedom Fighters".

Along with many treasured letters from the kids, was one from Head Master Ben Moyo of Muzezuri School in Mudzi, Mtoko:

"I want to thank you very sincerely for the goodies they received from you and for the wholesome book Frankly Partridge, it's a jewel, a masterpiece, some real work of art. I am proud to own it. Thanks too for the pamphlet. Indeed, I and all those I lead have much to thank you for." It was signed "Love, Ben".

My book: "Frank, profound and controversial" wrote Margaret Wasserfall (Look & Listen Publications Manager) "best describes a new book, aptly titled 'Frankly Partridge'." "He offers readers much food for thought... his ultimate aim." Mardon Printers published my book of philosophical observations about life and living, while Book Centre and Kingstons kindly provided entire window displays of the book! One cherished review was by D.L. Jordain in the Financial Gazette: "Being of a much older generation than Mr. Partridge, I found some of his concepts hard to swallow, but his zest for life and unbounded sympathy for the underdog will have an irresistible appeal to all generations. Rhodesians in particular will value this last attribute."

RHODESIAN MEMORIES

of many contributors

Well-known Rhodesian television personality, **Derek Partridge,** autographs copies of his recently published book, *Frankly Partridge,* described as "a fascinating insight into the man behind the screen image". It is about Partridge's experiences in the many countries he has visited, and about "many aspects of loving and living".

ILLUSTRATED LIFE RHODESIA

November 24. 1977 Vol. 10. No. 18

Around this time, my then-girlfriend June Barry (June Forsyte in BBC TV's The Forsyte Saga) came out to see why I was now in love with an entire country!

As a spin-off from my training Rhodesian trap shooters, I was asked by Staff Inspector Ian Holmes of the B.S.A. Police to instruct members of the Salisbury Urban Emergency Unit in the use of shotguns on moving targets at the Mashonaland Gun Club. Their rendezvous was mysteriously code-named Batcave! In 1980, Paul Meyer—the reason I came to Rhodesia—became one of the youngest shottists (18) to compete in the Olympics and, while in Moscow was asked if he knew Derek P... because, the questioner said... his shooting style reminded him of me! One shottist, Peter Panas, recently retired from managing a gun shop in California. Another coaching student was Deputy Minister of Information Andre Holland and his son Mike. Andre was a fifth generation Rhodesian, who remarried (Sally) and moved to farm in Mvuri. We stayed in touch for years, but if anyone knows where he is now, please let me know. Andre was the inventor--or part of the team—responsible for the Rhino armoured vehicle and also the banks of 9 HHO Cannons, which could be fitted to the front, back and sides of armoured vehicles.

Function memories: I was invited to be compere, judge or MC for: the Rhodesia Front Ball (the Guest of Honour was that unforgettable character, formerly Minister of Defence and then Foreign Minister, PK van der Byl); the Umtali Interflora show for the Border Patrol Welfare Fund; the Gwelo Model Show and the December Time Variety Show for the Terrorist Victims Relief Fund; Hopelands Fair for the Mentally Retarded; Lions Inter-High School Public Speaking Contest; Boy Scout Cooking Competition; St. John Ambulance Brigade Personality; Allan Wilson School Fun Night.

And then were the really tough ones like: Miss Salisbury Beauty Contest; Miss Mount Pleasant School Beauty Contest; Marlborough School Model Show; Miss Queen Elizabeth School Beauty Contest; Lancome Make-up Competition; Mabelreign Girl's School Beauty Contest; South African Institute of Welding, Ladies Evening; Miss Dominican Convent High School Beauty Contest; Lions Club of Mabelreign Glamourous Grandmothers Finals (with Janet Smith). I dated one of the very attractive (divorced!) finalists, as all the lovely contestants at the other functions were too young for me and, in any case, I've always preferred mature women! On RTV I presented the Rhodesia Jacaranda Queen Finalists. For the QueQue/Redcliff Cactus Carnival Queen

Contest, The Risco Review (Sep 77) headlined: "President and Partridge at Cactus Carnival", while the Midlands Observer headlined: "They are gorgeous" says DP!"

I have many fond memories of the truly lovely Rhodesian ladies... but that would be indiscreet! However, if anyone knows where South African Champion Hairdresser, Rina Blandino of Maison Rina is... please tell her I need a trim, as I've been unable to trace her!

I was delighted to have been invited to MC the Troops Ball, especially as the Chairwoman Maria Crampton wrote: "I would like to say, on behalf of my committee, how thrilled we are that 'Rhodesia's heart throb' (you) have accepted our invitation"; I was also pleased to be Guest of Honour at the M.O.T.H Ball for the Troops Comfort Fund (with Lt. Gen. Peter Walls); National Federation of Women's Institutes (with Janet Smith); Seki Provincial Authority Sundowner (with Senator Chief Chirau); Police Passing Out Parade, Tomlinson Barracks; as a guest at the launching of M.V. Sunbird (with the PM and the Cabinet); the Rhodesian Memorial Fund Dedication of Memorial Hall and, the Rhodesian Institute of Management.

I have to admit to being invited to speak at rather more women's organisations than men's! They included: Salisbury Mother's Club, Fleur de Lis Women's Club, St. Andrew's Women's Guild, American Women's Club, Marlborough Women's Association, Greendale Ladies Club, Salisbury Indaba Toastmistress Club and Rotary Anns. The men at eg: the Salisbury Toastmaster's Club, Salisbury 41 Club (Round Table) and the Rotary Club of Salisbury Central always me asked to share the secrets of being a successful public speaker. I said they would be disappointed with my simple answer: I didn't have any secrets, as I was the same person on, and off-camera. You have to be yourself--whatever that is—and if you pretend to be different from your real self, people will see through the façade and dislike and distrust you... especially in a TV close-up! We see personalities and actors on TV whom we warm to... and those we don't... just as in life, we meet people we instantly like... and those we don't. Many viewers liked my work on TV, but others couldn't stand me... some even sending hate mail and false accusations to Look & Listen and the papers, usually hiding behind what were found to be fictitious names and addresses. I told the club audiences it's better to polarize opinion into like and dislike, as that's preferable to being so bland that people don't have any opinion about you! If more viewers/people like what you do... that can be considered successful. If it's the other way... you're probably better off doing something else!

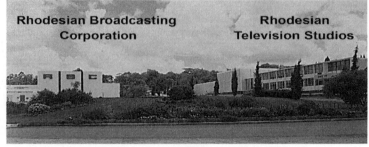

Then came the unexpected and ill-conceived decision to place RTV under the control of a bunch of bureaucrats and radio personnel at RBC Radio. None of them had any experience of TV and it caused so much friction, that Bill Basson, the Chairman of British American Tobacco was appointed to investigate. His 1977 Basson Report recommended the dismissal of RBC's entire Board of Directors and most of top radio management! For reasons not at first apparent, but later explained to me by Andrew Young, it was not implemented... and the results were disastrous for RTV and for Rhodesian viewers.

So, in May, 1977, Mike Hart-Jones and most of the producers, directors and their assistants, along with many essential engineering and technical staff--25 key TV production personnel, comprising some 70% of RTV's production staff--resigned in protest. This was a tragic, but very brave decision. It clearly showed how strongly they felt--as unlike in, say the US or UK, where there were many other stations to go to--they had nowhere else to go in Rhodesia.

Minister Ely Broomberg had been responsible for the ill-considered merger, but realised it had been a mistake and was trying to rectify it. He asked Mike to re-consider his resignation and to wait, pending his appointment of a new Director General to replace Deputy Director Generals Malcolm Gaven and John Baldwin, whose behaviour had been prime reasons for the resignations of Mike and his colleagues. So, Mike waited—unemployed—for two and a half months. Elly then made it very clear to new Director General James Neill that he wanted Mike and I to remain at RTV. But, when Mike met with him, the thoroughly unpleasant and ill-mannered Neill told Mike he didn't have time to worry about Mike's personal problems and "suggested" that Mike "move on".

Philippa Berlyn wrote to the PM, PK van der Byl and Elly Broomberg, deploring the situation and asking them to intervene. I met with the PM, several Cabinet Ministers and Military Chiefs to explain the true situation and the disgraceful way Mike had been treated by Neill. As a result, Elly Broomberg was about to restore TV's autonomy... and the resigned personnel, when very sadly, he unexpectedly died, thus allowing Neill to pursue his own agenda, So, unfortunately all our efforts were to no avail.

In my subsequent 30 years in British and American TV, I have never again met such a genius in the creation and production of TV programs as Mike... and I don't use the word "genius" lightly! It is heartbreaking to me that this friend and gifted producer chose to spend the rest of his life--not enriching the world of TV and film with his unique talents--but pursuing the aim of becoming an entrepreneur.

Presumably, following Neill's directive, Nick Critchlow, and Val Lunn (hastily appointed acting director of TV services) immediately tried to terminate "Frankly Partridge", but were unable to, due to my unknown-to-them contract with RTV. Johnny Clingen (new Head of Production) wanted to extend FP beyond the contract, but Neill refused. The newly empowered bureaucrats insisted that the last episode of the usually live FP show be pre-recorded... obviously they were afraid I'd "say something" on air... I probably would have! Mike's letter to RBC Chairman Basil Watts, (copied to the PM), described Critchlow as: "an inexperienced, non-Rhodesian, production assistant who was only promoted to producer/director due to the almost total exodus of RTV's highly professional production personnel."

Mike also wrote to RBC's Board of Directors, stating: "Derek has achieved more—in his few months here—for the Nation's morale than any other TV personality. The morale boost this man's sincerity has brought to Rhodesians of all ages and in all walks of civilian and military life, is incredible... and should not be lost to the country." He also told them that, in his ten years at RTV, he had never before seen the volume of fan mail received about me or my work. One of my favourites was: "Today I have seen you, and you said hallo to me and it made me very happy. Can you please send me a picture. I am a 6 year old Austrian girl and admire you. Your Patricia."

Then Janet and Derek Gordon-Farleigh started a nation-wide petition to keep me at RTV. In one week over 6,000 signatures were collected. Every day, for ten days, it made newspaper headlines, editorials, pictures and letters to the press. Coincidentally, Salisbury Council was looking for a Principal Officer, "a man of vision", to run Salisbury, so Meintjes, the Sunday Mail cartoonist, produced a cartoon showing RBC Chairman Basil Watts and Mayor Roy Wright standing in the doorway of my "new office", with the caption: "Well, that seems to have settled that little matter." The petition was presented to Neill and to Janet Smith, which elicited more editorials and pictures! Sadly, it was again, all to no avail. *People, whom Andrew Young described to me as: "... an extreme, right-wing power group which even Ian Smith can't control..." had won.

My diary noted: "It has been an unbelievably humbling and moving experience to have so many people in a nation of black and white people go out to bat for me. The right-wing extremists may have won the day, but they can never take away the total fulfillment and support Mike Hart-Jones and the people of Rhodesia gave me."

The Sunday Mail Sayings of the Week quoted from the open letter I wrote when leaving Rhodesia: "Placing RTV under the control of a bureaucratic establishment like RBC has been a disaster." The cover of the May 1978 issue of Talk magazine displayed "The Controversial Derek Partridge" and Elizabeth Shearer's article was entitled: "DEREK being frankly PARTRIDGE. She mentioned that I had an intense feeling of belonging in Rhodesia and that I was fiercely patriotic to this, my adopted country. At this point, as I had nothing to lose, she published a quote I mentioned from a South African writer which, I said, succinctly typified the Pockets Hill administration: "Political docility and mediocrity are the passports to promotion at RBC." She added that I intended to continue my one-man war against bureaucracy. Naturally, all this enormously enhanced my popularity with Neill and his "mediocre" minions at Pockets Hill!! My favorite quote concerning bureaucrats neatly sums them up:

"There's no reason for it... it's just our policy."

I received hundreds of letters regretting RBC TV's action, among them...

"Stay Kiddo, you make a lovely Rhodesian." from The Knights Concession;

"I felt some pains of how much all we Rhodesians were to miss you. Had it not been of those RBC TV people, we would be together here in Rhodesia." - Cosmell Chigorimbo, Salisbury;

"Your smiling appearances as a News Reader and on Frankly Partridge have brought to thousands of viewers, like myself and family, not only happy entertainment, but also a much needed boost to our morale during these times of doubt and uncertainty. As a very old Rhodesian, may I thank you for all you have done in the short time you have been here." – A.L. Tonkin, Salisbury.

"Thank you for all you have done for Rhodesia and Rhodesians. We will not forget." - Phyllis Port, Bulawayo.

Despite this "setback"(!) it was now time to revise 1977's original, WFR-assisted leaflet, so I returned to Rhodesia to do that. The revised version was expanded to 6 pages and written entirely under my name, not WFR's, so I took full responsibility for the contents. The publication was printed in Rhodesian green on white paper, covered 30 different aspects of life in Rhodesia and sold for Rh5c. The Herald headlined:

"Partridge puts out blunt new pamphlet."

The article continued that it was: "...written in a cold, objective manner". They quoted me as saying: "... its aims were entirely non-political."

"I have written it as a representation of what an outsider—like me—sees when coming to Rhodesia."

The Herald reporter asked: "... why was he prepared to spend his time and money projecting Rhodesia's image all over the world, in spite of his being a non-Rhodesian?

Mr. Partridge replied: "Rhodesia is the only place, out of all the many countries I know, where I have felt at home. My time in Rhodesia was the most gratifying experience in my life. I have strong feelings about this place."

The article continued: "All four parties in the transitional government, as well as the white opposition parties, ordered from a few hundred to a few thousand copies."

Later, Pat Bean, who Philippa Berlyn brought in to be WFR chairman after I left, wrote me that over 10 million copies of "Rhodesia - as it really is", had been circulated in 42 countries: four million of the first Women For Rhodesia version and a further six million of my revised version. The circulation was achieved by a combination of massive personal mailings by Rhodesians and Rhodesian government departments and by sending photostats of the leaflet artwork to the many Save Rhodesia organizations around the world. They then re-printed and distributed the leaflets in their respective countries. Shortly after, Philippa wrote me that WFR had ceased to exist.

Partly as a result of the revised leaflet, another trip was set--and partially sponsored by the Department of Information--to carry out some assignments for them and for Army HQ. In London I met with the pro-Rhodesian Chief of Commercial Information Services in the American Embassy, who was eager to distribute leaflets for the Department of Info. At BBC TV, I persuaded John Tisdall (Deputy Head of Current Affairs) and David Harrison (Assistant Editor Panorama) to pay for 8 Rhodesians (black and white, male and female) to be flown to Britain to be interviewed on Panorama or Tonight.

The leaflet was referred to by Peter Simple in his "Way of the World" column in the London Daily Telegraph on Feb 7th, 1978 as: "A drop of truth in an ocean of lies."

He closed with: "Great is the Truth and shall prevail."

A number of British MPs and US Senators commented favourably on it, as did national columnist William F. Buckley.

Senator Jesse Helms wrote: "Allow me—as a former newsman--to congratulate you on a job well done."

I had even sent one to the Queen... which was acknowledged in an October 12th, 1977 letter from the Foreign Office's Rhodesia Department, assuring me that Her Majesty had "noted my views"... sure!

Looking to locate specialised equipment for Army HQ (my contact was Captain S.D. Haarhoff, General Walls' assistant), I met retired US General Paul Van Hee, now an arms manufacturer. We discussed items that could be produced in Rhodesia, eg: a re-loadable anti-personnel mine, which fired 42, .22 long rifle cartridges in a broad pattern, effective up to 50 yards. There was a small anti-personnel bomblet which could be easily dropped from a spotter plane, without modification to the aircraft. I provided info about the Magna-Trigger Safety, which enabled a loaded and cocked pistol to be left in the open for easy access... but safe from terrs and children, as no one could fire it, except the owner, wearing a ring, which activated the magnetic safety catch, built into the pistol grip.

In New York, the News World asked me to write a series of articles based on the leaflet. Also in New York—just before he interviewed America's Ambassador to the UN, Andrew Young and Britain's David Owen—I gave Robert McNeil (of the highly respected PBS McNeil/Lehrer Report) information which, I was later told, altered the tone of his interview, so that it came out pro-Rhodesian.

These were the men who sold us down the river and, while they were being interviewed at RTV, I admit to having been taken in by Owen's smooth charm, but other colleagues in the newsroom distrusted him... they were right. I also admit that--after hearing Young speak--I warmed to him a bit, as he had the appealing gift of self-deprecating humour. A picture of me giving a copy of the RAIRI leaflet to Andrew

Young, in New York was published in the Sunday Mail on Oct 12th 1978. In the leaflet I had written that his actions were motivated by political ambition and... racism!

While in Washington during the visit of the PM and Rev. Sithole, the Washington Post published an op-ed article from me, refuting many false claims made by the NUF's Allan Savory. WNET, New York's Public Broadcasting TV, gave me airtime to state Rhodesia's case, which I then took to the American public on a speaking tour organized by The English Speaking Union. I showed audiences pictures of, eg: integrated Security Force units marching together, of blacks and whites participating in a marathon race and mingling at Borrowdale Race Track. Then, there were graphic pictures of atrocities committed by terrorists (the self-styled Freedom Fighters) against their own people... defenseless villagers—bayoneted or burned alive--as well massacres, torture and mutilation of soft targets, such as women, children and even babies; missionaries, nuns and priests, who had dedicated their lives to helping black people. Terrs—whose sources of funding included the World Council of Churches--generally preferred to avoid deliberate contact with Security Forces, as they knew the results were pretty much a foregone conclusion!

In Los Angeles I got my friend Whit Collins (a weapons expert and Senior Staff Editor at Guns & Ammo magazine) to arrange for: perimeter-guard sensor devices, eg: seismic, proximity, motion, microwave and body heat/odour; construction in Rhodesia of ceramic body armour; film of combat handgun training; a Hi-Standard 50 round (drum) 3" magnum, fully automatic shotgun, developed by the Marines for the Point Man in Vietnam, which discharged its 50 rounds in 4 seconds. I also provided Army HQ with a contact in the German arms firm, Heckler & Koch.

On my return from that trip, Keith Simpson wrote in the Sunday Mail about other presenters going over the border to work in SABC and SATV: "An exception however, is Derek, who has spent much of the interim as an unofficial, globe-trotting ambassador for this country..."

But what meant more to me than anything else, was an editorial in Illustrated Life and Talk which said: "... Derek "Frankly" Partridge is making a movie, starring opposite Jack Palance, but did <u>our</u> Derek appreciate one of the bargains on offer in Miami?"

That "our" told me I'd really been accepted as a Rhodesian... and to this day I read that and cry... just as I do when I read the last, treasured Xmas card from Philippa Berlyn, inscribed:

"Love from your country and Philippa".

Tragically, this wonderful lady was later killed when a Cessna 180 crashed near Karoi.

June 1979 was my last trip back to Rhodesia. As we approached Salisbury, the pilot of the Air Rhodesia flight from Jo'burg invited me to the cockpit... it was a very emotional, tearful experience... but greatly appreciated. Look & Listen wrote: "D.P. is back... with a job hosting two daily talk shows and news in Miami." They quoted me as saying:

"It's good for me professionally, but it's in the wrong country! This is my home and where I will always be in spirit."

To maintain my connections with my beloved, adopted country, I then wrote the L&L column "DP reporting from... Miami, New York, Bermuda, Rome, London (wherever work took me) for the next 3 years.

Mike Hart-Jones had built the opening of Frankly Partridge around my arrival at RTV in my BMW. After I left, this was parodied by Mike Westcott, riding a bicycle on "Disco Scene"... which provoked angry letters to The Herald from viewers, eg: L.L. Fowler of Avondale referred to RBC TV's "obvious immaturity", "this puerile parody" and "Derek had more professional artistry in his finger tips than the rest of the TV fraternity put together..." Keith Simpson headlined his Sunday Mail article, criticizing Mike Westcott: "Partridge hit below the belt."

Mike and I formed Rhodesian International Productions to make a film based on the leaflet. However, when it occurred to me--with Rhodesia's imminent demise--that R.I.P. was also Rest In Peace... we changed it to Flame Lily Productions! We came back to make the film and received clearance from Combined Operations HQ and the Ministry of Internal Affairs to film in operational areas and PVs.

Money was raised in the UK for the film... and then stolen by Malawian Peter Savage, whom Mike had entrusted to look after it.

That was the end of the film project!

On 12/4/79 Savage was convicted on an unrelated R100,000 fraud charge in the Jo'burg Regional Court.

In November 1977, when funds were also being raised by the Save Rhodesia Campaign in Cape Town to make the film based on the RAIRI leaflet, I was "anonymously" accused of violating Rhodesian Exchange Control Regulations. I chose to go to CID Fraud Section, swore an affidavit and insisted on their calling Brendan Willmer, National Director of SA's Save Rhodesia Campaign. With DSO Florens listening, he confirmed that the 650 Rand were with his organisation and had not been sent to anyone in Rhodesia. (An article in the 19/4/80 Herald said that Willmer had disappeared... along with funds he had received as a reward for "the capture or killing of Mugabe and Nkomo!")

Later, another Fraud Squad officer "anonymously" mentioned the names Cyril and Joyce Hartley and their daughter Janet Kaschula. By a strange coincidence(!), these were the three people who had tried to have me removed from WFR, but were outvoted 7-3 at a special meeting chaired—not by me—but by Women For Rhodesia President Philippa Berlyn.

I could only deduce that—due to my being known from RTV--they were not happy that WFR had taken away some of the limelight from their work at Co-Ord-A-Nation.

A letter from Joyce Hartley indicated that the three of them chose not act on my subsequent suggestion that they resign! Bill Ferris, the Director of the Department of Information was kept fully informed of these events.

The last thing I did before having to leave my beloved country and earn a living again in America, was to go down south to lecture for their Save Rhodesia Campaign. I also sold my gold watch to raise money for the Save Rhodesia Campaign, which was mentioned in the Feb. 15th, 1978 feature article about "The Pommie who's fighting for Rhodesia", in the Johannesburg Citizen.

One treasured piece of memorabilia is an ad from the Herald announcing that the PM would be attending not a Public, but a PUBIC meeting! To make matters even more amusing, it was on behalf of the candidate Reg Beaver... whose surname—to Americans—represents the part of the female anatomy... referred to in the ad!!

Another memory is intangible: On my last trip back home for Xmas 1979, I was with my friend, car dealer Alex Hasson... his small daughter—using a child's favourite gesture... the pointing index finger—proudly announced that was Frankly Partridge... Alex then told me that, at the time the program was airing, she had been between 2½ and 3 years old! The Herald reported "Partridge back" and that:

"He has spent much of the past two years living out of suitcases as an unofficial ambassador for Rhodesia."

Clairvoyant Bill McLeod wrote in his 1980 "Predictions":

"A very extroverted and controversial personality to hit Rhodesian TV was Derek Partridge. I was struck by the personality and vitality of the man. Although he is now in America, I feel he could return to Rhodesia and could even play a part in public affairs. A man of the future, I think, and one to be watched."

The book was sent to me by Joyce and Bill Blair of Borrowdale, with the inscription:

"May all the predictions come true—for you and this country which you love so deeply." Oh! How I wish they had...

My diary entry on 21/12/77, the day I left Rhodesia was: "If I never achieve anything else, I have more than fulfilled my purpose in life during my all-too-few years in Rhodesia. I've been fortunate enough to accomplish all I wanted to do and give to others and, I did not fall short of what I expected of myself. That this was endorsed by most people in the finest nation I've found in a lifetime of travel and that the love given me came from blacks, whites, coloureds and Indians, from children to aging pioneers, men and women, from Cabinet Ministers and Generals... to servants, make me an incredibly lucky man."

All the above happened in just two years (1976-78)... still the most significant years of my life!

My open leaving letter to all Rhodesians concluded: "As the inevitability of being forced to leave drew nearer, my 'TV smile' concealed a deep sadness... which will be with me as long as I'm away from Rhodesia. I'm painfully aware of the total truth of the words:

'Once you're a Rhodesian, no other land will do.'

Thank you, Rhodesians, for giving me more happiness than I have ever known before."

30 years later, I still feel exactly the same way... Paul and May Meyer, Celia Sparrow, June Soutter, Anne McCormack and especially Mike Hart-Jones (who became my best friend) and, all Rhodesians... there is no way I could ever thank you enough for providing me the greatest fulfillment and enjoyment of my life!

For a long time, I've wanted to show Joyce, my present wife of 12 years, my other "love affair". However, having been highly critical of Comrade Bob in my leaflet, I didn't want to find myself touring the country's jails! That evil maniac Mugabe's legacy will be that he starved, tortured and murdered his own people, enriched himself and his cronies, while destroying the country and its economy, turning the one-time "bread basket of Africa" into... a basket case. He is truly: "the Saddam Hussein of Africa".

A letter in The Herald from a Zambian said it all: "Before independence, we had everything... except a black government. After independence... all we had... was a black government..."

Similarly, in the former Soviet Union housing, medical care and virtually every important aspect of life was free, except the people...

On November 3rd, 2005, Christopher Dell, the United States ambassador to Zimbabwe, in his strongest criticism yet of Harare, said that "gross mismanagement and corrupt rule by President Robert Mugabe's government have plunged the country into crisis."

This statement is only a "few" years too late...!

A somewhat damp June Barry (June in The Forsyte Saga) with DP at Vic Falls

Casper the Cat by Richard Randall

You will find two schools of thought concerning the appropriateness of pet cats in safari establishments. One has it that they provide companionship and keep down rodents and snakes, and the other objects to them as obtrusive domestic elements (and bird killers besides) in what should be a pristine, biologically "pure" wilderness.

Casper was a cat who was oblivious to this perennial debate and was evidently quite secure in his residence at Camp X where he had resided for several years. Casper lavished his affection impartially on staff and clients alike. His lustrous tabby coat and large green eyes made him a firm favourite with the camp guests who plied him with tidbits from the table and saucers of milk at tea time. He preferred to sleep in the guest chalets at night (no one ever discovered how he got in) and many a tourist, on retiring, would find the cat fast asleep on one of the beds over which was draped a mosquito net. Each night Casper promiscuously selected a bed from a different chalet and, being a cute cat and a smooth operator, was rarely expelled from his selected quarters. He never really put a paw wrong until Miss Morsely came to camp.

Miss Morsely was a frail and elderly spinster on a first-time African safari, and full of notions of the dangers of the African bush, gleaned perhaps from a certain genre of African travel book popular several decades ago. Her apprehension, fuelled by an obviously nervous disposition, declared itself in her first questions to the camp manager : "Is it safe to walk around here? Aren't there lions around?" She was quickly told that lions had never been seen anywhere near the island on which the camp was built. This reply, however, did not seem to totally reassure her, judging from her insistence that a ranger accompany her to her room when she retired that night. Barely ten minutes after the ranger had returned from escort duty and had rejoined a small group at the bar, piercing screams were heard from Miss Morsely's chalet. The ranger and two other members of staff rushed to the chalet and urgently enquired of the lady what the problem was. They were answered by harrowing moans…

The thin reed door was forced open, and three torch beams revealed Miss Morsely and Casper both entangled and struggling in the mosquito net. It took some time to disengage the cat's claws from the net and throw him out; it took even longer to obtain any coherency from the ashen and trembling Miss Morsely. Several cups of tea and much soothing talk eventually fortified her sufficiently to enable her to recount her drama.

On going to bed Miss Morsely had neglected to tuck the mosquito net in under the mattress. The usual and not very serious consequence of such an oversight would be that a few mosquitoes would find ingress to their victims. Unfortunately for the good lady, however, that night Casper elected to sleep on her bed and craftily

135

insinuated himself under the net just after she had switched off the gas light. Without hesitation he leapt up onto the bed for a nice comfortable snooze.

It was a pity that he landed so accurately on Miss Morsely's face and that he had chosen the one soul in camp who would immediately take him for a much larger and homicidal felid. Her worst fears had been realised : there were lions in camp and there was one right here on her bed. With such personalities in such cases, the logic of the situation (size/weight of assailant, for example) does not assert itself....

Poor Miss Morsely's frantic struggles and shrieks terrified the cat who, in his vigorous attempts to break out (inflicting minor scratches on Miss Morsley in the process), got inextricably caught up in the net.

The next day, true to form and clearly unmindful of recent events, Casper punctually appeared at tea time with the guests whom he blithely proceeded to solicit for milk. Miss Moresly was there, too, and resolutely ignored her previous night's tormentor, who did not have the diplomatic good sense to stay away from her.

Rhodesia, "We Regret" by Rosemary Wilkins (aged 18)

A shot, a cry
Another death
Another grieving wife
Another "new communiqué"
Another fact of life.

A tear, a shrug
Another prayer
Another "one of ours"
Another cold statistic
Another bowl of flowers.

A wife, a man,
Another Dad
Another Mother's son
Another call-up paper
Another battle won.

A track, a spoor
Another lass
Another unpaid debt
Another "next of kin informed"
Another "we regret".

An eye, a tooth
Another kill
Another payment made
Another "ribbon" handout
Another "gong" parade.

A smile, a wave
Another kiss
Another "late deceased"
Another street collection
Another conscience eased.

A plea, a wish
Another hope
Another dream of "home"
Another "peaceful" answer
Another wish we'd known.

A Land, our Land?
Another's now?
Another's will imposed?
Another page of history?
Another chapter closed.

Arriving in Africa by Peter Pinder-Browne

It must have been in the very early 1900's when Grandfather, Alex McCready, who was born in about 1875 in Ulster, the north of Ireland, arrived in Cape Town. He had signed up on a freight boat as a crew member for the journey to South Africa, with the sole intention of jumping ship when he got there.

On arriving in Cape Town, he took shore leave and went to the usual sailor spots in the town.

When the time was right, he made himself look as though he had been attacked and went to the police station with the storey that he had been mugged and lost everything while in a dubious night club in the dock area.

He was prepared for the deception, because he knew that every sailor who went on shore leave had to leave his passport documents with the purser on board to ensure he would return.

He gave the policeman a very descriptive account of the happenings of the evening, how he had been cornered and had everything taken off him, passport, residence papers etc.

They asked him for his name. Grandfather was wide awake and he knew that the name McCready would be too easy to follow and he had checked that there were no colleagues named Wilson on his ship, so he gave himself the name of Alexander Wilson. The Police checked all the 'shore leave lists' and not finding any Wilsons missing, they issued him with fresh papers in the name of Alexander Wilson born in…. etc. This was the start of a new adventurous life in sunny South Africa.

We know very little about what he did in the first part of his life in South Africa, but one thing we know was that he met a widow from Graaff Reinet, Eastern Cape, who had three children and he married her. He had long since readopted his real name of Alex McCready, by which he was commonly known. They went looking for gold in the Northern Transvaal where my mother was born in Lichtenberg on the 12th of June 1908. It was a great occasion for this life loving Irishman, who, having celebrated his becoming a father, saddled his horse and started on the 100 mile journey to Pretoria to register the birth of his first daughter. He spent the nights along the way with old friends and celebrated further until he reached his destination.

On reaching the registry office he was asked to produce his papers, which he did and then what names he was to give the little girl. She is "Viola Patricia" was the answer. And when was she born? Some time in the early evening he said. And what date? This brought Grandfather into a bit of a tight spot. Miners are not so good with dates, so he asked what day is today. The 18th of June. OK, last night I was with Jimmy, the night before I was with Frank, before that it was Paddy and so they reconstructed that it must have been the 13th of June.1908.

Grandfather, complete with all the documents returned to Lichtenberg on horseback.

Two years later he moved to Southern Rhodesia with my mother then aged two.

Twelve years after that my Grandparents were running a Mica mine called "The Turning Point Mine" at Miama. The Mica was used in the electrical industry.

He decided that the time had come to buy a new car and had his eyes on a brand new Didion Button car.

When one bought a car in those days, they normally gave you a three day introduction to the handling of a machine and then let you take a driver's licence test before you were allowed to take the car home.

Grandfather completed the formalities, took the car out of the show room and went to the Salisbury High School to pick up his 14 year old daughter. They set out on the homeward trip, which up until then had been a10 day journey by ox-wagon.

As they went, Grandfather explained to mother all he had learnt about the car and driving, scaring mother half to death as he was concentrating more on the teaching than on the road ahead. By the time they had reached Trelawny, mother was completely informed about the techniques of driving a car, but still half scared to death by Grandpa's driving skills. After a short stop in Darwendale, Grandpa asked mum if she would like to have a bash. Mum thought it was a good idea, and decided it couldn't be any more dangerous then sitting next to Grandpa on the dirt road to the north, so she climbed into the driver's seat and took command.

After a few hairy incidents, they reached Banket for the night.

At breakfast the next morning, Grandpa decided that Mum's driving was definitely better that his own and they agreed that from then on, Mum would do the driving. They arrived in Miama safe and sound that evening. Grandma was very impressed with the car and the fact that she had two chauffeurs.

This situation of mother driving the car at her tender age, did not go unnoticed by the local constabulary, but there was no reaction, so Mum just continued driving the car when she was at home.

On Mum's 16th birthday, the 12th of June 1924, they had a very early visit from a handsome young constable with an envelope addressed to Miss V. P. McCready.

Mum of course opened it with great curiosity and found a freshly stamped driver's licence in her name. It was a present from the local police force.

Mum was never asked to take a drivers test.

Mum often told us twins about that episode and I think that she was a very good driver, although she did once 'oversteer' a Porsche in Salisbury when she was in her late sixties, it remained her only traffic accident.

Mother and Grandmother were not compatible, so as Mother was 16 now Grandmother, Isabel McCready found a suitable husband for her daughter. I think it was to get her out of the house as quickly as possible. The chosen man was a civil servant, Spencer Tanfield, who was about twelve years Mother's senior.

Mother did not make a big fuss, as she was also happy to get away from Grandmother, so a date was fixed for the wedding.

Now, even in those days, it was important to have all the documents for the formalities that were to follow. Mother asked Grandmother where she could find her Birth Certificate.

Granny answered: "In the big trunk under the bed in the guest room at the end of the passage".

Mum went down, found the trunk and found a whole stack of official documents including various birth certificates, but nothing that fitted to her.

She did however find a birth certificate for a "Viola Patricia Wilson, born in Lichtenberg on the 13th of June 1908".

This was the starting point of a whole lot of questions about where Grandpa came from and the answer was the story at the beginning of this article!

Northlea School Excerpts by Paul Sheppard

I was at Northlea during the period 1958 - 1963 but must confess that from an academic point of view my final year and others for that matter were totally wasted. However a hockey tour to Kenya was in the offing plus the opportunity to participate in an expedition to climb Mt Kilimanjaro (unfortunately cancelled due to political upheaval) and I was able to convince my long suffering parents that these were essential activities for my development. A fellow pupil by name Wendy Bullock also had some influence on my decision to stay.

The hockey tour to Kenya was fantastic. Joined by my two great pals from Northlea via Johnny Spence and Chris Barker we travelled by train to Beira, by sea on the Kenya Castle up the East Coast of Africa and then train again from Mombassa to Nairobi. Hockey games in Beira, Dar es Salaam, Zanzibar, Mombassa and Nairobi helped to relieve the monotony of the on board partying.

Our team had been selected from schools in both Rhodesia's and Nyasaland and I think was perhaps the only school team to have represented the Federation. It was also multi-racial which was somewhat Unique for the times.

On a different tack but on a similar note I recall when at Northlea playing many enjoyable games of Cricket against Founders (a school for Asian and Coloured kids) and was saddened on my return from Overseas to find that the Rhodesian Front had put an end to these contacts. I recall in particular a big fellow by name of Tarzan Patel who was pretty quick and lively especially on matting wickets. Many of those guys remain friends to this day.

Scripture classes were included in the curriculum in 1958 and my own denominations spiritual well being was taken care of by Mrs Broughton the wife of the then Headmaster. Assemblies in those early days were held in the Quad and those of us who fell foul of Mrs B were selected to read the lesson at these gatherings. It was a daunting experience for 12 year old boys and consequently the eccentric Mrs B was held in great awe.

For a time swimming was a compulsory Friday afternoon activity and I recall one occasion when Ray Suttle decided that all present should jump from the 3 m diving board. Everything proceeded smoothly until Andy Kyriakopoulous the little Greek fellow took his turn and it was discovered that he was a non-swimmer.

My brother Tony and Neil Dewar were classmates and friends and so it came to pass that I met up with Dave Dewar and we have remained friends for the past 47 years. Our first evening together was spent fruit raiding at Mr Haig's residence in Colenbrander Avenue. We were naughty little buggers.

Dave was a brilliant cricketer and I was keen and we spent many hours playing miniature cricket on his veranda. To level the playing field Dave agreed to bat and bowl left handed but in all the years we played I was never able to beat him.

140

Having an elder brother at the same school had certain advantages one of which was that long before I got to Northlea I had been forewarned about the intimidating RALT Suttle, at on our first Latin class we were told that henceforth we would have daily tests and that a 60% mark was the minimum acceptable. Those failing would be dealt with. One Terence Willox was the first to test the veracity of this threat and was severely beaten for his troubles. This had a salutary effect on my Latin career and I thereafter managed to stay half a step ahead of the basic. This is not to say that I did not on occasions cross swords with Ray and for baulking cadets, cross country swimming etc the outcome was invariably the same.

"Sheppard my heart is not really in this but bend over, Whack, whack, whack."

A beating that I cannot forget because of its severity was that administered by Mr Lionel Archer our Science Teacher. What I can't remember was what the punishment was for and all the guys in our class were on the receiving end. Perhaps one of the guys out there can remember what we did/did not do to deserve it. The lashes were administered in front of the girls which always made them harder to bear.

Kamativi is not a place one would normally associate with the game of Cricket but in 1960 Ray Suttle took a group of us to play there and had also lined up a game against Wankie.

The road to Kamativi even today is not the greatest and in those days was of the harsh corrugated type. We travelled in a VW kombie type vehicle and many of us suffered from car sickness and Ray made us run for a few kilometres through the hills. I can't for the life of me remember all the guys who were on this trip but I do recall that Collin Kendall was up on vac. from UCT and was part of the team. Can someone out there fill in the gaps. Kamativi is now a virtual ghost town, the mine having closed, and it is hard to imagine that it once supported a cricket team and had a most picturesque cricket oval nestled in amongst the hills.

To the uninitiated this village is on route to Binga where we often head to on our houseboat trips on Lake Kariba. One of our groups which includes Old Northleans Tony de Caila, Tony Carlyle and Keith Iversen have established a tradition which involves cracking the first frosty of the day on the way past the old school. As this generally happens at 6am it makes for rather a long day.

Sporting trips out to Falcon were memorable not only from the point of view of the keenly contested matches and the scrumptious teas and lunches served but also for the hair raising return journeys perched on the back of open lorries. Certain of our masters were quite partial to partake of the hospitality extended to them after these games and their ability to negotiate the low level narrow bridges at 8.30 in the evening often had to be taken on trust. We never said a word of course.

Northlea along with other schools used to send a platoon to participate in the annual Queens birthday parade held at Queens Sports Club. These were a pain but had to be done and one of our major problems was that our indefatigable leader who shall remain nameless invariably gave the commands for right turn eyes right etc on the wrong foot, this error of judgement causing much amusement and not a little consternation amongst our troops.

It was this same gentleman who said to Josh Berkowitz (a wily left arm spinner of cake cricket fame) "Joshua if you were leading the Jews they'd still be wandering". The same guy continuously had a ruler down his rods. Anymore clues needed?

At one parade it was particularly hot and troops were fainting in fairly large numbers all around us. Wors Keat had picked this up and whispered to the guys - "keep it up buggers we're the only platoon not to have had a casualty. Shortly afterwards the familiar cry of medic, medic rang out across the ground.

Wors had fainted and was unceremoniously removed from the arena.

Sport to my undying regret was my overriding passion at school and as Northlea was small in terms of numbers it was very much a case of if you were willing and able you were in and having no academic pretensions I was very much in. In addition to cricket, rugby, hockey, tennis, athletics, swimming there were other distractions to keep one's mind off the real world.

One of these was drama and my reason for participation having no interest/talent in the field was that rehearsals were often held after hours and enabled one to get out and about.

I recall that for one particular play evening rehearsals were held at the flat of the delectable Miss Balcilli in Fife Street. At the end of the evening we all trooped outside to our pile of bikes and mine which had been at the bottom had been knocked.

Bruce Millar was of course the supreme master and star of all our shows but I also remember some pretty amazing performances from the likes of Deborah Kahn, Michael James (a leg spinner of note who also developed into a fearless hockey goal keeper of no mean ability) and also Dave Dewar and John Abeles in I think the Importance of being Earnest which was performed in the Baines Hall.

We also participated in an Afrikaans/French choir coached by none other than Muller Rademeyer and the lines. 'Goud w silver het ek lief met al kartelrankjies' are indelibly imprinted in my mind. My apologies to Muller for any spelling errors.

Prior to the advent of television Friday entertainment was often provided by roof rattling sessions in the Plummer Street area of Northend. The procedure was thus --- two guys would be nominated to approach a house and knock on the front door. When opened they would enquire the whereabouts of a fictitious character Mr Scheckelgruber I think.

The shaking of heads and the closing of the door was the signal for the rest of the guys to let fly with rocks and any other missiles that came to hand. We would then all bomb shell and meet up again in an adjacent street to repeat the process. I had always fancied myself as a sprinter until one evening after the rocks had fallen and our gang were racing from the scene Norm Geras our front row forward not renowned for his athletic prowess breezed by in his inimitable upright style.

Highlights in the sporting arena were many and those that spring immediately to mind are these.

Playing in the first ever 1ST XV clash between the might of Milton and ourselves at Milton in I think 1962. We lost 17-3 and recall that we must have been conceding +/- 20 lbs per man in the forwards.

Tony Brous being red carded in a 1st XI cricket match played at Northlea (Guiness book of records stuff this).

Tony Brous and Dave Dewar putting on a century partnership against Plumtree who had Hunty William bowling at his best on a horrendous wicket.

Wyn Berry being hit on the body scores of times on a similar wicket and not yielding an inch.

Playing in a triangular hockey tournament in Gweru in which the top schools from Matableland, Mashonaland and Manicaland and Midlands participated and winning thus theoretically making us the top school boy side in the country.

Beating Chaplin 1st XV 8 -6 in a rugby match at Northlea. It was a classic. A friend of mine Allan Futter was the opposing hooker and perhaps 35 years later conceded that they had expected to murder us in the game. He also sheepishly admitted that they liked visiting Northlea because of our good looking girls and more specifically Carole Schiff.

A rugby tour to the Northern Transvaal where we played Louis Trichardt (thanks to their partisan ref this was one of the roughest marches I ever played in) Hans Merensky in Tzaneen and Capricorn in Pietersburg. John Sparrow our fiery but erratic strike bowler straying a little off line and pinning the silly mid-off squarely in the back.

So many many happy memories and my undying thanks go out to Ray Suttle, Brian Haddon, Muller Rademeyer, Frank Herbst, 'Linesman" Morton, Jim Annandale and a host of others who gave unstintingly of their time and more to ensure that we all became solid well rounded citizens. S. John - written in great haste and without much thought but hope this is of some use to you. .

Many Northleans benefited from the expertise of Miss Kets the mathematics teacher.

She had the dubious privilege of introducing us Form 1's to the complexities of Algebra and Geometry and to the mystery of the Pythagoras theorem. She was a wonderfully patient teacher and continues to teach maths at Girls College here in Bulawayo, as a means to supplement what must not be a pretty meagre pension.

She lives down the kopje from us in Hillside and amazingly still drives the same Green Morris Minor she had back in 1958.

"Jack Tar" at work during the completion of the Victoria Falls Bridge

The Statue of David Livingstome at the Victoria Falls

"….that scenes so lovely must have been gazed upon by angels in their flight."

Northlea by Tony Shepard 1955 to 1959

Four years ago. Jan and I are in Arles in the south of France on one of our globe-circling, backpacking trips. The guide book has suggested a certain pub may be able to provide accommodation at a reasonable rate. The rather large Frenchman behind the bar responded to my hesitant, " Bonjour. Avez vous une(or is it un?) chambre ?", by launching into a long explanation about the whereabouts of the aforesaid "chambre", the cost, the fact that only cash would be accepted and then he handed us a large key accompanied by a series of directions routing us through the backstreets of this very attractive town – all this in French!

I took the key and headed off. No problem. After several lefts and rights and various flights of stairs, we were there. And very nice it was too.

It took a while for it to sink in that I had, quite unconsciously, understood every word. When I finally understood why I'd had no problems, I immediately apologised to the ghost of dear old Mrs. Broughton, "Harpic", and realised that for all my lack of attention and adolescent criticism of her eccentric ways, she had taught me more than I had appreciated at the time – and furthermore it has stuck.

So too, has so much else of my education at Northlea. I still love History (thanks Jim and Bill) and this morning (this is the 40th year of my teaching career) one of the kids brought up a book in which was the phrase "Pax tecum". What did it mean? No problem with that one (thanks Ray).

These are but a few real world examples of just some of the benefits of my years at Northlea – in retrospect, it is easy to recognise what a diverse and talented group the staff were. They gave unstintingly, imposed a very firm and fair discipline and enabled me and many others to choose our own direction. I enjoyed it then, perhaps without appreciating it quite as I should and I certainly would like to acknowledge and thank all those teachers who had to deal with an often inattentive pupil.

Notwithstanding the above, school is not all academics and teachers, but is just as much a place of good times and the establishment of lifetime friendships. Sport was important – not as important to me as to others, but important and the opportunity to play in the best Matabeleland Senior School Hockey team ever with such stars as Keith Iversen and Dudley Morgan, plus my brother Paul who could play a bit and enjoy the brilliance of Col Kendall and myself playing inner and wing respectively is a cherished memory.

So too, a holiday I spent as I often did out at Richard Mirtle's farm. Bryan Haddon had lent us the pole vaulting gear and we taught ourselves the intricacies of this, passed on our wealth of knowledge and a year later it was included in the Sports Day events. If memory serves me right Kyrie was the first pole-vault champion.

Balmoral House was, of course, famous for its cross-country talent. Largely, I suspect, because Ray Suttle would brook no excuse from anyone not to participate. It took a while, but I actually began to enjoy it. Never did terribly well but enjoyed it and it enabled me to move up from the "Festina Lente" mile to the really serious one. It was the premier race on Sports Day. One year I ran third to Steve Cooper and Neil Dewar and thought I was a star, especially since I subsequently overtook Neil in the following Inter-School's competition. Such are our minor victories. So sport was good but there were other diversions like dances and parties.

In my final years, we had such a damn good time. It seemed like every weekend there would be some sort of hop and everyone got stuck in and enjoyed it. More amazing in this modern age there was no booze and nobody smoked and yet we had this thoroughly good time: lots of dancing, great music and a little snogging outside with some of the many lovely girls who kept up in some sort of line.

Years later I was chatting to Col Kendall who said that he and many others remembered this too.

Days Of Our Lives by Neil Dewar

To echo the title of Martin Meredith's book, the past is indeed another country. Much of Rhodesia will remain with me till I die – not only the specific memories but also the evocative images, the moods, the landscapes, the seasons (the yellow-brown grass in winter; the brown, bare dusty earth; the anticipation of impending thunder storms, the thunder and lightening; the flying ants, the heat and humidity of October, the jacarandas and flamboyants; black frost and guti; the fantastic cloud formations; -- one could go on and on). And then there were the people................ I deeply appreciate having been part of that particular society in the 1950's and '60s (moral and ethical denunciation of revisionist historians notwithstanding) and having taken out of it much of what made me who I am.

And so to Northlea. Mr Deerling, master of a sixth form English class comprising Edwil Williams and me, once told us to read as many biographies and autobiographies as possible. He asserted that, even if we did not know much about the subject, the very fact that a book had been written by/about an individual (and backed by a publisher) guaranteed that it would be interesting. More importantly, it would inform us greatly about the individuals' particular fields of endeavour and the social, economic, and political context within which events occurred. I've followed that advice in small measure and have often been struck by the almost unvaryingly unhappy childhoods/schooldays the protagonists recollected. For my part, the opposite obtained: my memories of school are overwhelmingly happy.

The school, of course did not exist in a vacuum. It drew on largely lower- and middle-class neighbourhoods and feeder schools where pretension was entirely lacking. Being the 'new kid on the block', it stood in strong contrast to the older, established schools over on the larney side of town. It attempted, with some success, to invoke a British public school ethos but it never quite carried it off, quickly acquiring its own 'corporate culture'. From the outset a 'pioneering spirit' prevailed where tradition did not yet inhibit behaviour, new challenges were met head on, and everything was 'do-able'. An exceptionally young 'gung-ho' staff acted both as catalyst and role models.

Memories of my first day at school are still vivid, largely because of the excitement and anticipation it elicited. I remember the disappointingly small scale of the place – just a number of classrooms tacked together with assembly held in what is now the quadrangle and Mr Broughton standing on the balcony. So many unfamiliar faces from different schools. Many were to become life-long friends. I was stuck next to one Bill Buckles for the taking of the first register.

"Name?" asked Ray Suttle.

"Buckles, Sir", the reply.

First name, address, telephone number.....etc. followed.

Then, "Date of birth?" 15 March, 1942 Sir".

"Next".... "Dewar, Sir" (first name, address, telephone number etc.).

"Date of birth?"..... "15 March, 1942"!!.

His reputation as a killer had preceded him and I could see that he thought we were taking the piss. I had visions of my senior school life being brutally limited to just one day!

I remember many of the seniors who I regarded with some awe, not least because of their sporting prowess: Tony de Caila, Vernon Wentzel, Tony Carlyle, Bill Cross (as he was then), Graham Hatty, Hilton Friend, Roy Stilwell, Ted Mirtle, Lance Penny, Johnny Youatt .... Very early on I played in a number of Sunday 'cross – the – colour – line' cricket matches with Indian teams (made up almost exclusively of Naidoos and Patels) that gave me a great sense of privilege and a ready introduction to some of the shops in Lobengula street.

My own first daily contacts were Messers Suttle (Latin), Annandale (History), Eddie Rademeyer (Maths), Coleman (French), Alan Morton (Woodwork), Mrs Suttle (Geography), Mrs Annandale (Music). Amazingly, the names of my first English and Science teachers elude me (Cherry??).

My present facility with maths and French is nil, reflected in my abject failures in the Cambridge Overseas School Exam.

The less said of my woodwork prowess the better.

Later influences were Mr Deerling (English), Mr Haddon (Geography) and the redoubtable Miss Leigh (Geography). Out on the sports fields Ray Suttle, Muller Rademeyer, Frank Herbst, and Brian Haddon dominated my life. Alan Morton was my first rugby coach teaching us to pass the ball with our fingers pointing down along its length and trying to get us to tackle a moving target (without much success).

Who could forget cadets with Jim Annandale in all his pomp and Staff Officer Horsefall (he of the cocky strut and fast lip which made each parade a dramatic comedy to a half-credulous audience). Polishing boots (using an iron) and brasses and preparing for the Queen's birthday parades were almost fun they were so different. Bertie Weston got so caught up in it that he went into the army full-time.

There was no hint of an impending war when all this would become 'for real' so I innocently enjoyed the fun. I've long forgotten Jim Annandale's facts and interpretations of British and colonial history but his hatred of all things American stays with me. Keith Iversen's bringing baseball bats and gloves into the classroom after break always guaranteed an outburst and the kit being tossed out of the window.

In fact, outbursts were common enough and I can remember witnessing physical dust-ups involving students and, on different occasions, Frank Herbst, Muller Rademeyer, Brian Haddon, and Joan Suttle (all quickly forgiven and forgotten).

Once, preparing for the dress rehearsal of 'HMS Pinafore', the support cast was given a run down on how to apply make-up and then the boys and girls were sequestered in separate rooms to undertake the task in pairs while the lead parts were individually made up by 'experts'. The guys started messing around in the male dressing room and soon most of the chorus members looked like Red Indians in war paint. Joan Suttle eventually walked in to see how things were progressing and went absolutely ballistic, grabbing a feather duster and laying about her indiscriminately, thrashing anyone and everyone within reach on whatever part of their anatomy happened to be in the way of the flailing bamboo handle.

On another occasion I remember Frank Herbst and Kenny Caple (Under 15) wrestling on the floor of the cricket nets for some forgotten misdemeanour. Ray Suttle was more the controlled assassin. I was so scared of falling foul of him that my parents tell me I used to recite Latin conjugations and declensions in my sleep. Many of the staff appeared to be entirely selfless, frequently sacrificing entire weekends for school events, something I took entirely for granted as we moved from one activity to another.

The school's 'pioneering circumstances' were reflected in our planting out the playing fields and collecting rocks and stones in buckets as 'hard labour' (the prevailing substitute for detention or getting whacked).

During one school holiday many of us helped my old man and Collie Kendal's father build the cricket scoreboard. In another holiday, we laid our own cricket nets (literal pick – and – shovel work, shoulder – to – shoulder with Ray Suttle while his small daughters wandered about). More often than not we made do with limited facilities and equipment. Having Brian Haddon often toss one of us the keys of his little black car (what was it?) in order to go home to fetch something, despite the fact that none of us possessed a car licence epitomized the attitude of casualness and trust that prevailed.

Sport was the hub around which my life revolved. I tried to keep up with my lessons and homework, was generally coerced to do so for which I am now grateful, but I couldn't wait for afternoon practices and weekend games. I suppose cricket was my first love, possibly because I was somewhat better at it than other codes, but I thoroughly enjoyed all the games I participated in.

Northlea was wonderful in all that it exposed one to. Besides cricket, I was, at different times, relatively seriously involved in rugby, hockey, athletics, swimming, tennis, and boxing. Golf in the holidays must be added to this list.

I wonder how often we cycled to the Bulawayo Golf Club (and occasionally the Harry Allen) with golf bags over our shoulders? Other sports in which I acquired an informed interest were Baseball (often going out to watch games featuring, in particular, Keith Iversen and Dave Judge) and cycling where Ken and Trevor Kendal excelled at Callies Sports Ground. Those whose attributes and style I envied but could never emulate included Collie Kendal (for his concentration and 'big match temperament'; Steve Cooper (for his training ethic and 'vasbyt'); Dave Judge (for his speed and evident fun he got out of competing successfully); Keith Iversen (for his virtuosity with a hockey stick and his cavalier approach); Bertie Weston (for his 'aggro' on the rugby field); and Joggie Van Staden (for his boxing prowess and sheer 'guts').

Individual achievements have long since faded but I do remember taking 5 for 7 against Tech, one of my victims being Brian Davison, an upstart U 15 in his debut first XI game (first ball nogal!). More generally, I remember the extremely high standards attained by many of my team mates. Northlea always had very good representation in Rhodesian school sides, an indication of the excellent coaching we received. Standards were set by others from the outset with Vernon Wentzel and Tony de Caila getting into the Rhodesian Nuffield side.

Other sporting memories include,

being broken-hearted when it rained on Saturdays and we couldn't play cricket – and the absolute boredom throughout such days;

playing in my first 'first team' game, facing Ant Grace of Plumtree and hitting it for four in an absolute state of fright (it was a full-toss);

picking up visiting teams at Northolt station early in the morning and taking members home for breakfast before the game;

having lunch prepared by the girls at school;

travelling away by bus and train to such schools as Plumtree, Chaplin, Guinea Fowl, Jameson, Que Que; Alan Wilson;

waiting for masters/umpires to finish their after game beers (plural!);

Ray Suttle making notes in his little black book throughout matches and conducting post-mortems immediately thereafter – possibly his greatest legacy was getting us to 'think' our sport and to respect the ethos underpinning it;

Ray Suttle putting a price on our wickets in the nets so that we would concentrate and protect them;

Going on a memorable tour to Kamativi and Wankie, organized by Ray Suttle, the year after I left school (Collie Kendal and I were 'guest performer's) with the likes of my brother, Paul Sheppard, Titch Robb, Tony Brouse, Rodney White, and Mickey Kettle);

Playing junior-level rugby games in white kit on absolute dust bowls with the dust eventually ringing our eyes and caking up our noses;

getting regularly drilled at rugby throughout an incompetent career;

rugby practices against the Police at the police camp.

training for, and running cross-country (always being the bridesmaid, placing second three times in a row);

running in the first 'multi-racial' sports meet at the Callies ground (the mile, with Steve Cooper in the starting lineup).

swimming in the Friday night galas at the Borrow St. baths (and ploughing up and down in the one mile race);

playing shallow-water water polo, a unique form of wrestling invented by Ray Suttle, at the North End baths for PT;

going to Herby Smith's gym in town and marvelling at the mastery of Joggie Van Staden for whom I had immense admiration and respect;

being made to fight Brian Robb with gloves on in the hall by Brian Haddon after an altercation in the play;

league hockey on Sunday mornings at the different sports clubs (OM's, Prunitians, Police ground, Queens, BAC);

making friends with many guys from other, opposition, schools whose company I still value all these years later.

Attempts to inculcate the arts and some culture were not entirely neglected. Aside from the obligation of engaging with English and Latin set works, I did perform in two 'extra-mural' stage productions, both of which I enjoyed immensely. The first was Gilbert and Sullivan's HMS Pinafore with Rob Williams, Jimmy Hewitson and Valerie Strachan taking the lead roles. Joan Suttle directed and the Bulawayo Philharmonic provided the musical accompaniment. The second was Shaw's Arms and the Man with John Mitchell, Edwil Williams and Barbara Schnieder in the main parts.

With hindsight, I do wish that we had been exposed to more music appreciation.

Talking of Rob and Jimmey, calls to mind our complement of 'Fairbridge boys' who added so much to the quality of the school. I regularly had friends home for the weekend – Jimmy Hewitson, Bill Buckles and Bill Sutherland in particular. Rob Williams and Gavin Schofiled later rose to prominence in their careers.

Riding our bikes all over Bulawayo is a standout memory, in particular morning trips to school with, separately and individually, Tony Sheppard and Wolfie Cesman. Getting to school early was often a priority as we had to meet Janet Lockley, who was always dropped off at about 7.00 am, so that we could crib her maths homework.

Being at a co-ed school was both a blessing and a curse.

The 'downside' was what the economists call 'cumulative negative externalities'. To one who was hormonally challenged/supercharged (randy, sharp, horny) throughout my schooldays, being surrounded by so many females was a source of anxiety.

Sex pervaded my waking (and dreaming hours) -- no names, no pack drill. In fact, most of the girls featured at one time or another. The fact that the free-love ethos of the hippie generation that we heard so much about in the US and Britain had not been embraced by our girls was a source of deep frustration. They embraced the music and fashion (except for burning their bras – another pity) but they would never go the whole ten yards.

All it took was a fleeting flash of female flesh to get me going and no, I did not go blind!.

I have fond memories of the dances we used to have, especially the dreamy 'up – close – and – personal' stuff at the end. And the all nighters in the Matopos on New Year's eve designed for the FINAL STRIKE! (but never delivering it).

School holidays were an intrinsic part of school life. I have vivid memories of messing round at different peoples' houses, visiting the fridge or pantry for whatever we could find, riding round aimlessly, in the evenings going out to listen to records, or wandering the streets fruit-raiding or occasionally roof-rattling, climbing over the wall of the Northend pool for a swim (when Robbie Robertson was superintendent). Later, watching TV and having hamburgers at the Muzzell's became an institution for a while. I often used to go through our back fence to visit Jenny Barbour, to listen to records and to kill a few hours.

How does one end off on reminiscences?

They go on and on like an expanding tree, each memory prompting new ones. Certainly get togethers of the sort we have periodically had in Cape Town usually including Ray Suttle, my brother David, Pat Dewil, Bruce Scott, Boetie Muzzell, Cedric Duncan and Johnny Spence flow seamlessly, lubricated by ever-increasing quantities of beer and stories embellished with every telling.

Cedric even tells us he was a good (the best ever?) wing for Rhodesia! Maybe we should all regard this as a 'work – in – progress' ……………………..?

Extract from KK dictionary (1953)

MISTAKE, vb. int, - posha. K.K. mastake. This word is used season in and season out as a sufficient excuse for any misdoing. "Why have you stolen my beans?" "Ini indaba wean jonjili lo nyemba gamena?"
"I have no excuse!" "Mena enzili mastake!"

The Bushveld by Eddie Cross, Bulawayo, 9th October 2004

Africa has a bug.

Its never been identified, has no name but all who have lived in Africa know it exists and that they might have it. Somehow it never leaves you once you're infected and no matter where you go – it never lets you go altogether.

At this time of the year I just love the wild open spaces that are called the bushveld. It is difficult to describe to someone who has never seen it, but all who have can instantly recall what it is like. It's October – yesterday it was 40 degrees Celsius in the shade and everything is dry and bleached. The tall grass is either burnt or white and the trees are either carrying a full flush of new leaves or are bare and still. Arriving at the edge of an escarpment, you crest a rise and there it is – stretching out to the horizon. Grey, harsh, beautiful.

It is not an easy land – it's full of strong contrasts and it is not forgiving. The soils are varied and are both rich and poor, rainfall is limited and then only for about 4 or 5 months a year. Nights are cool, early mornings fresh and crisp and the days hot with deep blue skies stretching as far as the eye can see. The long dry winter is followed by the violent storms of summer, rain on parched ground, that smell of the first rains on the dry earth, the flights of flying ants.

The nights are very special – the Milky Way blazing across the sky lit by millions of stars. The yellow moon rising above the earth and the springtime roar of the frogs, crickets and night birds. The flowering trees – the Knob Thorn with its mop of dense yellow flowers and thick scent. The new leaves of the Mountain Acacia and Msasa coloured from deep burgundy to light green, the splash of green as the wild figs and the Pod Mahogany comes out. The cicada beetles in the Mopani veld.

The anticipation of the rains and with it new life make this landscape very special as it teems with all sorts of life. Hundreds of different species of trees and shrubs, birds and animals – not forgetting the insect life.

The spectacles we often see – millions of Rose Beetles coming out at night. The splashes of red from the many varieties of aloes and the Erythrina. By comparison, the countryside in more gentle climes may be green and lush, but they have little of the character and lure of the African Bushveld.

The rivers, raging torrents in the summer, slow hot streams in the winter on wide beds of sand and stone. The long deep pools that hold all sort of threats – crocodiles, hippo and disease. The splash of the many varieties of fish from the famous Tiger to the grey Vundu.

Such country also breeds different kinds of people; perhaps Namibia is the best example of this with the proud Herero, the tall German/Afrikaners, the Sen and the people of the Namib.

But in Zimbabwe we have the Tonga, wonderful people who have lived on the flood plains of the Zambezi for centuries, The Venda of the Limpopo Valley – gentle people with great wisdom and a penchant for laughter.

I have a special place for the older people in the Bushveld, the deep furrows of time and the wisdom and humour in their eyes. Somehow the cynicism and shallowness of the modern world has missed them. They are deeply embedded in their land – unlike many of us who are just tourists and bystanders. To be among them is to be instantly at home, welcome and free and respected, always to come away with a small gift – no matter how poor your hosts might be.

Their dignity in rags, the hats with no crowns, the rough hands callused by years of hard manual work. The clinking of the cow bells on the oxen and donkeys as they forage for something to eat.

Some years ago I visited a Zimbabwean, who had reached the pinnacle of success in Germany, married a German girl and had settled in Munich. He told me that he had been to see the film Jock of the Bushveld" and had felt deep emotions when he had heard the call of the Emerald spotted Dove and had seen the dust rising from the feet of the cattle in the film. He said, after 20 years in Europe he could still smell the Lowveld and many times longed to feel the hot African sun on his arms and head.

Many look at us and ask why we stay?

No fuel, high prices, corrupt government, no freedom of speech and a daily diet of racism directed at all who are not drawn from the ruling elite and the tribe.

Why do we battle on – fighting a cause which many say is not ours?

Are we not aliens in a hostile world?

Then we travel to Europe and we discover that that is in fact where we are alien, to the US and find that we are strangers. We come home and find that we have more affinity to the people here than anywhere else.

This is our home in every way and we are right to fight for a better life for all the people who live here. Africa is only the "hopeless continent" because of leadership. We can help change that and so we fight on. This week we see that Blair's "African Commission" is meeting in Ethiopia. I sigh with despair as I hear them talk about debt relief and aid. These are not solutions – they may in fact simply make the situation worse.

Do you want to know why we Africans are poorer than we were 25 years ago? Just look at Zimbabwe. Give us aid – you might as well pour water on the desert sand. Erase our debt - You achieve little except to secure the balance sheets of the multilateral institutions that in many respects are partially responsible for our troubles and then invite a fresh round of State borrowing for all the wrong things.

No what we need is real democracy.

The freedom to vote for who we think will solve our problems best and if they don't – freedom to throw them out when they fail.

What we need is responsible and accountable leadership – in our villages, towns and cities and in our State House.

We look at the failure this week of the Asian countries to agree on a plan of action to force the Military Junta in Burma to give the people their rights and we sigh with frustration.

How long must we wait for the world to wake up to the real nature of such regimes and the plight of those who live under such dictatorships?

But for those of us who live under Mugabe – we have the Bushveld into which we flee when the atmosphere in the political jungle becomes just too oppressive or the problems in our factories cloud our horizons.

After a week on the Zambezi river or the lake, or a few days of hunting or simply a break away to a national park, we come back refreshed and with a renewed determination to see that we eventually win this war and see our beloved country given a fresh start.

"You and whose army.....?
Photograph by Steve Bailey.

And More of Northlea! By Wendy Iversen [nee Schiff]

Ah, Northlea! Fiona and I always said we could write a book on our years there! Fiona and I were practically joined at the hip, having been in the same class through Infant School at Baines Junior, prefects and House Captains together, in all the same Sports Teams, and involved in all the same schoolgirl pranks. In fact, Miss Gilchrist, our Sports Mistress, labelled us the "Terrible Twins" in the first term after our arrival.

I am sure most new pupils remember their first day at High School. Fiona and I stood outside the main entrance, in our green pinafores, to be scrutinised by the Senior boys, who made it their business to check out the talent, or lack of it. In any event, the sight of the Prefects in their imposing blazers [our Colours Blazers are still amongst the smartest I have ever seen, black, with a silver and green braid] will remain with me for all time.

Most of us rode to school, alongside Mr Coleman, our French teacher, and sometimes Mr Rademeyer, the Maths 'fundi', and the cycle track was a meeting place for many a courting couple. Keith used to wait for Fiona and I at the corner of Colenbrander and Main Street most mornings, and he was joined by Steve Cooper, Frank Cross or Dickie van Leeuwen, depending on Fiona's mood at the time! She had a variety of escorts in her Northlea years, whereas Keith and I remained an item throughout, and eventually married in 1969. We are still together 35 years later!

Fiona and I joined a class of real Bogs - possibly one of the brightest intakes ever , judging by our Cambridge results. The likes of Rodney Whyte, Nigel Scott, John Ogden, Rodney Firth, Roland and Phillip Simpson, to mention just a few. The girls faded into obscurity by comparison, although Arlene Scher and Margaret Dewar did manage to uphold the girls' reputation. Fiona and I were far more interested in the extra- mural activities, and as well as playing EVERY sport on offer, from Table-tennis to Softball, we also made our mark in the Cultural activities, such as Choir [Fiona couldn't sing a note - she only joined to keep me company], Drama, [where we managed to persuade Keith and Steve to take the part of Wiseman in the Nativity Play - I think the third Wiseman was Colin Kendall] - and considering that the only part Keith had ever taken previously was a tree, I thought this was a very noble effort! At least he MOVED this time round! And Scottish Dancing, which we really enjoyed. Fiona and I were the fourth couple in the Eightsome Reel, and danced with the seniors - Jen Barbour, my sister Nola, the Graham twins, Pam Mc Phail, Maureen Fenner- at the Showgrounds on Friday nights, when there were cultural evenings or functions. We were so sad when Miss Gilchrist left, and our dancing came to an end.

The Form One and Two girls were required to make lunches for visiting teams, and it gave us an opportunity to compare the talent. Lunches consisted of cold meats and salads - piles of potato salad, pots of boiled beetroot, mountains of lettuce and tomato, and our speciality - the mayonnaise - all made in the Domestic Science Rooms on the first floor, under the supervision of the Dom Sci teacher. We always upheld the manners of the Plumtree visitors to our boys, and Falcon, too, although they were very shy.

Northlea girls were asked to join Milton in their production of the Mikado, and a few of these liaisons ended in permanent ties. Ann Clark met her future husband Errol Wolhuter, in the Chorus, and they have recently celebrated their 39th Anniversary. We often reminisce on our Schooldays, as they are personal friends.

Our teachers were inspirational, unique and unforgettable. Fiona had a huge crush on Mr Marais, our blue-eyed, blond haired Science teacher, and was devastated when his fiancée arrived a term or two later, a petite, gorgeous little blonde, Miss Brewer , who taught Biology. I remember Fiona measuring Mr Marais' shoulders while he was dissecting a frog, and reporting they were over two rulers wide! There was Miss Leigh, who only had two blouses and two skirts in her wardrobe, and wore them on alternate days. She was brilliant - drew any map of any country without referring to a book - and had a memory for names second to none. Hers was the only lesson Keith was ever thrown out of. His class - the dreaded IV B's - had indulged in an ink bomb fight - and Keith's white shirt had been badly stained, so he took it off, put his tie and blazer back on , and boldly marched into Miss Leigh's class, only to be turned on his heels, and marched out again. Mr Riches, as the Art teacher, was one of my favourites. He broke his right arm in the holidays, and proved to be ambidextrous, drawing equally as well with his left. Margaret Dewar and I were privileged to accompany him to Life Drawing classes in the city on a Thursday night, where his private tuition proved invaluable. Mr Annandale, our History teacher, invariably sent Fiona and I to the loos for a drink of water, to quell our fits of giggling, and predicted failures for both of us at Cambridge level. He then had to apologise when we both miraculously passed! Savannah Smith's experiments never turned out, but we enjoyed watching the attempts, anyway. Another of our Biology teachers so inspired John Mitchell [our answer to Elvis], that he carried a dead dog to school, and boiled it for days in the Lab for its skeleton. The problem was it had been dead for quite a while, and the odour was horrendous, and permeated the whole school!

One of the downfalls of being a "pre" was reading the Bible Lesson in Assembly, and Keith paid me many Crunchies at Break to do his for him. By the time I was a Pre in Form IV, I was pretty used to it!

Breaktime was spent watching various forms of games that the Senior Boys engaged in. Either "Stingers" ,or "Bok-Bok", or equally physical activities. Most guys avoided «bucking" if Keith had the ball in Stingers! There was often Pipeband Practice, or Cadets at Break too. The girls got off lightly - just Tuckshop duties and the like.

Once, the Form Fours decided to try and get into the Guiness Book of Records, and piled into a telephone booth. I think they managed to squeeze in about twenty, and got their picture in the local newspaper, but I am not sure about the record!

Being in all the sports teams ensured lots of travelling, and Fiona and I loved the train trips, especially to Gwelo, Que Que and Salisbury. Memories of Jean Crampin singing "Shoo Fly Pie", with her banjo, climbing in and out of the windows, getting woken with the best coffee in the world - courtesy of Rhodesia Railways - climbing out at North Halt, bleary-eyed, at five in the morning. We were NEVER allowed to travel with our boys, for obvious reasons, but its amazing what fun a bunch of girls could have together!

In our Form V year, the Prefects uniforms were changed, and although we had mixed emotions about it, the new pleated grey skirts, apple green blouses, and straw boaters were very smart. We also were allocated a small Pre's room next to the Staff room, a new privilege.

There is so much more, but I hope sisters Nola and Carole and brother Peter will contribute, too. Northlea really was a very special school, and both Keith and I loved being a part of those early days - some of the best days of our lives!

Extract from KK dictionary (1953)

LETTER, n. tsamba, rugwaro. K.K. brief. "I have a letter from my brother to say that all my relatives are dead. I want to go home at once." "Mena bonili brief, yena pumili lapa broer gamena. Yena kuluma zonke lo mabroer gamena yena feeli. Mena funa hamba lapa kia manji manji." In other words he want to go and work on the adjoining farm. Insist on proper notice.

Vic Gane, Rhodesian Farmer by Chris

Vic was a bomber pilot from Canada during the Second World War and came to Rhodesia at the end of the hostilities. He farmed in the Hartley district on the banks of the Umfuli river and he brought with him the expertise learned from his father, who was among other things a boat designer and builder.

Vic's farm became a model farm with many innovations designed and built by him. The crops he grew included tobacco (of course) cotton and wheat. He bought a rusty pile of metal that was supposed to be a lucerne drier from a defunct factory, renovated it and improved it and then installed it on the farm, and then went into growing alfalfa to feed into the contraption. He had many projects advancing at any one time including a number of huge steel boats in various stages of construction.

One of these was, in my memory, over twenty metres long, which he called "The Kariba Queen'.

He took the Kariba Queen up to the Zambezi to launch it on that great river for trials. How this was achieved with the roads, as they were, is a mystery, as I imagine that he launched the boat at Chirundu. From there he went upstream into the Kariba Gorge.

The river was wild and untamed. There were large standing waves created by the force of the river encountering the twists of the course and the rocks embedded therein. The propeller cavitated through the whirlpools.

It was a wild ride, which must have reminded Vic of flying his heavy bomber through the hazards of fighters and flak over Germany.

On his way up the river they saw a group of men on the nothern shore who beckoned to The Kariba Queen. They were Italians, and they asked Vic if he would kindly take a cord across to the other side of the river for them.

Vic wisely refused, because with the state of the spate, if a wave had caught the steel cord, it would have ripped the transom out of the boat. It became apparent that these people were the first on site to build a wall across the river to create the Kariba Dam. When Vic passed the same spot downstream a few days later, the men had succeeded in getting a line across the river with the use of a rocket.

With Vic's adventurous attitude to life it would have been memorable for him to have been the first to pass a line across the river where now stands this huge structure.

He also could have been the first victim of Nyaminyami, the river God.

Operation Quartz - Rhodesia 1980 by R. Allport

The 1980 Elections

After the election of Bishop Muzorewa's government in 1979, Rhodesians hoped that Britain and the international community would recognise his administration and end sanctions. After all, British observers had pronounced the election free and fair in their <u>official report</u>. African voters had turned out in great numbers to vote for the Bishop, and, with a few minor exceptions, there had been no intimidation or coercion. The Rhodesians rightly felt that they had fulfilled the demands of the international community for African majority rule in Rhodesia, now renamed Zimbabwe-Rhodesia.

Nyerere of Tanzania and Kaunda of Zambia, however, objected at the Commonwealth Heads of Government meeting in Lusaka in August 1979, demanding that their protégés, Mugabe and Nkomo, leaders of the two main terrorist groups seeking power, should be included in any final arrangement for majority rule in Rhodesia. Their pressure was instrumental in causing Thatcher to withhold recognition. The fact is that Muzorewa had been democratically elected into power by a 67% majority, whereas his critics, Kaunda and Nyerere, were both heads of one-party dictatorships with shaky economies. (Kaunda had even been unable to provide a red carpet for the Queen at the Lusaka meeting and had been forced to borrow one from "arch-enemy" South Africa...)

Pressure thus mounted for the Rhodesians to hold new elections, again monitored by the Commonwealth, but this time including Mugabe and Nkomo's parties. Tired of the war and sanctions, and with the increasing level of white emigration seriously affecting the economy, Muzorewa was eventually forced into going along with an agreement for a new election.

Because Rhodesian security forces were increasing their cross-border raids on terrorist bases in Zambia and Mozambique Presidents Kaunda and Machel persuaded Nkomo and Mugabe to moderate their conditions for participating in the new election. Mugabe, for example, had initially demanded that the Rhodesian security forces be disbanded prior to the election and that the country be policed by a combination of the terrorist forces. This was a condition to which the Rhodesians would never agree, as it was a patently transparent attempt by ZANU to ensure its forces would have de facto control of the country prior to the election, and allow him to influence the voting and ignore any result unfavourable to ZANU. The resulting distrust that Rhodesians felt for Mugabe's methods and manoeuvrings was probably the prime reason behind the preparation of a contingency plan.

Eventually agreement was reached for the holding of new elections. Commonwealth monitoring forces arrived in Rhodesia and the terrorist forces of ZAPU and ZANU began to send their men to Assembly Points throughout the country.

At midnight on 28 December 1979 a ceasefire came into effect. The majority of white Rhodesians hoped or expected that Muzorewa would again secure a majority vote. However, it did not take long for experts such as John Redfern, Director of Military Intelligence, to work out that this would not come to pass. For one thing, thousands of armed ZANLA terrorists remained at large inside the country. In their place in the Assembly Points were thousands of youngsters masquerading as guerrillas, leaving the real terrorists free to intimidate the population and influence the voting. Commanders of the Rhodesian security forces informed General Walls of this, and he tried to persuade Lord Soames, the temporary governor sent out by Britain to preside over the election, to disqualify ZANU. Soames gave Mugabe several warnings, but took no further action to prevent ZANU from taking part in the election.

Prior to the election a military intelligence paper was prepared by Rhodesian officers, setting out the possible courses of action for opposing ZAPU and ZANU, and preventing them from winning the election. A second intelligence paper predicted a victory for Mugabe and warned that this could precipitate a rush of victorious terrorists into the capital, Salisbury, confronting white civilians and the security forces. Further studies described what would be "Vital Assets Ground" in the event of this happening and detailed action that would need to be taken to retain these strategic areas. The papers also stressed the need in this case to swiftly "neutralize" the terrorist Assembly Points. Members of COMOPS and Special Branch involved in drafting these papers appeared to be convinced of the need for some sort of pre- emptive action to prevent the country from falling into chaos.

Operation Quartz

These intelligence papers probably formed the basis of the plan that was given the code-name "Operation Quartz". This plan envisaged placing Rhodesian troops at strategic points from which they could simultaneously wipe out the terrorists at the Assembly Points and assassinate Mugabe and the other terrorist leaders at their campaign headquarters. The strike would be assisted by Puma helicopters of the South African Air Force and would involve the participation of elite Recce units of the South African army. Clearly the Rhodesians had discussed Operation Quartz with their counterparts in the SADF and obtained their approval and co-operation. Lord Soames had already agreed to allow 400 South African troops into the country in order to protect the Beitbridge area, the main route of escape for whites if the situation were to degenerate into chaos and all-out war. In fact the number of men that the SADF sent across the border was closer to 1,000, although some were later withdrawn following protests by Mugabe.

Operation Quartz was apparently based on the assumption that if Mugabe were defeated in the elections it would be necessary to carry out a strike against ZANU to prevent its forces from attempting a coup and taking over the country by force. The plan presupposed a victory by either Nkomo or Muzorewa, or, more likely, a coalition of the two. ZIPRA forces had in fact already begun joint training exercises with the Rhodesian forces, and undoubtedly their leaders had been given an idea of what Op Quartz would entail. Nkomo was not popular with the whites, however, and there was a distinct possibility that the white troops would ignore orders to avoid clashing with ZIPRA.

Although the full details of Operation Quartz have never been made public, some aspects of the plan have been revealed by former members of the security forces. It was divided into two parts: Operation Quartz, an overt strike against the terrorists, and Operation Hectic, a covert strike to kill Mugabe and his key personnel.

The Assembly Points had been agreed on as part of the Lancaster House Agreement and were simply huge camps where thousands of terrorists were congregated. The Rhodesian security forces had been tasked with monitoring the pre-election activities and keeping the peace. Most of the front-line units were therefore already in positions within easy striking distance of the terrorist camps. Attacks on the camps would be preceded by strikes by the Rhodesian Air Force.

The covert part of the plan - Operation Hectic - was to be carried out by the elite troops of the Rhodesian Special Air Service (SAS). 'A' Squadron of the SAS would assassinate Mugabe, while 'B' Squadron would take care of Vice-President Simon Muzenda and the 100-man contingent of ZANLA based in the Medical Arts Centre. 'C' Squadron was designated to take out the 200 ZIPRA and ZANLA men with their commanders (Rex Nhongo, Dumiso Dabengwa and Lookout Musika) based at the Audio Visual Arts building of the University of Rhodesia. As far as possible, the ZIPRA men would be given an opportunity to escape, and had possibly been informed of the plan beforehand.

The SAS squadrons were to be backed up by tanks and armoured cars of the Rhodesian Armoured Car Regiment, together with a surprise weapon in the form of hitherto undisclosed 106mm recoilless rifles in the Rhodesian armoury.

Eland armoured cars would support 'A' and 'B' Squadrons, while the Rhodesian T-55 tanks would support 'C' Squadron by pounding the Audio Visual Arts building into rubble prior to the attack by the troops. At first it was intended that all eight of the T-55 tanks would be used against the university buildings, but later four of them were sent to Bulawayo to assist the RLI Support Commando in the attack planned for a large Assembly Point in the area.

The tanks were secretly put onto low-loaders and moved to a forward assembly area at the King George VI barracks. Rehearsals with the tanks had taken place at Kibrit barracks, and the planning was thorough and detailed. The tanks would fire approximately 80 high-explosive rounds into the building at point-blank range, after which a single tank would ram the security wall around the university. With foresight, the troops had even removed the front fenders of the tank concerned, so that debris from the wall would not get caught under them and foul the tracks! This was the command tank and during the preparations the CO was in close contact with SAS Major Bob MacKenzie, whose troops would subsequently enter the building and clear it. Trooper Hughes, who took the unique photos shown here, was loader on this particular tank and he recalls that the tanks were also equipped with spotlights and fully stocked with extra 12.7 and 7.62 ammunition in addition to the main gun load.

The SAS teams would use this breach to storm the building and clear it of terrorists, marking each cleared room with a sheet draped out of the window. The SAS men were well-prepared for their task, equipped with AK-47s, body armour and stun grenades, similar to those used by their British counterparts. The operation would be over before the terrorists were aware of what was happening.

As the voting drew to a close, the troops of the SAS, RLI and Selous Scouts waited eagerly for the code word 'Quartz' to be given. They were impatient to get to grips at last with the enemy that had always used classic guerrilla hit and run tactics. There can be no doubt that if the order had been given the terrorist forces would have been decimated within hours. Their superior numbers would have counted for little in the face of an attack by the small, but highly motivated and effective Rhodesian troops.

The signal was never given.

Three hours beforehand the operation was cancelled and Mugabe was announced as the victor, his men jubilant in the streets of Salisbury, while the Rhodesian troops watched in silence.

The reason for the cancellation of Operation Quartz is not known, but there are several possible explanations.

Lt.Col. Garth Barrett, commanding officer of the SAS, believed that it had been compromised by someone at the upper planning levels who was secretly working for the British. A credible theory as several earlier attempts to kill Mugabe had been seemingly dogged by bad luck - meetings where ambushes had been laid had been cancelled at the last minute and Mugabe narrowly escaped several bomb attempts on his life. Nkomo too, had narrowly escaped a well-planned and executed attempt on his life by the SAS in Zambia. It was almost as if they were being warned beforehand.

Another theory is that the operation was compromised by ZIPRA men who had been informed of the plan, either on purpose or by accident. Their close proximity to the ZANLA forces would have made it difficult for them to keep their own preparations secret for very long.

A third possibility is that once General Walls realised that Mugabe had won the election he cancelled the operation on the grounds that it had been intended only to be implemented if Mugabe were to lose the election and attempt to take power by force.

Walls later claimed in an interview that he had not known of Operation Quartz, but then went on to explain that he had not ordered a coup because it would not have lasted 48 hours in the face of world opposition. Ken Flower, head of the CIO, certainly knew of the plans, since they had been given to him by a Special Branch officer. Interestingly, he made no mention of Op Quartz in his memoirs.

Monday March 04, 1980 - 0900hrs. History in the making - opportunity lost? Blakiston-Houston Barracks members of RhACR 'E' Sqn listen to ZRBC election result broadcast - Op Quartz is over, forever.

The realization sinks in. Mugabe the new Prime Minister - ZANU PF is the ruling party. Some cry, some laugh, the foreign soldiers plot their escapes - in the background the roar of African soldiers cheering at KG VI Barracks grows louder!

Ian Smith also reportedly told Ian Hancock in an interview in July 1989 that he had spoken to the security force commanders at a meeting in his Salisbury house just prior to the elections, and said that Walls had assured him that Mugabe would not win, but when pressed by Smith, Walls had admitted that there was a contingency plan to stop Mugabe. It seems very unlikely therefore that Walls was unaware of the existence of the Op Quartz plans.

Even after Mugabe's election victory had been announced, troops of the security forces waited in tense anticipation and the situation remained uncertain until Walls went on television that evening and announced that "anybody who gets out of line or for whatever reason starts disobeying the law will be dealt with effectively and swiftly..." This carefully- worded statement signalled the end of any hopes that Operation Quartz might still take place.

According to the journalist, Pat Scully, details on Op Quartz became public after Mugabe decided to get rid of Peter Walls, following the latter's caustic comments about Mugabe in TV and Press interviews in South Africa. By accusing Walls of having been the mastermind behind the whole plan, Mugabe would be able to dismiss him and at the same time distract public attention from the 'Tekere Affair' (Edgar Tekere, one of Mugabe's cabinet ministers, had been arrested for the murder of an elderly white farmer), which was giving Mugabe a lot of bad publicity abroad at the time.

Nathan Shamuyarira (Minister of Information) therefore accused Walls in the House of Assembly on 15 August of treason and claimed the following:

1. Op Quartz involved a military takeover of the country on 4 March, the day of Mugabe's election victory.

2. ZANLA troops had been purposely massed in assembly points so that the Rhodesian Air Force could take them out en masse.

3. ZIPRA was not to be attacked, in hopes of promoting an alliance between Nkomo and Muzorewa after ZANLA had been neutralised.

4. Op Quartz was cancelled a bare 3 hours before it was due to be launched, because Walls felt that it could not succeed in view of Mugabe's overwhelming victory at the polls.

John Ellison, a 'Daily Express' (London) foreign editor, who originally broke the story, later claimed that the version given by Shamuyarira in the House of Assembly had been deliberately distorted to implicate Walls. Op Quartz, according to Ellison, was simply a contingency plan that had been drawn up 6 weeks earlier and was designed to protect the coalition government (Nkomo-Muzorewa) which many believed would be the outcome of the election. The operation would thus have been carried out, if it proved necessary, in support of a legally elected government.

General Walls flatly denied Shamuyarira's claims, saying he had never heard of Operation Quartz, but Mugabe refused to believe this, demanding that Walls leave the country as soon as possible. Walls had already pointed out to Mugabe that he did not have sufficient control over the 3 ex-terrorist forces, and in an interview in August on SABC-TV predicted that trouble was coming. He was right - three weeks later shoot-outs between ZIPRA and ZANLA started...

The Operation Quartz signals

That Op Quartz was in fact seriously considered by the security forces and that preparations were detailed and far-advanced at the time of the election is shown by the existence of some of the original signals sent to units of the army. Copies were kept, against orders, by some of the officers, and a number of these originals are now in the possession of the Rhodesian Army Association, which is preparing a history of the war.

Signal 1
(dated 27 February 1980)

0 271245B FM JOC THRASHER TO AIG 73 BT T O P S E C R E T G673 SUBJ
REDEPLOYMENT OF FORCES IN THE EVENT OF MUGABE WINNING THE ELECTION.
1. SITUATION. IN THE EVENT OF MUGABE WINNING THE ELECTION CMM A CONTINGENCY PLAN HAS BEEN DRAWN UP WITH A VIEW TO ENSURING THAT THE VITAL ASSET GROUND IS SECURED. IN THE EVENT OF THIS HAPPENING CMM THE FOLLOWING POSSIBILITIES EXIST CLN
A. THE ASSEMBLY PLACES ECHO AND FOXTROT EMPTYING.
B. THE MOVE OF LARGE ORGANISED GROUPS OF CTTS INTO THE TOWNS CMM RURAL AREAS AND ONTO THE LINES OF COMMUNICATION.
C. THE ASSISTANCE OF FRELIMO TROOPS BEING GIVEN TO MUGABE TO TAKE OVER THE COUNTRY.
2. MISSION. TO SECURE THE VITAL ASSET GROUND OF JOC THRASHER CMM INCLUDING THE MAJOR AREAS OF EUROPEAN POPULATION (URBAN AND RURAL) AND THE COMUNICATION ROUTES TO SALISBURY AND BIRCHENOUGH BRIDGE.
3. EXECUTION.
A. GENERAL OUTLINE. THE EMPHASIS OF DEPLOYMENT WILL MOVE FROM THE TTLS TO THE VITAL ASSET GROUND WITH ALL REDEPLOYMENTS TAKING PLACE ONLY REPEAT ONLY ON RECEIPT OF CODEWORD QUARTZ WHICH MUST BE DONE AS SOON AS POSSIBLE. THE MAIN TASK WILL BE TO ENSURE THAT AREAS OF STRATEGIC IMPORTANCE AND EUROPEAN POPULATION IS SAFEGUARDED AT ALL COSTS.
B. SUB JOC RUSAPE.
1. GROUPING. UNDER COMMAND ON RECEIPT OF CODEWORD QUARTZ
A. 3 INDEP COY RAR
B. 8 RR MINUS C1 COY 8RR AND ANTI TANKS PLATOON
C. K COY BSAP SUPPORT UNIT
D. SFA DETACHMENTS AS ALREADY DEPLOYED IN YOUR AREA IN SUPPORT ON RECEIPT OF CODEWORD QUARTZ FIRE FORCE BRAVO
11. TASKS. A. DEPLOYMENTS TO TAKE PLACE AS FOLLOWS CLN
1. 3 INDEP COY RAR INYANGA AREA
11. TWO COYS 8 RR HEADLANDS AREA
111. TWO COYS 8 RR RUSAPE AREA

1V. ONE COY 8RR INYAZURA AREA AND ONE COY 8RR OLD UMTALI AREA.

V. K COY BSAP SUPPORT UNIT PENHALONGA AREA WITH ONE TROOP DEPLOYED TEA ESTATES HOLDINGBY TTL.

V1. SFA TO BE WITHDRAWN FROM THE TTLS AND PLACED UNDER COMMAND SUITABLE COMPANIES FOR THE PROTECTION OF FARMERS.

V11. THE DEFENCE OF HEADLANDS CMM RUSAPE CMM INYAZURA CMM INYANGA CMM DOROWA MINE CMM PENHALONGA AND THE TEA ESTATES CMM MUTASA DC'S CAMP CMM RUDA.

V111. THE PROTECTION OF ALL EUROPEAN FARMERS AND CIVILIANS.

1X. THE LINE OF ROAD FROM UMTALI TO MACHEKE.

X. THE LINE OF ROAD FROM INYANGA TO RUSAPE AND INYANGA TO UMTALI WITH EMPHASIS ON THE FORMER. NOTE CLN THE LINE OF RAIL SHOULD NOT BE CONSIDERED AS A PROTECTION TASK.

X1. TO BE ABLE TO REGROUP AS A CONVENTIONAL BATTALION WITHIN EIGHT HOURS.

X11. TO PROVIDE ONE COMPANY WHICH IS CAPABLE OF REINFORCING UMTALI WITHIN FOUR HOURS

X111. PROTECTION OF ODZI BRIDGE

111. BOUNDARIES. NO CHANGE EXCEPT WEDZA TTL REVERTING UNDER COMMAND SUB JOC MARANDELLAS ON RECEIPT OF THE CODEWORD QUARTZ.

(A) 3 BDE DEF PL

(B) ELMS SELOUS SCOUTS

(C) A COY BSAP SUPPORT UNIT

(D) C COY GUARD FORCE

(E) SFA DEACHMENTS AS ALREADY DEPLOYED IN YOUR AREA. IN SUPPORT OF RECEIPT OF CODEWORD FIRE FORCE BRAVO

11. TASKS. DEPLOYMENTS TO TAKE PLACE AS FOLLOWS CLN

(AL 3 BDE DEF PL ODZI

(B) SELOUS SCOUTS AT GRAND REEF

(C) A COY BSAP SUPPORT UNIT VUMBA/BURMA VALLEY

(D) C COY GUARD FORCE ODZI AREA

(E) SFA TO BE WITHDRAWN FROM THE TTLS AND PLACED UNDER COMMAND SUITABLE COMPANIES FOR PROTECTION OF FARMERS.

(F) THE DEFENCE OF ODZI

(G) THE PROTECTION OF ALL EUROPEAN FARMERS AND CIVILIANS

(H) THE UMTALI/SALISBURY ROAD WITHIN YOUR BOUNDARY

(J) THE UMTALI/BIRCHENOUGH BRIDGE ROAD

111. NO CHANGE EXCEPT SABI TTL REVERTS UNDER COMMAND SUB JOC ENKELDOORN

1. GROUPING. UNDER COMMAND ON RECEIPT OF CODEWORD QUARTZ CLN

(A) 4 RR MINUS C COY

(B) F COY BSAP SUPPORT UNIT

(C) ONE TROOP RHACR

(D) ELMS 3 ENGR SQN

(E) SFA DETACHMENTS AS ALREADY DEPLOYED IN YOUR AREA. IN SUPPORT ON RECEIPT OF CODEWORD QUARTZ CLN FIRE FORCE BRAVO

11. TASKS. DEPLOYMENTS TO TAKE PLACE AS FOLLOWS CLN

(A) 4 RR COMPANYCASHEL

(B) 4 RR COMPANY MELSETTER AREA

(C) 4 RR COMPANY MT SELINDA AREA

(D) 4 RR COMPANY CHIPINGA

(E) F COMPANY BSAP SUPPORT UNIT MIDDLE SABI AREA
(F) THE DEFENCE OF CASHEL CMM CHIPINGA AND MELSETTER
(G) THE PROTECTION OF ALL EUROPEAN FARMERS AND CIVILIANS
(H) THE PROTECTION OF CHIPINGA/BIRCHENOUGH BRIDGE ROAD
(J) THE PROTECTION OF BIRCHENOUGH BRIDGE/UMTALI ROAD
(K) PROTECTION OF BIRCHENOUGH BRIDGE
 (L) TO BE ABLE TO REGROUP AS A CONVENTIONAL BATTALION WITHIN EIGHT HOURS
111. BOUNDARIES. NO CHANGE. D. SUB JOC MARANDELLAS.
1. GROUPING. UNDER COMMAND ON RECEIPT OF CODEWORD QUARTZ CLN
(A) 10 RR COY
(B)2 1 POU COY
(C) L COY BSAP SUPPORT UNIT
(D) E COY GUARD FORCE
(E) SFA DETACHMENTS AS ALREADY DEPLOYED IN YOUR AREA. IN SUPPORT ON
RECEIPT OF CODEWORD QUARTZ FIRE FORCE BRAVO
11. TASKS. DEPLOYMENTS TO TAKE PLACE AS FOLLOWS CLN
(A) 10 RR COY MACHEKE
(B) E COY GUARD FORCE WEDZA
(C) POU COY AND L COY BSAP SUPPORT UNIT MARANDELLAS AND SURROUNDING
FARMING AREA
(D) SFA TO BE WITHDRAWN FROM THE TTLS AND PLACE UNDER COMMAND SUITABLE
COMPANIES FOR PRETECTION OF FARMERS.
(E) THE DEFENCE OF MARANDELLAS CMM MACHEKE AND WEDZA
 (F) PROTECTION OF ALL EUROPEAN FARMERS AND CIVILIANS
(G) THE PROTECTION OF THE MACHEKE/SALISBURY ROAD WITHIN YOUR BOUNDARY.
NOTE CLN THE LINE OF RAIL SHOULD NOT BE CONSIDERED A PROTECTION TASK
111. BOUNDARIES. NO CHANGE EXCEPT WEDZA COMES UNDER COMMAND ON RECEIPT
OF CODEWORD QUARTZ. E. SUB JOC ENKELDOORN.
1. GROUPING. UNDER COMMAND ON RECEIPT OF CODEWORD QUARTZ
(A) COY RAR (EX BALLA BALLA)
(B) COY 10 RR
(C) G COY RDR
(D) C COY BSAP SUPPORT UNIT
(E)S1 COY BSAP SUPPORT UNIT
(F) SFA DETACHMENTS AS ALREADY DEPLOYED IN YOUR AREA IN SUPPORT ON
RECEIPT OF CODEWORD QUARTZ FIRE FORCE BRAVO
11. TASKS. DEPLOYMENTS TO TAKE PLACE AS FOLLOWS CLN
(A) RAR COY AREA ENKLEDOORN
(B) C COY BSAP SUPPORT UNIT AREA ENKELDOORN
(C) COY 10 RR AREA FEATHERSTONE
(D) G COY 1 RDR AREA FEATHERSTONE
 (E) 1 COY BSAP SUPPORT UNIT AREA FEATHERSTONE
(F) SABI SFA DETACHMENT TO BUHERA
(G) REMAINING SFA TO BE WITHDRAWN FROM TTLS AND PLACE UNDER SUITABLE
COMPANIES FOR THEPROTECTION OF EUROPEAN FARMERS.
(H) THE DEFENCE OF ENKELDOORN CMM FEATHERSTONE AND BUHERA
(J) THE PROTECTION OF THE SALISBURY/UMVUMA ROAD WITHIN YOUR BOUNDARY
(K) PROTECTION OF ALL EUROPEAN FARMERS AND CIVILIANS
111. BOUNDARIES. NO CHANGE EXCEPT SABI TTL REVERTS UNDER COMMAND ON
RECEIPT OF CODEWORD QUARTZ. F. 3 RAR TAC HEADQUARTERS.

1. COMMANDER CLN LT COL LEAVER
11. 2IC CLN MAJOR G MOSTERT
111. GROUPING. UNDER COMMAND ON RECEIPT OF CODEWORD QUARTZ
(A) 5 (INDEP) COY RAR
(B) 6 (INDEP) COY RAR
(C) C COY 4 RR
(D) C1 COY 8RR
(E) ANTI TANK PL 8RR
 (F) TWO TROOPS RHACR
(G) ELMS 3 ENGR SQN IN SUPPORT ON RECEIPT OF CODEWORD QUARTZ FIRE FORCE
BRAVO IN DIRECT SUPPORT ON RECEIPT OF CODEWORD QUARTZ O BATTERY RHA
1V. TASKS.
(A) TO PROVIDE WITHIN TWO HOURS A BATTLE GROUP CONSISTING OF CLN
(AAL THREE COMPANIES
(AB) ONE TROOP RHACR
(AC) ANTI TANK PLATOON
(AD) ONE TROOP RHA
(AE) ELMS ENGRS
(B) THE DEFENCE OF UMTALI V. BOUNDARIES. NO CHANGE TO CURRENT URBAN OPS
BOUNDARIES. BATTLE GROUP WILL BE GIVEN ITS BOUNDARIES BEFORE DEPLOYMENT
BY THIS JOC. G. C COY (FERUKA COY) RDR.
1. GROUPING. NIL.
11. TASK. TO PROVIDE PROTECTION ON THE FOLLOWING BRIDGES CLN
 (A) TANGANDA VN 425 766
(B) CHANGADZI VN 341 947
(C) NYANYADZI VP 391 166
(D) MURARI VP 475 328
(E) UMVUMVUMU VP 495 396
(F) WENGEZI VP 502 440
(G) WHITEWATERS VP 554 640
(H) MPUDZI VP 554 640
(J) INYAZURA VQ 148 302
(K) LESAPI VQ 080 532
(L) MACHEKE UQ 804 938
(M) UMTALI VQ 570 101
(N) MANICA VQ 566 222
(O) ODZI (INYANGA ROAD) VQ 674 553
(P) NYAKAPINGA VQ 682 581
(R) INYANGOMBE VQ 700 782
(S) UMTALI VQ 423 067 H. CO-ORDINATING INSTRUCTIONS.
1. SUB JOKS RUSAPE AND CHIPIGA MUST PLAN THAT IN THE EVENT OF 4RR AND 8RR
BEING REDEPLOYED ON A CONVENTIONAL BASIS CMM AN ALTERNATIVE

PAGE 11 RBVDGCR 010 T O P S EC R E T PLAN FOR THE COMMAND AND CONTROL OF
THE SFA BE IMPLEMENTED.
11. THE DETAILED PLANS OF WHERE TROOPS ARE TO BE DEPLOYED CMM THEIR TASKS
AND TIMINGS ARE TO BE SENT TO THIS JOC BY NO LATER THAN 031200B MARCH 1980.
THESE PLANS ARE TO INCLUDE SPECIFIC DETAILS AS TO WHAT VITAL INSTALLATIONS

ARE TO BE GUARDED WITHIN THE TOWNS CMM I.E. AIRFIELDS CMM PTC INSTALLATIONS ETC.
4. ADMIN AND LOG. DETAILVNHWILL BE FORWARDED LATER.
5. COMMAND AND SIGNALS.
CODEWORD QUARTZ IS FOR THE IMPLEMENTATION OF THIS PLAN. NO TROOPS REPEAT NO TROOPS ARE TO BE REDEPLOYED UNTIL ADDRESSEES RECEIVE THIS CODEWORD.
6. NORMAL BATTALION AND SUB JOC NETS TO BE USED. SIGNAL NET FOR 3 RAR TAC HEADQUARTERS TO BE GIVEN LATER.
7. ALL ACKNOWLEDGE. BT

Signal 2

P 010952B FM SUD JOC CHIPINGA TO JOC THRASHER BT T O P S E C R E T G1. YOUR G673 SUBJ REDEPLOYMENT REFERS.
ONE. 4RR COY DEPL AS FOLS. A COY TO CHIPINGA BASED AT BATTLE CAMP. B COY TO REMAIN BASED AT MELSETTER, D COY TO REMAIN BASED ORIBI RIDGE, E COY EX UMTALI TO BASE CASHEL.

TWO. ELMS 4RR ATK TO CASHEL, ELMS 4RR ATK AT BIRCHENOUGH BRIDGE, 1SEC 4RR MOR AT BIRCHENOUGH BRIDGE, ELMS
4RR RECCE TO BIRCHENOUGH BRIDGE, MELSETTER AND CHIPINGA.

THREE. ATT PERS, F COY BSAP TO MID SABI BASED NEAR CLUB, 1 TP RHACR TO REMAIN AT CASHEL DURING PRESENT UNCERTAINTY IN SUP OF E COY 4 RR.

FOUR. TASKS FROM NORT TO SOUTH. E COY (CASHEL) I. TO PROTECT THE REMAINING WHITE ELMS WITHIN EFA. II. TO GUARD THE POLICE STN AND TEL EXCH. III. TO DENY ACCESS BY THE EN TO THE ROUTES INTO RHOD AT VP 844 338, EN CAN BE STOPPED EFFECTIVELY AT VP 790 358 AND VP 783 383, ALT ROUTE AT VP 844 398, EN CAN BE STOPPED AT VARIOUS PTS ALONG ROUTE UP TO VP823 398 THEN VP 59 42. IV. TO PROTECT BRIDGES AT VP 617 407, VP 589 414 UMVUMVUMVU. V. TO EFFECTIVELY PATROL RDS WITHIN AREA OF RESP. VI. SHOULD REQ ARISE, ALL EUROS WITHIN AREA TO BE LAARGERED AT COY BASE PRIOR TO BEING MOVED. VII. POLICE STN HAS PETROL PT, ALL AREAS ON GENERATED POWER.

B COY MELSETTER. I. TO PROTECT REMAINING WHITE ELMS WITHIN THE AREA. II. TO GUARD RESERVIOR, PUMP STN, PORK PIE REBRO, TV REBRO ESC SUB STN, PRIMARY SCH, VILLAGE CLINIC, HOTEL AND VILLAGE PETROL PTS. III. TO EFFECTIVELY PATROL ACCESS RD TO AREA VP654
157 WHERE RESP REVERTS TO E COY 4 RR, ALSO RD TO AREA VN 671 838, WHERE RESP REVERTS TO A COY 4 RR. IV. TO PROTECT BRIDGES VP 695 057 BIRIWIRI, VP
787 054 NYAHODI, VN 675 894 SILVERSTREAMS, VN 659 852 CHIHONDE. V. SHOULD REQ ARISE, ALL EUROS WITHIN AREA TO BE GROUPED TO CHIMANIMANI HOTEL. VI. AREA IS ON ESC POWER, HAS NO STD.

A COY CHIPINGA. I. TO PROTECT WHITE ELEMNTS WITHIN EFA.
II. TO GUARD PTC, HOSPITAL, WATER STORAGE TANKS, FILTRATIONS PLANT,PUMP STN, DAM, SCHOOL, FUEL STNS X 3, ACCESS RDS 3 RD BLOCKS, ESC SUB STN.

III. TO EFFECTIVELY PATROL ACCESS RDS TO VN 632 792, TO VN 426 795 WHERE RESP TAKEN OVER BY D COY 4 RR.
IV. BRIDGES WITHIN AREA OF RESP ARE OF A MINOR GRADING AND CAN BE BY-PASSED IF NEC.
V. POLICE STN AND CMED HAVE ADDITIONAL FUEL PTS.
VI. POLICE STN AND HOME AFFAIRS ESTABLISHMENTS TO BE RESP OF SINGLE SERVISES.
VII. SHOULD EUROS HAVE TO BE REGROUPED, SCHOOL AND HOTEL WILL BE USED.
VIII. AREA IS ON ESC POWER AND HAS STD.

TAC HQ 4 RR. TO REMAIN IN POSN AT CHIPINGA ARMY CAMP AS A MOVE WOULD CAUSE A LOWERING OF MORALE WITHIN THE AREA.
I. TO ASSIT THE BASE MAN POWER ON TASKS CARRIED OUT BY A COY 4 RR. TO GUARD THE CHIPINGA AIRSTRIP. III. TO ASSIST THE DC AND ACC WITH ANY REGROUPING OF EUROS SHOULD THIS BECOME NEC.

F COY BSAP SP UNIT. I. TO PROTECT WHITE ELM WITHIN THE EFA. II. TO GUARD THE MAIN PUMP STN, ESC SUB STN, GMB STARAGE SHEDS, SLA WKSHPS, THE MAIN AIRFIELD AT CLUB. III. TO EFFECTIVELY PATROL THE ROADS WITH AREA OF RESP TO VN 426 759 WHERE RESP HANDED OVER TO A COY 4 RR. IV. NO BRIDGES IN AREA AF ANY CONSEQUENCE. V. FUEL PTS EXIST ON MOST HOLDINGS. VI. SHOULD EUROS HAVE TO BE REGROUPED THEN CLUB FACIL WILL BE USED. VII. AREA IS ON ESC WITH AUTOMATIC PARTY LINE.

D COY 4 RR. I.TO PROTECT WHITE ELM IN AREA OF RESP. II. TO PROTECT EURO ENCLAVES AT JERSEY AND ZONA. III. TO DENY ACCESS BY THE EN TO THE ROUTE FROM ESPUGABERRA AT VN 74 73. THIS PLAN TO BE DRAWN UP IN CONSULTATION WITH CO 4 RR AND OC ATK.
SHOULD REQ FOR REGROUPING OF EUROS WITHIN AREA ALL PERSONS TO BE ESCORTED TO THE MAIN AREA WITHIN CHIPINGA.

FIVE. SHOULD 4 RR BE RE-DEPLOYED ON A CONVENTIONAL BASIS THEN SFA MUTAMBARA UNDER 4 RR OFFICER WOULD BE BROUGHT DOWN AS FOLLOWS: I. HQ SFA TO BE EST AT HOME AFFAIRS SFA CAMP IN CHIPINGA.
136 EFF. II. CASHEL ONE PL SFA   20 MEN. III. MELSETTER ONE PL   30 MEN. IV. CHIPINGA ONE PL   40 MEN. V. MT SELINDA   20 MEN. VI. HQ   26 MEN.

SIX. THE SFA WILL IN CONJUNCTION WITH THE RESOURCES AVAIL FROM HOME AFFAIRS IN EACH AREA TAKE OVER THE GUARDING OF ALL KEY PTS AS DETAILED FOR 4 RR COYS.

SEVEN. HOME AFFAIRS AND POLICE WILL COMBINE WITH TPT TO ASSIST WITH THE MOVING OF SFA FROM CHIKOWA TO THEIR RESPECTIVE LOCS.

EIGHT. TWO ADDITIONAL OFFICERS EX 4 RR WILL BE ATTACHED TO THE SFA FOR THE DUR OF THEIR TASK SHOULD REDEPLOYMENT OF THE ARMY BECOME NEC.

NINE. IT IS NOT ANTICIPATED THAT TANGIBLE ASSISTANCE WILL BE FORTH-□ COMING FROM POLICE RESERVE AS MOST MEN IN THIS AREA ARE FARMERS AND WILL NOT LEAVE THEIR PROPERTIES. SHOULD A REGROU- PING EX FOR EUROS BE

UNDERTAKEN THEN POLICE RESERVE WILL BECOME AVAIL FOR URBAN DUTIES AS
FAMILIES WILL BE SAFE.

TEN. CERATIN ESTABLISHMENTS HAVE MILITIA IT IS ANTICIPATED THAT A COMBINED
MEETING WITH ACC, DC, POLICE WILL TAKE PLACE TO COORD THE USE OF MILITIA IN
THE ABOVE ROLE.

ELEVEN. AIRFIELDS. THE AIRFIELD AT TILBURY AND THE MAIN STRIPS AT BOTH
CHIPINGA AND MID SABI WILL BE GUARDED. ALL OTHER AIRSTRIPS WITHIN THIS
AREA WILL IF REQ BE RENDERED U/S. TWELVE. TMGS. AFTER RECEIPT OF THE
CODEWORD EIGHT HOURS WILL BE REQD FOR THE REGROUPING AND RE-
DEPLOYMENT OF SFA. VEHS FOR THIS EX RESP OF BSAP AND HOME AFFAIRS. BT

Signal 3

Y 022130B FM JOC THRASHER TO AIG 73 BT T O P S E C R E T G720 QUARTZ REPEAT
QUARTZ. THE REDEPLOYMENT IS TO BE EFFECTED BY 031900B MARCH
1980 WITH THE FOLLOWING CHANGES.
1. SUB JOC RUSAPE.
A. A1 COY 8 RR MOVES UNDER COMMAND 3 RAR TAC HQ UMTALI. ASSEMBLY AREA
SHOWGROUNDS.
B. FORCE LEVELS IN ASSEMBLY PLACE ECHO TO REMAIN INCLUDING CURRENT FORCE
LEVELS AT RUANGWE.
C. K COY SP UNIT MINUS ONE TROOP TO REMAIN AREA ASSEMBLY PLACE FOXTROT.
D. 3 INDEP COY PLATOON AT NYAMAROPA TO RETURN INYANGA AREA. NYAMAROPA
BASE TO REMAIN OPEN AND POLICE AND HOME AFFAIRS DETAILS TO GROUP
TOGETHER.
E. FIRE FORCE ECHO MOVES UNDER COMMAND AND IS TO POSITION INYANGA
BARRACKS.
2. SUB JOC UMTALI.
A. A COY SP UNIT TO REMAIN ON CURRENT AMBUSH TASKS. B. 3 BDE PLATOON TO
POSITION VUMBA.
3. SUB JOC CHAPINGA. A. A COY 4 RR TO REMAIN DEPLOYED SABI TTL ON PRSENT
TASK.
4. SUB JOC MARANDELLAS. NO CHANGE TO FORCE LEVELS. A. L COY SP UNIT TO
POSITION MACHEKE. B. RAR TRAINING COY TO POSITION MARANDELLAS. C. COY 10 RR
MOVES UNDER COMMAND SUB JOC ENKELDOORN.
5. SUB JOC ENKELDOORN. A. RAR TRAINING COY RAR MOVES UNDER COMMAND SUB
JOC MARANDELLAS. B. 10 RR COYS TO REMAIN UNDER COMD AND POSITION WITH TAC
HQ IN AREA FEATHERSON WITH G COY RDR UNDER COMMAND. C. C AND I COYS
SUPPORT UNIT TO POSITION AT ENKELDOORN.
6. FORCE HATTY. A. COMMANDER MAJ HATTY. 8 RR TO PROVIDE TAC HQ. B. GROUPING.
1. UNDER COMMAND.
(A) 5 INDEP COY RAR
(B) A COY 4 RR
(C) C COY 4 RR
 (D) C1 COY 8RR
(E) K COY SUPPORT UNIT MINUS ONE TROOP.
11. IN SUPPORT. FIRE FORCE BRAVO. C. TASKS.
1. MAINTAIN PRESENT RSF FORCE LEVEL IN ASSEMBLY PLACE FOXTROT.

11. PRETECT/REINFORCE ELEMENTS RSF IN ASSEMBLY PLACE FOXTROT SHOULD NEED ARISE.
111. PREVENT CTT BREAKOUT FROM ASSEMBLY PLACE FOXTROT.
1V. DEFENCE OF BUHERA. V. TO REGROUP THE SFA IN THE SABI TTL FOR THE DEFENCE OF BUHERA TOWN AND THE LOCAL ENVIRONS.
7. 3 RAR TAC HQ. A. COMMANDER LT COL LEAVER. B. 2IC MAJ CAMPBELL. C. GROUPING.
1. UNDER COMMAND.
(A) 6 INDEP COY RAR.
(B) A1 COY 8RR.
(C) ANTI TANK PLATOON 8 RR.
(D) THREE TROOPS RHACR.
(E) ELEMENTS 3 ENGR SQN.
11. IN DIRECT SUPPORT. Q BTY RHA.
111. IN SUPPORT FIRE FORCE BRAVO. D. TASKS. NO CHANGE.
8. COORDINATING INSTRUCTIONS. A. ALL SFA LESS THOSE IN PV'S TO BE REGROUPED AND PLACED UNDER COMMAND OF SUITABLE COYS FOR DEPLOYMENT IN TO VITAL ASSET GROUND. SFA LO'S TO REMAIN WITH SFA.
B. ALL H.AFF AN POLICE BASES WHICH CAN BE DEFENE BY THE DETAILS AGAINST DETERMINED ATTACK ARE TO REMAIN OPEN. THIS IS LEFT TO THE DISCRETION OF THE SUB - JOCS AND THOSE THAT CANNOT BE DEFENDED SHOULD BE CLOSED. C. **ALL CTTS WHO ARE NOT WITHIN THE LAID DOWN CONFINES OF THE ASSEMBLY PLACES ARE TO BE TREATED AS ILLEGAL AND SHOT**. D. IT IS APPRECIATED THAT THE SFA REGROUPING WILL PROVIDE A MAJOR PROBLEM ESPECIALLY REGARDING TRANSPORT. HOWEVER SUB JOCS MUST MAKE THE BEST PLAN POSSIBLE. E. CMF MEMBERS ARE NOT TO BE INFORMED OF THE REGROUPING AND POSITIONING OF TROOPS.
9. COMMAND AND SIGNALS. O - GROUP THIS HQ 030900B FOR SUB JOC

PAGE 5 RBVDGCR 004 T O P S E C R E T COMMANDERS CMM SB REPS CMM LT COL LEAVER (3RAR) CMM MAJ HATTY (8RR).
10. NOTE. THE DEPLOYMENT IS A PRECAUTIONARY MEASURE AND DOES NOT INDICATE PRIOR WARNING OF THE RESULT OF THE ELECTION BT

The Rhodesian T-55 Tanks

Before 1979 the Rhodesian Army had not possessed any tanks. In October of that year they received eight T-55 tanks from South Africa, confiscated from a French ship, the "Astor", which had been transporting a heavy weapons consignment from Libya for Idi Amin in Uganda. Amin's regime collapsed on the day that the ship docked in Mombasa and it was redirected to Angola. The ship called in to Durban where the cargo, including ten Polish-built T-55LD tanks (built in 1975), was seized, South Africa at that point considering itself to be at war with Angola. Two of the tanks were kept by the South Africans for evaluation. The remaining eight were transported to

Rhodesia, together with SADF advisers for the purpose of training Rhodesian crews. The rumour was spread that the tanks had been captured in Mozambique, in order to obscure South Africa's part in the deal. The tanks, now part of the Rhodesian Armoured Car Regiment - in a newly-formed "E" Squadron - were driven around on tank transporters for several months in order to give the impression that the Rhodesians possessed a large number of heavy tanks. On arrival the T-55s had sported the original Libyan camouflage scheme. Major Winkler ordered them repainted in American camo, which was eminently unsuitable, and finally the South African instructors had them painted in anti-infra-red South African camo, which proved perfect for Rhodesian conditions. The tank crews came from 'D' Sqn RhACR, regular force soldiers who had signed on for a minimum of 3 years. Trained crews were vital if the tanks were to be used to maximum effect and it was necessary to ensure that the crews would remain in the Army for some time. A few of the men had tank experience already, but initially there was a lot of experimenting and reliance on the manuals, until Army HQ arranged for proper training by members of the SADF School of Armour.

Command of 'E' Sqn was given to Captain Kaufeldt, an experienced tanker from West Germany. More recruits from the RLI and Selous Scouts arrived to fill the gaps and acquitted themselves well in their new task.

The Soviet-manufactured radios were removed from the tanks and replaced with the South African radios and headsets used on the Eland 90 AFVs. These used a throat-activated microphone system and were far superior to the Soviet models. In Soviet tanks the radios were operated by the loader, in addition to his task on the main gun. The Rhodesians, reasoning that the loader already had enough to keep him occupied, moved the radios to the tank commander's position. The tank crews were issued with brand-new Soviet AKMS assault rifles and were eager to test them in battle conditions. They were destined to remain unused.

Frederick Courtney Selous 31.12.1851 – 4.1.1917

Selous was a British explorer and hunter famous for his exploits in East Africa.

He was born in London, and was educated at Rugby and in Germany. His love for natural history led to the resolve to study the ways of wild animals in their native haunts. Going to South Africa when he was nineteen he travelled from the Cape of Good Hope to Matabeleland, reached early in 1872, and was granted permission by Lobengula to shoot game anywhere in his dominions.

From that date until 1890, with a few brief intervals spent in England, Selous hunted and explored over the then little-known regions north of the Transvaal and south of the Congo basin, shooting elephants, and collecting specimens of all kinds for museums and private collections. His travels added largely to the knowledge of the country now known as Rhodesia. He made valuable ethnological investigations, and throughout his wanderings - often among people who had never previously seen a white man - he maintained cordial relations with the chiefs and tribes, winning their confidence and esteem, notably so in the case of Lobengula.

In 1890 Selous entered the service of the British South Africa Company, acting as guide to the pioneer expedition to Mashonaland. Over 400 miles of road were constructed through a country of forest, mountain and swamp, and in two and a half months Selous took the column safely to its destination. He then went east to Manicaland, concluding arrangements there which brought the country under British control.

He took part in the Matabele War (1893), being wounded during the advance on Bulawayo. While back in England he married, but in March 1896 was again settled with his wife on an estate in Matabeleland when the native rebellion broke out. He took a prominent part in the fighting which followed, and published an account of the campaign entitled Sunshine and Storm in Rhodesia (1896).

In World War I Selous participated in the fighting in East Africa as an officer in the 25th Royal Fusiliers, where he was killed in a minor engagement at Beho Beho in January 1917.

Captain Jack Malloch flying his Spitfire nearly forty years after being shot down in one over Italy in the Second World War.

This particular aircraft was retired in 1954 and spent nearly twenty years on a plinth at New Sarum. Jack did a deal with the Air Force which concerned his DC-7 being used as a transport aircraft. She was rebuilt by Engineers at Afretair with unofficial help from Air Force personel, and flew again in 1980. She crashed with Jack on board in March 1982. Officially the crash was caused by a thunderstorm, but others calim that he was shot down by a SAM 7 fired by the Zimbabwe Army.

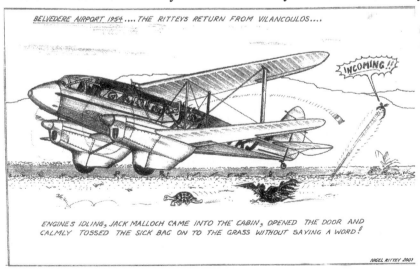

BELVEDERE AIRPORT 1954....THE RITTEYS RETURN FROM VILANCOULOS....

INCOMING !!!

ENGINES IDLING, JACK MALLOCH CAME INTO THE CABIN, OPENED THE DOOR AND CALMLY TOSSED THE SICK BAG ON TO THE GRASS WITHOUT SAYING A WORD !

NIGEL RITTEY 2001

Bulawayo in the 50'ies by Stanley R. Maiden

When I received a honourable discharge from The Royal Air Force in 1952 in England, my wife and I made plans to immigrate to Rhodesia. My wife's parents had immigrated there two years earlier. They were living at Turk Mine, a small community 40 miles from Bulawayo. Her father worked with the ESC, The Electric Supply Commission. Arriving in Bulawayo late October 1952 via Union Castle Ship, "Capteown Castle" at Cape Town, followed by a 3 day train journey to Bulawayo, we were met by her parents. I had promise of employment in my contract to work for Rhodesia Railways . At this time my wife was eight & half months pregnant with our first child.!! We spent the first few days with her parents at Turk Mine, following which I returned to Bulawayo to report to Rhodesia Railways offices to commence work.

My "single living quarters" were supplied and supervised by Rhodesia Railways at minimum monthly rental. I recall the area was called "Railton Single Quarters" .

Close by was the cafe/restaurant. It was there, as I was having a meal, I suddenly remembered I needed to contact the hospital, "The Lady Rodwell". I knew that with my wife's forthcoming checking into the hospital for the birth of our first child; it was about two weeks later after our arrival in Bulawayo late October. I called the hospital to confirm my wife's admittance to see if she had as yet been admitted.

A nurse answered my phone call. This was November 13, 1952. I enquired if Mrs. Elma Maiden had been admitted yet. The reply......

"Congratulations, Mr. Maiden, you have a son!"

One memory I have never forgotten was this. I dropped everything, phone included, raced out of the restaurant and grabbed/ the first bicycle available and rode the six miles to the "Lady Rodwell Hospital" to see my firstborn whom we named "Wayne".

During our 10 years in Bulawayo we were blessed with two more sons, Paul, in 1954 and Daryl in 1956. They were both born at the Mater Dei Hospital in Bulawayo. Our last address in Bulawayo was 47 Hampshire Drive, Hillcrest, Bulawayo.

1962 following my promotion to Driver 1st. Class, I was transferred to Northern Rhodesia , as it was known at that time, to a small community named Choma. In 1964, we immigrated to the United States where I entered Abilene Christian College in Abilene, Texas. I began full time preaching in 1966 in various parts of the United States. In 1995, I stepped down from full time preaching and now serve as one of twelve elders with a congregation of the Churches of Christ in Springfield, Missouri. The most important event in my life during my 10 years in Bulawayo was this: I became a Christian in August 1958. Rhodesia was a great country I will never forget.

Drifting by Mike Beresford

Let the wind blow my thoughts where it will,
Let them drift on the clouds in the sky.
Let me close my eyes and find calm in this world,
Serene as a river that quietly flows by.

Bring back to good times, the joy and the laughter,
When we sang for no reason but singing,
When tomorrow was just a new day coming after'
The good day in which we were living.

Give me the mountains I climbed in the sun,
And the rivers I rambled through forested glades,
The strength that was mine at the time I was young,
When promises given were promises made.

Let me sail once again on Kariba's blue waters,
With the honk of the hippo and fish eagle calls.
Let God find a place for His sons and his daughters,
Where they will find peace when the cloak of night falls.

Give me time with a loved one with whom I can share,
All hopes and the depths of my dreams.
And we shed our concerns with the ghost of despair
And discover what life really means.

I welcome my memories of those good times past,
For they tell me that life's not a lie,
That I'm here for a reason and as long as I last,
There's a promise as great as the African sky.

"We have also had our land taken from us!"
photograph by Steve Bailey

"Ambush" by Chris Higginson extract 'Reluctant Assassin 1'

I'm lying now in the baking heat and sighting down the way
I've time in hand to now repeat what happened yesterday
How terrorists, they came into, that peaceful country kraal
And killed and raped and pillaged there, to keep their kin in thrall

They must have come soon after dawn before their prey had risen
And lighted bits of grasses torn from now their victim's prison
Then tossed the burning bits of straw upon their kinfolk's huts
And gunned those down, who would escape, with shattered bone and guts

The children's heads were smashed upon that central ancient tree
Where tribal elders used to sit, to argue then agree
There must have been lack of control they killed like rabid dogs
Madness was their frenzied goal like savage boar or hogs

But animals stoop not this low this is a human trait
To victimise the helpless so survivors can narrate
To others, what the cost is of non co-operation
The villagers were caught between the forces of the nation

It has been so through history, this con-trol of the lands
The Cossacks came in hoards from East, with savage warlike bands
The settlers of America, declared a war on those
Who had been there before them, with guns and clubs and blows

The English herded Boers into the camps then burned their farms
The Romans ruled the then known world, with fear and force of arms
The Eastern countries too have had their rule by dynasty
There seems not to be any where from violence we are free

And so I lie in ambush state, to kill this latest crowd
Of killers who will meet their fate, so then I can be proud
To join the line of slayers, that stretch back in my past
In one more little incident, in which I have been cast

"Looking Back and Forward" by Mike Beresford

I was born in Africa and its seasons shaped my soul,
I knew my place beneath the sun, the warm earth made me whole,
Those arching skies and brilliant stars fixed my position there,
That brooding space my boundary, the far horizons clear.
I belonged to Africa and knew no other home,
I had no wish to leave her and no wish to roam.
The heat, the storms, the droughts were all familiar scenes to me,
The hills, the plains, the valleys and the bronzed Msasa trees.

It's tempting to resist my fate, to look back and complain
At the stealing of my birthright, and who, or what, to blame,
At the loss of those I loved and knew and the places I have known.
Nine tenths of life is travelled but the rest is moving on.
Regrets and blame are for the past and I must walk the track
That takes me on this journey, where there is no turning back,
I must embrace the changes that old England holds for me
And see the old with eyes anew where I was meant to be.

There is beauty here in England and it's steeped in history,
It's the land of both my parents and my ancient ancestry.
So I must look beyond the dross and open up new doors,
And blend my life that's yet to come with what has gone before.
I do not have to be there to hear the Hueglin's song,
It lives forever in my mind where memories belong.
When I sail through the sunset, the truth will set me free!
' Take me out of Africa - but leave Africa in me'

Wedding Charter by anon

I am reminded of one particular trip on an Air Rhodesia Dak, in the very early 70's. My wife's best friend was still living in Blantyre then when she decided to get permanently hitched. There was a good size contingent of guests, mostly the young and poor like me, all from Salisbury and all wondering how the hell we could get to Blantyre on the cheap and in double quick time.

A scheduled flight on Air Rhodesia/Air Malawi Viscounts was too costly, and driving was out. I took myself off to the Air Rhodesia Head Office, introduced myself to the lass at the desk, and asked if I could, "Please charter a Dak to fly to Blantyre to attend a wedding pissup on a Saturday afternoon, and be back in time for sebenza on Monday morning."

The lass went to speak to the bwana who came out and said - sure thing young man, sign here.

I then scrambled to find the loot from the 27 other piss artists, which I achieved that same day, and just at first light on the appointed Saturday morning, our group was airborne heading for Blantyre in a throaty Dak.

I had not really read the small print in the contract - the paragraph that stated that a full service bar was included in the price. Bring it on baby, and by the time we landed at Chileka some 2.5 hours later, the party poured off the plane and into a fleet of cars belonging to people who had offered to accommodate us for the night.

The Air Rhodesia Crew was invited as part of the party of course, and the festivities carried on very late into the night.

On the Sunday late afternoon, the visitors were dropped back off at Chileka for the 2.5 hour pissup at 10,000 feet back to Bright lights, and we all made it back to work on Monday, on time, serious babalaas notwithstanding.

The Mushroom Stew from Stu Grover

I wish to recount a true incident which took place in the late 70's in Que Que

For those of you who know this area well, you will remember that as you left QQ on the way to Redcliff and Gwelo there was a residential area on the left as you were leaving the outskirts of the town. It was here that there were 2 bachelors who shared a house and who enjoyed the good things in life - Beer - Braai's and watching Saturday rugby.

One such Saturday after making the necessary purchases for the forthcoming Saturday afternoon they proceeded back to their dwelling to prepare for the afternoon's rugby followed by a braai. 'Que Que ites' will remember just after the rains there were always 'locals' on the side of the road who would sell you a bucket of fresh wild mushrooms for about 2 dollars. Thinking that these would be an added treat for the day they purchased a bucket of said mushrooms and continued home.

On arrival it was decided that they would cook up the mushrooms and eat them as snacks whilst watching the game. During the cooking of the mushrooms consideration was given to whether these were in fact mushrooms, or whether they could in fact be poisonous toadstools. They decided that it was better to play it safe they completed the cooking of the now undecided items, and then they placed a portion of it in the dog's dish. They instructed the house boy to keep an eye on the dog and let them know if anything happened.

Beers were opened and they proceeded to watch rugby. At half time they were assured the dog was still in good health so they dished up a goodly portion of mushrooms each, restocked themselves with refreshments, and continued to watch the 2nd half of the rugby.

Just before the end of the game the house boy came running in and informed them the dog was dead. Without even a thought they dashed out into the car and off to casualties. They explained the situation to the nurse on duty and they were admitted and placed I, a ward and had their stomachs pumped out. They were kept under observation for the night and then as there appeared to be no more complications they were then released on Sunday morning.

Arriving home in a weak but 'happy to be alive' state they decided that they should at least do something for their dog.

They asked the house boy where the dog was, only to be informed,

"Baas, eet is still next to the road where the car ran it over! "

Sweet Potatoes With Orange by Audrey

6 Servings

This vegetable is excellent served with Pork or Lamb. It can be prepared well in advance and baked just before serving.

1 kg unpeeled sweet potatoes, scrubbed.

4T (60ml) butter

1 ½ T (225 Ml) custard powder

½ cup (125ml) brown sugar

1 cup (250ml) freshly squeezed orange juice

1 tot orange liqueur or 2 t (10ml) orange essence

1 t (5ml) grated orange rind

1 T (15ml) lemon juice

½ t (2.5ml) salt

Boil the sweet potatoes in their jackets until done. Cool, slice.

Arrange slices in a buttered, ovenproof dish.

Make a sauce by melting the butter. Blend the custard with sugar and add to the butter. Mix well with a wooden spoon.

Add the orange juice. Simmer until smooth.

Add the liqueur, rind, lemon juice and salt. Stir and simmer.

Pour the sauce over the sweet potatoes in the dish.

Pre- preparation can be done to this stage.

Bake at 150C (350deg F) for 30 minutes and serve.

Kwe Kwe Vryheid Farm by Franci

Dusk falls gently onto churning dust that dances this way & that.

Flickering lights from a million fire flies show the herd of cattle their way home.

Heads down, milling, bellowing cows return to the kraal, anxious to find calves left behind.

Jumping about on wobbly legs calves rush forward to be nuzzled by a wet nose with a familiar smell or merely pushed aside.

The faithful old herdsman stands a while, content that all is well.

He closes the gate and slowly makes his way home for his evening meal.

"My Ouma" by John Theron

My grandparents trekked to Rhodesia pre 1920s and I would like to have a story of my gran's included if appropriate. Their surname was Kriek and they moved onto a farm called "Girlie's-dale" in Enkeldoorn where they had a large herd of cattle.

The rindepest wiped out their herd and Oupa Kriek walked from Enkeldoorn to Salisbury to look for a job.

He got a message through to Gran to say that he'd found a job building the prison in Umtali and that she was to take their kids in the wagon and meet him there. She loaded up the family and had just one helper to lead the oxen.

She had three daughters 8, 7 & 2 plus her baby son.

Gran says that one evening on the trek they came to a 'spruit' (small stream) and she thought it would be a good place to spend the night as there was grazing there for the oxen. She stopped slightly past the spruit and she was sitting on the tail gate of the ox wagon when an impi of Matabele came running down the road towards them and stopped about 20 metres away.

By then Gran had a grasp of the black lingo and even though she was concerned to be a woman on her own in the middle of nowhere.

She called the impi leader to approach her.

He came about halfway forward and she asked him if he knew that she had died and come back to life.

He scoffed at the idea.

She said, "This is true!"

He scoffed again, so she said, "If I want I can take my leg off and put it here beside me, or I can take my eye out and put it back again!"

He thought this was funny but still scoffed at her words.

She said, "No, this is true! I can even take my teeth out!"

She then removed her false teeth.

That was the last she saw of them.

My Gran's party proceeded safely to Umtali.

"A Quiet Chat" by Diane Stucke.

I used to work at the Veterinary Research Station on the Borrowdale Road, which was not far from the Horse Race Track. My father was a trainer there and we were both involved in the racing activities at the track. We had many visitors who used to arrive to order and collect vaccines for their farm animals, and I got to know some of them quite well.

While the orders were being prepared they would sit on the desk in my office and we would chat about subjects, usually relating to farming matters. There was one gentleman I remember in particular. He was a quiet, modest man and he would wait patiently, like all the others for his order to be filled.

I would make him a cup of tea, and we would chitchat about the weather, labour problems and the difficulties that sanctions were creating for the farmers who were doing their best to feed the growing population.

I often think back to that time, and wonder how many other Prime Ministers in the world today would come into an office the way he did, with no bodyguards and security and join the queue without any pretence of self importance.

From the KK Dictionary by S E Aitken-Cade (1953)

DRUM, n. — ngoma. K.K. ngoma. Very noticeable over the week-end. Properly sterilized these percussion instruments make fine sundowner tables. The more sundowner tables the less noise from the compound.

FORGET, vb .tr — kuriarwa, kukanganwa. K.K. kashewa. One of the most common excuses for the non-execution of tasks. "Why haven't you washed the dishes?" "Ini in daba wena aikona gezile maplates?" "I forget." "Mena kashewili."

OLD, adj. – sharuka. K.K. madala. "Where is my old coat?" "Upi lo madala bachi gamina?" – "Well tell the cook to bring it back!" "Longilli, chella lo cook yena pendusa yena!"

MILE, n. – Try to express distance in terms of time. Along the main roads it is possible to indicate distance by mile posts, but in general you should figure out the distance as at three miles per hour. Or less!

Memories of Falcon – by Colin Bewes

I went to Falcon in 1975 on a minor scholarship from Springvale, as did my brother Nick two years before me in 1973. If we had not had the scholarships I doubt we would have gone to Falcon as my folks were not that well off.

Anyway, I was unusually put into a different house to Nick - he was in Oates and I was in Hervey this was at the request of my parents, who cannily predicted that this would ensure that I would not have someone else to fight my battles in the same house. As it turned out, I got teased quite badly at Falcon but by my final years my parents' strategy had paid off and I think I am stronger for it now.

My first week at Falcon was the usual junior's journey of unknowns, having arrived exhausted surviving the overnight train from Salisbury, finding out who was your friend, who was your foe, and who to avoid altogether, finding out that everything your brother had told you about discipline, chores, pointless exercises etc was absolutely correct discovering all of a sudden that your prefect (Creswell) kept snakes in his study and thought it was hilarious to dangle a Yellow-belly an inch from your face as you tried to concentrate on your Wilbur Smith during afternoon rest. One of the odd things I noticed straight away was that those in Form 2 who had already done a year at Falcon were somehow regarded as a cut above us Johny-come-latelies – both by the seniors and by themselves ....compensation, I guess, for the fact that they had missed out on a year at the top of the pile at their junior schools!

Charlie

What made my first week or two at Falcon a lifelong memory was the night when, just after lights out, Head of Hervey, Mike Renahan, came into the dorm and did a fine job fielding questions and answers about Falcon in general until the subject of Charlie came up. As Renahan explained, Charlie was a miner who was a bit of a sour puss, but he did have an attractive wife. Apparently he had found out that someone, McKenzie (or some Scottish name) had been having it away with his wife. When he confronted the culprit he was thrown down the mine shaft for his pains. It did not end there because Charlie survived the fall, but broke his leg and, being thus immobilised, expired eventually through starvation. The leg break explained why a dragging noise could be heard when Charlie was about in the house corridors and his motivation for haunting (especially) the junior dorms was to find and be revenged on any descendants of McKenzie. The precise name is probably lost by now because the cops would often change it to fit one of the new juniors at the beginning of the new school year. They would also, of course, impersonate Charlie with admirable realism (looking back). Anyway, after Mike Renahan had explained most of the story about Charlie, someone in my dorm asked,

"If Charlie spent all that time down the mine shaft, can you smell him if he's coming close to our dorm?"

Mike's reply was simply, "Yeah, Charlie stinks..."

He did not get any further because there was an earth tremor that lasted about 10 seconds. Naturally, this was capitalised on by Mike and the result was that not many of us in that Hervey junior dorm got ,much in the way of sleep that night. Every sound - mostly those from the loo cisterns nearby - was magnified, and I think there was at least one attempt at impersonation ...or was there?

Building Hervey's gardens

I forget which particular misdemeanour we were all guilty of in my second year at Falcon, but there was a concerted effort to develop the Hervey gardens, which consisted of three main tasks, namely:

- putting gravel on all the pathways this was achieved by sending all those on balck marks or fatigues to the quarry below the laundry with wheelbarrows to load and cart slate gravel back to Hervey.

- building up a terrace below the junior dorms of Hervey. There was quite a lot of hardcore we were able to use left over from building work on the lower VIth study block, but there was also an huge amount of soil that had to be put there and levelled off. I forget where this came from, but you can guess which group of pupils had to shift it into shape!

- grassing over and nurturing the lawn on the junior dorm terrace. Sowing the lawn was the easy bit. Encouraging it to turn into a proper lawn took a lot longer, involving hundreds of black marks' worth. I think in the end the cops gave up the pretence and went on about house duty etc to justify all the hard labour. I particularly remember coming up with cunning watering devices to make the process more efficient - e.g. a series of plastic drinks bottles pierced with a geometric design to achieve the right spread of water. As it was quite thick plastic and the piercing tool was my compass, you had to pierce at precisely the angle you wanted the water to come out. The result was pretty acceptable as we used that lawn for sleeping out and also for more than one end of year house party. House parties were a highlight of the year that most people looked forward to the first few I remember were at the swimming pool, so the usual braai was combined with various pool-related games or mucking about. The last one I had was on the Hervey junior dorm lawn / terrace and the braai was topped off by various musical interludes ...John Hopkins came up with a guitar from somewhere. I think it must have been a general policy towards 1977/78/79 that evening activities outside the security fence would be asking for trouble and of course the pool was very much outside.

I can't remember exactly when the security fence went up, but it must have been in 1977/78 when the war was getting pretty serious. Must have been about 10 to 12 foot high and surrounded the entire school except for, as mentioned before, the swimming pool (don't remember the lower part of it that well, but would imagine it included the laundry, stores and squash courts too). I guess it must have been more of a visual deterrent which, combined with the presence of the army camp a mile down the road, must have been enough to put the opposition off the idea of attacking the school. Certainly, it was no deterrent to us and any FOB who lived inside that fence must surely remember climbing over it to engage in one illegal activity or other, myself included.

The War

Despite being willing to climb over the security fence, the war was never that far from my mind in my time at Falcon. Most at Falcon in the mid to late 70s had brothers or other close relatives involved in the security forces and, of course many came from farming families whose homes and lifestyle carried great risk. My brother Nick was in BSAP Ground Coverage in the late 70s and my father did a lot of flying to remote airstrips until his untimely death in August 1977 as well as worrying about relatives, we were daily reminded of the war when reading the Chronicle during the after lunch break occasionally, announcements in assembly or at dinner really brought it home to us as boys we had known were reported killed - Bruce Burrell, an all-rounder and head or captain of everything worth leading at both Springvale and Falcon was the announcement I especially remembered. Less impact, but remembered all the same were the deaths of Gordon MacLachlan (his younger brother Andy was in my dorm) and the first Viscount disaster, in which, Brenda, the sister of Grant Pearson, another dorm-mate, died. Whilst boys at schools in peaceful countries might have talked in their spare time about football and girls, current affairs loomed large for us at Falcon in the 1970s. Consequently I often worried about the possibility of an attack on the school and what would I do if it happened.

Cadets

Some of the best times many of us had was in the Lower VI, playing soldiers in Cadets. The idea of being drilled by various masters was immediately funny to most of us, but it did have its benefits; for example, if you liked guns you got to do some free shooting and to learn how to use an FN 7.62 Nato rifle – the best part of this of course was doing 'Jungle lane' in the mine dumps, walking slowing along one of the river courses next to a mine dump followed by our instructors who would activate the target boards. Equally enjoyable was the mountaineering module, in which we all learnt to abseil and climb, which worked out fine for most of us until the day that one of our number disturbed a wasps nest on the way down the quarry we had been driven to. The highlight of Cadets came at the end of the year when were kitted up and were given our co-ordinates with which to map-read our way to Cadet Camp in the Mullangwani Hills. I really don't know how we managed to get there since the map-reading skills of my stick leader got us to a point where the landmarks we were expecting to see did not exist (aka lost!). Our radio procedure was not much better but I guess it saved us a cold night in the bush. The camp was run in 1978 by a tough cookie called Gus Henderson; there is some debate between Tim Sinclair and I over whether he was ex-US Marines or ex-Paras, but his provenance is immaterial – suffice to say, he appeared to know his subject well. The ultimate evidence of this came one afternoon when Gus demonstrated how to shoot an MAG from the hip. Having pointed out a small area on a distant hill as his target, Gus proceeded to tear up the bush on said hill and achieve an amazingly tight grouping …which was extremely fortunate, for he had not been firing many seconds before a very agitated figure was seen to scramble, leap and generally exit the target area at high speed down the side of the hill. This turned out to be Clive Elworthy (Oates 79) who had lost his wristwatch on the hill during the morning's skirmishing exercise.

Girls at Falcon

Actually, it's not strictly true that girls were a rare object of discussion at Falcon. In 1976 or 1977 the College was blessed with the presence of some of the bravest girls on the planet Louise Menashe, Felicity Taylor, Joy-Anne Cox, Margi Goodburn, Catherine Stewart and one other. Whatever they did, wherever they went, whatever they said became the subject of gossip around the school, including, of course, rumours of which lucky boys might have been making 'progress' with any of them. There was always an invisible line that had to be crossed if you decided to interact in any way with this minority. The 'line' was the risk that your motives for talking to, smiling at, looking at any of the girls might be mis-interpreted by the rumour-mongers for example, if you talked to them, were you trying to make out? If you looked at one of them, was it the one generally considered to be the most attractive or least attractive etc for example, (I can confess it now!) I had a particular attraction to Joy-Anne Cox, but I had to be very careful about admitting this to anyone because a few people had decided they did not like some aspects of Joy-Anne's appearance, and admitting an attraction to her could therefore make you an object of derision yourself. All in all, a bit of a nightmare, but more for them than for us, as I found out many years later when I met Felicity Taylor and Margi Goodburn at FOB events. I am told that Joy-Anne did very well for herself after Falcon and those who knew her confirmed what a really nice person she is!

Violence under the stars

One of the few privileges allowed to us when no-one had misbehaved recently was the practice of sleeping under the stars. The metalwork beds used by everyone up until Form IV were easily transportable from the dorms to the house gardens and it was an absolute joy to be able to gaze at the stars on a cloudless night whilst listening to LM Radio on your earphones, eating saved-up tuck etc.

Of course, you could also position your bed next to that of your friends and talk the night away with them, shutting up occasionally when a passing prefect barked for peace and quiet. This was fine most of the time, but on one occasion one of my dorm-mates carried it a bit far and, as well as keeping the noise levels up, decided to start chucking stones my way. I think it was Richard Bates but it's probably a good thing that I can't remember exactly who it was, because I eventually lost my rag and went over and hammered the face of the culprit with my right fist. Stupidly, I really did use a hammer action and, although gratified to see two beautiful black eyes on my victim's face the next day, I also spent a night of extreme discomfort and, after a visit to 'the San', it became apparent that I had broken my hand. This was double punishment because it happened just weeks before I sat my 'O' Levels - as you can imagine, writing them was excruciating, though, I don't think it affected my results luckily.

Brandy - Hong Kong style

If you asked the right questions and knew the right people and, most importantly, those people thought they could trust you not to blab your mouth off, there were a number of ways in which to procure illegal substances such as cigarettes (not a priority for me as I was only ever a 'social' smoker) and booze, e.g. Ouzo, Brandy or whatever spirits were available in Rhodesia at the time. The method was simple. On a certain day of the week (Tuesdays I think), a minibus drove to Bulawayo to transport various musical types to receive lessons from their respective teachers. At least one of these pupils would, with co-operation no doubt bought from the driver, divert on the way back to an establishment that sold the requisite goods. Then an unscheduled stop was made on the way back, just after the airfield, in order to cache the haul for later recovery. The one and only time I made use of this procurement facility was when a group of us from Hervey had planned a Saturday bush exeat and decided that brandy would make a very good mixer for the bottles of Coke we had bought for the occasion. My 'wholesaler' was Abo Davies, and, true to his word, he delivered up our order of 4 bottles of locally made brandy.

The location of the bush exeat remains a somewhat hazy 'north-west' of the College, but needless to say, it was sufficiently removed from the risk of meeting anyone who might give us away. Our 'party' started at around 10.00 a.m. and went on 'til 5.00 p.m. I don't remember much between the hours of 12 noon and 4.30 p.m. but I was told later that I had been doing cartwheels down the side of the hill on which we were carousing. I guess the magic ingredient was the concept of Brandy & Coke, Hong Kong style ....one of our number had recently returned from a holiday in Hong Kong and insisted that over there the measure was one part Coke to seven parts brandy. Naturally we all thought this was an excellent concept and adopted it for the day. When we eventually staggered back through the College gates I was sure Mr McQuade ('Curly')had spotted my less-than-coordinated demeanour, judging by the quizzical look he gave us as he drove in, but fortunately we did not receive a summons from him. The thumping headache I had later, which forced me to abandon the Saturday night movie, was punishment enough!

Incidentally, during my last year, there was a strong rumour doing the rounds that on one of the Army's first aid demos, someone had made a deal involving the supply of drip kits, because these were found to work wonders for those suffering from bad hangovers! Tim Sinclair knows more about this!

Afternoon Tea at DET's

One of the best friends I made at Falcon was Guy Turner. Being the headmaster's son, this opened quite a few doors closed to most. For instance, there were many visits to the Turner household in which Guy and I engaged in pellet gun shooting in his garden (the G'way birds were a particular target!), handling what I presume was DET's Sten gun, putting the world to rights generally and - at 4 p.m. sharp on those afternoons we happened to be there, enjoying Earl Grey tea and cake, courtesy of Mrs Turner.

If not at Guy's home, I spent a lot of time in his study, again either putting the world to rights or trying to work out the answers to Twik Van Wyk's maths assignments - Guy was rather more clued up than I was in Pure & Applied Maths and the 'team' homework sessions probably benefited me more than Guy. There was also a time when Guy tried and failed to teach me guitar, but the less said about that the better. More memorable perhaps were the occasional forays into the junior dorms on Friday nights to instigate pillow / water / tieflick fights.

Friendship with Guy led to an introduction to one of the sons of Twik Van Wyk, who was in the year above us. Dave (??) Van Wyk had developed a cottage industry using a slats of metal that had seen previous use in the railways plus a lathe and a few other choice tools. Like many others I put in my order for an oversize Bowie knife with its 12-inch blade. Dave did a fantastic job, with handle finished off in brass and leather. Only problem was, I never really had a use for this monster of a weapon so only ever used it to impress friends and girlfriends. It also needed a lot of maintenance since the blade was not stainless steel!

Coffee Cigarettes

In my last year at Falcon I became a prefect 'by default' when Johnny Marais was de-copped for nearly setting the stage alight whilst smoking in the ceiling of the assembly hall.

As prefect, I was put in charge of the Hervey lower sixth block - not a problem as far as the main block was concerned, but next to my study were three recently converted studies in which resided the 'criminal Christophers' - Chris Hughes, Chris Hart and Chris Matthews. These three were dyed in the wool rebels, prone to taking literally ANY opportunity to drink, smoke or generally misbehave. At the same time, they were all three very genuine and likeable people. My dilemma therefore was in deciding how to keep some semblance of order in the lower sixth block. It did not take me long to realise that I was never going to change Chris, Chris and Chris, so after the first couple of occasions when I caught them smoking in their studies, I sat them all down and came to an 'accommodation' with them the essence of the unwritten agreement was that I would help them to keep out of trouble (e.g. the prefect's greater 'mobility' gave me earlier and more accurate warning of approaching housemasters or unsympathetic College prefects). In return, my three potential troublemakers undertook to exercise greater discretion than they might otherwise have done, especially whilst in the lower sixth block. Surprisingly this arrangement worked very well and I ended the year with very few embarrassments and good friends with the three Chris's.

Occasionally I engaged in a little 'social' smoking with the three Chris's I remember one Friday night when, having nothing much else to do, we experimented with making cigarettes out of paper and coffee, and a few other substances. Sadly - since we had a plentiful supply of coffee grounds - the experiments were a complete failure the coffee did not burn that well and the taste was not that great. Oh well, enquiring minds!

Perfect learning environment

One of the enduring legacies of having gone to Falcon was the quality of teaching staff. Sure enough, some of the teachers were quirky, but somehow they managed to bring out the best in you...

- Ike Stewart's passion for history kept me enthralled at the subject to the point where revising the finer points of the Napoleonic wars was actually fun, and I still remember a lot of it!

- Twik Van Wyk's dry humour and equally dry teaching style was certainly a challenge I think his comment to me of "Bewes, you are never going to pass Pure & Applied Maths" was just the goad I needed to pass that 'A' Level, and the lessons spent desperately trying to understand the advanced scribbles on the blackboard were interspersed with moments of high comedy - once I was gazing absently out the window as Mrs Marais walked across the lawn when suddenly Twik was twisting my ear backwards and offhandly quizzing me, "Bewes, you never seen Mrs Marais before?"

- the late 'Batman' Prentice, whose disabilities provoked many a mean under-breath jibe from most of us, but whose teaching was every bit as high as the Falcon standard.

- Anne Hoole must have done her head in keeping us in order but she certainly brought the Shakespeare and Hardy, even Joseph Conrad to life even now, if ever Far From the Madding Crowd, Taming of the Shrew or Romeo & Juliet (the Zeffirelli version of course) is on the TV, I find myself irresistibly drawn to watching it again. If the films of these books were not in the School Movie programme, Anne made sure we saw them one way or another and, equally, made sure we knew what licence the film director may have taken.

- Ashby, teaching 'A' Level Economics, made the subject truly interesting and taught the subject well enough to last a lifetime, reinforcing this with persuasive exhortations to read The Economist from cover to cover ...I still find myself asking the same questions when I read that magazine!

- and DET ....even in the rebelliousness of teenage years, I think all of us recognised the excellence of his teaching in fact, for me, admiration of DET's thinking made me anticipate his annual prize-giving speeches all the more keenly - and they are still some of the best features of the Falcon Magazines of the 1970s.

As well as having fine teachers, the environment itself was highly conducive to learning naturally, the fact that Falcon was a boarding school was an enormous factor in this but my memories of revising for 'A' Levels testify to deliberate policies that worked in our favour. In the 6-8 weeks leading up to 'A' Level exams, we found that we were given increasing amounts of free periods, designed to allow us time to absorb what we needed to in order to pass and excel in the exams. Having the responsibility for revision shoved squarely on our shoulders (with subtle prodding and occasional checkups) seemed to do the trick thus we were able to plan days that started with an early morning swim an hour or two of intensive revision an hour or two of light revision catching rays at the swimming pool - maybe revising with a friend a cross-country run perhaps one or two lessons in which to be further drilled in the main areas we needed to cover for the exam all rounded off by an evening of mixed revision and socialising - or sometimes just the socialising if enough progress had been made!

Thank you Falcon.

"Rogues and Scroungers" by Chris Cooke.

I have very vivid memories of going to Beira every Rhodes and Founders. This was a special time for me, as, not only was it going to be a glorious 4 or 5 days by the beach camping in Dad's canvas bell tent, but it was also my birthday (July 12).

I remember the excitement starting as we set off in the car for Umtali. The holiday really started when we stopped at a lay-by at dawn, and out would come the primus stove, which Dad would pump up, while Mum produced the bacon and eggs. We would gleefully gobbled all this down while waving to cars passing us 'enroute' to the same destination. I also remember arriving at the Pungwe river where we would drive onto the pontoon, which was then pulled across by some very strong men.

'Doctor Jim Kennedy of Ndanga' by Doctor Bob Doy

Extract from A Doctor's Odyssey - Memories of a Guy's Man (ISBN 1-4137-4735-3)

I spent almost 15 years in Rhodesia as part of a lifetime in the practice of medicine around the world. My experiences are contained in my book mentioned above.

I have devoted five chapters of the book to Ndanga, which was a district of 7500 square miles and a population (then) of around 300,000 people. I was the sole doctor for these people from 1960-1964. A predecessor was Dr. Jim Kennedy and it is he who deserves to be remembered in this book of Rhodesian Memories. I am enclosing a few relevant excerpts that I will be happy for you to include.

"The second doctor stayed even longer, from 1932 until he was compulsorily retired in 1959 and my immediate predecessor appointed. His name was Jim Kennedy, the man who created Ndanga and who made it, and himself, a legend in his lifetime. A history of Ndanga or a biography of Dr. Kennedy, they must be almost synonymous, would be richly rewarding and perhaps one day, when Zimbabwe has rediscovered the importance of its past in its present, they may be written.

Jim Kennedy was a man of great energy and drive and found that he was unable to work within the narrow confines of the hospital as he found it. He soon had the staff and local people extending it by building rows of Kimberley brick, thatched huts, each twelve feet square, until the place looked like a large African kraal.

He believed that his patients would feel more at home in familiar surroundings with their relatives, and he used the force of his personality and presence to persuade entire families to be admitted. He also had another motive for doing this; he believed, I am sure rightly, that all the local inhabitants needed treatment for something or other, be it sepsis, chronic malaria, bilharziasis, worms, malnutrition, or any one of a host of other ailments with which the population was afflicted. He would thus take the opportunity of giving various members of the family whatever treatment he thought their particular case merited while he had them at the hospital. Even when a standard-pattern District hospital was eventually built with permanent materials Jim refused to use it for its designated purpose. Feeling as he did that his people would prefer their familiar way of life to sleeping in beds in communal wards with non-family members, the new hospital was used solely as a, largely empty, store-house.

Travelling the district

However, he did not confine himself solely to hunting on these expeditions.

If he came to a fairly populous area with numerous kraals in the vicinity and decided that they needed a hospital there, he would persuade the people to build one. It would consist of the usual Kimberley brick and thatch huts with three additional huts a short distance away where he could stay when visiting. The perimeter of all the hospitals, including Ndanga itself, was marked by an edging of large stones and at the rural hospitals a double line of similar stones enclosed a path leading to the "doctor's house."

All these stones and the bottom three feet of the huts were regularly whitewashed and the covering had become so thick over the years that the Public Works Officer in Fort Victoria delighted in showing me a fragment from a corner of one of the huts that at first glance could be mistaken for part of a tibia!

As he had neither permission nor funds with which to build these rural hospitals, Jim paid for the labour with salt. This was an interesting throwback to the times when salt was used as currency - the word salary is derived from the Latin word for salt. How he explained the enormous consumption of salt and whitewash and the continuing rise in the consumption of medical supplies I never discovered, but either through indifference or incompetence at Head Office he got away with it for years.

By the end of his time he built nine rural hospitals but when I took over one had been absorbed by a neighbouring district and one had been handed over to a mission hospital, leaving seven as part of the Ndanga hospital complex. Having built the hospitals he had to provide access to them, at least from Ndanga, and so he had tracks carved out of the bush and kept open for wheeled vehicles. Thus he was the first person to open up that part of the country to communication and his roads eventually appeared on the maps and were taken over and maintained by the District Administration.

Since neither the hospitals nor the patients in them existed officially, he was unable to draw rations for them and patients had to supply their own food while in hospital. This was often inadequate; under-nutrition was one of the conditions requiring treatment and so Jim combined his hunting activities with the feeding of his patients.

He once confided to me that he had killed eight hundred and fifty buffaloes during his twenty-seven years at Ndanga (which works out at one every eleven days) and bitterly regretted that he hadn't been able to make it a thousand! Eventually, of course, the Ministry of Health had no option but to recognise the status quo and take the rural hospitals on to the establishment and staff and equip them.

This then was the unit I was to take charge of to the best of my ability: a District hospital and seven rural hospitals providing medical care for around three hundred thousand people and occupying an area of about seven thousand five hundred square miles...

...Jim was not merely a product of Empire, he was the sort who built empires. A man in the stamp of Clive, Raffles and Rhodes.

An imposing figure of a man, an unselfconscious, arrogant racist who believed in the supremacy of all things British.

Not for him the racism of the Nazi or the Afrikaaner. Miscegenation might be beyond the pale but so was extermination or oppression.

He laboured long and selflessly in the service of those who were unfortunate enough to be inferior.

He ruled his kingdom by divine right, if not the divine right of kings then at the very least the divine right of being British..."

"I also need space for my family, please…..?"
Photograph from Steve Bailey

You know you are a Rhodesian... by 'anon'

You know you are a Rhodesian if you can still remember Sally Donaldson's voice on the radio, if you saw Grease four or five times and failed your driving license at least once. If you still wear trainers without socks, and horrify people by eating dried, raw meat. If you miss the smell of rain on a hot, tar road, and a whiff of red stoep (verandah) polish takes you back to Christmases by the pool and makes you long for a great, bed-rattling, window shaking, earth tremoring, all-kids-and-animals-in-the-parents-bed storm.

If you went to school in Zimbabwe you were taught real subjects like history and grammar and you are probably still convinced day scholars are pampered mommie's boys. You surely sang rude or witty words to hymns in school assembly and you are still absolutely certain your A-levels were harder than most first-year university courses today. And of course you know, or still write to, someone who went to Prince Edward, Saints, Falcon, Marymount, Peterhouse, Chaplin, Guinea Fowl, Churchill Umtali High School or Gwebi Agricultural College.

At your school, instead of being counselled, unruly students were beaten - and it worked. And it was no use complaining to your father, because he thought this was a good idea. Now you bore or frighten your children with harrowing tales of your deprived upbringing - when TV started at 17.00 hrs and kids were expected to ride push bikes to school.

Rhodesians have their own dialect. Traffic lights are robots, crocodiles 'flatdogs', while Koki pens are Neons to this day. What is this thing called polystyrene - you call it kaylite - and 'muush' is still part of your vocabulary - as is braai, kopje, fundi and lekker (translation - barbecue, hill, expert, nice, and by the way, 'muush' also means 'nice').

If you are a Rhodesian you know all about playing in sandpits and on jungle-gyms and you had avocado, mango, guava and paw-paw trees in your garden. You still remember the taste of gemsquash with melted butter, mealies and Mazoe Orange Juice, and yearn for bream fried on the side of a dam, five minutes after it was caught. You can still sing 'Ag Pleeze Daddy' and treasure Wrex Tarr's Chilapalapa LP's. Of course you still know the words of 'Cockie Lobbin' and all the Abba songs. You remember Jacaranda trees in bloom on Selous Avenue and own at least one ivory, soapstone or wooden carving.

You are an ex-Zimbo if you or someone very close to you did wheelies on the Enterprise Road outside Gremlins; lost some teeth, or worse, on the rockslide at Mermaid's Pool; spat from your bedroom window at the Monomatapa onto the pool deck, then ducked your head in quick. Or perhaps you injected Cane spirit into a pocket of oranges to beat the booze ban at the Rugby at Police Grounds - or sat at Castle Corner in the cricket grounds, then couldn't remember who won the match. You think the All Blacks are the Zimbabwe Tennis Team, and you recall carefree, noisy days at Lake Mac, before the hyacinth took over.

Rhodesians know how to drive on strip roads and most collected speeding tickets while racing to make the Beit Bridge border post by 6 pm. Remember the 'Coke' cans you collected on trips to South Africa, because they were so cool, and all that enthusiastic hooting and waving when you spotted another 'Rhodesian car while travelling 'down South, because the number plate said S... or B... or G'?

Old habits die hard so you still can't get your head around the idea of throwing away a glass Coke or beer bottle, instead of taking it back for the deposit. And you still find it hard to discard anything which, in your humble opinion, could be fixed. You hate washing your car and mowing the lawn, while ironing is something other people do.

It goes without saying that you've never carried your own golf clubs, and you think golf carts are for weaklings. When you hear crickets in July you immediately think of Christmas beetles and after an afternoon rain you expect to see chongololos plus a 'few' flying ants. You will never forget sitting for hours, sometimes days, in a petrol queue - and not getting any.

As a Rhodesian you used to believe that people in England and the USA, or wherever, had to be much better at everything than you were - until you visited those countries and found they were inhabited by ordinary beings living ordinary lives. So it wasn't too difficult to adapt to new circumstances, but it can be lonely.

Rhodesians still think the most haunting sound in the world is the cry of the fish eagle, and you long for the soft morning glow that brightens the Mashonaland sky between 5 and 6 am, and highlights the Msasa trees.

I hope, far-flung Rhodesians, you all have someone who also remembers...

Extract from KK dictionary (1953)

ONE, adj. – imwe. K.K. munya, wani. "One at a time, Gentlemen, please!" "Gena wani wani you momparas!"

Late Rains by Richard Fenner

I've trudged my way from Kariba   to the Portuguese border line
I've tracked through the Valley in summer's heat, with the stick in a skirmish line
I've humped my pack and my rifle,   and my ammo and canteens too
And I've sweated me dry 'neath the weighted sky when the rains are overdue

I've watched the mealie stalks turn to dust and the trees to a parchment brown
And the rivers shrink 'til the fish can't drink, and even the lions lie down
I've slogged through the kopjies rock by rock, scratched to bits by the bush and the thorn
While the birds just sit, and the cheetahs quit, in the face of a blazing morn

I've seen God's riches wither and die, seen might bleached down to bones
On a fruitless march to a waterhole to find that no-one's home
I've stumbled on crazy-paved earth where the rivulets used to flow
And trod shimmering rocks that melted my socks as the heat swelled from below

Heat that hammers at you like an anvil, Satan's fires raised on high
And all you can do is turn pleading eyes to a merciless, washed-out sky
In search of the slightest hint of a breeze, some sign of a brief respite
From the furnace that sucks at your very soul as you pray for the fall of night

I've staggered my way into evening   with a pebble inside my cheek
I've cursed the dust and the heat and the flies and my kit and my poor damned feet
And longed for the day when the noon grows dark, and the thunderheads storm and roil
When the lightning snakes, and the rainclouds break, and bring blessed end to this toil.

When in just a day, in its magic way, the bush starts to turn to green
As sap bursts back through the raindrop's touch, the most beautiful sight I've seen
And the zebras prance, and the daisies bloom, and the gnu dash to and fro
As the rains bring new life to Rhodesia's land - the most beautiful land I know.

Extract from **"At the Going Down of the Sun" by Charlie Warren BCR**

I joined the Rhodesian Light Infantry in June 1974, when I was 18. I don't know why I joined. I guess it was due to the fact that I was a rebel when I was young, and my mother always used to tell me that the army would sort me out.

I heard this so many times I wanted to crap in my rods.

Eventually after I matriculated in South Africa I went back to Zambia where my parents both owned good businesses and were established members of the horseracing fraternity in Kitwe. My Dad owned and trained a string of horses and stayed on a large plot in Garneton outside Kitwe. My Mom owned a swimming pool business in Kitwe. My folks got divorced and we, my brother and I, were sent to boarding school in South Africa.

We stayed with family on both sides and spent our lives being passed from pillar to post. In July 1970, Kevin, my brother, and I were up in Zambia on holiday. We had to have our teeth done at the dentist's in Kitwe before flying back to boarding school in SA. Anyhow the day came and we both had to be put under, as there was a lot of dentistry to be done. I was first and then Kevin.

I awoke from the anaesthetic to find that Kevin had been given the wrong drug by the anaesthetist and had died during the dentistry work. I was stunned and couldn't handle it.

I was sixteen at the time and he was fifteen.

I had gone the straight and narrow route until then and I don't know why I changed. But as time went by, I started drinking and smoking and rebelled against any authority and discipline. I was always in trouble at school and threatened anyone in authority with the worst and actually carried out some of my threats, although nothing was ever proved. I pranged cars, partied until all hours of the morning, spent a night or two in police cells (at the age of 17 - something I'm not proud of today) and caused great embarrassment to my parents.

During my travels through Rhodesia to Zambia one school holiday I happened to see a recruiting poster, advertising for the Rhodesian Army. I was finishing my Matric year and thought that this was the career move I wanted. Anyway this was put on the back burner and I kind of forgot about it, although I had already made enquiries about enlistment, and had asked the officer at the recruiting centre to send me some application forms to my school in SA. These duly arrived towards the end of my final year and when they did, I thought to myself

"Yeah right, as if I want to be stuffed around by some a*holes with a bit of power for the rest of my life, and to sleep in the rain and freeze in the cold and eat shitty army food, stand guard and lie awake in ambushes, shitting yourself, not knowing how many gooks were going to walk into your piss-willy ambush, whether they would kill you, or you would be killed, or one of your buddies would end up on the slab".

I promptly filed the application forms in my holiday suitcase and forgot about them.

On my last trip to Zambia on holiday to see my folks, I had packed everything in my suitcase and had put all my kit on top of the application forms. I got back to Kitwe and began seeing my buddies. The parties started and my Mom started telling me I was drinking too much and I should slow down and so on. One thing led to another and I started looking for work in Kitwe, but to no avail. I was young, white, and had no experience in anything. It was depressing. I needed a job to fund my partying. My folks were certainly not about to give me money to drink and smoke.

I was bored the one day and decided to go through my suitcase and sort out a few odds and ends, and there they were- those application forms. I pondered on these for a few days and eventually sat down and filled them in. I went for a medical with our family doctor who was dead against me signing up. He said Zambia and Rhodesia were having some ugly political problems and Zambia had closed its borders to Rhodesia. He told me that if the government found my application forms I could be jailed at 18 for treason. I went ahead with the medical anyway and gave one of my buddies the forms to post for me in Salisbury on his way to university in SA. I then forgot about the whole story.

I was getting flak from my Mom as I had gone back to partying on weekends in between fishing trips and hunting trips - with no thought or plans of any work. One day as I was nursing a rough hangover she said to me,

"The army will sort you out my boy. I suggest you do something with your life, as I am not going to support your bad habits."

The penny dropped and I said to her that I should look for work in Rhodesia as no white boy is going to get work in Zambia. She reluctantly agreed and I made plans to go and seek work in Rhodesia.

I drove to Salisbury with a buddy of mine and stopped in at the recruiting centre and spoke to the recruiting officer. He said my application had been approved and that the papers were ready for me to sign. I told him I would return the following day. I went out to a pub called the Coq d'Or, had a few drinks and then booked into a hotel where I considered my options.

The next day I returned to the recruiting centre and some WO2 (Schoultz - I think his name was) took me through to the recruiting officer's office and told me to take a seat. A Major Lamprecht came through and greeted me like a long lost son and offered me refreshments and then asked me if I was sure that this is the career I wanted.

I thought, "Sh*t man, if this is what army life is going to be like - tea served by a Sergeant Major and seated in the Major's office like I owned the joint and him singing sweet praises about how the army was good for a young man, that it was a stable job and all that sh*t."

So I said to him that I was ready to sign on for three years.

He gave me his expensive pen and I signed on the dotted line.

He stood up, shook my hand and welcomed me to the Rhodesian Army.

"You are in the Regular Force for three years; I hope you enjoy it."

He then he called the CSM and said to him,

"Brief this recruit and get him to Cranborne Barracks. Intake 139 has already started basics; see if you can get him on that intake."

I saw the CSM's eyes light up and he said to me,

"Do you know where Cranborne Barracks are?"

I replied I didn't. He then snapped,

"When you address me, you call me 'Sir', do you understand recruit?"

I just stood there and thought "f*ck...".

I could still make it to the SA border; this sh*t was not for me. He must have been reading my mind because he called for a lance corporal to take me through to the barracks. I was stuffed and it was too late for me to do anything about it.

Anyhow we arrived at the main gates of the barracks and I was directed to the RP's office. In front of the office were white painted lines. I ignored these and went straight into the office and introduced myself, but omitted to tell them I had just enlisted. They asked what I wanted and I then told them I had just enlisted.

Then the sh*t hit the fan.

Out of nowhere another four of them appeared, all shouting different sh*t at me at the same time. Eventually I understood that I had to stand on the white line outside and wait to be acknowledged. I doubled outside and stood in the sun nursing a hangover while the bastards ignored me for about an hour, other than hurling obscenities at me every few minutes. This was the first taste I had of the Rhodesian Light Infantry, and I knew I was in for friggin' hard time...

Garrett Locomotive #422 15th Class with contributor Stanley Maiden at Ggungubane Siding in 1956.

"Morning Light" by Chris Higginson
Extract from Reluctant Assassin 1

My parents are still asleep and I am up now so I decide that I am going to go out.

I dress. I can still smell the residue of smoke in my shirt from the fires at the compound last night. I should change it, but the generator is off, so the lights will not work and I cannot be bothered to search around in the dark for another shirt.

The dogs are all asleep.

There is nobody about as it is early morning Sunday. I can still hear a last lone drummer tapping an irregular beat from the compound. He sounds as though he is the last survivor of the night's celebration. There are no crowds or tractors this morning. Only the insects are rasping and rubbing their single note songs.

The moon is gone, but there is enough starlight to see shapes. The east is lightening. I make for the kopje at the back of the house. It is a stiff climb. I find my rock, where I sat before.

It is cool through my short pants.

The sun is coming fast and the light in the sky is changing as I watch the cloudless horizon. The air is refracting luminosity into colours, through reds, oranges and yellows until a spear of sunlight lances across the land.

A radiance around me bathes the trees with a warm light. Most of the trees are still without leaves, because the rains are still to come and it has been dry for months.

But the Musasa trees.... they are different.

They burst forth with leaf before all the other trees.

First scarlet, which shades to red and then transmutes to brilliant lime green that becomes dark green when the rains start. These are the most astonishing autumn colours in the world and these trees display them in the tropical spring.

They stand out in the arid country, all by themselves.

Candles of colours that stand ranked on the eastern sides of the kopjes, and in the golden horizontal morning light all the crimson and green leaves seem to be luminous. The sight is a special gift from somewhere. I can smell the freshness from the leaves and the flushes of coloration saturate my mind. I can almost feel the softness in the air.

Above me, the light transposes the clouds of leaves of the trees into an aura that seems to bathe the area in a soft glow. I do not know if it is caused by the reflected light from the young leaves or the soft first rays of the sun.

It does not last.

Gentleness in Africa is a transient thing.

The sun is now climbing above the horizon. It means business. No more will it refract around corners.

The world wakes up and takes stock.

Birds try out their voices before launching into their territorial battle cries.

One, which I learn later is a Heuglin's robin, starts his dawn calling nearby. The

203

words of his song are said to be "Don't you do it! Don't you do it!" He repeats it a dozen times each phrase rising in note and volume to a crescendo of expectation. Then I see him. He has a little black head with a white stripe through the eye and a deep orange breast.

I fall in love with him.

Here is a little bundle of energy, who knows he is beautiful and loves exalting his life with a song that would bring tears of joy to a king.

He represents all the things that I am not.

His celebration of life will enhance mine.

I think I am beginning to find that natural solitude feeling that I am looking for.

Now everything is beginning to stir. The pigeons are landing in the top branches of the trees around me to warm up in the first rays of the sun. The Flycatchers will take over these branches later when the insects start moving and buzzing along their urgent flight paths between the bushes. The Fire Finches and Blue Waxbills are getting an early start. They land on the tall grass stems and bend them low so that they can then pick off the seeds.

I cannot tell how long I sit simply wondering at each new experience, as I watch the morning unfold.

I jump down from the rock where I have been sitting and make my way back down the path.

From a distance, I can see there is a commotion at the house. My father has a shotgun, a deck chair and a paper. My mother is obviously arguing with him and is holding her arms stiff sideways. Chigamba is wringing his hands in distress about something.

"Nyoka Bwana! Big snake! Like the one that bite baas John and my mother. It is the same one. Make very much poison!"

He had seen the snake going into a hole in the wall where the bathroom pipes emerge. It would not matter normally, but this hole is near the kitchen door and he is NOT happy. The snake is now under the built-in bath. Probably, it has been living there for some time.

A small crowd is gathering. Amazing how quickly this happens in Africa where, when something interesting occurs, people emerge seemingly from nowhere. My father wants to settle down with a beer, the shotgun and the paper and wait for the snake to come out.

My mother is not satisfied with this. She wants something done! Smoke it out!

She gets two of the crowd aside and tells them to start a fire and put some pieces of tyre into it. She wants to make smoke with the burning rubber and then thrust the pieces into the hole where the snake has taken refuge. Daniel, who is Kaise's second son, is banging on the bath inside to frighten the snake into the open.

That is sure not to work.

The crowd is beginning to enjoy this. One man pinches another, who leaps into the air with a shriek as he thinks that the snake has somehow bitten him from behind.

They all find this hilarious.

My father is philosophical and settles in his deck chair. Mother is not entertained at this lack of action and discipline. The pieces of rubber are now burning and bubbling and Mateus pushes them into the hole with a flat plank. Black smoke pours out of the hole.

No result.

Mother decides that we must flood the snake out. Mateus pulls the end of the hosepipe, which drains water from the water tank and feeds it into the hole. The others have positioned a couple of sand bags in front to dam the water.

Smoke and water pour forth. Still there is no snake.

Now, she decides, we are going to gas it out. She gets a box of Calcium Carbide crystals from the office. When you mix these crystals with water, they give off a flammable gas, which they use in the 'Baboon Scarers' to make explosive noises. These explosions sound like shotguns firing.

She throws a couple of handfuls into the hole and stands back to check the result.

It is spectacular.

There is a huge bang.

The bathroom windows blow out, bricks fly, water sprays and everybody runs.

My father lies tangled in the deck chair.

The bathroom is destroyed.

The snake is dazed, but still alive in the rubble. The crowd surges forward with sticks, all shouting for courage and they dispatch the snake in short order.

After the fuss dies down my father takes me aside, very seriously, to explain:

"Now, my boy! Listen very carefully! If you see a snake, like this one, or any one then you must come and call Mummy or me, see? You must not go anywhere near it! All right? Now what do you do if you see a snake?"

"I take a big stick and I beat it and beat it... and beat it"

How this aligns with the tranquillity of two hours earlier is something that I still have to learn.

Extract from **"The Kitchen Kaffir Dictionary" by S E Aitken-Cade** circa 1953

THE usual dictionary is made up of two sections, English and the other language. This means that you have two chances of making mistakes. In this dictionary there is a great improvement, for by inserting extra words the writer increases your chances to three or four. In addition to the usual very concise note about each word, you may find yourself engaged in reading a whole page devoted to the practical application of the word. This will provide the author with a lot of fun and fill up space like anything. If you have one of the ordinary dictionaries, you've had it; but if you read this dictionary, you've got it coming for a long time.

Most dictionaries proceed in an alphabetical manner, and there is no reason to depart from that hallowed custom. General remarks on the etymology of the English language are specifically excluded. K.K. stands for Kitchen Kaffir, a useful but incoherent language. The idea behind the dictionary is to provide the farmer with a vocabulary of Shona, but the author cannot agree that this will ensue. Any similarity between this and Webster is purely coincidental.

ABLE, to be, vb. int.—kwanisa. But more generally rendered in K.K. as enza. "Wena asi enza—?" Are you able to—?"

To this opening gambit you can add the various English words indicating the job you want done. "Wena asi washing? Cooking?"

The general reply will be "Ya Boss," which means: — "Yes. I'll have a stab at it."

"I'll try anything once" or "I don't understand but I'm willing to oblige."

If the reply is in the negative it will be "Aikona," meaning "No," "I don't want to," "Don't like washing," or "Am I a wage slave?"

ABOVE. adv. and prep.— pamsoro, kumsoro. K.K. pezulu. "Put that above that."— "Faka lo pezulu ga lo.' "Take the one on top."—" Tata lo lapa pezulu."

ABUSE, vb. trans. — tuka. (Revile). Use English.

ABUSE, n.—See ABUSE, vb. trans.—Egyptian, Urdu, Italian or broad Scots useful.

ACCUMULATE, vb. trans.— unganidza. K.K. is expressed by a sentence into which the noun is slipped as desired. "Faka zonke munya indaba."— Put all together." "Faka zonke lo gwaai munya indaba lapa." —"Put all the 'baccy together there."

ACCUSE, vb. trans.—mangara. A fairly useless process as you can accuse until you are blue in the face without getting any satisfaction. It is a favourite week-end pastime for your native employees. You will often find two or more boys standing outside the kitchen first thing Sunday morning to "Mangara."

To save endless bother intone the following in a firm voice: — "Buya kusasa, mina nika wena brief, wena hamba lapa Police."   "Come in the morning, I'll give you a letter, you can go to the Police."

ACCUSTOMED, vb. int—jaira. Are you accustomed to this work?" is rendered. "Wena jaira lo sebenza?" "Is that ox accustomed to the yoke?"—" Lo mombe yena jaira joke?"

Yoke is English, Jok or Juk is Afrikaans, but the, wily Munt has it right, it's a joke.

ACHE, vb. int.—panda. K.K. cheesa. "Lo skop gamma yena cheesa." —" My head aches." Cheesa also indicates that the sun, water or temper is hot.

ACROSS see CROSS.

ADD (add together), vb. trans.—unganidza. Add together is used in the same sense as accumulate.   See also INCREASE.

ADDRESS, n.—kero. As most of the rural natives are working for somebody who has a Postal Bag or Post Box they have their mail delivered c/o their employer. Hence " Kero (care of) for " address." "What is your address?" —" Ini lo kero gawena?"

ADVICE, n.— Unpalatable in any language.

ADVISE, vb. trans.—raira. See ADVICE, n.

ADZE, n.— mbezo or semo. A most useful tool especially for new settlers. Not to be confused with badza. Most natives are adept with it and can chip poles and planks into shape quite competently.

AEROPLANE, n.—ndeke More commonly, "Furayi machine." In extreme cases the staff may insist on saying "Viking" or Spit."

AFTER, adv., prep. and conj.— shure. See WHEN. K.K. By and bye. In common use all over the Colony in conjunction with "longisa." "I will attend to you afterward."—" Mina longisa wena by and bye."

"I will see you later."—" Mina bona wena by and bye." Don't get these two confused.

AGAIN, adv.—zwakare. K.K. Futi. "Do it again."— "Enza futi." "Come again"—" Buya futi."

AGO, adv.—kare. Long ago— kare kare. K.K. kudala and kudala sterek.

AGREE,vb. int.—tenda. K.K.vuma. "Do you agree?"— "Wena vuma?"

Also used by the staff when you send them down to the compound for a malingerer. "Yena aikona vuma, Boss," means "He won't come, Boss."

It is also used to indicate non-agreement on the part of mechanical equipment— Lo tractor yena aikona vuma," The word is also widely used by the European section of

the community.—" I tried the Bank for an overdraft but the manager wouldn't vuma."
"Yes, I asked Flossie but she didn't vuma."

AGREEMENT, n. —chitenderano". Never means the same thing to any two people so why should we go into it here? Watch all Europeans like a hawk. Watch agreements with Africans like two hawks.

AIR, n—mweya, mphepo. K.K. mweya, moya. "Open the door and let in some air."—"Vula lo door, yena gena mweya." "This tube is punctured, mend it and fill it with air."— "Lo chube yena ponchilied, longisa yena, faka mweya."

ALARM (to be alarmed)— karuka. K.K. saba. "I am alarmed (afraid)." — "Mena saba."

ALIKE, (to be alike), vb. int. — fanana. K.K. munya indaba. This confuses the issue and gets us back to "accumulate." But in K.K. the sentence goes like this. "This and this are alike."— "Lo na lo yena munya indaba."

But when you are grading the confusion heightens. "This and this are alike, put them together."—" Lo na lo yena munya indaba."

ALIVE, (to be alive), vb. int.— pona. K.K. izwa. "The ox is not dead, it is alive."— "Lo mombe yena aikona fele, yena izwa."

This word is also used to indicate understanding. "Mena izwa, Boss."— "I under stand, Sir." "He doesn't understand."— "Yena aikona izwa."

ALL, adj.—eshe. KK. zonke. "Bring all the cattle (oxen, cows)."— "Buyisa zonke lo mombe." "Yena tatile zonke."— "He has taken all." Zonke can be used for everything.

ALLOW, vb. int—tenda K.K. vuma. Use in the same fashion as AGREE. "The Boss will not allow." —"Lo Boss yena aikona vuma."

ALONE, adj.—oga, ega K.K. kupella (see ONLY). "He came alone."— "Yena buyile, yena kupella." "I cannot go alone." "Mena aikona asi hamba, mena kupella." The latter sentence comes up any time after sundown.

ALSO, adv.—zwe. K.K. futi. One of the most satisfactory words in the KK. group.

Bring one more."— "Buyisa munya futi." "Bring that one also.''— Buyisa lo muya futi."

Is used to indicate recurrence. The tractor is dead again."— Lo tractor yena fele futi."

ALWAYS, adv. — mazuwa ose (literally "every day"). K.K. zonke skat. "Why do you always come here?"— "Ini indaba wena buya kuno zonke skat?"

Why do you annoy me all the time?" —"Ini indaba wena shupa mena zonke skat."

AMONG, prep.—mukati, pakati. KK pakati. Also used for INSIDE. "Put me among the girls."— "Faka mena pakati ga lo vasikana."

"He is inside the house."— "Yena kona pakati ga lo kia."

AND, conj.—na. K.K. na. This is easy. Use "na" all the time. When you have mastered one of the local dialects you will find variations but until then stick to a simple "na."

ANGER, n. —shungu, hasha. KK cheeky. "The lady was very cross." — "Lo Nkosikaas yena enzile cheeky maningi." This is used too show that an ox is bad tempered. "Boss up lo mombe, yena kona cheeky maningi."— "Watch out for that ox, it is bad tempered."

ANIMAL (wild), n. — mhuku. K.K. into (thing). "Into ga lapa shut-in."— "A thing of the woods," Any unidentified creature of the wilds is referred to in this manner in KK.

ANOTHER, adj.—mwe. K.K. futi. Yes, the same old word again.

"Tell me another."— "Chella mena munya futi."

"Give me another.—" Nika mena munya futi."

"Will you have another?"— "Wena funa munya futi ?"

ANSWER vb. Lv. — pindura, dayira. KK. Pindura, kuluma (talk). "The Boss does not answer."— "Lo Boss yena aikona pindura (kuluma)."

"Pindura" is also used for " Turn round" or "Turn over." Very confusing.

ANT, n. There are oodles of names for ants so don't try to get them all at once. Juru is the name used for termites and swoswe will do for all the others in the opening stages. "Go to the ant thou sluggard."— Hamba lapa majuru, wena loafer."

Having no poetic background this will be lost on the staff. "Ants in the pants," has not yet been translated, so we can render it as:— "Juru lapa kapadula."

ANT-HILL, n —churu. These are a great nuisance and hard to eradicate. After an ant-hill has been broken open and ex posed to the air to oxidise it is useful as compost. Also excellent stuff used in moderation for bricks. Makes good tennis courts. Termites or white ants perform the function of the British earthworm. Unlike the earthworms they attack houses too.

ANVIL, n.—shanguriro. KK. simbi. "Heat the iron and bring it to the anvil." "Cheesa lo simbi and buyisa lapa simbi." Simbi is used for all metal.

"Chaiya simbi." —"Ring the hell." "This bolt is broken."- "Lo simbi yena fele."

ANY, indef. adj.—Just how indefinite you will discover. Usually expressed in K.K. thus:

"Give me any thing." "Nika mena lo wena funa." Literally: "Give me what you like." "Indeed, there are not any." "Sure, azeko."

APPOINT, vb. tr.—gadza. KK. use enza (made). "I have appointed him my boss-boy."— Mena enzili yena Foroman gamena."

ARISE, vb. int—simuka. KK. gerrup. In general use simuka." Natives will sit clown as a sign of respect. It is not polite in their custom to stand before a superior. When a boy comes and squats down in front of you to discuss something, take it as a sign of respect and show your superiority. The same applies when boys pass in front of you when there is plenty of room behind. They are not showing any rudeness, they are merely conforming to their custom. In the old days it was dangerous to allow any one to pass at your back.

ARM. n.—ruoko, ruwoko K.K. mawoko. "Bamba lo mawoko gayena."— "Hold his arms."

ARMPIT, n.—hapxe Skip this one. It is a terrible word any way.

ARRANGE, vb. tr. — gadzira K.K. longisa "Arrange my personal kit in the chiffonier." "Longisa lo pashla gamena lapa mabokisi ga lo paraffin." "The drawing room is in a mess arrange it tastefully." "Lo kia yena mubi, longisa yena."

ARRIVE, vb. int.——swika. KK fika.. "When the Boss arrives, give him some refreshment." "Skat lo Boss yena fika, nika yena whisky." (Tea, Coffee, Pepsi-Cola.)

ARROW, n—musewe. You're no Robin Hood. Use a shotgun. Agincourt is out in this atomic age.

AS, adv.—sa. Unbelievable but true. Proves that the native mind works in the opposite direction to ours. KK. Fanika. "Do as I tell you." " Enza fanika mena kuluma wena."

ASK, vb. tr — bnvanza. K.K. funsa (foonsa). "Ask the Boss, where is the key?" "Funsa lo Boss, upi lo key?"

ASP, n.—nyoka. K.K. nyoka. All other snakes nyoka. Stomach-ache is also nyoka.

ASHAMED, to be, v.—tsweruka. Seldom, if ever, used. They seldom, if ever, are. No one seems to have bothered to invent a KK. word for this unused term. After all, why waste time?

AT, prep.—pa, ku, KK. lapa. "Is the Nkosikasi at home?" "Lo Nkosikasi yena kona lapa kia?"

AUTHORITY, n.—simba. (syn. strength). "He has no authority (power) to do that." "Yena azeko simba ku enza lo!'

AVOID, vb. tr. (by running away) tiza. K.K. baleeka. "The bossboy is running away." "Lo bossboy (foreman) yena baleeka." "The boy who broke the plate is avoiding you." "Lo muntu yena bulaleeli plate yena baleekili."

AVOID, vb. Tr., work—KK. Loafer. "He is avoiding work." "Yena loafer,"

AWAY, to be, vb. Int –po. K.K. azeko, "The Boss is away." "Lo Boss azeko." (Lit. Not').

AXE, AX, n.—demo. This is one of those almost universal words. "Bring me my axe." "Buyisa mena lo dema gamena."

That is all we are putting into the A list. It could have been reduced even further, but that would have left us with a bare 20 lines of print. Words like arpeggio, astronomy, arthritis, and alimony have been left out. We debated about "astonished," but agreed that natives are never astonished, and seldom impressed. We now pass on to the Bs. There are some Bs we have had to leave out, but any farmer, old or new, can fill them in from memory. They are universally understood.

"Sorry, Caption got lost." (Ed.)

Or was it broken?

Pom Christmas by Mike Beresford

So once again it's Christmas but what a change in scene,
The lights are on at midday and outside it's really mean,
They forecast gales on Christmas Eve and fog on Boxing Day,
Watch out for ice on all the roads and frost is on the way.
If you're lucky and it snows on you it soon will turn to slush,
Don't think of Christmas shopping and avoid the Christmas rush.

I'd gladly face the mozzies and the flies if it were warm,
And watch a chongololo making haste across the lawn.
I wish I had a flame lily but most of all my wishes,
I wish I had a houseboy to clean the bloody dishes.
Alas, this will not happen and that is very clear,
So have a happy Christmas and a similar New Year.

"So just where is my Pride now....?"
Photograph by Steve Bailey

Rhodesian 'Bike Tour 1960 by Chris Higginson
Extract from Reluctant Assassin 1

I come over the crest of the hill too fast. The road disappears from beneath my wheels. I clamp on the hand brake, too tight with panic. The cable snaps and my BSA 650 and I are off the road and though the ditch, now dodging trees.

She rears and bucks.

Time goes in slow motion.

Boulders float past.

I examine the bark of trees, in detail, as they sail slowly by.

Almost, with leisure, we come back to earth. I have her angled just right so we bounce back into the air. But the bounce is too vigorous. We drift apart in the air. She goes to one side of the Msasa tree. I examine the tender new leaves in passing, as I glide past on the other.

The impact happens in stages. My feet land first. My knees bend into my chest. My breath whooshes out. I try to hold my hands in front. My arms can't take the strain and slowly bend. My face slides slowly into the dirt and I cartwheel into a heap.

It is quiet. There is dust. The bike is silent. It is really quite peaceful. I wonder if I should allow myself to drift on, in this tranquil world. I am watching the green, green leaves against the blue, blue sky, above me. The picture of tender lime coloured leaves dappling the sky imprints itself on my mind.

It is too beautiful to go... Yet.

The pain starts.

Head hurts. Gravel rash on my hands. I feel my face- my hands are now covered with blood. Damn. How am I going to explain that away? I sit up and I move each limb, one at a time. Oddly, everything seems intact. The bike is lying on her side. She also seems to be intact.

I heave her onto her wheels. My homemade crash bar is bent back and seems to have taken most of the impact. The hand brake is useless with the broken cable. I feel the compression of the engine by pushing the kick-lever with my foot and it feels still good. I give her a kick and she growls back to life. I can see a path weaving back towards the road so I snake my way along it. As I approach the road I can hear a car coming. I know my face is a mess so I crouch low over the bike as though adjusting something on the engine. The car stops and a woman's voice calls out.

I look up.

She nearly faints.

"Oh God!" she says, "I'll call an ambulance! Wait there I live just up the road. I'll be back!"

Now I am in trouble.

She roars off.

And so do I, in the opposite direction.

Damn. Now there is going to be an enquiry about the accident that never happened. It will not take them long to find me. I get back to the college, still in a mess, grinning bloodily at each car I pass. Fortunately one of the boys at the college wants to train to be a doctor. He is delighted to have a real patient with whom to practice. He swabs and cleans my face and sticks bits of plaster here and there.

I hide my BSA at the back of the building. 'Digger' looks at me and my facial repairs and doesn't say a word.

The Police come.

Nobody knows anything.

Now I know that this is the end of my puttering around the back streets of the suburbs of Bulawayo and sneaking off occasionally to the Matopos.

I am going to have to get legal. My Beesa and I could be pulled off the road for a dozen infringements. It is time to trade her as spare parts.

And so I meet Harley.

He (not 'She') has seen better days. He is a Harley Davidson

750 cc Vee Twin, from the War. The story goes that he was transported back from the North African campaign, in the back of a Dakota. He was supposed to have been won in a poker game from an American dispatch rider.

Either that or he was stolen!

He is all I can afford. The second hand bike shop needs the floor space and nobody else would want to be seen dead, on such a machine. 'Harley' and I go home together, now that school is over. We 'blatter' up the road to Salisbury. This is now the new tar road that has been constructed between the two largest towns of the country and which has replaced the old strip tar road. It still has its undulations, but is luxury compared to the potholes and temporary repairs of the old road.

My mother has forgotten that I am coming home. It does not surprise me. At least I have the bike, which is better than the time I had to walk the fifteen miles home from the Hartley station when she forgot the previous time. She gets on with her life and I get on with mine.

She has not even noticed that the bike is different.

However, she notices that I am.

Perhaps there is a sort of swagger to my walk, or something in my eye, but she knows with female instinct that something about me has changed.

I am now due to go to the Salisbury Polytechnic to start an Engineering course, but I have some time before I start. I decide I am going to tour. I do not have much money so I will plan to sleep in the bush and then spend what little I have to keep 'Harley' fed.

I pack him with a blanket roll, a semi-waterproof suit like the Africans use, on the farm irrigation gang. I make a sheath for the stabbing spear that Paul my Zulu friend gave me and I hang a witch doctor's necklace on the handlebars. This will ensure that the bike will not be touched or even approached by any African. In fact, while I have 'Harley' in the sheds, nobody will even go in there, with this powerful evil magic hanging on her.

I tell Mum that I am off to see a school friend in town. She nods absently and away I go in the opposite direction. I decide to go and see the low-veld where the government is building dams and a canal system to irrigate a huge area of dry bush. I am also curious about the green stones, which my father brought back from his hunting trip in the Sebungwe, years before. Although I know that it is unlikely that I will find where it was that he found them. I do not think he knew where he was on that trip most of the time.

My mother doesn't want to talk about the past and where they went or what they did, while he was researching the medical effects of fear while hunting lion.

Nostalgia is not part of her make-up.

Her past is put in a box and forgotten.

I 'blatter' past Beatrice and stop in Enkeldoorn for lunch. I am careful not to go into the pub, as I have heard stories of how the locals lock visitors into a 'jail' in the pub and then make them pay for the drinks. I take the road south through Fort Victoria and then down the escarpment. I 'vibrate' my way to the new town of Chiredzi. This is where they are building the new sugar mill. I meet Ted, who is now involved in developing the irrigation side of the new projects. He was my father's lion hunting companion from eighteen years before. He came back to Rhodesia after the War with medals including a Polish VC. He won't talk about how he won them, except to say he thought that there were others who deserved the recognition more than he did.

There are jobs available here but not for me, as I have not yet done my military "call up". They do not want to employ me, only to have me disappear for three months for army training. I still have to do the military service after I finish my schooling.

"Come back later!" They say.

While I am motoring around looking at the clearing operations, the heavens open and Triangle gets its annual rainfall in three days. The place is swamped. The dirt roads between the embryo towns become rivers of mud. I am soaked in the warm rain in spite of my efforts to keep dry with the 'waterproofs'. In the undulating countryside the water collects in the dips. The roads are awash. In one of the low spots I fall off into the swirling brown water. 'Harley' almost disappears. All I can see is his one wide handlebar sticking up out of the mud. I pick him up somehow and push him out of the mess of mud and water. He is clean in moments from the solid downpour of rain. Water streams out of his exhaust. I fear the worst. I test the compression with the kick-start. It seems good. Second kick and he starts, making his 'potato-potato' noise as though nothing has happened. I fall in love with him on the spot.

He is a faithful friend indeed, almost as good as a horse.

I decide that I will go north from here, across the Birchenough Bridge, which spans the Sabi River. This is a spectacular single span suspension bridge that still has the ashes of it's namesake in one of its pillars. By the time I get there the rains are gone for the moment, but the water is flowing deep and strong in the river.

"Sometimes the river is only sand, from bank to bank." says the barman at the little hotel at the western end of the span. It is still morning and I see he is shaking and fidgeting as he does his stock take of the bar. He pours a beer for himself and it disappears. His shaking is now less noticeable than before. It must be lonely here. I have a coke and move on. I want to see the tea estates in the Chimanimani Mountains.

The Chirinda forest is where I stop for the night, mesmerised by the butterflies. Perhaps the rains have stimulated their breeding. There are clouds of them. I used to keep a Hawkmoth collection at home as I was fascinated by the way they fly and hover as they feed like humming birds in the dusk, until it was destroyed by the Africans, when my mother moved my few possessions out of the spare room while I was at school. I did not have the heart to start again. These butterflies with their luminescent and iridescent colours are a collector's dream. They filter between the shafts of light that stand like bars in the thin mist of the forest, where the canopy allows the isolated rays of the sun to penetrate to the forest floor. They are so bold that they come to investigate me and fly around my head as they carry out an inspection. I have the strange feeling of understanding their type of group intelligence of the insects due to their concentrated numbers.

Silly, cannot be true!

I should 'collect' them instead.

However, if I were to carry a butterfly net, on a motorbike, I would project a strange contradictory image. Perhaps not.

I spend one night near the Bridal Falls, with Harley camped in the forest. Everything is wet with mist.

There is an eerie feeling here when it is dark.

I am not sure if the sounds I hear during the night are falling screams. I spend most of the night with my back against a tree, my spear in one hand and my witchdoctor's necklace in the other. The unhappy spirits leave me alone.

I move on in the morning feeling I am not welcome here.

As we progress along the route Harley is slowly shedding bits of himself along the way. The vibrations loosen everything in turn. Bits of mudguard fall off, the rear-view mirrors disappear and the headlight keeps becoming detached. Things I tie to the back carrier keep getting themselves untied, so I feel regularly with my hand behind my back, until, one time, I find the whole carrier has escaped. I find it, by going back, lying in the road with a puzzled African staring at it wondering what it is. He would no doubt have re-cycled it into something useful like a grill for a fire if I had not rescued it.

Nothing goes to waste in Africa. I pass Hot Springs and keep shaking along until I get to Umtali. I pass through. I do not like towns. I do not have nothing against this one in particular, but I feel that these are places where people live behind gates and hedges, all locked into their own self-inflicted cells. I decide to 'blatter' my way up the Vumba road to see my old school. It is now a missionary centre. I don't miss it, but the shapes of the mountains and the way the forests clothe the clefts on them, are like familiar friends.

The pass in the mountain range called Cloudlands still exerts that strange emotional pull that it had for me when I was at school here. I decide to spend the night in 'fifth forest' with Harley hidden behind bracken and creepers. As I sit unseen in the forest while the odd rare car goes by, I get that sense of superiority that I am sure a leopard feels as he surveys his domain from his favourite tree. This is the forest where there are those wonderful lianas, or 'monkey ropes'. When you detach them from the ground, they make natural swing from the branches high above. It is too tempting. I cut one and start a few experimental swings. It feels good. In moments I am swinging out over the void of the slope, high above the bracken and nettles below.

I hear a cough.

Like a smoker's cough.

It is a leopard's cough. They test reaction this way, of a potential prey, to see what caution they need before attack.

My hair stands on end. In seconds I am back on Harley. He roars a throaty response, as we wheel spin away down the road.

I really must pay more attention. Playing like a monkey in a forest with leopards about is stupid.

I carry on along the road to Leopard Rock Hotel. Leslie Seymour-Smith, who built the hotel, is no longer there. He and my father had tried gold prospecting in these hills. They came back with quartz rocks, which, when you wet them with saliva, gleamed with speckles of gold. They believed that an ancient people who had come here to mine gold had made the mountain terraces here.

Who knows, but the forests still have the wandering spirits from the village that was crushed by the mountain. The villagers, apparently, would not help an old crone who came to them for help, so she cursed the village and they were all killed when the mountain split in half and fell down on them.

I move on to Inyanga. I pass the Troutbeck Inn, pausing only to buy fishing trace and hooks from the reception and then I putter my way up the winding road to the Conemara Lakes and 'World's View'. I don't stay long, because it is wet and cloudy, although I love the smell of the pine forests and sound of the wind as it swishes through the trees. It is so different to the rest of the country.

Below the Troutbeck Dam is a small stream, in front of Herbert McIllwaine's cottage that I know well so I poach a couple of trout using worms. Fresh trout in the early morning, fire cooked, is a special treat. They taste even better with the knowledge that if Colonel Mac should catch me I will be peppered with his 12-bore shotgun. A little danger is good for the appetite. I must get back down to warmer altitudes. It is chilly at night in the mountains even at this time of the year.

Harley and I cruise down to Rusape, and then we pass through Salisbury, to take the Kariba road. I spend the night at the Sinoia Caves, another place with wandering spirits. I want to see the Kariba dam as it is finished now. I had been here years before, while it was being built. A group of farming friends, with my parents, had taken three days off to do a safari here. We had made a camp where the Sanyati River joins the Zambezi, but of course that place is now all under water.

The road winds down the escarpment. When I came here the first time the road was gravel and crowded with huge trucks delivering materials to the dam site. Now it is tarred, but it is still tortuous. Harley and I take our time. It is hot and there are places in the road where the tar is soft and almost melting. I wonder why I was in a hurry to leave the cool mountains of the Eastern Highlands.

I stop at the side of the road in order to commune with nature. I can see a Mohobohobo tree, which has fruit that is good to eat.

There is also a Baobab with cream of tartar pods hanging down. The seeds are covered with a powder that is like sherbet and is refreshing to suck. I wonder if I will be able to dislodge a pod by throwing a stick at it. The trunks of most of the baobabs are difficult to climb because of their large girth and smooth sides, unless they have been distorted or damaged.

I prop Harley on his side stand. He clicks quietly to himself, as the hot metal exhaust system cools. I go and squat behind some bushes out of habit which is strange as there is very little traffic and if a car was to come, I would hear it from far. As I am engaged I see a young elephant bull emerge from the trees on the far side of the road. He is full of himself and shakes his head at Harley.   When he does this, his ears crack like whips.

Harley does not move.

 I do not either.

He comes across to the bike to investigate and starts sniffing around with his trunk. He burns the tip of it on the cooling vanes. He squeals with rage and rips off the remains of the windscreen, knocks Harley over and stomps off back into the copse of trees from where he came. Harley is lucky to have not been more seriously hurt. What I do not know, is that his silencer is now loosened. A few miles further down the road it falls off. I stop and tie it back on with a bungee elastic net, called an octopus and some barbed fencing wire. Off we go again. Several miles further on there is a huge roar and I get a great slap on the back that winds me. I think that the Thundergod has got me. The silencer has fallen off again, hit the road and arched round on the springy bungee and slammed me on the back. I am lucky that it has hit me flat and not with the pipe end first. This time I tie it with tambu and barbed wire.

This is the true African 'fix it all' system.

At Kariba I 'blatter' up to the church on the top of the hill, built to commemorate the people who died building the dam wall. I see that people are avoiding looking at me, as I sit on the bike and admire the view. I must look too much like a scruff.

Where to now?

I would like to follow the lake, but there is no road, and it would be impossible to 'bundu-bash' along the escarpment.

I watch the sun lowering across the lake. There are plenty of places to camp by the shore. Up here on the hill, the smart houses are near the top, and the size and importance of the houses and their occupants decreases as one goes down the hill. On that basis, I should be camped by the water's edge. I cannot cross over the dam wall to Northern Rhodesia, or Zambia, as it is now called as the 'Federation' has broken up and I need a passport. I glide down the hill with the engine off. I see a telephone kiosk.

Hell, I had better give my mother a call.

I get Chigamba the cook.

"Yes baas... baas Charles, he not here... No... Oh, you baas Charles! Oh... Yes baas... Madam, she not here... No, she not coming for tonight... Ah! Me tell Madam you not coming for tonight... But Madam, she not here! How for I tell Madam? She not here... Oh! I tell Madam tomorrow, you not coming for tonight! ... But she know tomorrow, you not here for tonight... Why I tell Madam tomorrow, you not here for tonight?"

I cannot answer that, so I give up.

Down by the water's edge there are many little fish, keeping in the shallows for protection. Every now and then there is an eruption in the water as a larger fish snaps at them. I try my line with a bit of corned beef for bait. Whatever it is just snaps the line off. An African fisherman is amused at my efforts and shows me a tiger fish that he has caught with a steel trace. It has interlinking teeth, as sharp as a cat's. I swap a fish from him, for a tin of condensed milk. Not a tiger as he tells me it has too many bones but a good-looking bream.

He shows me how to suspend it over a fire on a flexible stick.

We talk about important things, like fish and food and how the lobola price has gone 'too much, very much high', with the earnings from the new hotels spreading into the local population. It seems everybody wants a bicycle AND a radio these days.

The next morning I have a stroke of luck. I meet Vic, who has a farm across the river from my mother's farm and a little upstream. He was one of the people who came on the safari to the dam construction with us years before. He now has his boat at Kariba. It is called the Kariba Queen. He used to ride the rapids here before the dam was built. He designed and built the 'Kariba Queen' himself. His father was a boat builder from Canada, but Vic had gone off to the war as a bomber pilot, volunteering and flying in the RAF. Vic is a huge man and always seems to be having fun. He simply knows that life is great and he makes it so for those around him. Perhaps wartime taught him that. He tells me he is going to do a run up to Binga, at the other end of the lake with some people who want to start a ferry service. He will take my bike and me! There is enough space on his small ship.

I leap at the chance.

Vic's boat is remarkable. It simply flows through the water. There is no wake and no bow wave. It seems to progress with so little effort and yet at what seems to be a good speed.

We stop at Bumi Hills and I sleep on board. In the evening we watch the elephants come down to the water's edge to drink and frolic. They must be following their old paths, retained by memory from the years before the dam was created, to the Zambezi, and now for them the river seems to be at a continuous flood level.

From there it takes us two leisurely days to get to Binga. The guests trawl for tiger fish. The sun sets ahead of us into the water. Drowned trees pass by. Harley doesn't make a sound. This is a peaceful way to travel. I am sorry to leave them at Binga. I 'blatter' my way to the top of the hill, and watch as the boat curves out into the lake on its return journey. The fish eagles are riding the air currents and now, away from the water, it is getting hot again.

Now my route is to take the gravel road through Wankie to the Victoria Falls. Wankie is where the coalfields are and it is where the smoke used to rise from the underground fires burning the coal before they were brought under control. It is always heated like an oven here. I do not stop. Even the hills are black and then in the distance I see the smoke in the flat plain ahead.

However, this is not smoke, it is mist. Rising up from the dry, sun baked bush-veld. It is the spray from the Victoria Falls. From this distance I cannot yet see the river, but the spray seems to rise up hundreds of feet into the air. It takes me a couple of hours to get there.

The relief by the river, from the heat of travel, is wonderful. I have to stay and absorb the moisture through my skin, now burned dark brown by the sun and wind. The forest along the lips of the gorge is in permanent rain and the roar of the falling water drowns my hearing. Little bushbuck drift between the trees and the birds drink in flight.

It is the time of the full moon so I wait for nightfall.

And it comes.

The lunar rainbow.

There is rain, but no cloud to obscure, the moonbeams in the mist. But the moon rainbow does not have the colours of the sun's rainbow. That is what makes it so pure and ghostly. And the people who are drinking in the bars and hotels are missing it all!

It is hard to leave the security of all this abundant water, for the dry country roads, that stretch hundreds of miles to the South to Bulawayo. But I have to move on.

The guards will not let me go into the National Game Park at Wankie on my way south because Harley is not a closed vehicle. The lions here have not been trained that human meat is forbidden. So I decide to head back to the Matopos one last time.

This time, among the granite domes, I do not have to be anywhere urgently. I can spend a couple of nights here. But I sleep up a tree as there are plenty of predators about. I decide that for the first time I will try some Matabeleland dagga, because that is what the Matabele use to commune with their spirits.

They say it works better than the Mashonaland stuff.

And so, with my spear and necklace and a fire, I try some.

    I don't see any spirits,
        but I can hear the resonance of the rocks.
          These are the ancient 'Singing Stones',
            of the Matabele.

But the song that I hear seems, much older than that.

"How can you possibly know what I understand?"
Photograph by Steve Bailey

History of Rhodesia by Pete in Oz.

For the benefit of any readers who may not be aware of Rhodesia's real history, and who might be misguidedly giving any credence to the foreign press, here are some genuine factoids about the pre-1980 Rhodesian situation.

1. When the pioneers arrived in the area, the Matabele (an offshoot of the SA Zulus) were in firm control. They hunted and chased a few thousand Mashona around the bush, and considered them to be their cattle - to be herded and used. The pioneer's first mistake was to stop this carnage. If they hadn't, the Mashona would have been annihilated.

2. By 1890, neither the Matabele nor the Mashona had a written language or anything more advanced than our stone age ancestors.

3. From those beginnings, the white settlers built a rich, fair and prosperous land in which every citizen had food, education, employment, hospitals, roads, clean water, power, the right to earn a vote and an impartial police force and judiciary which applied civilised law as it was intended.

4. Yes, the government was paternal, being elected from two voters rolls which ensured that the black politicians remained in opposition and could not take control of the management of the country. We knew what would happen if they did, and our assertion of their inability to govern a country has since been absolutely proven.

5. Prior to the insurgencies which were managed and financed by the Russians and Chinese the largest single item on the Rhodesian budget was African Education (13%). Hardly the policy of a "repressive regime". Every piccanin was within reach of a school and clinic or hospital. Interestingly, the remote schools and clinics were the first targets of those that the foreign press call "Heroes". Hundreds of black teachers and nurses were cruelly tortured and murdered, in many cases by those who are stealing farms today.

6. Like rats in a laboratory, when given "death control" in the form of plentiful food and good medical services, the Masona and the Matabele began breeding uncontrollably. From a few tens of thousands they grew to a seething mass of millions within 50 years. By 1980, 400,000 white Rhodesians found themselves not only defending their country from outside insurgents, but entirely financing and supporting 5,000,000 blacks.

7. The nail in the coffin was driven in by the Americans. Concerned about the Cuban access to good oil in Angola, Kissinger initiated dialogue with the South Africans, who were desperate for any sort of contact with the western world. The slopies agreed to help the yanks remove the Cubans (which they did) and, as part of the new "accord", betrayed us. Without the SA support, we could not continue.

8. Not implementing op Quartz was our second big mistake. Before handing the country   over we should have removed the poison and the filth. We had full control and the ability to do it right up to the last hour.

Now that civilised management has been removed, the country is reverting to the stone age. Unfortunately we inadvertently allowed an artificially huge population to build, so that now they are utterly destroying the flora and fauna in a desperate struggle to survive.

Mugabe has very sensibly removed any possibility of the povos (commoners) being fed by either local farmers or food from the west, so hopefully the situation will not last for too long.

AIDS is also helping, but it is a race against time.

The Tsetse Fly or the Air Force Will Get You

Bombs are bursting, bullets bash and bodies blow apart
Shrapnel slivers slice and slash, as blood bleeds from my heart
Rockets roar as Hunters soar with aftershocks of sound
While spirits flee, released and free, from corpses on the ground

Metal eagle! Mighty! Regal! Spitting death from High
Howling! Yowling! Engine growling, as I lie and die
I am killed, my limbs are stilled, no more to terrorise
As I'm to die, it's better I am slain by Gods not flies

Chris Higginson

The Kudu from Mary D.

In 1973 my boyfriend was driving me home one night from the Norton Sports Club. I had only recently arrived in Rhodesia as a nurse from Groote Schuur in the Cape. He said to me:

"Would you like to see a kudu?"

I thought that this was a proposal along the lines of, "Do you want to see my etchings?"

"Really!" He said.

"A whole herd of them. They come to graze under the trees on the road to Kent Estate. Everybody here protects them. They are almost tame! Sometimes they move to another farm by jumping over the fences. One friend of mine, on this very road, experienced them jumping over his car and the fence in one leap!"

All this sounded too good to be true.

"Yes," I said, "I would like to see them!"

He turned off the dirt road we were travelling on and went a few hundred metres, and there we saw them standing quite at ease. I was spellbound that here were these wild animals living at peace in this farming area, unmolested and fearless.

It was here perhaps that my love affair with this, my new country of choice, began.

We continued home, weaving to avoid the resident owl who would not move from his appointed place.

"He has more right than I!" said my boyfriend.

Then we had to stop for a nightjar that was having a midnight dust-bath in the middle of the road. After a minute he deigned to fly off, trailing his long wing feathers behind him like banners.

A tiny duiker watched us pass, standing sideways with his eyes shining like lamps from the reflexion of the car's lights.

This was so much more beautiful than the neon lights of the city.

I still miss my friend.

I wonder, if he had survived the war, just how he would be involved with wildlife and its preservation now.

Perhaps, in a way, it is better that he didn't.

'Chrispin, the Shona Driver' by Fred Ericsen-Miller

I was assistant manager at the Wise Owl in Umtali, from 1970 to '73.

Coney Fleming, that Icon of Umtali Boys High, was the manager.

When the Pearce commission arrived and stayed at the Wise Owl, they insisted that their driver share all the same facilities that they had.

Lord Pearce, was very definite on this point, even when his one driver asked if he could eat at the back with his own people.

So shall we call the driver Crispin? He was a 50 yr old Shona, of limited education, but well brought up and very courteous. He was slightly balding and had a ready smile for all.

That evening, the six people of the commission came in and sat in the lounge before supper and insisted that their driver join them which, very reluctantly, he did.

You could see Crispin's discomfort, which was not so much because he was seated with them, but more at having to make conversation with them. This was, to say the least, an arduous task.

Never instigating any conversation, he just made courteous replies and gave an awkward smile when he could not understand the Pompous British accent.

Well, our waiter arrived and A La Carte menu's were handed around, including one to Crispin. With his limited education he was certainly not well enough versed to know what Chateau Briand(sic) was. As the Lords placed their orders, it got closer to Crispin's turn. His fidgeting spoke volumes for his discomfort..

Lord Pearce placed his order then turned to Crispin and asked in his best British accent:

"What would *you* care to have , My Man?"

Crispin asked what He, Lord Pearce, was having.

Lord Pearce said "Chateau Briand." (Forgotten how it is spelt)

Then Crispin asked, "Sah, what eez that?"

Lord Pearce described it as "Delicious best beef fillet, with a tasty sauce on it".

Crispin, said he would have the same.

Conversation carried on as normal, with the occasional nod from Crispin, who, by now was trying to talk to one of the Waiters.

The waiter, being a Manica, was not too pleased about talking to a Shona.

Dinner was called and they all moved in to the dining room.

Crispin was seated next to Lord Pearce and the meal was served..

Crispin's look of wonder at the huge piece of meat, with all the trimmings and garnishing, that was placed before him was sight for me to savour for many years.

He just sat and stared at it.

When he looked up, he saw Lord Pearce was slicing delicately at his steak with a steak knife.

He looked back at his plate and then, with pleading eyes, looked up and opened his mouth to say something.

Lord Pearce, motioned him to go ahead and eat and enjoy the meal.

Poor Crispin.

He had a look of sheer mortification as he sliced the first slice and he saw this RAW meat staring at him.

He looked and looked, as if it would get more cooked the longer he looked at it, but the meat refrained from obliging. He tried to put some in his mouth, but stopped, and looked at it again.

He chanced a hopeful sideways glance at Lord Pearce, who dismissively said.

"Eat up, my man!"

Crispin put the food in his mouth, then with one or two chews his face turned purple, almost blue and then back to black.

He swallowed the offending meat in one gulp, almost choked, swallowed hard again and then with a pleading look to the Lords, and to Lord Pearce himself, asked..

"Plleeeease Sah,do u mind if I go and eat Sadza with my people at the back?"

Lord Pearce was gobsmacked.

He looked at each of his entourage, as if looking for help, then, disdainfully dismissed Crispin, with a look of utter disbelief, which I am sure to this day soured his meal and the milk in his coffee afterwards.

I last saw Crispin smiling and enjoying a big pot of sadza and conversation, having forgotten about tribal differences, which was more befitting his nature and tradition.

This was something that the Commission never learned, which I did, and that was 'you can't put a square plug into a round hole!'

When I pointed out to Lord Pearce how happy Crispin was with his own kind, he just retorted that it was 'us' who had suppressed 'them' so much, that they felt "uncomfortable in our company".

'nuff said!

I left Rhodesia soon after.

Rhodesia in the Fifties by Angela Peterson. (nee Storey)

I was a student at Bulawayo convent 'til 1956, then went to Townsend and then did one year at the old UCRN in Salisbury in 1958. So for me Bulawayo was about being a teenager and Salisbury about being then a young woman.

Remember the Exhibition in 1953, with the Queen Mother and Princess Margaret coming to town? I'd never seen anything like it before: there was real ballet in Bulawayo! And the park right opposite - so peaceful - movies at the Palace Cinema and the others who's names escape me.

My first boyfriend who stood me up one Saturday matinee.............(shame on his little black heart1)

OK Bazaars on one corner and Greatermans opposite. Meikles and Haddon & Sly and Saunders with the bakery on Abercorn Street just down from OK Bazaars. Naakes, the frame shop, on Fife Street.

It's hard to think that was all 50+ years ago and probably no longer exists. I met my husband-to-be in the lounge of the Shelborne Hotel on Boxing Night 1959. I had three children in Rhodesia - twins at the Lady Chancellor Nursing Home in 1961 and another daughter at Mater Dei in Bulawayo on the last night of 1962.

I can remember sitting on the veranda of our house in Hillside and thinking that I could never, ever imagine anywhere else I would ever want to live. It was unique.

And then my husband's work led us to leave Rhodesia in 1965 and head for the United States where I've lived ever since. But in my mind those 15 years I spent there are like a shining oasis of peace and sunshine with jacaranda and flamboyant trees - 'strips' on the road to the Falls and the Agricultural Show every year - guavas and pawpaw and granadillas - all so wonderful after England and the War.

I have a good life here, but the brilliant golden pool of memory that was Rhodesia is something that warms my heart always.

A Brief History of Central Africa by Eddie Cross

Countries have character – Zimbabwe is no different and it is very special. It is a small country – only one third the size of Zambia but it sits astride the transport corridors of southern Africa, linking the great forest States of the continent to the arid plains of the deep south.

It spans the great divide of the continent and has a wide variety of climate – from the cool, misty Eastern Highlands to the hot, dusty lands along the Limpopo and the Mopane and Acacia forests of the Great Zambezi basin.

But most of all it is its people who set it apart from all its neighbours. The only really indigenous inhabitants are the San – of whom only a small group remains – perhaps several hundred in all. Then there are the Shona – migrants from the coastal plains of West Africa and the Nguni people in the south – also migrants, but from East Africa. All together there are perhaps 10 tribal groups with the only other significant migrants being a small community of white Africans of European decent and several thousand people of Asian decent.

Its history goes back perhaps a thousand years – no more. In 1200 AD the first major wave of migrants arrived and quickly established the Monamatapa Kingdom in the south of the country. Building links with the great civilizations of Asia and the Mediterranean, these people became the first to mine gold and other metals and the evidence suggests a community that dominated the whole of the Central African region. They were not a military people and were cultivators and pastoralists – creating dominance by their intellect and social cohesion and effective defence systems.

The next invasion was not so benign. To the south a major genocide had taken place as Chaka, the Zulu King and the inventor of the stabbing spear and Zulu war techniques, sent raiding parties into the central highveld plains to wipe out the people who lived there and who had refused to become vassals. When the first white Boer settlers arrived on the highveld, they found no people – only burnt villages and the bleached skeletons of the thousands who had died.

Two Impi's of the Zulu nation sent to take part in the "Mfecane", failed in their mission and instead of returning home to disgrace they fled north, crossing the Limpopo river – then regarded as the northern boundary of Zulu dominance and settling just north of the Matobo Hills.

There, these 40 000 men quickly established precedence – they simply wiped out two minor tribal groups and subjected the others to becoming vassals. Under the Nduna, Mzilikazi, they subjected the rest of the region, including the vast swathes occupied by the Shona people, to periodic raids to both establish just who was the boss and to extract tribute, women and cattle. The Ndebele Kingdom was essentially an extractive one – they grew nothing and just took whatever they needed to thrive and survive.

By the time of Queen Victoria, the Ndebele were threatening the kingdoms of the Batswana, the Bamatongo and tribes as far north as Malawi and Mozambique. To restrict their activities and influence appeals to the British Queen saw the establishment of protectorates in both Botswana and Zambia. This marked the first constraint on the freedom of pillage for the Ndebele people.

The first white settlers arrived as hunters, prospectors and missionaries. They trickled in from the mid 19th Century and then arrived in numbers in an organized way when the pioneer column arrived in the new Capital, Salisbury in 1896. The Ndebele did not welcome their arrival while the Shona saw the newcomers as perhaps an ally against the pillaging activities of the Ndebele.

Initially steering clear of the Ndebele, who had a well deserved reputation as a fighting force, the white settlers soon found they could not subsist with the raiding activities of the Ndebele – it was simply too disruptive and dangerous. So an edict was issued to the leader of the Ndebele – his forces were not to cross the Shangani River. For Lobengula, that tall, mild natured man who was Mzilikazi's successor, this edict was an act of war. The Ndebele could not live with any further restrictions to their raiding activity.

They immediately moved several thousand men towards the new borderline and issued an ultimatum of their own to the settlers. The stage was set and in three separate battles – the first at Shangani, the second in Gubulawayo and the third in the north, in the Lupane district, Ndebele military might was broken by a combination of the gatling gun and ruthless pursuit.

By these means the country called Rhodesia came into being. In 1923 they decided to remain an independent State – outside the Union of South African States that was being formed and to become a self governing Dominion within the British Empire. No cognizance was given to the interests of the Shona and Ndebele people and the technical and managerial skills of a tiny band of settlers of European origin dominated. The extent of the influence of this tiny minority is difficult to explain – but a similar situation existed in India where the British Administration never had more than 5000 English civil servants in its ranks and yet they dominated that vast continent and their influence lives on today.

The numbers of white settlers grew slowly until the Second World War when suddenly Rhodesia was selected to play a key role in the training of pilots for the Royal Air Force. Large temporary settlements were created in Salisbury, Gwelo and Bulawayo and thousands of men and women passed through this tiny African country to be trained and to go back and fight in the war in Europe.

At the end of hostilities many of those who had briefly lived in Rhodesia came back to settle and with them some 1100 ex pilots of the RAF. These new settlers were well-educated, serious characters that wanted to put their roots down and make a life for themselves after the horror of the European conflict. They became the core of a new breed of Rhodesian that was to make an indelible mark on the life and history and even the character of the country.

Immediately following the arrival of these new Rhodesian recruits, the Federation was formed and this gave rise to a decade of rapid growth and development – albeit with a backdrop of growing discontent by the subjugated black majority peoples. By the end of the Federation experiment, the white community had grown to 250 000, including 6 500 farmers and hundreds of miners and industrialists. 40 per cent of these settlers were of Scottish decent and this does something to explain their character and determination.

Perhaps the greatest influence on the country however, came out of the Missions. Spread across the country they were, by 1962, responsible for 90 per cent of all the educational activity in the country and at least 60 per cent of health services. Missions were a huge business, driven by the desire of overseas Churches to proselyze in Africa and the acceptance by the Rhodesian government that these institutions were a cheap way to meet the needs of the majority black population.

But you cannot educate a man and still keep him shackled. By 1949, the black majority had started to develop the instruments of resistance and power that would over time result in the settlers being defeated. In 1949 these fledgling forces mounted their first campaign – a general strike that paralyzed the country for a short while and for the first time brought out the army to protect civilians.

It was not until 1962 that the first shot was fired in this conflict – the first use of live ammunition by the armed forces since the turn of the Century. In 1964 the Nationalists split into two factions – Zapu and Zanu and these then dominated the political scene until independence was finally achieved in 1980.

With no effective external control over the local settler administration and the deep roots set down by the whites in Rhodesia it was never going to be an easy transition. In 1964 the government had no choice but to take the leaders of Zanu and Zapu and detain them indefinitely. This decision was partly based on the threat they posed to the government and partly to halt the internecine violence between the two groups who were largely divided on ethnic grounds.

In 1965, the then leader of the White Community, Ian Smith, himself a former pilot from the Second World War, defiantly declared independence from Britain on a unilateral basis. This shattered the fragile legal standing of the Rhodesian government and brought it into conflict, not only with the emerging States of Africa but also the international community. Both Zanu and Zapu immediately initiated the establishment of military wings externally – Zapu with the primary support of the Soviet Union and Zanu with the support of the Chinese government. The stage was set for war.

After several skirmishes in the preceding years, the civil war broke out in earnest in 1972 when some 600 Zanla guerrillas attacked remote communities in the north east of the country. By Christmas 1972, Rhodesians were at war with themselves.

The Americans describe the Rhodesian war as a "low intensity guerrilla conflict". That it certainly was but both sides gave no quarter. The casualty rate as a percentage of the forces deployed ranked with those in Viet Nam and when it finally came to an end in March 1980, some 150 000 men and women were involved in active military duty on one side or the other.

Faced with insurmountable odds the Rhodesians did a remarkable job with the tools at their disposal – exhibiting ingenuity and courage on a significant scale. Specialist forces such as the SAS and the "Fire Force" units were undoubtedly amongst the most outstanding fighting men in the history of conflict. Many of their exploits will be talked about and debated for many years to come.

But it was to no avail and when the South Africans with a final ultimatum eventually confronted Ian Smith, he had no choice but to do the honourable thing – to settle the dispute on the best terms he could garner. By then it was too late to really have much influence and at the final talks in London, the fate of the small, uncertain white minority was essentially sealed by the US and the United Kingdom.

We now believe that it was the British administration under Lord Soames who were responsible for the subsequent victory by a minority Nationalist leader, Robert Mugabe who came to power. Their rationale was quite simple – we want a fast transition to someone who can stop the war and maintain the peace. To them. That was Mugabe, who although he had led the talk's team for Zanu, was still a minority figure with insignificant military influence.

The assassination of Josiah Tongogara in Mozambique completed the picture and gave Mugabe an unfettered run for President – a post he won with over 80 per cent of the vote in March 1980.

Mugabe had never wanted to take control of a functioning State – his first preference would have been to lead an army in to Salisbury, a smoking ruin with the entire white community dead or driven into exile. As a dedicated intellectual Marxist, Mugabe wanted to establish a State similar to that which the Khmer Rouge tried to create in Cambodia – a peasant socialist republic.

Instead he found himself with a constitution that prescribed his power and influence for 10 years, a powerful opposition in the form of Joshua Nkomo and Zapu and an administration with a large and embedded white component. He had a large army with no loyalty to himself and when the first real conflicts arose with the revolt and attempted coup in 1983, he had to use the remaining elements of the Rhodesian Army and Police to suppress the revolt.

He decided he had to deal with Nkomo first and in 1983 he launched the now infamous Gukurahundi – or "wind". Over three years a special force created by Mugabe and made up of soldiers from his tribal minority and trained by the North Koreans, murdered up to 30 000 people in Zapu strongholds. They denied them food in times of drought and channelled development funds and aid away from the same areas. By 1987, Nkomo had had enough and he capitulated and signed a "Unity Agreement" with Mugabe. It was the end of Zapu as an organisation.

After 1990, the way was open to deal with the other problems but by this time the mismanagement of the fundamentals in the economy were creating difficulties. Mugabe was no longer the "golden boy" of African politics and domestic and international criticism had begun to mount.

Attempts by Zanu to reduce the influence of the Church on life in Zimbabwe were a complete failure. The Missions had done their job too well and any attempt to reduce Christian influence in education was rebuffed – not by outsiders but be Civil Servants whose roots were in the old system. Mugabe did not want a capitalist economy – he wanted a centrally planned and directed economy that he could use to support the State in its wider ambitions – a desire frustrated by a strong private sector that was doing a reasonable job.

Even in the sphere of the Trade Unions – an institution he distrusted as much as Ian Smith had – for different reasons, he had trouble. They insisted on their independence from the State and demanded economic and political reforms that were contrary to Mugabe's ambitions. By 1997, the trade unions were Mugabe's major headache.

Then in 1997 Mugabe began to make the mistakes that will destroy his legacy in African history and will eventually remove him from power. He responded to an appeal by a former friend from Dar es Salaam and President of the Congo for help. He dispatched 13000 troops, aircraft and heavy equipment to the Congo to defend his friend's new hold on power after the collapse of the Mabuto regime.

This was followed a year later by a belated effort to placate the neglected war veterans who demanded and were paid huge reparations for their participation in the struggle for independence. The combined impact of these two measures put the economy into a downwards spiral that has lasted a remarkable 6 years and has reduced the average Zimbabwean to penury.

The statistics are dismaying for a country not at war – GDP has declined by half, exports have also fallen by half, life expectancy is down to 34 years and falling, agricultural output is down 80 per cent and we have not been able to feed ourselves for 5 years. Inflation now stands at an all time high and is in the hyperinflation category and still rising. In 1980 one Zimbabwe dollar bought US$1,40. Today one US dollar buys you 200 000 Zimbabwe dollars.

But for all the trauma and conflict, the country is still what it always has been, a friendly, peaceful place with delightful, hard working people. The bush is still there and with it the wilderness with it's roaring lion and coughing leopard. The great Zambezi River with its white water rapids and the fighting Tiger fish. The wonderful quiet evenings and the crisp mornings with the Heuglins Robin calls and the warm moonlight nights with the soft calls of the nightjar.

Most of all it is still home – even if we are a long way from our roots. One day soon, we might get a government that will recognise us for who we are – just people trying to contribute in any way we can and in the process making life better for ourselves, our families and the wider community.

Phineas by John Wiseman

My father died when I was 18 months old in 1940, leaving my mother with a mine and a farm in the Que Que district. One day on the way back to the mine, we saw a bundle in the road near the Baobab tree about 12 miles out of Que Que on the Gokwe Road. Mother stopped the pick up and got out to investigate. It turned out to be a black infant aged no more than a few hours. The Infant was taken into Mother's care and brought to the mine. On arrival at the mine, Mother phoned the Police to report the incident and then went off to the compound to find a wet nurse for the child. Eventually mother found a suitable woman and after promising payment for caring for the infant, left him in the care of the wet nurse.

The police investigated the incident, but never did find the child's mother. My mother named the infant Phineas, and ended up paying for his upkeep thereafter.

Mother however believed that everyone had to earn his keep, so when Phineas was about four years old he was given the job of goose boy. His duties involved letting the geese out of their pen every morning, keeping an eye on them during the day and returning them in the evening. For this, Phineas was allowed to have tea and sandwiches with the house servants, in the morning, and was given lunch. The situation remained satisfactory over the years, as Phineas went to school, was promoted to feeding the dogs and cats, cleaning the swimming pool, and eventually, he was taught to become a groom. Phineas adored the horses, and proved to be a very good groom, and all went well until some years later, whilst we were sitting under the mulberry trees having a sundowner, and my sister's favourite stallion came home with a saddle but no one in the saddle.

Enquiries revealed that Phineas had illegally, saddled the horse, and ridden off to a nearby beer drink. He had tethered the stallion behind a hut, and then went off and imbibed more than a wise quantity of beer. However, what Phineas had not noticed was that the stallion had been tied next to the mosese, at which he had been eating with the proverbial horse's appetite. When Phineas eventually decided to go home, it was a matter for debate who was the worse for wear.

Anyway, Phineas trying to impress his drinking cronies set off with great gusto at a full gallop. What happened after that was never accurately verified, but suffice it to say that when Phineas was found, he was hanging about fifteen feet down a disused mine shaft by his leather belt, which was snagged on a piece of round iron protruding from an old timber support. Phineas was rescued and was told that he was clearly too unreliable to look after the horses, so he was promoted to work on the mine, where his job was to watch the belts driving the machinery. When they began to slip, he was to stop the machine, apply belt dressing to prevent the slip, and then re-start the machine.

All went well for a couple of months, and then unbeknown to us, he decided to become a bit more efficient, and not stop the machine before applying the belt dressing. Sadly, the inevitable did eventually happen, and Phineas' clothes got caught between the belt and a pulley, and Phineas was dragged into the works and killed.

A picture form the days when a Rhodesian pound was a pound and bought a dozen beers with snacks on the side.

Now a zimbeer costs 45 tons of one cent coins!

The Jolly Poacher from Belinda Sherwell

Sing this song to the tune of Waltzing Matilda, with an indigenous African accent.

Verse1.
Once a jolly poacher sat by the Limpopo, under the shade of a baobab tree,
He sung as he sat as he waited for the in-yamazan *(wild game) you'll come a twisting matwetwe with me.

Chorus
You'll come a twisting, you'll come a twisting, you'll come a twisting matwetwe with me, as he sung and he sat and he waiting for the in-yamazan, you'll come a twisting matwetwe with me.

Verse 2.
Down came a reed buck to drink at the Limpopo, up jumped the poacher and bumbered him quickly, and he sang as he shoved that reed buck in his mielie sack you'll go down well with sudza and tea.

Chorus
You'll go down well, you'll go down well, you'll go down well with sudza and tea and he sung as he shoved that reed buck in his meilie sack you'll go down well with sudza and tea.

Verse 2.
Down came the boys mounted on their Yamahas down came the chaps from the BSAP. Who's that jolly reed buck you got in your melie sack you'll come to Gwana-Gwanzin-gwe with me.

Chorus
You'll come to Gwana, you'll come to Gwana, you'll come to Gwana-Gwanzin-Gwe with me.
                    HOW! Do you know what happended next?
Verse 3.
Up jumped the poacher and he jumped into the Limpopo – saying "you'll never make me a restrictee"
And his voice my be heard as you pass by the Limpopo

HOW! I'm such a fool for jumping in the Limpopo because in Gwana the scoff is all free.

Eastern Highlands Bike Ride by Bernie Boshoff

I finished my military service in July 1968, and joined Air Rhodesia as an apprentice radio technician in August at the princely wage of 30 pounds per month. 5 pounds went in tax and deductions, and another 5 pounds in rent to my parents. Without their help, I could never have lived on the remaining 20 pounds, and I will be forever grateful to them. By 1970, I had acquired a second hand Honda CB350 motorcycle which cost me a massive $620. Our currency had gone metric by this stage. My motorcycle helmets cost me a lot more than that these days!

During this year, I had to take some leave, though I didn't have enough money to go on any fancy trips, so after a few days kicking my heels around home I got bored, so I decided to go on a tour of the Eastern Highlands on the bike. On the first day, I shot up to Inyanga and spent the night at my parents small farm. My dad recommended that I go down the Honde valley and visit the Aberfoyle tea estate, where they had a country club that would take guests overnight. Although the war was already affecting tourism in the area, I wasn't too worried and thought that was a good idea.

So the next morning I set off to the Honde.

The roads were all dirt except the stretch which descends the escarpment from the Inyanga highlands to the Honde valley floor. This is a fearsome bit of road, very steep and with tight switch backs. Many African busses and trucks have severe accidents here because the drivers cook the brakes on the way down, then run off the road and over the edge.

This wasn't a problem on the bike and I enjoyed the ride down. The valley floor is some 3000 feet lower than the Inyanga tablelands and the climate is completely different. You go from mountain forests and trout streams to lowveld heat and Baobab trees within a couple of miles. The tea estates are up at the North end of the valley, and to get there, you first have to go through about 20 miles of Tribal Trust Land (TTL). I didn't have any trouble here, except that I began to worry about fuel. I didn't know if I could get fuel at Aberfoyle, and if that proved negative, I didn't think I had enough to get out of the valley again. However, I soon spotted an African store that had a fuel pump and I managed to get some there.

At the North end of the valley, the climate changes again. The tea estates are tucked up against the base of the escarpment, directly under the mass of Mount Inyangani. The rainfall here is over 100 inches per year, and the air is hot and humid, perfect for tea. The natural bush is Tarzan of the Apes type jungle, with massive trees, thick undergrowth, and numerous cool streams running down from the mountain. The scenery is fantastic, with Mount Inyangani looming over you on the one side, and the flat, hot plains of Mozambique stretching away into the distance on the other. After an interesting ride through the tea estates, I finally arrived at the Aberfoyle club, and went in. I had arrived just in time for lunch, and I was the only customer present.

There were about 6 waiters, a barman, and the whole kitchen staff with nothing to do except serve me. I felt like royalty, and had a fantastic lunch finished off with a lemon steam pudding that I can still remember 35 years later, and all at a subsidized club price.

After lunch, I booked a room and then went exploring. The club was like something you would see in a James Bond movie. There was a swimming pool, tennis courts, and a beautiful golf course carved into that imposing jungle. And through the middle of this ran a fairly large stream, still cool and clear from the mountain, where you could go trout fishing. The bird life was fantastic, mostly exotic parrots and parakeets, the like of which I had never seen before. And all this just for me, I was a bit overwhelmed and didn't know what to do with it all.

Fortunately, that evening a few guys from the tea estate arrived. At first, they looked at me like I was something the dog had brought in, but when they saw the bike, the ice was broken. Nearly every guy worth his salt has a bike somewhere in his background. We soon ended up in the bar, and I couldn't believe my eyes. The country had been under sanctions for 5 years already, and you couldn't get Scotch Whisky anywhere else in Rhodesia, but this place had whisky. Man, they had 6 shelves, each about 6 feet long, and they were lined from end to end with bottles of Scotch, and no two were the same brand. I didn't know there were that many types in the world.

I love Scotch whisky, and it was all at club prices. I started at one end of the shelves, determined to taste all the Scotch in the bar. I don't remember how far I got. The next morning, I woke up with a thick head, but after a good breakfast, I felt better, and set off on more adventures. I rode back up the valley and turned South towards Umtali. From there, I went up the Vumba Mountains and had lunch and a beer at the Leopard Rock hotel, but I couldn't afford to stay there, so I carried on and stopped for the night at Hot Springs where I camped for the night. I couldn't face another piss up there, so I had a quiet night, and resumed my travels the next morning in good condition.

From Hot Springs, I back tracked slightly, and rode up to Cashel, and then through to Melsetter, Skyline Junction, and back to Birchenough Bridge for lunch and a beer. I then intended to ride through to Fort Victoria, but my map showed a road going through Bikita and Zaka to Buffalo Range. I had never seen the lowveld sugar estates, so I thought, what the hell, I would give that road a try. So, when I got to the Bikita turn off, I took it. Bad decision.

I soon realized that I was in the middle of a huge TTL, and instead of there being one road, like the map showed, there were dozens of them, going every which way, and all unmarked. At every junction, I took the biggest looking road, or the one heading South. There was a different feel to the Africans here. The Adults seemed hostile, and the children all ran away when they saw me. I suppose most of them had never seen a motorbike before. Fortunately, I was travelling fairly fast, and none of them could react fast enough to do anything about me. I soon began to regret my decision to take this road, and I wanted to turn around, but the fuel situation had raised it's head again, I didn't have enough to go back. I had to get to Buffalo Range.

The TTL was even bigger than I first imagined. I thought it would never end. Soon, the sun went down, and the next thing I was riding in the dark with no directional guidance. I was getting really worried when I suddenly came to a fence and a cattle grid, and I was out of the TTL and into bush. Thank God, I rode another mile, then decided to stop before I got seriously lost. I switched off my lights so no one would see me, and I rode about half a mile into the bush and stopped for the night. I didn't put up my tent or light a fire because I was still too close to the TTL, and I didn't want to be attacked in the middle of the night. In the army, I had slept in the bush many times, but this was different, there was not a single sound the whole night. There were no insects, no night birds, no animals, no people, just total silence, it was quite eerie.

After a restless night, with no dinner or breakfast, or anything to drink, I woke at dawn and got going.

It turned out that I was only about 10 miles out of Buffalo Range, but I had got there too early and nothing was open, so, as I still had a little petrol, I went on to Triangle. There, I managed to scare up some breakfast and a load of fuel, but with the flat country, and miles of sugar cane, there was nothing interesting to see, so I carried on to Ngundu Halt, and turned towards Fort Victoria. I got there around midday, and stopped for the usual fuel, lunch, and a beer.

While I was having the beer, a young man, about 30 years old, came into the pub and sat down next to me. He was a South African ex biker, and had seen my bike outside. We were soon chatting, and he told me about his life. About 10 years earlier, he rode from Jo-burg where he lived, up to Kimberly to attend a big party. While he was there, he was chatting up some girl, and to make conversation, he asked her where he could get some diamonds. Kimberly is famous for it's diamond mine.

The girl asked if he was serious, and of course he said yes. So she said wait here, and off she went. About half an hour later she returned with a bag of rough diamonds which her dad had stolen from the mine, but was too afraid to sell. Well, he was also afraid of taking the diamonds, but to save face, he offered her 100 Rand for them, which was all he had, and to his amazement, she accepted that. So he took the diamonds back to Jo-burg, and after some very careful negotiations, he managed to sell them for 5,000 Rand without getting caught.

With the 5 grand, he bought a small plot of land outside Jo-burg, but instead of trying to farm it, he just improved it by putting up fences, clearing bush, and putting in a borehole. He then sold the block at a profit, and bought a bigger one, and did the same again. By the time I met him, he had just bought a huge ranch near Triangle, and was improving that, with no intention of actually farming it. I bet he is a very wealthy man today, he had taken a little bit of luck and turned it into a huge fortune in a short time with hard work and intelligence.

Well, after that interesting conversation, and a few beers, I was about out of money, so I decided to run for home. I got on my trusty Honda, pointed it towards Salisbury, and opened the throttle to the stop. I lay on the tank to keep out of the wind, and roared home at about 100 Mph all the way. What a great little bike, 200 miles flat out, and it was still idling like a Swiss watch when I got home.

Any British bike of the day would have spat it's pistons out on the road if you tried that.

"Anyone for Darts?"
Photograph from Steve Bailey.

This is my Rhodesia by Patricia Wilsenach

Reading the article on your "Rhodesian Memories" book had me thinking on what my real Rhodesian memories were.

Were they the black rain of the burning fuel depot just outside Salisbury that coated our faces for a week after the first flames shot into the night sky.

Arriving at work to find your desk on its side with its legs blown off, the windows of your office in shards on the floor and the little church next door a shattered shell of its former glory.

Flying to the Falls in a straight up ,straight across and straight down again pattern to avoid the missiles that killed your friends in the two Viscount disasters, or being questioned by the MP's because you were in the wrong place at the wrong time and seen talking to an Intelligence Major [whom you happened to work with] and a member of the S.A.S [Your brother] within an hour of each other.

Having your school friend's Mother come and explain to the class that they will never see their friend again as she has been shot and killed on the way back from her holiday in S.A. and that from now on you will travel in convoy to and from Beit Bridge or for that matter to the Rugby teams next game in a small town some distance from Salisbury.

Are these the memories of Rhodesia? Yes and No.

Rhodesia to me is, running barefoot down the hot tar road that appears to disappear in translucent waves just a few feet in front of you. The frail Flame Lilies forcing their way through the sandy soil to blaze in all their glory at the side of the road whilst the wild Dahlias shake their heavy heads as the wind tosses them to and fro between the long roadside grass.

Circling Kariba's runway , around and around whilst the airport officials, waving long sticks, chase the Elephants off the tarmac so the plane can land.

The myriads of flying ants floating in clouds across the land, the dragonflies and water skiers darting across the surface of the pools and lakes. The beautiful collection of large flowering trees and vivid and varied flora and fauna.

Going camping on the family farm and spending half the day chasing the pet bush pig around in the veld that you become so exhausted you forget to check your sleeping bag before you climb in it , and then are rudely awakened by the cold wet feeling of a snake crawling over your foot as you slide into your bed!!

The dark thunderstorm clouds hanging over the city or the heavy blue skies before a hail storm. The vivid sunsets that warm the sides of the buildings in the evening. Most of all the people ,strong and sensitive, supporting and helping each other, laughing and crying together but picking up the pieces when life wants to knock them down and smiling when things are good again.

That is my Rhodesia.

'Charlie Prince' dictated by Bill Bell

Charles Prince was the Chief Air Traffic Controller at Mount Hampden airport, which was situated close to Salisbury on the Sinoia road. He ran his piece of 'airspace' with an iron hand, which stemmed from his many years as a flight instructor.

He usually dressed in a similar way to the 'Air Force Uniform (Tropical) Dress' code, which included the 'Dysentery Bags' made infamous during the Second World War at the many Flight Training Centres situated around the country.

There are many stories told about Charlie Prince (Mr Prince to his face!) over the years, but one that springs to mind is when the "God Botherer" was in town. This was one of group of Missionaries that had fairly free rein in the sixties to run their flights to and from their various Mission Stations to Mount Hampden.

Charles christened them "God Botherers" and he had various names for different clubs and institutions associated with aviation. For example "Spraying Knuckleheads" was his expression for dropping parachutists, which used to infuriate 'Buster' Brown of the Parachute Club.

These Missionaries were Americans who were financed, ostensibly, by American Church Groups. As a result they had more modern equipment than the charter companies and flight schools that used to operate out of the same airfield.

One morning one of the missionaries parked his new Cessna 185 near the Control Tower. He prevailed upon Charles to come and see this new addition to the Missionary Fleet as it was equipped with all the latest navigation and radio aids.

Charles approached the aircraft with caution while the 'God Botherer' went through his speech extolling all the facilities and equipment inside the cockpit.

There was a small compartment door located on the right hand side of the Instrument Panel which had a logo which said that it "could and should be opened in the event of an emergency".

The 'GB' opened the door and out popped a bible.

On the front cover of the bible were the words, "GOD IS OUR PILOT", in large capital letters.

Charles glowered at it, then said in his authoritative voice,

"When you join my circuit, You take Command!"

He stomped back to his Control Tower with his moustaches at the 'high port'.

I remember Mt Hampden when Charles Prince was running the club and the control tower there. My dad (ex bomber pilot) and Percy Newton (ex spittie pilot) shared a two-seater chipmunk. VP-YKW. They used to take turns going up around dusk and doing ridiculously dangerous aerobatics such as banking between the two flagpoles which stood in front of the control tower and doing slow rolls along the runway with the lower wingtip within a few feet of the deck. My brothers-in-law, Ian and Ninx Kluckow also spent a bit of time there as they had a C182 for getting back and forth to the farm at Doma.......   Pete.

I remember the evening when Percy Newton paced out the distance between the control tower and the flag pole, and Charlie Prince came out of the tower, with moustache bristling and fist waving saying:
"Don't you bl**dy dare".
The problem was that the distance was less than the wingspan of the aircraft, so Percy had to bank the machine to get it through the 'slot'.
There were lots of crazy b***ers there, because they all had war experiences, and a lot of them did not take authority seriously.   Anon.

My parents belonged to Mashonaland Flying Club when they were first building the club house, and in fact my mother was the first woman private pilot licensed in the country.
Her instructor was 'Scott' Robbie, whose party trick was to fly over the airfield with a Tiger Moth, upside down. A 'Body' would fall out of one of the cockpits onto the runway, whereupon the aircraft would stall dive and spin, and the land with a perfect 'three pointer' in front of the control tower on the grass, apparently without a pilot.
All fantastic pilots, but also seriously nuts.
Great fun to fly with.
Lots of stories about them all.......   Anon.

Talking about characters, I remember Andre Holland when he was farming in Rhodesia. He went to a fancy dress ball dressed as Dracula. The party continued until after the "small hours", so he went straight from the party to where his farm workers were assembled for the reaping of the tobacco leaves.
He stood high on the trailer and directed operations, with his cloak swirling around in the morning breeze.
The Africans were mightily impressed, and their status in comparison to the other farms' labourers rose to new heights with such a charismatic and masterful 'Boss'. Anon.

Roasting Stuffed Chicken

The following cooking technique was sent to me in an apparent attempt to help novice cooks judge when to remove the roast chicken out of the oven in a condition when it is cooked , but not dried out.
Please refer all claims to your house insurance company.

6-7 lb chicken
1 c melted butter
1 c stuffing
1 c uncooked popcorn
salt & pepper to taste.
Preheat oven to 350 degrees.
Brush chicken well with melted butter, salt and pepper.
Fill cavity with stuffing and popcorn.
Place in baking pan in the oven.
Listen for the popping sounds.
When the chicken's ass blows out the oven door and the bird flies across the kitchen, the chicken is done.

Brother Conway from D Turner

We lived in a small suburb called Westwood and as a young boy I well recall a very kind and gentle catholic missionary called Brother Conway who would regularly call on my mother and offer one or two words from the bible. He was especially fond of me and my reserved nature and would often "advise" my mother to keep my wayward cousin at bay, as he would have a bad influence on me. Although I was only 4yrs old at the time I still have vivid memories of him sitting and sipping a cup of hot tea whilst talking in his gentle voice to my mum.

I was saddened when he was transferred to Musami Mission as this meant an end to the visits.

You can imagine my horror even as a little boy a few years later when The Herald reported that some missionaries had been killed by insurgents and the gentle priest, who I had grown fond of, had been among those mercilessly slaughtered.

242

'Morning Has Broken' by Robin D.W. Norton

Morning has broken, like the first morning
Blackbird has spoken, like the first bird
Praise for the singing! Praise for the morning!
Praise for them springing, fresh from the Word!

After so many years away from the Rhodesia I knew, the hymn 'Morning Has Broken', reminds me of the early morning starts I had when I used to drive to what was then Mount Hampden Aerodrome to have flying lessons with Harry Allen, who was at that time working as Chief Engineer for Field Aircraft Services at Salisbury Airport.

As a young lad I used to listen to LM Radio beamed from Lorenco Marques and at 6am every morning at that time, in the early 1970s, they used to play the Cat Stevens version of this song, which coincided with the last few minutes that I could get LM Radio as, with the sun and daytime, the radio signals could not make it to Salisbury, (well, not on my radio).

For me the important memories I have are almost all to do with aircraft, working for Fields we were close by the Air Trans Africa hangar, the site and sound of the big four engine DC7s and Super Constellation firing up the engines with clouds of smoke and the deep rumble as the engines settled into idle, later the powerful roar as the aircraft took off from 06, slowly getting louder and louder until they flew by still at low level heading off to who knows where.

I remember the friendships of that time and being able to go and ask for help and spares from other companies on the airport. They were happy times for me; even though the job itself was not what I was cut out for so I left Fields Aircraft Services after I qualified as a licensed engineer. My flying too was very limited, as I got my PPL on Piper J3 Cubs of the Mashonaland Flying Club aircraft. My PPL flight test was conducted by Charles Prince who, when he died young, had the airport named after him. Mount Hampden became Charles Prince Airport which name it retains to this day.

Other Salisbury Airport memories include the smell of the kerosene from the Air Rhodesia Viscounts as they started up their engines ready for the early morning departures around the country and South Africa, then the silence as the Airport went quiet until the Rhodesian Air Force based at New Sarum across the runway got started and came to life.

The C47 Dakotas often flew, I still recognise the sound of the Pratt and Witney 1340 engines on the very few occasions you get to hear them in the skies here in the UK.

The Canberras were also based at New Sarum and the Hunters used to come up from Thornhill, Vampires too were often deployed which all added to the interest especially when they arrived back from a sortie, arriving in pairs for a fast run down 06 to break over the tower before landing. Another type not to be forgotten, the little liked Aermacchi Al60 Trojan with its distinctive propeller noise caused by the prop tips nearing the speed of sound, I had quite a lot to do with them.

My real regret is that I was a very young and immature teenager. I was not at the airport long enough to make more friends and contacts and be able to mix with 'old' people, 'old' being relative as even 30 years old to me then was getting on a bit! Even so, the likes of Jack Malloch, Ken Rogers, Mike Saunders, Charles Prince and others who were and still are great names within Rhodesian Aviation, not forgetting Harry Allen who encouraged me and reminded me how privileged I was. I chatted to them all they all made a lasting impression on me. In more recent years I am grateful for the contacts I have made with many of the pilots and other people connected with Rhodesia and the aircraft world.

All I can say is it has been wonderful and incredibly interesting.

I first submitted photographs of aircraft before I left school in 1970, Flight International published some of my photographs, I then used to write and take photographs for Wings over Africa on a regular basis and then for the Durban based magazine, World Air News whose Managing Editor is Tom Chalmers, an ex corporate pilot. Some 35 years later in 2006 he will be using my aircraft photographs from Farnborough 2006 and then later on images taken from the National Air Races held in Reno, Nevada. Just proves how not much changes, as I still retain my intense interest in big and powerful radial piston engines.

My thanks to all my Rhodesian friends and acquaintances.

I certainly have not forgotten you even if you have me!

The Silent Pool in the Sinoia Caves

The Silent Pool at Sinoia, Rhodesia consists of a blue pool 270 feet long by 150 feet wide situated 150 feet below ground level in a cave. Part of the pool is open to the sky through a wide shaft. These caves are situated some 80 miles northeast of Salisbury on the road to Zambia. The fantastically limpid water has a dry season visibility of 200 to 300 feet with a temperature of 72°F all the year round. The flat silt floor at nearly 340 ft would appear to be the bottom of the cave, or perhaps part of a very large mud shelf. The pool is known by the local Africans as Chirorodziwa - the Pool of the Fallen. Apparently in the 1830s the warlike Angoni Tribe was moving northwards, when they raided the nearby villagers and threw them into the pool from the hole at ground level.

A White Rhodesian's Apologies   Anon

We want to say we're sorry for trying to help you up
Assist you climb the ladder of success
We tried to feed you all, and help you sip the Cup
But all we did was make a bigger mess.

We thought that bringing doctors, and hospitals to life
Would be the way to earn your gratitude
We're sorry that we fought against the plagues and strife
And malnutrition from the lack of food

We're regretful for the training, and free education,
Rebuilding of the schools you burned to ash
We recorded all your languages, taught maths to all the Nation
We should have known that this to you was trash

We're so regretful for, the farms and mines and trading
That we brought to full and fine production
And that we made employment so that poverty was fading
The clothes and cars we lured you with seduction

We're sorry for the roads and bridges and the trains
Because you kill yourselves with accidents
Forgive us for the dams to irrigate when rains
Fail. Blame us and not coincidence

We're apologetic for the charities we started
We should have known that these were foreign things
And as for paying all taxes, we were too open hearted
We should have treated you like your own kings

But now you have it back and taken what was ours
You're making what you wanted all along
It must be right and proper because the planet powers
Agreed that you were right and we were wrong

So we've taken all our sons, our daughters and our wives
And moved to places where these standards are
Longed-for and desired, we've started brand new lives
We hope you will forgive us from afar

247

"**Appendix A**" of a document commissioned by the United States Army called "Lessons for Contemporary Counterinsurgencies, "The Rhodesian Experience".

I am indebted to the 'Rand Arroyo Center' for permission to publish these extracts written by authors **Bruce Hoffman, Jennifer M. Taw and David Arnold**.

Many former Rhodesian police, army air force and intelligence officers currently living in South Africa, Great Britain, Canada and the United States consented to be interviewed for these documents obtained from the 'Rand Arroyo Center'. Many have requested to remain anonymous. The following can be acknowledged however. Dr Richard Wood, Professor of History at the University of Natal, who was a former Rhodesian Intelligence officer who has provided information from his book on the History of Rhodesia and from official documents from the PM Mr I. D. Smith's office. We can also acknowledge the contributions from General Walls and Wing Commander Peter Briscoe.

THE RHODESIAN SECURITY FORCES

THE RHODESIAN ARMY

The Rhodesian Army's command structure and organization were modelled directly on the British Army. A Lieutenant-General commanded the Army and was responsible to the Minister of Defence. Later in the conflict, when COMOPS (a combined operations organization) was created, its commander exercised operational control over the Army as well as independently commanding the Army's special forces. As Rhodesia had very limited white manpower upon which to draw for professional military service, a large part of the Army consisted of national service and reserve personnel. Initially, all regular combat units were staffed with full-time career soldiers, but after 1972, when national service was increased from 18 to 24 months, inductees were drafted into some of the Army's special forces. In addition, many foreign volunteers, mostly from South Africa but also from Britain, the United States, France, Australia, and New Zealand, served in the Rhodesian military.

THE RHODESIAN ARMY SPECIAL FORCES

Rhodesian African Rifles
The Rhodesian African Rifles' (RAR) two battalions were composed of black soldiers led by white officers. The black soldiers' knowledge of tribal cultures, ability to speak various tribal languages, and bush skills enabled them to obtain local intelligence that the average white soldier could not hope to acquire and they could

function better in Rhodesia's harsh climate and terrain than the average urban-born and raised white trooper. Although the RAR first proved themselves capable soldiers fighting with the British in Malaya more than a decade before, their initial performance in Rhodesia was poor, giving them a bad reputation among other Army units. Improved training, however, raised the RAR's performance, and by the end of the war many RAR personnel were participating in elite force operations, such as the various Fireforces.

Rhodesian Light Infantry

The Rhodesian Light Infantry (RLI) was originally conceived as a light infantry unit but later changed its tactical mission and structure to a commando organization as it became more actively involved in the counterinsurgency campaign. The battalion was made up of four commando units of about 90 men each. They were trained as paratroopers and provided the backbone of the Fireforces. The RLI also participated in most of the major external operations and cross-border raids. Because of their proficiency, they were classified as "Special Forces" and, after 1977, came under the control of COMOPS.

Special Air Services (SAS)

The SAS was modelled on the elite British unit of the same name and fought beside the British in Malaya during the 1960s. During the early stages of the Rhodesian counterinsurgency campaign, the SAS was employed mainly in tracking insurgents. Later, the unit was expanded into a regiment comprising A, B, C, and D squadrons and for the remainder of the conflict was employed in clandestine external operations. Volunteers from various units were rigorously tested for mental and physical stamina before being accepted by the SAS and then were extensively trained in parachuting, canoeing, bush craft, explosives techniques, and other special tasks. The unit maintained a high standard of efficiency and achieved a very high rate of operational success.

Selous Scouts

The Selous Scouts were formed at the beginning of Operation Hurricane in 1973 and tasked with obtaining intelligence on the size and movement of insurgent groups. Like the SAS, most Selous Scout personnel were volunteers who had undergone a stringent selection course before being trained in parachuting, insurgent tactics, bush survival, and weaponry. Surrendered or captured insurgents whom the Rhodesians had "turned" were also included in the unit. Their inclusion was critical because the information these recent defectors provided kept the unit current on insurgent tactics and operating procedures. Because of their success, the Selous Scouts doubled in size over the course of the conflict. and eventually some 420 members were deployed on active service. Their role was similarly expanded to include external operations, and they became responsible for training and administering the combat tracking units in addition to their "pseudo" operations role.

Greys Scouts

The Greys Scouts were a mounted unit trained specifically for tracking on horseback. They could thus cover more ground than trackers on foot and could more easily escape insurgent ambushes. Personnel were recruited from the regular Army and trained in equitation. The unit was also used for patrolling and occasionally on cross-border raids. Because it was classified as special forces, it was also under the control of COMOPS after 1977.

The British South Africa Police (BSAP)

The BSAP was Rhodesia's national police force and was responsible for maintaining law and order throughout the country. Although it was modelled on the British police system, the BSAP was more like the Royal Canadian Mounted Police in its development, structure and organisation. It was commanded by a Commissioner of Police who, in turn, was responsible to (and appointed by) the Minister of Justice (later, Minister of Justice and Law and Order). The BSAP was organised into branches, the most Important of which were the Duty Uniform Branch, Criminal Investigation Department, Special Branch, Support Unit, and Police Reserve.

Duty Uniform Branch

The Duty Uniform Branch performed most of the routine police work. They were also responsible for riot and crowd control and the staffing of Police Anti-terrorist Units (PAW). Ranks of constable and above were "de facto" reserved exclusively for white personnel until 1976, but there was nevertheless heavy recruitment of black personnel in the lower ranks.

Criminal Investigation. Department (CID)

Serious crimes, or those of a more specialized nature, were handled by detectives in the Criminal Investigation Department. The CID had posts at all the major police stations both in the urban and rural areas. It drew its personnel from the Duty Uniform Branch, and successful applicants underwent further training and probation before being granted the permanent rank of detective. As in the Duty Uniform Branch, black detectives were recruited but were confined to the lower ranks.

Special Branch (SB)

Special Branch was responsible for internal political intelligence. It drew virtually all its personnel from the CID, was administered by the BSAP, headed by the Director of the Internal Affairs Department, and controlled by the CIO. In the early stages of the conflict, SB agents penetrated the highest levels of the insurgent armies.

SB's role thus expanded to external intelligence as insurgent recruits, including undercover SB agents, were sent out of the country for training. Even after the Rhodesian military developed its own intelligence unit, the Army and Air Force continued to rely primarily on the Special Branch for intelligence.

Support Unit

The support unit was the BSAP's paramilitary wing, and it was organised along similar lines to the Rhodesian African Rifles. Its white personnel who commanded the sections and platoons of the unit, were drawn from the ranks of the Duty Uniform Branch. Although the members of the support unit received extensive military and riot-control training, they were organised along military lines, and were heavily armed. Until the start of the rural insurgency they performed only ceremonial duties. It was not until 1976 that the unit was used to its full potential as a paramilitary force, at which time it performed successfully.

Police Reserve

The Police Reserve was developed as one means of overcoming the manpower shortage in Rhodesia. Several specialized reserve units were formed to supplement and relieve the regular police. This enabled routine police crime-prevention duties, critical in preventing urban infiltration as well, to continue to be carried out even in times of emergency. In the 1970s, Rhodesia's national service was expanded to embrace the police reserve. All white Rhodesian men were required to complete two years military service after leaving high school and although this service was initially restricted to the Army and Air Force, it was later expanded to include the police, prison services, and Internal Affairs Department. Those who joined the police received much the same training as regulars, and then transferred to the A-Reserve or Field Reserve.

The Field Reserve.

The Field Reserve comprised all white volunteers who, before the rural insurgency, supplemented riot squads in urban and rural areas. As the rural insurgency grew, however, the field reservists were employed on various static guard duties, convoy protection, and defending white farms in the operational areas. When Police Anti-Terrorist units were formed, many were composed entirely of field reserve volunteers. In 1977, after several bombing attempts in the urban areas, the reservists were used for cordon and search operations.

The A-Reserve.

The A-Reserve comprised volunteers who, after receiving training in law and police duties, worked one shift month at their local police stations. In emergencies, the reservists were expected to take over normal police duties, releasing the regulars for other assignments.

The Special Reserve.

The Special Reserve was formed at the height of the black nationalist unrest during the early 1960s. These reservists were white homeowners who patrolled their own neighbourhoods at night and were given limited powers of arrest. "Key Point Special Reservists" were employees of vital installations such as power stations, strategic factories, communication stations, and other important non-military facilities who were trained specifically to protect these facilities.

The Police Air Reserve Wing.

The Police Air Reserve Wing consisted of volunteers (usually farmers) who owned their own aircraft and assisted the regular police in emergencies for air reconnaissance and search, and, occasionally for casualty evacuation as well. During counterinsurgency operations in the area, the senior Air Force Commander assumed command over the local Air Reserve Wing. In these instances, the Air Reserve Wing was often used as a telstar, circling at high altitude to relay radio messages between security force units operating on the ground and their area JOCs.

The African Field Reserve.

The African Field Reserve was established to involve blacks in combating urban unrest during the 1960s. Although many blacks were successfully recruited in the initial drive, maintaining the reserve proved difficult. Not only were blacks reluctant to be involved because of threats made by black nationalists, but those blacks who did join were relegated to menial duties. Nonetheless, the African reservists provided the police with a large pool of manpower that could be called upon during emergencies and this was extremely valuable, especially during the first wave of urban disorder.

Police Anti-Terrorist Units.

In 1966, following the first serious guerrilla infiltrations into Rhodesia, the police started training personnel in counterinsurgency tactics. Special Police Anti-Terrorist Units (PATU) were established, composed of five volunteers (typically four white and one black) from the regular police. When they could be spared from their routine duties, they were assigned to two-week tours of duty in rural areas. Because of their limited firepower, the PATU sticks were initially deployed on the fringes of operational areas, primarily on reconnaissance missions. As the security forces faced mounting manpower constraints however the PATU sticks were deployed on combat missions, often in conjunction with the Army.

South African Police (SAP).

The South African police served in Rhodesia between 1967 and 1974. Despite being a police unit, the SAP operated as a virtual military force in Rhodesia for most of the conflict. The SAP initially was commanded by the Rhodesian Army. The SAP provided its own air support in the form of Allouette 111 helicopters. Its air crews, consequently, came under the command of the Rhodesian Air Force. Most of the SAP personnel were employed on patrol duties along the north-western border, although some were deployed in the Operation Hurricane area. SAP personnel were also seconded to the BSAP or the Rhodesian Special Branch for other duties. While the helicopter units performed well in Rhodesia, the SAP ground units had an uneven record, enjoyed few successes, and experienced a higher casualty rate than the Rhodesians largely because they operated on their own, as Army units, in unfamiliar territory and against tribes with whom they were unfamiliar. To rectify these weaknesses, the Rhodesian police trained several SAP units as PATU. Operating with and under the control of Rhodesian PATU units, these enjoyed increased success.

THE RHODESIAN AIR FORCE

The Rhodesian Air Force command and rank structure was based on the British Royal Air Force. It was commanded by an Air Marshal who, like his counterpart in the Army, was accountable to the Minister of Defence. The RhAF was never a large air force. In 1965. it consisted of only 1,200 regular personnel. At the peak of its strength during the insurgency, it had a maximum of 2,300 personnel of all races, but of these only 150 were pilots actively involved in combat operations. These pilots however, were able to fly all of the aircraft in the Air Force inventory, which gave the RhAF a considerable amount of flexibility. Pilots were rotated through the various squadrons partly to maintain their skills on all aircraft and partly to relieve fellow pilots flying more dangerous sorties.

The Department Of Internal Affairs

The Department of Internal Affairs (IAD) personnel were the acknowledged experts on tribal culture and mores and therefore played a prominent role in the conflict. IAD officers served at the Joint Operational Centres and were heavily involved in implementing such civic measures as the protected villages programme. The paramilitary "Guard Force," which was responsible for the security of the protected villages also came under IAD control.

White Internal Affairs personnel received extensive training in African tribal law and customs and were required to speak at least one of the tribal languages. Despite this it is evident that many of the senior officers failed to fully appreciate the black population's nationalist political aspirations. This became clear when IAD assessments of black political opinion were at odds with Special Branch's assessment. Unfortunately, though IAD was wrong in several of these cases, IAD senior personnel had the government's ear and IAD assessments were generally accepted over those of Special Branch.

Appendix C of a document commissioned by the United States Army called "Lessons for Contemporary Counterinsurgencies, "The Rhodesian Experience", with kind permission from the Rand Arroyo Center.

CROSS-BORDER RAIDS

Throughout the conflict various elements of the Rhodesian Air Force and Army conducted numerous operations and raids outside of the country's borders (see Fig. C.I). The more important are summarised here by the units that conducted them. In this respect, the various so-called "hot pursuit" raids that were carried out into the north-eastern border area of Mozambique during the beginning of Operation Hurricane are not covered because these operations were being conducted in a country that at that time was friendly to Rhodesia and had authorized the raids.

This map shows the positions of various external raids carried out by Rhodesian Security Forces, described on the following pages.

THE RHODESIAN SPECIAL SERVICES (SAS)
AND THE RHODESIAN LIGHT INFANTRY (RLI)

The SAS was the best equipped and trained of all the Rhodesian units for clandestine operations. Like their British counterparts, this was one of their prime functions, although, as it transpired, it was only during the last years of the conflict that they were used extensively in this role. Before 1972, the CIO used small units of the SAS to conduct clandestine operations into Zambia. Of the two missions that have been reported in the open literature, neither was successful. In one an explosive device accidentally detonated just as the group was about to cross the Zambezi river into Zambia, killing several operators and causing the mission's abandonment. In a later operation, a group of SAS were successfully flown into Lusaka but were unable to complete their mission and left without sustaining any losses.

The RLI conducted numerous hot pursuit raids into Mozambique during the early days of Operation Hurricane after the Portuguese abandoned the country to FRELIMO and conducted several external operations of a conventional nature against insurgent bases in conjunction with the SAS.

1. Operation Big Bang: South West Zambia. August-October 1978 (Fig. target A). This operation, involving 48 SAS personnel, was to eliminate a large ZIPRA base camp just on the Zambezi River. The raiders crossed the Zambezi River by boat and then proceeded on foot to the camp and attacked it, killing nine insurgents and capturing or destroying vast quantities of equipment. The SAS suffered no casualties.

2. Canoe Operations: Cabora Basa Lake. Mozambique, January 1977 (Fig. target B). This operation involved 12 SAS troops who used canoes to sneak into Mozambique via the Cabora Basa Lake and conduct several hit and run raids against ZANLA and FRELIMO bases and installations. The group operated on the lake for six weeks while they mined roads, ambushed vehicles carrying FRELIMO and ZANLA forces, and attacked several insurgent camps. At the conclusion of the operation, the Rhodesian force had killed at least 20 FRELIMO guerrillas (including the commanding officer and his second in command, as well as the Political Commissar

of Mukumbura). The SAS sustained no casualties. At later stages during the conflict, the SAS and Selous Scouts conducted other canoe operations with similar success.

3. Attack of Chioca Garrison: Mozambique, March-May 1977 (Fig. target C). This operation involved an attack on a ZANLA camp near the town of Choica in the north-eastern border area of Mozambique by a force of 22 SAS personnel who were transported by helicopter to a point 11 miles from their target. From there, they proceeded on foot under cover of darkness to the target. The camp was attacked at first light with explosives, mortar, and automatic weapons, resulting in its complete destruction and the deaths of at least 38 insurgents. One SAS member was killed.

Following this attack, ZANLA insurgents moved into the town of Chioca. A group of 16 SAS operators then returned to Mozambique to carry out a series of ambush and mine laying operations. In May, this force was supplemented by an airdrop of 12 more SAS who conducted a dawn attack on Chioca, destroying an unoccupied ZANLA camp. By the operation's conclusion, the SAS accounted for 24 enemy killed in ambushes for only two of their own, who sustained slight wounds from enemy mortar fire during the occupation of Chioca.

4. Ambush of ZANLA insurgents between Chioca and Tete: Mozambique, October 1977 (Fig. target D). This ambush was conducted by 12 SAS operators after a CIO radio intercept had revealed that 24 ZANLA insurgents would be returning to Mozambique from the Operation Hurricane area. The raiding party was air dropped at night into an area some 31 miles from the intended ambush site. After arriving at the

site, the SAS waited for 10 days until the insurgents arrived. Twenty-one insurgents were killed and only one ZANLA person escaped the ambush. The SAS suffered no casualties.

5. Operations in Southeast Mozambique: October-November 1977 (Fig. target E). In October 1977 the SAS took over external operation in south-eastern Mozambique from the Selous Scouts. Their first mission was to disrupt ZANLA convoys on the road south of the town of Mapai, just over 50 miles from the Rhodesian border. Twenty-two SAS troops were dropped from an Air-Trans-Africa DC-7. Four of them sustained sprained and broken limbs during the jump and were left hidden in the bush while the remaining force ambushed a three-truck convoy, destroying one vehicle and killing 20 ZANLA insurgents. The other two trucks managed to turn around and escape but were subsequently destroyed by RhAF Hunter jet fighters. Three SAS personnel were wounded in the ambush.

In November, a stick of 16 SAS men were parachuted 75 miles inside Mozambique to ambush a motorized convoy bringing ZANLA insurgents and their equipment to Mapai from Maputo. While preparing the ambush site, they encountered a small group of FRELIMO/ZANLA and killed three. Before they could change the ambush site, the convoy arrived and the leading truck, carrying ammunition, hit a mine and exploded. The burning truck prevented the others from continuing so the insurgent forces retreated into defensive positions for the night. The SAS requested an air strike for the next morning and, after first light, a Lynx and Hunters arrived and destroyed or damaged 21 of the remaining vehicles. ZANLA suffered over 50 casualties. The SAS sustained no losses.

6. Operation Dingo: Mozambique, November 1977 (Fig. targets F and G). This operation consisted of an attack on two large ZANLA bases in east and northeast Mozambique. The first attack was launched against the larger of the two camps, called Chimoio, which held some 11,000 insurgents and was situated about 56 miles east of the Rhodesian) border city of Umtali. The attack began with a bombing run by RhAF Canberras, followed by Hunters, Vampires, and Lynx. Virtually every available RhAF combat aircraft was used in the operation. A combined force of 97 SAS and 48 RLI paratroopers then sealed off two sides of the camp while the third side was covered by 47 heliborne RLI troops. The fourth side was contained by helicopter gunships. For the helicopters to refuel, the Rhodesian force had to create a temporary staging base inside Mozambique. The camp was taken after a day's fighting and some 2,000 insurgents were killed. The Rhodesians suffered losses of one soldier and Vampire pilot killed and about eight other personnel wounded. Large amounts of equipment were either captured or destroyed while captured documents revealed a considerable amount of useful intelligence.

Twenty-four hours later the same Rhodesian force attacked the Tembo camp housing about 4.000 insurgents. It was situated northeast of the Cabora Basa Lake 140 miles from the Rhodesian border and required that the Rhodesians establish two helicopter refuelling bases in Mozambique. The same basic tactics were used, but as the camp was in two parts, it was not possible to envelope it as easily as at Chimoio. As a result, large numbers of insurgents were able to escape into the bush during the Rhodesian assault. Nevertheless, some 86 insurgents were killed, a large quantity of equipment was destroyed, and the Rhodesians sustained no losses.

7. Hot Pursuit: Botswana, February 1978 (Fig. target H). This operation was mounted on a ZIPRA camp just across the border with Botswana near the Kazangula ferry by a force of 28 SAS following an insurgent on an SAS patrol just inside the border with Rhodesia. The SAS force tracked the insurgents to a camp across the border and killed 17 to 24 ZIPRA insurgents and Botswana Defence Force members found there. No casualties were sustained by the SAS.

8. Attack on ZANLA Barracks: Tete. Mozambique, May 1978 (Fig. target I). This was another canoe operation on the Cabora Basa Lake involving eight SAS operators who attacked the Battariao Barracks in the town of Tete. Time delay explosive charges destroyed the buildings after the SAS had left. An unknown number of ZANLA insurgents were also killed. The SAS team sustained no losses and was later evacuated by helicopter.

9. Operation Elbow: Southwest Zambia, January and June 1978 (Fig. target A). An SAS force attacked a ZIPRA base known as BK camp on the Zambian side of the Zambezi River east of the Victoria Falls. They killed 27 ZIPRA insurgents and also laid land mines on surrounding roads that caused several casualties among Zambian police and military personnel. ZIPRA subsequently established another camp further inland that the SAS again successfully attacked. By June, ZIPRA had moved back 20 miles from the river and bad set up a base at a mine that was assaulted by a force of 12 helicopter-borne troops who made their way on foot to the ambush site. The Rhodesian force had to remain in their ambush positions for 11 days to attack three heavy Soviet made trucks packed with fuel, ammunition, and new ZIPRA recruits. All the vehicles were destroyed and 69 ZIPRA insurgents were killed. Several more guerrillas including a senior commander were killed shortly afterwards when their vehicle detonated a mine laid by the SAS before they left the area. The SAS suffered no casualties.

10. Operation Gatling: Central Zambia, October 19, 1978 (Fig. targets J and K). This attack was part of an operation involving three ZIPRA bases deep inside Zambia. An air strike was launched against a base called Freedom Camp and is described in the external air operations chapter. Immediately after the bombing run, a raid was mounted on the Mkushi camp situated 93 miles northeast of Lusaka. The operation consisted of an air strike by some of the same aircraft involved in the Freedom Camp attack followed up by 120 SAS paratroopers and 45 SAS heliborne troops (including an 81 mm mortar unit). Approximately 600 insurgents were killed and large quantities of arms and equipment were either captured or destroyed. One SAS member was seriously wounded. At the conclusion of this raid, the Rhodesians struck at ZIPRA's CGT-2 (Communist Guerrilla Training) camp 62 miles east of Lusaka. An air strike was similarly followed by a vertical envelopment conducted by RLI paratroopers and heliborne troops. To provide refuelling for the helicopters, the Rhodesian force established temporary staging base inside Zambia. The RLI attack on CGT-2 camp was not as successful as its predecessors since the insurgents, having heard of the other two attacks, vacated the base and only 51 were killed.

11. Operation Shovel: Tete area, Mozambique, December 1978 (Fig. target L). This attack involved the destruction of a railway bridge on the Moatiye/Beira line by 20 SAS paratroopers dropped into the area by the RhAF. Despite several initial setbacks. the bridge was destroyed just as a train was crossing it. The SAS suffered no casualties. Shortly afterward, a group of 12 SAS ambushed a ZANLA supply convoy, destroying the lead truck with an RPG-7 rocket. Although the remaining vehicles managed to turn around and escape, most were destroyed the following day by an RhAF air strike conducted by Hunters.

12. Operation Inhibit: Southeast Mozambique, December 1978 (Fig. target E). 20 SAS paratroopers dropped into Mozambique just south of the border town of Malvernia to ambush vehicles transporting ZANLA supplies from Maputo. While the SAS were preparing their ambush position, a group of heavily armed ZANLA insurgents suddenly appeared. The Rhodesians killed 45 guerrillas; only one SAS trooper was killed.

13. Attack on the Mavuze Hydro-electric power station: East Mozambique, January 1979 (Fig. target V). This was a joint operation conducted by the SAS and MNR. The power station, located about 25 miles east of the Rhodesian border city of Umtali, was destroyed with a 75 mm recoilless rifle.

14. Operation Neutron: Mozambique, March 1979 (Fig. target F). This operation involved the infiltration of a two-man SAS team into the Chimoio area to ascertain the location of the new camp and direct an air strike on it. Upon the air strike's successful completion, the SAS team was evacuated by helicopter after the insurgents discovered their presence and had wounded one of the SAS troopers in the legs. Two months later another two-man SAS team returned to the area and successfully directed another air strike on a camp of 150 ZANLA insurgents.

15. Attack on Beira Fuel Depot: Mozambique, March 1979 (Fig. target L). This ambitious operation was carried out by a joint SAS-MNR force on the fuel depot located in the port of Beira. The target was 186 miles from the Rhodesian border city of Umtali and the force was transported by helicopter under cover of darkness to a point just outside Beira. From there, the party made their way on foot to the target, which was attacked with rockets and automatic weapons. A bomb concealed in a suitcase simultaneously destroyed a nearby oil pipeline. All targets were successfully destroyed and the team left without suffering any casualties. The fire created by the attack on the fuel depot raged for days and was only extinguished after fire-fighting experts with special equipment were flown in from South Africa.

16. Operation Gatling: Attack on Nkomo's House, Lusaka, Zambia, April 1979 (Fig. target M). The intention of this attack was to kill ZIPRA leader Joshua Nkomo at his house in Lusaka and also destroy a large ZIPRA armoury in that city. Forty-two SAS men, dressed in Zambian military uniforms and driving a Land Rover with Zambian markings, were ferried across the Kariba Lake and then drove to Lusaka. Although the Rhodesian force destroyed both the house and the armoury, Nkomo was away and thus escaped an ambush. Two SAS soldiers were wounded but succeeded in returning to Rhodesia with the rest of the group.

17. Operation Dinky: North Botswana, April 13, 1979 (Fig. target N). This operation involved the destruction of the ferry across the Zambezi River at Kazangula on Botswana's main road link to Rhodesia. Twelve SAS troops conveyed a 242 1b specially prepared charge strapped to a bicycle across the border to the ferry site on foot. The charge was laid in the water in one of the ferry docking areas under cover of darkness and detonated by remote control The ferry was completely destroyed and the SAS team returned to Rhodesia without suffering any casualties.

18. Operation Carpet: Lusaka, Zambia, June 1979 (Fig. target M). This operation was a raid on the ZIPRA intelligence headquarters in Lusaka, Zambia to destroy the facility, obtain documents, and perhaps capture some high ranking ZIPRA intelligence officers as well. It was carried out by 28 SAS troops who were transported right into the intelligence headquarters compound by recently acquired Bell helicopters, which had the range to reach the target. The attacking force, which was fired upon by ZIPRA guards as it landed, breeched the security walls with a specially made explosive device and then cleared the building of all defenders before destroying it with explosives. Only one ZIPRA intelligence officer was captured, the other two being absent at the time of the raid. A large number of documents were also captured before the building was destroyed. While the attack was being conducted, the RhAF dropped fuel for the helicopters to use on their return flight, which was carried out without incident. The SAS suffered one casualty, the commander of the raid, who was killed when one of the team's explosive devices caused a brick wall to collapse on top of him.

19. Operation Chickory: Lusaka, Zambia, June 1979 (Fig. target M). This operation involved an air strike followed by a ground operation conducted by 50 SAS men against a very large ZIPRA camp near Lusaka. The small force of ZIPRA guarding the camp put up very light resistance. The air strike destroyed large quantities of equipment. The raiding force returned to Rhodesia without suffering any casualties.

20. Operation Uric: Gaza Province, Mozambique, September 1979 (Fig. target E). This operation involved the destruction of all the major road and rail bridges from Malvernia along the Rhodesian border to Barragem, Mozambique. Its objective was to force ZANLA insurgents to walk an extra 200 miles to reach the Rhodesian border from their inland camps. In addition, the Barragem irrigation canal was to be destroyed and the town of Mapai attacked. The targets were first subjected to air strikes involving virtually every combat aircraft in the RhAF. This was followed by a ground force attack of 360 troops drawn from the RLI and SAS who destroyed the bridges with prepared explosive charges. As in previous operations a staging area for refuelling the helicopters was established in Mozambique. The attack was carried out and all the bridges were destroyed except the road one at Barragem, which was left partially in use. The assault on Mapai, however encountered very heavy resistance from the defending forces, and the Rhodesians lost two helicopters in the attack.

21. Operation Norah: Mozambique, September 1989 (Fig. target Z). This was a combined SAS-MNR operation to destroy a tropospheric scatter station. a highly sophisticated radio communications centre located on a mountain 102 miles from the Rhodesian border. The force consisted of 32 troops who were taken by helicopter to a remote area in Mozambique a two-day march form the target. The force carried out the attack under cover of darkness and although the centre was not completely destroyed, it was heavily damaged. The force withdrew under heavy fire without sustaining any casualties but were nearly captured by FRELIMO forces reacting to the attack.

22. Sinking of Dredgers: Beira Harbour. Mozambique, September 1979 (Fig. target L). This Was another combined SAS/MNR attack on the Mozambique port of Beira. Originally, several targets were to be attacked, including the telephone exchange and two dredgers. The attack on the telephone exchange had to be abandoned, but limpet mines were successfully placed on the two dredgers and a floating dock. Both dredgers were sunk and created problems for FRELIMO in keeping the harbour free of silt. The raiding party withdrew without sustaining any casualties.

23. Attack on Chimoio: Mozambique, September-October 1979 (Fig. target F). This operation involved another attack on the Chimoio complex involving ground troops supported by artillery, armoured cars, and aircraft. The battle was conducted over two days against very heavy opposition. This time the insurgents were well trained and difficult to dislodge from their bunkers; few casualties were therefore inflicted on them. The artillery was instrumental in stopping an armoured counterattack by FRELIMO using T -34 tanks. The Rhodesian forces were withdrawn after this.

24. Operation Cheese: Zambia, October 1979 (north of D in Fig.). This operation involved the destruction of a road and rail bridge that linked Zambia with Tanzania. The bridges were located 200 miles north of the Rhodesian border on the Chambezi river and were destroyed by a force of 16 SAS men who parachuted into the area and then made their way to the target by canoe. The SAS team then hijacked a large removal van to make their way south to a point where they were picked up by RhAF helicopters.

25. Destruction of Rail Bridges: Tete, Mozambique, October 1979 (Fig. target I). This operation was a follow-up to the earlier destruction of the rail bridge near Tete and involved the destruction of three more bridges. Three SAS groups carried out the attack, returning to Rhodesia without sustaining any casualties except for one group that was severely stung by a swarm of bees and required hospitalization on their return.

26. Operation Tepid: Zambia, October 1979 (Fig. target P).

This attack was carried out against a ZIPRA camp on the Zambezi River near Kariba by a combined force of helliborne SAS and RLI troops following an initial air strike. The operation was not a success mainly because the ZIPRA forces were well dug in and could not be dislodged. The camp was eventually abandoned by the ZIPRA forces who escaped and sustained light casualties. A Rhodesian Lynx was hit by ground fire during an earlier strike but managed to return to Rhodesia where it sucessfully effected an emergency landing.

27. Operation Dice: Zambia. November 1979 (Fig. targets K and P and north of map). In hopes of blunting an unexpected conventional ZIPRA invasion of Rhodesia three SAS teams destroyed three road bridges on the Chirundu Lusaka Road having been inserted into the area by helicopter. A few days later another team was airlifted into Zambia and destroyed a road bridge just south of Lusaka. The following day two simultaneous attacks were conducted using the same tactics against a road bridge east of Lusaka and a road and rail bridge connecting Lusaka and Tanzania to the north. All were successfully destroyed. Another double operation was carried out the next day, this time against a road bridge east of Lusaka that was the country's main communications link with Malawi. The other target was a road bridge near Kariba Lake. Both were destroyed. The SAS suffered no casualties.

THE SELOUS SCOUTS

Although the Selous Scouts were originally asked to obtain internal intelligence on insurgents by posing as guerrillas, they became increasingly involved in external operations as the conflict escalated. Some of these operations were of a clandestine nature, to which they were suited, while others were of a more conventional type.

1. Kidnapping of (ZIPRA) terrorists from Francistown, Botswana, March 1974 (Fig. target R). An eight-man team comprising four European and four African Scouts was clandestinely infiltrated into Francistown to kidnap several terrorists and bring them back to Rhodesia for interrogation. The raiders captured four occupants of the ZIPRA headquarters and drove them back across the border to Rhodesia without incident.

2. Kidnapping of ZIPRA official from Francistown. Botswana, September 1974 (Fig. target R). Another team of Scouts (two Europeans and one African) was infiltrated into Francistown to locate and kidnap a senior ZIPRA official. After several false leads and some reconnaissance, the team finally located their man and abducted him, after a fierce struggle. He was then placed in the back of a car and taken across the border to Rhodesia. However, the team left behind false passports, a radio transmitter, and weapons in a hotel room, along with an unpaid bill. One of the European members of the team had to return to the hotel where he paid the bill, collected the weapons and radio, and departed for Rhodesia without incident.

3. Raid on Caponda. Mozambique, March 1975 (Fig. target Y). Twenty Scouts staged an assault on a ZANLA staging base 55 km north of Rhodesia. They travelled to and from the target on foot. After a 24-hour march, the unit came upon the terrorist base only to find it deserted. A cholera epidemic had broken out among the terrorists and the camp had been evacuated. The unit returned safely to Rhodesia.

4. Mozambique, January 1967 (Fig. target C). This operation involved a helicopter borne assault by 15 Scouts against a ZANLA transit camp that was destroyed.

5. Operation Traveller: Attack on Caponda base, Mozambique, April 1976 (Fig. target V). This operation involved another attack on the ZANLA staging camp that was plagued by a cholera epidemic. The attacking force consisted of a 20 man patrol that marched into Mozambique, attacked and destroyed the camp, killing seven terrorists and wounding 16 others. The raiding party returned to Rhodesia on foot, several of them having been injured.

6. Operation Detachment: Raid on Chigamane, Mozambique, May 1976 (Fig. target T). This operation involved an attack on a ZANLA base 108 (km) inside Mozambique. Twenty European and African Scouts dressed in FRELIMO uniforms travelled in four military vehicles disguised as FRELIMO vehicles. The ZANLA terrorist base was attacked and destroyed with rockets, mortars, and machine guns. The raiders returned to Rhodesia safely.

7. Operation Long John: Attack on Mapai. Mozambique. June 1976 (Fig. target E). This operation involved an attack on a ZANLA base in Mapai, 48 miles inside Mozambique by 58 Scouts travelling in four trucks and two Scouts cars. all disguised as FRELIMO vehicles. Along the way, the raiders disconnected telephone lines and sabotaged the railway line. The column was allowed to enter the terrorist base by an unwitting sentry. Once inside sappers destroyed 13 Mercedes busses used to transport terrorists to the border (one bus was spared and was taken back to Rhodesia as a souvenir). In addition. the insurgents' entire armoury was seized and brought back to Rhodesia before an air strike was called in to destroy the base. Nineteen terrorists were reported killed and 18 wounded; one member of the raiding party was killed and a few were wounded.

8. Nyadzonya/Pungwe Raid, Mozambique. August 1976 (Fig. target U). This operation involved a raid on a large ZANLA base 60 miles inside of Mozambique by a Scouts column comprising ten trucks and four armoured cars, again disguised as FRELIMO vehicles. The Scouts in the first four vehicles were also dressed in FRELlMO uniforms. They cut the telephone lines leading to the town where the terrorist base was located, then drove straight into the camp. They then opened fire on the unsuspecting insurgent terrorists drilling on the parade ground, killing at least 1,028. Fourteen important ZANLA insurgents were captured and taken back to Rhodesia for interrogation. On their way out of Mozambique the raiding party blew up the Pungwe Bridge to prevent any pursuit and returned to Rhodesia safely. In a separate action, the covering team deployed to block the column's escape, ambushed a Land Rover whose six occupants were found to be senior ZANLA officers; all six were killed.

9. Operation Maradon: Attack on Jorge do Limpopo and Massengena, Mozambique, October 1976 (Fig. target E). This operation involved an attack against a ZANLA base at Jorge do Limpopo, 36 miles inside Mozambique. The strike force travelled a circuitous 350 to 400 km round-trip route, and two reconnaissance teams (one of three and one of two men) were parachuted into Mozambique in advance of the column. Upon entering Mozambique, the raiding party laid Claymore mines on roads and booby-trapped the rail line. Telegraph and telephone lines were also cut. The column then launched a succession of attacks, destroying a FRELIMO garrison, derailing a troop train (and killing 36 of the terrorists on board), and destroying a large water reservoir, along with railway switching points and several enemy military vehicles. A senior FRELIMO commander was also killed. On November 2 the Scouts returned to Rhodesia, having destroyed the terrorists' logistical base of support. They disrupted communications between Jorge de Limpopo. Ma1vemia, and Massengena, wrecked two trains, destroyed all motor transport in the area, and sowed land mines in various spots. This operation effectively undercut ZANLA's operational capacity and weakened insurgent morale.

10. Operation Ignition: Attack on ZIPRA. Francistown, Botswana, November 1976 (Fig. target R). This operation involved an attack on ZIPRA's headquarters in Francistown by a team of Scouts. Its purpose was to destroy a stockpile of suitcase bombs intended for use in Rhodesia. The raiding party used previously captured. insurgent suitcase bombs to destroy the headquarters building and the stockpile of bombs, wounding five insurgents in the process.

11. Operation Aztec: Attack on Jorge do Limpopo, Mpai, and Madulo Pan, Mozambique, May-June 1977 (Fig. target E). This operation involved an attack on several ZANLA bases 138 miles inside Mozambique by a motorized column of 110 Scouts disguised as FRELIMO soldiers. A railway line, the terrorist bases' chief source of supply, was also destroyed. In addition, military vehicles and equipment were destroyed by RhAF air strikes flown in support of the raiders.

12. Operation Vodka: Raid on Mboroma ZIPRA camp, Zambia, December 1979 (location not known). This operation involved a raid on a ZIPRA prison camp 96 miles inside Zambia containing 120 opponents of the terrorist organization along with some African members of the Rhodesian security forces. A team of 42 Scouts were parachuted into the camp after it bad been softened up by an air strike. Resistance was quickly overcome: 18 guards were killed and six were captured. Only 32 prisoners were freed, because the remainder were outside the camp on work details. In the evening, the raiders and freed prisoners were airlifted back to Rhodesia from a nearby airfield.

13. Operation Petal I: Botswana, Mach 1979 (Fig. target W). This operation involved the kidnapping of Elliot Sibanda, a senior ZIPRA intelligence operative, by a team of Scouts who crept across the border into Botswana and laid an ambush. Although badly wounded, Sibanda was captured and brought back to Rhodesia alive.

15. Operation Petal 2: Francistown, Botswana, April 1979 (Fig. target R). This operation involved an ambitious raid to kidnap the ZIPRA. southern command. The raiding party consisted of a small column of two armoured cars and some other trucks disguised as Botswana military vehicles and Scouts dressed in Botswana military uniforms. The column crossed the border and drove to the house being used by ZIPRA and arrested its occupants. Before the victims realized what had happened, they were back in Rhodesia.

RHODESIAN AIR FORCE

The Rhodesian Air Force was actively involved in many of the cross-border raids by delivering the ground forces to the target by helicopter or parachute drop, extricating them at the conclusion of an operation or by means of a so-called "hot extraction" if they got into more trouble than they could handle. Most instances have been covered in the summary of the ground force external operations. On occasion, however, the air force did undertake external air attacks on their own, even though in most instances, the best results were usually achieved by a combined air and ground force operation. Good results were also achieved by the air force being directed onto the target by small reconnaissance units operating externally. There were, however, several very successful air strikes mounted against ZIPRA camps.

1. Attack on arms dump: Tete, Mozambique, December 1978 (Fig. target I). A high-ranking ZANLA official captured by Special Branch gave information about a large arms dump of insurgent weapons stored in a hangar in the town of Tete. A single

Hunter jet was dispatched and destroyed the dump, the hanger, and the surrounding buildings with a single rocket. This attack was subsequently followed by a ground operation (see SAS Operation Shovel).

2. Attack on ZANLA vehicles: Tete area, Mozambique, December 1978 (Fig. target I). Hunters were directed onto a number of ZANLA vehicles by SAS operators after they had destroyed the Moatiye/Beira bridge (see SAS Operation Shovel).

3. Operation Newton: Attack on Chimoio Camp, Mozambique, March 1979 (Fig. target F). An intensive air strike involving Canberras, Hunters, Lynxes, and helicopter gunships was directed onto the camp by a small SAS reconnaissance team operating in the area (see SAS Operation Newton). The following day RhAF Hunters returned to attack several FRELIMO armoured personnel carriers that had been brought up to evacuate the wounded. As the aircraft were about to attack, one was nearly hit by a SAM-7. Both aircraft took evasive action and then swept down to destroy one armoured personnel carrier and inflict casualties on FRELIMO and ZANLA personnel.

4. Operation Gatling: Lusaka, Zambia, October 19'18 (Fig. target M). Two ground force operations were conducted in Lusaka. The strike was timed to occur at 8:30 &.m. during which time the camp personnel would be on parade. Taking part in the operation were eight Hunters, four Canberras, and helicopter gunships. To give the latter the necessary range, a refuelling base had to be set up within Zambia. To be successful, the timing of the aircraft over the target had to be perfect.

First in the air were the helicopters, followed by the Canberras and the Hunters. All flew at tree-top level to avoid radar. The Hunters hit the target first with bombs and rockets, followed by the Canberras which dropped bombs. Finally, the gunships came in and strafed the camp with 20 mm cannon fire. While the attack was taking place, some Hunters were dispatched to attack any Zambia Air Force MiGs that scrambled to intercept the RhAF planes. At the same time, the commander of the Canberra force contacted the Lusaka air traffic control and warned them to keep all aircraft, including the MiGs, away from the target area. The Zambians complied with this request and, after the attack was complete, all Rhodesian aircraft returned without suffering any loss. Conservative estimates put ZIPRA casualties at over 1,000 dead and many others wounded.

5. Operation Vanity: Attack on ZIPRA camp, Angola, February 1979 (north of map in Fig.). This operation involved an air strike on a ZIPRA base deep inside Angola. The strike force consisted of four Canberras supported by a top cover of Hunters. As the base was at the extreme limit of the Canberra's range, ZIPRA was not expecting the attack and complete surprise was achieved. The Canberras flew at 39,000 feet, dropping down to tree-top level for the final run into the target. It had just been raining when the attack was mounted and all the insurgents were sheltering inside the barracks. As a result, there were many casualties. All aircraft returned to Rhodesia.

Insurgency And The Black Nationalist Organisations

With kind permission from the Rand Arroyo Center to publish these extracts written by authors Bruce Hoffman, Jennifer M. Taw and David Arnold.

Background Of The Conflict

Although Rhodesia was a British crown-colony before 1965, its constitution, unlike those of the neighbouring British colonies, afforded it control over domestic affairs, with Great Britain retaining only the right to intervene in matters involving foreign governments. Even when the Federation of Rhodesia and Nyasaland was formed in 1953, the government of Rhodesia retained control over its own internal affairs, limiting the federal government's responsibility to such matters as defence and foreign affairs.

After the 1956 Suez crisis led the British government to accelerate the granting of independence to its other African colonies, black nationalists in the Federation's three territories began to step up their own demands for an end to colonial rule. As Britain had done in its other African colonies, it granted independence to the two northern territories of the Federation only after assuring, through constitutional legislation, that political power would revert to the black majorities. Britain could take no similar steps in Rhodesia because of that colony's tradition of self-rule. Nonetheless, the British refused to grant Rhodesia its independence until the white-minority government formally began to transfer power to the country's black majority. While in office, the moderate Rhodesian United Federal party (UFP) had sought to ease tensions with both Britain and domestic black nationalists by agreeing to a new constitution that reserved 15 parliamentary seats for blacks. The blacks, however, rejected the UFP overture as insufficient, arguing that progress toward majority rule would be too slow. Mounting civil unrest, accompanied by increasingly strident black nationalist demands for immediate majority rule, caused the whites to replace the UFP in the 1962 general election with the conservative Rhodesian Front Party, which promised to decelerate the drift toward majority rule and restore law and order in the country. By 1965, talks between Rhodesia and Britain on majority rule and the related constitutional issue had stalled. The Rhodesian government accordingly unilaterally declared the country independent of Great Britain (an action popularly referred to as UDI). Britain responded by immediately imposing trade sanctions against Rhodesia, including an oil embargo, that were subsequently embraced by much of the international community as well.

Strategy And Tactics

When it became clear that the Rhodesian government was not going to enfranchise blacks nor allow them to organize for political power, the two principal black nationalist groups. the ZAPU and its offshoot the ZANU, began gradually to abandon their reliance on urban riots and demonstrations as a means of pressuring the government and instead directed their efforts toward organizing a rural guerrilla insurgency. The initial strategies of both organisations were very similar and fairly simple. Their plan was to foment sufficient violence and unrest in Rhodesia to compel the British and other western countries to intervene militarily and restore order, thereby paving the way for black majority rule. With training, uniforms, and weapons provided by several communist countries, both ZAPU and ZANU began to infiltrate heavily armed groups of guerrillas into Rhodesia from Zambia between 1965 and 1969.

The entire campaign was a complete failure. After crossing into Rhodesia the insurgents attempted to establish bases in sparsely populated areas. The security forces, however, were able to track them easily and capture or kill the poorly trained insurgent bands before they were able to mount any attacks. The guerrillas were also exposed by Rhodesian police Special Branch agents who had penetrated the nationalist movements and kept Salisbury informed of infiltration plans and guerrilla movement. Finally, the local tribal population either feared the insurgents or were indifferent to their cause and therefore were reluctant to assist them. Thus, the security forces were frequently able to intercept insurgent bands before they even crossed he border and often captured them without a struggle. When the insurgents did attempt to fight, they were devastated time and again.

ZANU recognized the inadequacy of both this strategy and the penalties of poor training and ill-preparedness sooner than ZAPU. As early as 1965, ZANLA (Zimbabwean National Liberation Army) troops were withdrawn from the field to be retrained by communist Chinese advisers in Maoist rural guerrilla warfare techniques. ZIPRA (the Zimbabwean Peoples' Revolutionary Army, ZAPU's army), however, stubbornly clung to this strategy of blind rural insurgency until 1969, by which time it had been decimated by the Rhodesians and had to suspend operations for a year to regroup.

By 1970, however, ZIPRA was forced to change its strategy. With the Soviet Union's support and encouragement, ZIPRA began to concentrate on developing a conventional army, while deemphasizing the use of the guerrilla units that hitherto had spearheaded the struggle. Instead of waging the kind of extensive guerrilla campaign inside Rhodesia that ZANLA planned to implement, ZIPRA's goal was to invade Rhodesia with the conventional army it was building and then, after consolidating its control over the country, wipe out its rivals in ZANLA. The invasion plan envisioned two motorized columns, supported by tanks and jet aircraft. entering Rhodesia from Chirundu and Victoria Falls and then converging on Salisbury. Rhodesian intelligence, however, learned of ZIPRA's intentions and pre-empted the invasion by destroying ZIPRA's staging bases in Zambia. ZIPRA, accordingly, was forced to recommence its infiltration tactics, seeking to obtain support from the Matabele tribal territories as a means of offsetting ZANU's strong popular support in other parts of Rhodesia. ZIPRA also increased pressure on the Rhodesian government by escalating its attacks on white Rhodesian civilian targets. It was responsible, for example, for shooting down two

Rhodesian civilian airliners with SAM-7 missiles in 1978 and 1979, killing a total of 107 persons.

In contrast to the Soviet revolutionary warfare doctrine embraced by ZIPRA, ZANLA (as previously noted) was heavily influenced by Mao Zedong's teachings, emphasizing the need to win the loyalty and support of the local population as a prerequisite to a successful rural insurgency. ZANLA, however, was not in a position to implement this strategy until 1971, when it established an alliance with FRELIMO, the black nationalist guerrilla movement then fighting the Portuguese in Mozambique. As FRELIMO already controlled the Tete district bordering north-eastern Rhodesia, it was from there that ZANLA recommenced its offensive operations.

The first ZANLA incursion from Mozambique took place in December 1971, and its fighters were able to operate along the border area for almost a year before the Rhodesian forces learned of their presence. Their success was a direct reflection of how thoroughly and completely the organization's cadres had subverted the tribal territories adjoining the Mozambique border before moving any fighters into the area. These advance teams spent time and effort in cultivating the local populace, becoming familiar with their traditions and beliefs while gently establishing ZANLA's influence over the tribesmen. Particular attention was devoted to learning about local grievances and then offering practical solutions to these problems. The ZANLA cadres were respectful and tried to interfere as little as possible with tribal routines. Soon, tribesmen were not only helping the insurgents to conceal themselves from the security forces but were providing assistance transporting arms and materiel across the border into Rhodesia.

The greatest dividends however, were paid in the intelligence network that ZANLA was able to develop among the local populace. The guerrillas were thus able to identify police ground coverage personnel and district commissioner staff, as well as suspected government informers and sympathizers within tribes. The insurgents dealt with the latter in a summary and brutal manner to dissuade others from cooperating with the authorities. In this respect. ZANLA was much more violent in its relations with civilians than ZIPRA. Nevertheless by fostering this powerful combination of fear and support, ZANLA effectively limited the number of tribesmen willing to inform on the organisation.

Although ZANLA began to attack white farms after December 1972, the organisation's main emphasis was on mine-laying, both to disrupt rural commercial traffic and to inhibit security force mobility and patrolling. Because Rhodesia's economy was largely based on exports of farm produce from the north-eastern border area. ZANLA's mine-laying strategy was a particularly effective form of economic warfare. It was also easy to implement given the combined ease of insurgent infiltration from Mozambique and ZANLA's subversion of the local population. Supporters within the local population, in fact, were often trained by ZANLA to lay the mines themselves.

ZANLA, however, suffered a series of reversals in 1974. Improved Rhodesian rural countermeasures, coupled with a power struggle within the ZANLA high command-engineered by Special Branch that culminated in the assassination of ZANU's external leader in Zambia, Herbert Chitepo and led to the arrest of ZANLA leaders in Zambia dealt a serious blow to the organisation. Nevertheless, the 1973 coup in Portugal that prompted Lisbon's decision to grant independence to Mozambique and Angola assured FRELIMO's eventual control of Mozambique. This unexpected development. combined with a South African-imposed cease-fire in Rhodesia, tilted the balance back in ZANLA's favour.

Following the release in 1976 of the leaders imprisoned after Chitepo's assassination, ZANLA renewed its offensive. FRELIMO now governed Mozambique; and during 1977-1978, ZANLA forces were able to expand their area of operations from Tete province to the entire length of the eastern border with Rhodesia. Floods of recruits from Rhodesia joining the insurgent movement were hastily trained and sent back across the border- where their sheer numbers began to overwhelm the already hard-pressed and over-stretched security forces. Despite suffering heavy casualties, the ZANLA guerrillas were effective in disrupting Rhodesia's economy by targeting road and rail links with South Africa. Although traffic was never completely stopped, the insurgents were able to overextend the security forces while subverting new tribal areas.

Although ZANLA failed to disrupt the 1979 elections that brought Bishop Abel Muzorewa to power, the insurgents were nevertheless in the ascendancy. Despite agreeing at the British-hosted Lancaster House Constitutional Settlement in 1979 to cease activities and remain in specified assembly points until new elections could be held in Rhodesia, ZANLA sent tribesmen to take the insurgents' places in these areas and thus were able to continue offensive operations. Through both voluntary and coerced tribal support, Robert Mugabe, ZANLA's leader, was accordingly assured electoral victory and in 1980 became Zimbabwe's first Prime Minister.

While the Rhodesian security forces were successful in controlling the insurgency until 1969, by the mid-1970s the situation had changed dramatically. Clearly, several factors were responsible for the insurgents' change of fortunes, not the least of which was the reassessment of strategy and tactics that followed their initial failures. Key, however, was the insurgents' ability to operate from bases in countries bordering Rhodesia. When Zambia shut down ZANLA's bases in that country following Chitepo's assassination, for example, the organization suffered a severe setback. When ZANLA gained access to the Tete district of Mozambique and later to the entire eastern border area, however, its position with regard to Rhodesia was strengthened immeasurably. Internationally, the insurgents were also at an advantage. While Rhodesia functioned under international trade sanctions and was forced to make political and military concessions because of its dependence on South Africa's rail lines and ports, the insurgents did not operate under similar constraints and indeed received advisory and material support from communist bloc countries. Moreover, while the security forces suffered domestically from a chronic manpower shortage the insurgents could draw strength and support from the majority black population and therefore ensure a steady flow of recruits. The insurgents were also generally more familiar with the bush. had a better appreciation of local customs and were less readily identifiable than most members of the security forces. .

Of the two insurgent groups, ZANLA was clearly the more successful. Its form of Maoist rural guerrilla warfare took full advantage of the local population through patience and preparation, blunting the security forces' ability to gather the kind of intelligence on ZANLA that the Rhodesians used so effectively against ZIPRA's conventional force build-up. Instead of emphasizing direct combat, as ZIPRA had intended with its Soviet-trained and influenced standing army, ZANLA avoided engaging the security forces directly and instead sought to win through a strategy of attrition by overextending the Rhodesian forces and by attacking economic targets. Finally, ZANLA's emphasis on gaining the loyalty of the population paid off when national elections were held in Rhodesia in 1980 and Robert Mugabe was voted into office.

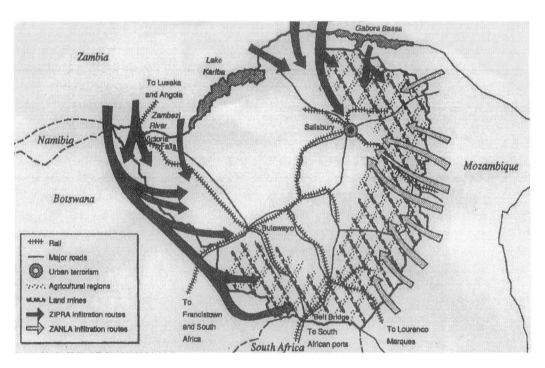

The War Against Rhodesia.

Mine survival vehicles developed during the Bush War include the Leopard, the Crocodile, the Puma, the Rhino and the Pookie.

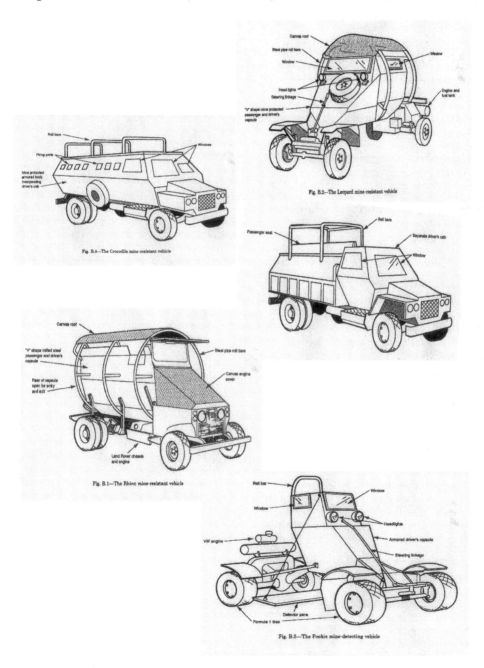

Fig. B.2—The Leopard mine-resistant vehicle

Fig. B.4—The Crocodile mine-resistant vehicle

Fig. B.1—The Rhino mine-resistant vehicle

Fig. B.3—The Pookie mine-detecting vehicle

Security Force Organisation And Operations
Extract from Rand Arroyo Center Document for the US Army

The history of the Rhodesian counterinsurgency is one of constant security force adaptation to new insurgent tactics. At the outset of the conflict, the security forces' excellent intelligence network allowed them to curb insurgent infiltration from Zambia into Rhodesia. Then, as the numbers of insurgents crossing into Rhodesia burgeoned, the security forces formed special tracking teams and emphasized "track and kill" operations to intercept the infiltrators before they could stage any attacks. Although these operations were extremely successful, after the insurgents changed their tactics in 1970, the Rhodesians found that they in turn needed to readjust their countermeasures. Drawing on Britain's experiences in Malaya and Kenya during the 1950s, they developed effective mine-countermeasures created special units to gather intelligence, penetrated both black nationalist armies, skilfully exploited the rift between ZANLA and ZIPRA, began their own external operations, and developed quick. reaction attack units. The flexibility that the security forces demonstrated in developing these countermeasures was directly responsible for their tactical successes and stands in stark contrast to the counter insurgencies fought by the Portuguese in Mozambique and, arguably, by the government in El Salvador, where security forces have shown themselves to be more rigidly wedded to inappropriate or ineffective tactics and doctrine.

Security Force Organization And Attendant C3 Issues

In 1965, the Rhodesian police still ran virtually all Rhodesian internal defence operations. ZANU and ZAPU were just beginning to supplement their tactics of urban unrest with more serious rural insurgent operations, infiltrating armed groups of communist-trained guerrillas over the Zambian border into Rhodesia. But because Special Branch had so thoroughly infiltrated ZANU and ZAPU, the police were able to stop most incoming insurgents at the border. Aided by the element of surprise, police interdiction was simple and fairly non-violent. On April 28, 1966, however, the police, supported by Air Force helicopters, fought the first battle of the war against seven ZANLA insurgents outside the town of Sinoia. The Battle of Sinoia clearly demonstrated the need for cooperation among the various branches of the security forces. The police won the battle decisively, but not without luck. They failed to call in the Army. despite the scope of the action, and did not communicate effectively with the helicopters overhead. Nor were the police themselves adequately armed or trained for military encounters. Accordingly, following the engagement, cooperation among the Air Force, Army, and police was formally institutionalized. The government outlined a system of responses to insurgent actions whereby incidents that progressed beyond the control of a single service would be handled by a special joint operational force representing the police, Army, and Air Force. Thus, the institutional barriers among the military services themselves as well as between the military and civilian coordinating agencies were mitigated.

Accordingly, "Joint Operation Centres" (JOCs) were established throughout the country composed of local commanders of equal or similar rank from each of the armed services who met on a daily basis to determine tactical operation decisions through a process of consensus. The Criminal Investigation Department (CID) and/or Special Branch (and thus the CIO, to which Special Branch was responsible) were also represented on the JOCs, as was the Internal Affairs Department. This was especially important at the tactical level when the lack of any organizational structure to guide joint operations or direct the flow of intelligence from other services could seriously undermine operational performance and success. The JOC system was thus effective in integrating all five entities responsible for Rhodesian defence: the police, the Special Branch. the Army (and its special forces), the Air Force, and the Internal Affairs Department.

Until 1977, the Operational Coordinating Committee (OCC) stood at the apex of the JOC system. The OCC was responsible for the planning and execution of all combined security force operations, and its members included the national commanders of the police, Army, and Air Force, as well as the CIO Director General. The problem, apparent through the entire JOC system but especially acute at the most senior level, was that no single commander had overall authority or seniority over fellow committee members. Accordingly, all decisions had to be reached through an arduous system of consensus, with each member retaining the responsibility for ensuring that his service carried out agreed-upon command decisions. Issues that could not be decided in the JOCs and sub-JOCs were thus referred up the command structure to the OCC, where top commanders debated their forces' appropriate role in each operation. Those issues not resolved by the OCC were referred further up the line to the Prime Minister. This resulted in critical tactical delays and meant that security forces were driven by no overall national strategy.

In response to this situation and to the tension it engendered between the Army and police in particular, the various services began calling for a "supremo": a single supreme commander with the authority to direct the entire security force structure under a unified strategy. The Prime Minister, Ian Smith, was initially opposed to the idea, arguing that he served as the supreme commander and that the OCC already referred controversial matters to him for policy decisions and subsequent enforcement. Eventually, however, after the services' demands intensified, Smith agreed to establish a more coordinated system of command, eventually creating the Combined Operations Command (COMOPS) in 1977 and appointing Lieutenant General Peter Walls, the Army commander, as its head.

Walls, as head of both COMOPS and the National Joint Operations Centre (NATJOC), which replaced the OCC and to which COMOPS reported, was ostensibly endowed with the authority to exercise command over all the security forces and relevant civil agencies. In practice, however, the appointment of a Supreme Commander did little to improve the command situation, since he still lacked any real authority over the other NATJOC members, most of whom had been members of the OCC. For the most part, Walls functioned as little more than a chairman and NATJOC was little more than a looser version of the OCC. Moreover, NATJOC proved itself even less capable of meeting the demands of war than its predecessor organisation. To ensure compliance with any directive, the order had to be approved through NATJOC rather than through COMOPS. In other words, directives had to be approved not only by the Supreme Commander but by the relevant security force commanders as well. War by high-level committee continued. The situation was further complicated by the fact that in the reorganization, COMOPS obtained control over the operational planning functions of the various services but did not incorporate their planning staffs. Without the logistical staff necessary for detailed planning, COMOPS should have limited itself to coordinating the overall war effort along broad strategic guidelines. Instead, it became directly involved in the planning and execution of individual operations. The results were a spate of logistical and intelligence problems, animosity between the various security force commanders and the Supreme Commander, and continued neglect of the need for a unified strategic plan.

In the final result, COMOPS did not meet the expectations of the security forces or the government. No doubt the Rhodesians had expected the appointment of a Supreme Commander to yield the success of the similar command structure in Malaya under General Sir Gerald Templer. The fact is that Templer, as High Commissioner in a British colony, had enjoyed an absolute power that could never have been given to a Rhodesian commander. Ian Smith never relinquished his control over the counterinsurgency campaign, and he refused to give free reign to the "supremo." He therefore should have provided more leadership in developing an overall strategy. As it was, the tedious decision-making problems of OCC were compounded by the continued degeneration of inter-service relations and a further fracturing of the command structure that occurred even after COMOPS was created.

Countermeasures Against Urban Terrorism

The British South Africa Police (BSAP) was Rhodesia's national as well as metropolitan police force and, like the Rhodesian military, was based on the British model. Its principal units and departments were the Duty Uniform Branch; the Criminal Investigation Department CID). which was responsible for serious or specialized crimes; Special Branch (SB), which handled all internal political intelligence; a paramilitary support unit; and the Police Reserve. In addition to the usual police duties of maintaining law and order, the Rhodesian police force was responsible for investigating crimes of subversion and for gathering intelligence on subversive groups and activities.

As the insurgency began to spread in the late 1960 and urban unrest intensified, the Police formed 24-hour riot squads: small. mobile stand-by units, manned by regular police on a rotating basis. For effective responses to more serious terrorist incidents, the police also created "Urban Emergency Units." which were widely publicised in hopes of deterring the terrorists from carrying out any attacks. These countermeasures, combined with the police force's usual preventive activities. enabled the BSAP to completely stifle insurgent operations in Rhodesia's cities. This success was mostly the result of information obtained by police from an extensive informer network. combined with effective public awareness campaigns.

Police intelligence was used to detect and apprehend terrorists and suspected terrorists, to uncover terrorist safe houses and arms caches. to undermine local support, and to disrupt terrorist communication and planning. Special Branch's network of informants and intelligence sources was so good that insurgents travelling to Salisbury merely to visit relatives and not for any operational purposes were often intercepted and arrested before they even entered the city. Bombings were effectively deterred by posting security guards to control access to shops, stores. and businesses; teaching emergency procedures and search methods to businessmen and shop clerks; and encouraging the public to report any unattended parcels or suspicious objects.

Rural Pacification And Security

The Rhodesian counterinsurgency campaign demonstrated that low-tech and improvisational solutions can be effective in LICs (low intensity conflicts) and that it is not necessary to spend huge amounts on sophisticated high-tech weaponry and materiel Like most contemporary Third World countries confronted with the costs of fighting a protracted insurgency, Rhodesia had limited financial resources to draw upon. The international trade sanctions and arms embargo imposed on the country throughout the conflict placed an additional burden on the already financially constrained security forces. Thus, the Rhodesians were compelled to discover low-cost, adaptive. and novel solutions to a variety of logistical and operational problems.

Countering Landmines

One of the most serious threats to Rhodesia, for example, was the landmines laid by guenillas on roads throughout the country's principal farming areas. Like many Third World countries, Rhodesia's economy was based on agricultural exports. Hence, it was vital that the roads and communications links criss-crossing the country's farm region be kept open to both commercial traffic and security force patrols. The threat was not only economic but political and psychological as well. The Rhodesian governmental apparatus, for example, was breaking down in many areas as officials found it increasingly difficult to travel in areas with heavy insurgent activity. More serious, however, were the potential effects that the mining could have on security force mobility. The Rhodesians had been horrified to discover that similarly widespread insurgent mining of roads in Mozambique had reduced the mobility of their Portuguese counterparts in that country and had turned them virtually into a "garrison army" whose personnel feared leaving their fortified barracks and posts to go out on patrol.

Engineers in the Rhodesian police force and Army devised several innovative and inexpensive modifications to ordinary military and commercial vehicles that dramatically reduced the deaths and injuries suffered by passengers when these protected vehicles struck mines. Indeed, mine-related casualties were reduced by 90 percent and injuries by 20 percent. These simple measures included filling tires with water and air to dissipate explosive force, designing wheels that would blow clear of the vehicle and thus not damage the axle, and mounting special V-shaped capsules on chassis to deflect the blast. Not only were they effective in keeping the roads open to traffic and bolstering security force morale, but they also enabled the Rhodesians to take back and retain control of the countryside and thereby deprived the guerrillas of the freedom of movement essential to their operations.

Overcoming Tracking Problems
The security forces were similarly successful in overcoming some of the difficulties inherent in tracking small guerrilla units and bands of infiltrators through rough country in harsh climatic conditions. Within the Army, special four-man tracking teams were organized and trained for extended operations in the bush. The tracking teams worked in threes: one group in pursuit of the guerrillas, one following the trail backward in hopes of encountering other guerrillas or discovering a hidden arms cache or valuable insurgent documents, and one leap-froging ahead to try to pick up the trail more quickly. The teams were supported by a larger section of troops, who would move forward and engage the insurgents once they were located by the trackers.

Botanists, recruited from local universities, taught the trackers how to live off the land (as the guerrillas did), recognize changes in an area's natural ecology that would indicate a guerrilla presence, and identify from broken brush or faintly trampled grass the tell-tale signs of movement. Instead of fatigues and combat boots, the trackers wore tennis shoes and shorts. Increased comfort while operating in the often intense midday heat was not the only reason for this attire. Tennis shoes made less noise than boots, were lighter, and made less of an imprint on the ground, thus making it more difficult for the trackers themselves to be tracked. Similarly, by wearing shorts, the trackers were forced to walk around the brush, rather than through it, reducing both noise and physical signs of movement. There is perhaps no better example of the Rhodesians' commonsense approach to complex problems than the special communications gear used by the trackers to maintain contact with one another: ordinary, inexpensive dog whistles. Though inaudible to the untrained human ear, the whistles were an effective means of communication between persons attuned to its distinctive pitch.

Fireforce Operations

Perhaps the most successful counterinsurgency tactic used by the Rhodesians was the joint Air Force and Army "Fireforce," a heliborne reaction team developed in the early stages of Operation Hurricane. Using helicopters provided by South Africa, the Rhodesian Air Force devised this particularly effective means of vertical envelopment. The original Fireforce typically consisted of four Allouette m helicopters, each manned by a pilot and technician/gunner. Three of the helicopters, referred to as "G-cars," were used to transport four fully equipped troops, while a fourth helicopter, called the "K (for kill)-car," carried a pilot who was the senior Air Force officer, a gunner-technician and the Army unit commander, who directed the operations below. The "K-car" could also be used as a gunship when required (hence, its appellation).

The four helicopters were supported by a fixed-wing aircraft equipped with rockets and machineguns. In the early stages of the conflict, this was usually a single-engine Aeromacchi-Lockheed AL-60 Trojan. A particularly noisy aircraft, the AL-60 generally preceded the helicopters, effectively blotting out the noise of their engines and helping to maintain at least a modicum of surprise about the impending ground attack. The initial helicopter-deployed contingent of 12 Rhodesian Light Infantry or RLI, the Rhodesian Army's commandos, or paratroopers would be supported by additional ground troops, who also carried fuel for the helicopters.

Later in the conflict, the regular Fireforce unit was expanded to six helicopters and was referred to as a "Jumbo Fireforce." This number of helicopters and troops was about as large as a single commander could effectively control Other variations consisted of a heliborne mortar unit that would be deployed from the "G-car," which would then act as the unit's aerial spotter. The lack of helicopters prevented the creation of more Fireforce units as the insurgents increased their area of operations. To relieve the situation, a stick of paratroopers was added to each Fireforce complement. The paratroopers were transported over the targeted area in a World War 2-era DC-3 Dakota fixed-wing transport plane and then dropped to support the smaller heliborne-deployed force already on the ground.

The Fireforce was used most successfully in tandem with information on insurgent locations obtained from static observation posts, Selous Scouts "pseudo-operations, and other ground intelligence sources. As an immediate reaction force, it could be also scrambled whenever any ground forces required support. This was a great morale builder for the average soldier, who knew that assistance was only 30 minutes away at the most. Demands on the Fireforce continued to increase during the closing years of the conflict, to the point where it as not unusual for it to be deployed as often as three times a day in certain heavily contested areas.

Police Anti-Terrorist Units

The increasing demands placed on the Army's limited number of combat personnel led to the formation of special Police Anti-Terrorist Units (PAW) for service in rural areas. Each PATU consisted of five policemen who were released from their routine duties for two-week operational tours in the bush. The teams lived in encampments that functioned as temporary police stations, complete with prisoner facilities. The PATU's mission was to maintain order, enforce the law, and gather intelligence. The police teams were especially effective in areas not yet subverted by the insurgents, where the local population was generally cooperative. Because they felt secure and protected, these villagers or tribesmen often readily provided information on insurgent movement and activities. Most PAW teams however, were deployed in areas that had been thoroughly subverted by the insurgents and thus could accomplish little. If not already sympathetic to the guerrillas, the local population in these areas were nonetheless reluctant to cooperate with the authorities for fear of insurgent reprisals. The PATU were therefore relegated to carrying out trivial patrol duties rather than fulfilling the active counterinsurgent role that was their' primary mission.

In addition to the PATU, police reservists performed static guard duties in rural areas as part of the "Bright Lights" programme. Their task was primarily to protect isolated farms from guerrilla attacks. The programme was difficult to maintain, however, as manpower demands throughout the entire security force structure intensified. As an alternative in one area, PATU sticks would conduct random night-patrols of farms, checking the black workers' compounds as well as the farmers' residences. This tactic was largely effective in deterring insurgent attacks on the farms since the guerrillas never knew where or when the PATU sticks would be patrolling. The police also regularly organized convoys to protect commercial traffic along rural roads and were responsible for developing the first mine countermeasures. As a result of these measures, the insurgents were never able to fully close down the country's roads.

Small Unit Tactics and Special Operations

The Rhodesians' emphasis on special operations for both tactical objectives and intelligence gathering stands in stark contrast to the prevailing military view of special operations as an adjunct to conventional operations and not as a viable and independent instrument of war. The Rhodesians' heavy reliance on small, elite special operations units admittedly was dictated by manpower shortages and the overall strain imposed on the country's already outnumbered and overcommitted security forces. Indeed, approximately 50 percent of all regular training was in the form of small-unit tactics. Nonetheless, the weaknesses that necessitated this approach actually proved to be a source of strength in prosecuting an effective counterinsurgency and reemphasized the ineluctable axiom that small, lightly armed and highly mobile guerrilla bands are best fought by similarly small, lightly armed and highly mobile government forces.

Rhodesian special operations units, for example, carried out 42 cross-border raids (and provided information crucial to the success of five Rhodesian Air Force attacks) of which all but five were complete successes. Two of the five failures resulted from poor intelligence, including the April 1979 attempt to kidnap ZIPRA leader Joshua Nkomo. More than 4,000 insurgents were killed in the operations that specifically targeted the enemy units whereas total security force casualties were only 19 killed or wounded. Of the remaining operations, involved the destruction of insurgent assets and four the kidnapping of enemy commanders or senior political officials. The Rhodesians also used these raids as a means to exploit rivalries within insurgent organizations, upset relations between the organizations and their host governments, and dissuade those governments from providing assistance to and supporting the insurgents' struggle. Certainly, the most successful operation was the 1975 assassination of Herbert Chitepo, head of ZANLA's political department, in Lusaka, Zambia. The former head of the Rhodesian CIO estimated that the operation set ZANLA back two years in its struggle against Rhodesia.

Cordon Sanitaire

The Rhodesians were less successful with operations that suffered more distinctly from a lack of clear and consistent military strategy at the national level. Given the Rhodesians' serious deficiencies in manpower and material, unrealistic assessments further undermined the Security Forces' performance. These operations seemed to develop identities independent of reasonable strategic considerations and were initiated, and often prolonged, with neither sufficient regard for resource constraints nor clearly defined, broad strategic objectives.

The "Cordon Sanitaire" (or Corsan), for example, was originally envisioned as a physical obstacle to prevent insurgent infiltration. From the start, however, its effectiveness was problematical and little was done to modify its defects. Minefields were planted along 518 miles of the Mozambican border, with the intention of. creating a depopulated, mined, fenced, and paroled area that would either deter insurgent infiltrators or at least make it easier for intruders to be discovered and tracked from footprints left in the soft, raked earth. In practice, however, mines were often detonated by animals or uncovered by rain, rendering them ineffective.

The reason for the barrier's failure was mainly the lack of manpower devoted to patrolling it. Whereas control points were supposed to be established every six miles from which reaction forces could be deployed, too few personnel were assigned to patrol the Corsan. Thus, even when insurgents detonated mines, the remainder of their infiltration party was often able to escape back across the border before security patrols arrived. The insurgents even found ways of breaching the Corsan by digging trenches across it that similarly went undetected because of infrequent security force patrols.

Civic Action Measures

The Rhodesians had less success with various rural civic action programmes. Although the extremely limited finances available for these programs partly explains their failure, the Rhodesian military's tendency to treat civic action as an adjunct or afterthought and not as an integral part of the counterinsurgency campaign irrevocably undermined any prospect of their success. The protected villages program, for example, was modelled on the highly successful British system that had been implemented in Malaya 20 years before. Yet the Rhodesians ignored several important lessons of the British experience.

The Malayan protected villages program, for example, had been the cornerstone of the British government's "hearts and minds" campaign to wean popular support from the communist guerrillas. Its success was based on the premise that only when the people felt secure and protected from the guerrillas would they cooperate fully with the government. The British also recognized that the programme had to be aggressively and effectively "sold" to persons who were being forced to leave their traditional homes and resettle in new government-built villages. Accordingly, the government embraced a two-pronged approach involving actual physical measures to improve the relocated villagers' standard of living-electricity, indoor plumbing, etc.- alongside a sophisticated psychological warfare campaign directed by an information department that the government created specifically for this purpose.

In Rhodesia, however, the "hearts and minds" dimension of the British approach seemed only an ancillary objective. Rather than providing for the security of the civilian population, the Rhodesian military saw the protected villages as a means of relocating persons from one part of the country to another to create depopulated, rural "free fire" zones where the security forces could operate with impunity. This misplaced emphasis is apparent in the minimal amount of money that the Rhodesians spent on the new villages and the attendant failures either to improve the relocated tribesmen's standard of living or to develop an organized pro-government psychological campaign. Worse still, once the tribes were settled into their new villages, the government provided little if any protection from guerrilla attack, or intimidation.

Although the Army's neglect of civic action was the inevitable consequence of inadequate finances and an overcommitted military establishment already stretched thin by an escalating insurgency, institutional inertia combined with an almost reflexive inclination to discount the importance of non-military countermeasures played a considerable role as well. The same organisational apathy, for example, thwarted Operation Favour, the government-sponsored self-defence program. Local militias were armed with cast-off, antiquated weapons and accorded only the most rudimentary training, rendering them incapable of defending either themselves or their villages. The militias were further disadvantaged by their personnel: unemployed men from urban areas who were recruited without regard for their lack of tribal affiliations with the people they were defending or familiarity with the bush. The militias consequently lost credibility with the populace, particularly after they began to harass and intimidate the tribesmen they were supposed to be protecting.

The militias also performed poorly against the insurgents. Moreover, the ease with which the guerrillas disarmed the militiamen sowed suspicion within the security forces about the militia's loyalty and dependability. Thus, rather than providing an additional layer of protection for the villages, the way in which the Rhodesians organized, equipped and supported the militias made the villages doubly vulnerable. They were specifically targeted by the guerrillas (who saw them as threat to their rural hegemony) and distrusted by the security forces (who regarded them as potential, if not actual, "fifth columnists") who refused to come to the militias' aid when the villages were attacked.

Special Operations-Intelligence Gathering

As police difficulties in obtaining information from the rural population increased in the early 1970s, the Rhodesians began to investigate alternative intelligence-gathering techniques and sources. By 1973, their'attention had fastened on so-called "pseudo" (or "counter-gang") operations. This technique, whereby security force personnel posing as insurgents circulate among the population gathering information on guerrilla movement and activities as well as on local sympathies, had been pioneered by the British during the Mau Mau uprising in Kenya nearly two decades before. The Rhodesians experimented with "pseudo" units as early as 1966, but this inchoate effort was both unsophisticated and unnecessary, given that the vast majority of rural blacks at the time were either politically indifferent or opposed to the insurgents.

In the rapidly deteriorating security conditions of the 1970s, however, the idea was resurrected. With the encouragement of the Prime Minister and senior CIO and Special Branch officials, a new unit known as the Selous Scouts was established in November 1973. For administrative purposes, the Scouts were placed within the Rhodesian Army's command structure, though the Special Branch commander coordinated and directed the unit's intelligence-gathering function. Some of the original pseudo operatives joined the new force, and additional personnel were recruited from the Army and Special Branch. Captured or surrendered insurgents were also enlisted. Their inclusion provided for the constant flow of up-to-date information on insurgent operations and behaviour necessary for the Scouts' successful charade.

The Rhodesians spent a great deal of time and effort on "turning'" insurgents - that is, persuading them to switch allegiance and serve with the government forces. Their approach was patterned on the methods that had been used so successfully in Kenya. Prospective candidates were thoroughly screened and then given the choice of joining the Scouts or facing prosecution under Rhodesian law for terrorist crimes (conviction for which carried the death penalty or long prison terms). Those who chose to join the Scouts were formally absolved of any crimes they may have committed while serving in the insurgent ranks, were paid an attractive salary, and had their families relocated to special, protected, and comparatively luxurious Selous Scouts' encampments. Previously "turned" insurgents-who provided living proof of the benefits of service with the Scouts were often used to persuade their recently captured or surrendered former comrades to join the unit. Selous Scouts recruiters also looked for prospective candidates among wounded insurgents. These casualties would be earmarked for special treatment. They would be quickly evacuated from the battlefield, given excellent medical care and recuperative attention, and thus encouraged to come over to the Rhodesian side.

The first Selous Scouts unit was ready for operational duty in January 1974 and was deployed in the Operation Hurricane area. The units generally operated in eight-man sections (a number selected because it was the size of the typical insurgent unit), dressed in insurgent uniforms or clothing, and carried the same weapons the insurgents did. The Scouts' missions, it should be emphasized, was not to engage the insurgents in combat but to determine their size and location and then report this information either to "Fireforce" teams or ground combat units, which would take over. To avoid confusion and prevent other government forces from mistaking the Scouts for actual insurgents, any area that they were operating in was "frozen" -that is, no other security forces were allowed in its vicinity. The Selous Scouts proved extremely effective in providing the security forces with useful and timely intelligence. According to one internal assessment undertaken by the Directorate of Military Operations, the Selous Scouts were responsible for a staggering 68 percent of all the insurgent kills and captures in their areas of operation.

External Intelligence Gathering

The CIO's Branch 2 was responsible for almost all external intelligence-gathering operations. Obviously, the black front-line states surrounding Rhodesia were of considerable interest to CIO, and Branch 2 had an extensive network of agents supplying intelligence from Zambia, Botswana, Mozambique and even Angola. The agents in Zambia included people living along the border, many of whom belonged to tribes hostile to the Zambian government. These agents provided considerable information on ZIPRA bases in these areas. CIO also mounted a concerted intelligence-gathering effort against the Soviet and Peoples' Republic of China embassies in Lusaka, Zambia. The success of these operations, however, was more the result of Russian and Communist Chinese underestimation of CIO's intelligence-gathering abilities, leading to lax security, than of CIO's sophistication. In addition, liaison continued throughout the conflict between Zambian intelligence and the CIO for the exchange of information of mutual interest.

The CIO also had agents in Angola and Mozambique who provided information on insurgent activities in these countries, especially in the urban centres and ports. Many of the agents were Portuguese nationals who had remained in the country after independence. While they were never able to penetrate the insurgents' bases, the agents nonetheless monitored insurgent activities in the cities and reported the arrival of arms and equipment shipments. The also kept track of FRELIMO security operations in Mozambique and of Cuban activity in Angola. Special Branch, however, did succeed in placing agents on the insurgent bases. Many, in fact, were sent with insurgent recruits for guerrilla training in Communist-bloc countries.

Information from agents was relayed to Salisbury by various means. In Zambia, blacks met with their Special Branch officers simply by crossing the river into Rhodesia. Special Branch also operated an extensive courier system that funnelled information from Lusaka to Salisbury. White agents were able to communicate clandestinely by telephone, usually by calling contacts in South Africa on the pretext of talking about business matters.

The Rhodesians also frequently used other countries' intelligence agencies, including the American Central Intelligence Agency and Britain's MI5 (domestic intelligence and counterintelligence) and MI6 (overseas intelligence). One senior CIO maintains that it was not unusual for intelligence organisations to continue to maintain contact even though formal relations between their governments may have been strained or actually severed. In fact, throughout the conflict virtually all important external intelligence on Soviet and Chinese contacts with ZIPRA and ZANLA was obtained from the CIA. MI5, and other western intelligence organisations. The animosity that existed between the Rhodesian and British governments after UDI, for example, did little to affect intelligence exchanges between the CIO and MI5 or MI6; the British services were unsympathetic toward ZANLA and ZIPRA because of their ties to various Communist countries.

Close ties were also maintained between the CIO and the Portuguese and South African intelligence communities, as well as with France, Italy, and Greece. Many opportunities for such exchanges were opened through the course of normal business :relations involving the circumvention of the international trade sanctions imposed on Rhodesia (more colloquially know as "sanction breaking"). Apparently, countries prepared to buy Rhodesian goods or supply the country with materials were also prepared to provide a considerable amount of information.

Destabilisation And Disinformation Operations

In addition to intelligence gathering, Special Branch, Branch 2, and the Selous Scouts were actively involved in covert destabilization and disinformation operations. The exact extent of these has not been fully revealed, but the few operations for which there is some information available provides some idea of their nature and success.

During the early sixties, the split between ZAPU and ZANU had an extremely detrimental effect on the nationalist struggle. It is assumed, though inconclusively proven, that Special Branch may have exploited the rivalry between these two movements whenever possible, using agents of influence strategically placed in both organisations combined with various disinformation tactics. These tactics were certainly used in Zambia after UDI to help foment the rivalry between ZANLA and ZIPRA. Peter Stiff, for example, recounts the sabotage activities in Lusaka of two British veterans of the British SAS who worked for CIO and were assisted by a white Zambian farmer and his wife. This foursome conducted several attacks against both ZANLA and ZIPRA targets that were made to appear as if they had been staged by the rival insurgent organization.

The most successful of these operations was the assassination of the ZANU's national chairman in Zambia. Herbert Chitepo, done in such a way as to suggest that his death by a car bomb was due to factional fighting within that organisation. This incident provoked the anger of Zambian president Kenneth Kaunda, who had allowed the nationalist organizations to operate in his country only on the express condition that there was no internecine violence. When Kaunda learned that dissident ZANLA elements were suspected in Chitepo's murder, he ordered the arrest of all senior ZANLA officials (including military commander Joseph Tongogara), the expulsion of the organisation's fighters, and the suspension of all ZANLA activities in Zambia. The arrested officials were brutally interrogated until they falsely confessed to involvement in Chitepo's murder, while other alleged conspirators were shot. The overall result was a severe setback for ZANLA operations that, according to Ken Flower, the head of the CIO, cost ZANLA an estimated two years in its war against Rhodesia.

Rhodesia's most ambitious external destabilisation operation was the formation of the Mozambique National Resistance Movement (MNR. later to be called RENAMO). The Rhodesians hoped in the long term to undermine and ultimately overthrow FRELIMO and replace it with a pro- western government and, in the short term, simply to use the MNR both to further disrupt ZANLA operations in Mozambique and to provide intelligence about the insurgents and their bases. The genesis behind the MNR idea lay in the Mozambican population's increasing discontent with FRELIMO. That insurgent organization had been completely surprised by the Portuguese decision to withdraw from Mozambique and thus was unprepared to assume power in 1974. FRELIMO rule, accordingly, was generally inept and quickly alienated the population. As increasing numbers of Mozambicans fled their country, the CIO decided to launch a disinformation campaign using a large, powerful and impossible to jam transmitters that the Portuguese had given to the Rhodesians when they left Mozambique. These broadcasts described the fictitious activities of a nonexistent resistance movement in Mozambique that the Rhodesians called the MNR.

The ruse worked only too well. Shortly after the broadcasts began, FRELIMO deserters began crossing in droves, seeking to join the resistance movement. The CIO was therefore forced to create a real organisation to preserve its ruse. Because Rhodesia itself lacked the resources needed to supply a clandestine army, the CIO turned to other countries, primarily in South Africa, for the funds and weapons the

MNR required. Training was provided at first by former Portuguese soldiers, but the black recruits distrusted their former colonial masters and responded better when the Portuguese trainers were replaced by former Rhodesian SAS troopers now working for the CIO. In their search for a leader for the movement, the CIO found André Matangaidze, a former FRELIMO platoon commander, who had fled to Rhodesia in 1978 after escaping from a FRELIMO re-education camp. The CIO tested Matangaidze's leadership ability by sending him with a small band of men to free the inmates at the camp from which he had escaped. Matangaidze succeeded and was appointed the commander of the MNR.

Subsequent MNR operations were equally successful, and support for the movement grew rapidly in both Mozambique and Rhodesia. The Rhodesian Army in particular was impressed by the MNR's success and threw its full support behind the movement. In 1979, the MNR began to work very closely with the Rhodesian SAS. They carried out several joint raids, including the attack on an oil storage farm in Beira, Mozambique; the sinking of ships and subsequent blocking of a harbour in a Mozambican port; and the disabling of a FRELMO tropospheric scatter station. Unfortunately for the Rhodesians, the MNR was formed only toward the end of the war and thus had little effect on ZANLA, although it did destabilize the FRELIMO regime and later was exploited by the South Africans as a bargaining tool against Mozambican support of the African National Congress (ANC). Although the MNR did not achieve the objectives for which it was originally established and had little effect on the outcome of the Rhodesian conflict, some of the Rhodesian intelligence officers and special operations personnel involved in the formation of the MNR and the attendant disinformation campaign in Mozambique claim that had these efforts been initiated earlier in the conflict, the FRELIMO government might well have been overthrown and the insurgents deprived of their operational bases in that country.

Disinformation operations were carried out within Rhodesia as well. Perhaps the most controversial were atrocities against civilians allegedly undertaken by the Selous Scouts disguised to appear as, and thereby to discredit, the insurgents. Among the crimes that the Scouts allegedly committed were the murders of white missionaries, attacks on tribal villages, and the murders of insurgent contacts, whom the Scouts had accused in front of witnesses of being government collaborators. Although both Special Branch and Selous Scout officers categorically deny these allegations, some former police officers maintain that many of the Scouts' disinformation attempts were in any event amateurish and did more harm than good.

The Rampadshan by Professor R. Trevor Jones, O.B.E.
Consulting Orthopaedic Surgeon, Salisbury from Sandra Andersen.
Originally printed in the Central African Journal of Medicine in 1960.

Rampadshan is the name given by the Bechuana people to a sandal made out of an old motor car tyre. It means "father of the roads." The Manica and Mashona make a similar sandal and call it "Washu."

Essentially it is a piece of motor tyre or ox hide cut to the shape of a foot and held on to the foot by thongs like the Roman sandal of old. 'This footwear has been used by Africans for years, and a good pair of rampadshans will last for as long as ten years.

Wars, industrial and motor accidents have been responsible for a great increase in the number of amputations. Their numbers have and will still increase with the growth of the Federation. No artificial limb can replace a normal limb. The evolution of the modern articulated limb is a classic of man's ingenuity, but even to-day many amputees prefer the old-fashioned pegleg.

There are very many more African than European amputees in this country. The loss of a limb in an African is a great disability. In most cases he is no longer fit for his previous employment, and on returning to the reserve finds, his disability even more serious.

An African amputee is fitted with either, with an articulated limb or a pegleg. The pegleg costs about £25, while the articulated limb costs £65 or more. For the African, the pegleg is more suitable because it does not require all the care and maintenance of the articulated leg. Not only this, but the man with a pegleg can walk farther, is more agile than the man with an articulated leg. Again, the rubber end of the pegleg lasts longer than the shoe of the articulated leg.

The pegleg. has, however, many drawbacks. Of these, the most important are that there is no foot and the wearer is always self-conscious of his disability. Secondly, he cannot easily walk through the soft ground, fields and mud, and for the African farmer this is a serious handicap.

The best articulated foot does not stand up to the African's demands for long. Admittedly he has a foot, but this limits his activities even more than a pegleg. The ankle joint requires constant attention and the shoe fitted to the artificial foot has a relatively limited life. When the shoe wears out it is frequently beyond repair. It is then discarded and for economic reasons not replaced. The beautifully made calf skin covered artificial foot is then exposed to the rigours of African wild life. In a short while the foot and ankle joint are damaged beyond repair.

It became increasingly important to produce a foot not only cosmetically pure, but efficient and robust enough to stand up to all the demands of the African's vigorous and strenuous life as a landsman.

The orthopaedic technicians at the Government Orthopaedic Centre in Salisbury, led by Mr. Miller and Mr. Ecob, solved this problem with inspired thought and energy. After a year's experimenting they have now produced an artificial foot which is not only superior to the best articulated foot, but is easy and cheap to manufacture.

The "rampadshan" foot consists in its simplest form of a piece of motor tyre fixed to a pegleg with a wooden footpiece nailed on to the dorsum of the tyre sole and a lighter piece of tyre extending from this to the anterior aspect of the pegleg.

The advantages of this foot are obvious. It is easy to produce. There is no costly and delicate ankle joint mechanism requiring constant care. The wearing parts can be easily replaced and by the most unskilled person. The wearer can sit on his haunches.

All degrees of inversion and eversion are possible, and any extreme of these movements occurs at the foot and not at the amputation stump. The amputation stump is accordingly not subject to the same strain as in other types of artificial legs.

The wearer has an easier and more natural gait. When the shoe wears out there remains years of life in the motor tyre sole of the pegleg. Apart from this, a person with this sort of artificial foot can walk through mud, ploughed lands and water without fear of damage to the artificial foot.

In all respects one must regard this foot as a revolutionary advance in artificial limbs. One can confidently anticipate that it will replace all other forms of artificial feet.

The staff of the Government Orthopaedic Centre should be congratulated on the skill, thought and energy that they have displayed, and it is anticipated that the amputees of the world will be eternally grateful to these men.

With great foresight the Department of Health has patented this foot. By doing so the Government has prevented the exploitation of a simple principle, saved the country thousands of pounds and ensured through royalties another stable source of national revenue.

A Few Adventures with Wildlife in the Valley

While I was in the BSAP we were doing a patrol west of Chirundu, in conjunction with some RAR contingent. These guys set up an ambush position, and then (as they do) fell asleep. The MAG Gunner woke up when his MAG fell over, and looked into the face of a lion that had knocked it over!. He screamed and sh*t himself. His mate next to him set off a flare, and in the light they could see that a whole pride of lions was circled around them. The MLWC (main lion what counts) had gone to have a sniff at him before they started their meal!

Another RAR guy woke in the night in "camp" with a lion's nose almost touching his. He got such a fright that he went nuts and they had to casevac him!

I was on patrol in the valley west of Chirundu and we wandered into a herd of elephants. It is amazing how difficult they are to see in certain circumstances. The chief Jumbo alerted us by picking up a stick and rapping it on a tree to get our attention. We slowly backtracked and found another route around the herd.   Ian.

Wildlife was a definite problem. A jumbo caught one of our blokes, whilst he was taking photos of it near Kariba. He didn't realise how close it was, and then he tripped whilst trying to exit fast. The jumbo did the complete tango on him, "kneeling" him and then whacking the remains against a tree. The guys who scraped up the remains for burial said that the coffin was basically packed with damp sand. Pete

I did NS in 2 Indep at Kariba and all the crew had plenty experiences with wildlife, more so than with gooks. Can't remember the guy's name but a Hyena snatched at him while he was asleep. Fortunately he had been using his webbing as a pillow and that was what the Hyena ran off with. We spent the next day tracking the beast and retrieving ammo pouches, water bottles, grenades etc. Kevin

A mate of mine was doing his national service and for some unknown reason his stick decided to sleep on a game trail. He was doing the guard duty, sitting up in his sleeping bag, when a lion came up, took a mouthful of his shoulder and started to pull him from the sleeping bag and into the bush. I think there was sh*t, shouting and shooting for awhile, but the main thing was that the lion left him. Made the papers in Rhodesia at the time, think it was early 70's. Mike

The first patrol we went on, the young driver woke with an elly baby feeling his face with it's trunk. He screamed, the mama became aggressive and the whole stick dived into the Zambezi until Mrs Jumbo calmed down.
One of our stick was woken up by a hyena pulling him in his sleeping bag out of his bivi? The animal had the foot of his bag, fortunately for him.

My mate lost his whole chilly bin (cooler box) to hyena. It was filled with prime rump steak and beer. They chewed through the box and ate the nyama but he managed to save the beer. Hugh.

Never mind hyenas - the worst I saw was a bloke who got an ant in his ear - he had his .375 out and was going to use it, we stopped him and drowned the ant with precious water - he wouldn't hold still enough for me to piss in his ear. That was near the vlei that was a game park outside Vic Falls.

Valley Patrols by Bernie Boshoff

In the army, when we finished training and were sent to Kariba, my first patrol was down the gorge below the wall. We had to walk in those days, I believe later on they got power boats to do the patrols. Bet there was a lot of skiving and not much patrolling then. Anyway, on this occasion, 3 of the wall flood gates were open, and the river was really high. We circled around Kariba village, and got to the river about a mile below the Wall. At first, the walk was relatively easy, but further down, there is a long stretch where the gorge walls rise straight up out of the water to a height of nearly 2000 feet. To get around an obstacle at the waters edge that may be only 50 feet wide, you had to climb up 2000 Ft, go along the top 50 Ft, then climb back down 2000 Ft. All the while, we could see huge crocodiles shadowing us in the water hoping that we would fall in.

All the mountains in the Kariba area are made up of loose crumbling rock, and as we climbed, we were all dislodging rocks which were tumbling down onto the guys below. At one point, we got to a part where we needed a rope to continue, but of course we didn't have one, so we joined several of our rifle slings together to make one. Our best climber managed to get up unaided, and he then fastened the sling rope so the rest of us could climb up. As I was waiting for my turn to climb the rope, someone above dislodged a rock about 4 pounds in weight, and it hit the guy standing next to me square on the head.

I heard the thump, and looked round into this guys face. I saw a sheet of blood flow down his face like a curtain, and his eyes start to roll up as he passed out. We were standing on a tiny ledge many hundreds of feet above the water, and the crocs, so I grabbed the guys webbing and held on desperately hoping he wouldn't drag both of us off the ledge. Fortunately, he came around fairly quickly and was able to stand after a few minutes, but his confidence was destroyed, and we had a hell of a job to get him up the rope.

After a whole exhausting day of climbing up and down, we had only progressed a couple of miles down the gorge and were looking for somewhere to camp, but everything was vertical. Finally, we found a tiny beech at the waters edge, about 6 Ft wide and 50 Ft long. 20 of us lined up like sardines to sleep, with our feet nearly in the water, and our heads up against the cliff.

That night it was really dark, no moon and overcast. I lay there trying to sleep, but thinking about those huge crocodiles which would only have to stick their jaws out of the water 12 inches to grab one of us and pull him in. To make matters worse, it sounded like a leopard had grabbed a baboon just around the corner from us. The screams were terrible, and were echoing up and down the gorge for what seemed like hours.

Didn't get much sleep that night.

The next day, we again had a hell of a struggle making progress down the gorge. We came across a smooth rock slide that went straight into deep water at an angle of about 75 degrees. We couldn't climb over it so we had to go across it. Several guys got across OK, but the guy in front of me lost traction and slid down into the water. As he slid, he had both hands trying to claw into the rock, and he rubbed all his finger tips off. When he hit the water, with full kit and rifle, the air pockets in his kit initially kept him afloat, but they soon filled up and he began to sink. I saw the look of desperation on his face, and he began to thrash wildly. Fortunately again, one of the guys who had already crossed, managed to reach him just as he went under, and pulled him up by his hair. Somehow, the guy managed to hold onto his rifle through that ordeal.

At some time during this day, we were up about 100 feet above the water when a Canberra bomber from our air force came flying up the gorge level with us. He came passed so close that I could clearly see the pilot through the canopy, in fact, I think I could have shot him. What a magnificent sight, but he was taking an awful risk, he didn't see us at all, and we weren't hiding.

That afternoon, we were again contemplating another 2000 foot climb to get around an obstacle at the waters edge. Across the river on the Zambian side, we could see a small African village tucked onto a small flat spot near the river. What a beautiful setting that was, completely isolated, you could only get to it by boat. The next thing, an African fisherman from the village came passed in his canoe, carved from a single solid tree trunk, and he came over and offered to help us.

This guy was completely primitive, and probably didn't know that he lived in Zambia, or that this was Rhodesia, and we were at war. We could have shot him for crossing the river illegally, but that didn't occur to us or him. He ferried us 2 at a time around the obstacle, and set us down on a lovely beech where the Chimwa river joined the Zambezi. As payment, we each gave him a tin of food out of our rat packs, and he was delighted.

The beech was much bigger than the last one, and so nice that we decided to camp there. That night, the fisherman came back across and threw his nets near us in the river. He made a good catch, and came and gave us a massive Tiger fish, about 30 Lbs, and a huge Mozambiqua Bream, about 10 Lbs. We carved fillets off these and grilled them over our camp fires, I have never tasted fish so nice, especially the Tiger fillets, which were even better than the Bream, much to my surprise. I was always told that Tiger was inedible, that's bull**** - trust me.

The next morning, we left the Zambezi and started up the Chimwa gorge, which was mostly dry except for a few stagnant pools. This didn't make the going much easier, though we were able to stay on the river bed all the way. There were several dry waterfalls which we had to climb up. Towards evening, we were again looking for somewhere to camp. We came across a small pool in a deep gorge with a bit of clear sand to camp on. As we approached it, there was a tremendous thrashing in a clump of reeds, and an angry Rhino came stamping out and charged off up the gorge.

We settled down to camp, but because we were away from the Zambezi, and it was winter, as soon as the sun went down, so did the temperature. In fact, we were soon freezing, so we thought, to hell with the gooks, let's light a fire. Being in a deep gorge, there was little chance of it being spotted, and we soon had a roaring bonfire going, and settled down around it to sleep. It was a beautiful moonlit night, and we could hear hyenas whooping up and down the gorge.

Sometime during the night, the guard schedule broke down, someone fell asleep on guard and never woke up the next guy. Somehow, in the morning, our lieutenant missed this vital point, but I noticed tracks all around our camp, hyena tracks. A hyena had come into camp and circled right around us, coming as close as 2 feet to our heads. We were sleeping with our feet towards the fire, and our heads out. I've heard tales where a hyena has bitten the face off a hunter while he slept in the bush. That sent a shiver up my spine.

That was the last night out on this patrol, and the next morning we made it to the old abandoned Chimwa mine, and were picked up by truck. That patrol is forever burned in my memory, it was through some of the most beautiful and scary country I've ever seen. The Zambezi river is magnificent through there. It's up to half a mile wide and very deep. The water is crystal clear, and surges and swirls in whirlpools. It would be totally impossible to swim against it.

In my next most memorable patrol, the army sent our platoon into the Matusadona Mountains on the other side of Lake Kariba for a week of intensive patrolling. They took us across the lake by boat and up the Sanyati Gorge to the second crossroad, where they dropped us off in the West side gorge.

From there, we marched up the West side crossroad gorge for two days, then split up into squads of 6 or 7 guys, and patrolled out into the Matusadona Mountains. This area is very rugged and covered with dense bush. There are no roads, no tourists, no hunters, no Africans, nothing. As a result, there is heaps of game in there, and we were constantly bumping into all sorts of animals at close range. The only way to get around, was to follow the numerous elephant paths, or walk up the dry stream beds, the bush was too dense to walk through.

One of the other squads was walking up a dry stream bed with high, nearly vertical banks, when they came face to face with a bull elephant. The elephant took one look at them and immediately charged. We had been warned that if we shot any elephants for whatever reason, we would spend the rest of our lives in DB, so the guys turned and ran. The lead guy went about 20 metres, when he spotted a place where he could scramble up the bank, but he tripped and fell on the way out. When they got back to the main camp, there were 3 distinct boot prints on his back and he was really angry. His mates had run right over him when he fell and left him to the elephant, which fortunately didn't complete his charge.

My squad was following an elephant path around the side of a steep hill when we stopped for a break. As we rested, we heard a massive crash as a big tree fell over, it

291

could only be an elephant, and my mate wanted to have a look, so the 2 of us sneaked off and stalked up to where the noise came from. Sure enough, a huge bull elephant had pushed over a tree and was picking at the roots. But my mate wasn't happy to watch from 100 metres away, oh no, he wanted to get closer. So we stalked up to within 15 metres of the brute. By now I was pretty nervous, the bull was awesome, and could have reached us in 2 steps. At this point, I remembered that my rifle safety catch was on, so I very carefully and slowly eased it off. The elephant heard that tiny click and fanned out his ears and took a step towards us. I nearly wet myself. The elephant was close enough to see us now, they have very weak eyesight, and he took a good long look at us, then turned with an angry snort and ambled off. I had to sit down for a couple of minutes because I couldn't stand any more.

After many more adventures which I will leave for another time, we walked back to the lake. We reached the flat area on the shores of the lake in the afternoon, and were hot and tired, and walking without paying attention. Suddenly the ground began to rumble under our feet. We stopped and looked, and saw that we had walked right into the middle of an enormous herd of buffalo, there must have been 2 to 3 hundred animals, and they were stampeding all around us. We could only watch in fear as the noise and dust enveloped us, but they didn't run us down.

I saw more game on that trip than I ever had before, or ever will again.

By Train to see Wrex Tarr by Paul Mroz

My only claim to fame with Rhodie Celebrities went something like this:

It was Salisbury in the early 70's when I was visiting some of my old mates .

We had travelled from Umtali on the overnight train to Salisbury, you remember, the old coaches with the wood interior, green leather (maybe) seats in the compartments with photos of scenic spots in Rhodesia hidden behind thick glass attached to the top bunks.

"RR" etched in the glass mirrors.

At the end of each corridor , a canister of water.

At the Umtali station , I had sat watching the platform from our compartment window for my usual amusement , the late arrivals for the 3rd and 4th class coaches, running down the platform with huge bundles on their heads to catch the departing train after the Guard had blown his whistle and waived the green flag. Being a wee bit sadistic , this somehow drew my mirth. It was time to hit the corridor and look out the other direction , not much to see but the shunting yard of Umtali station. Odzi was the first stop as I recall, milk cans loaded , mail dropped off, my folks called out mentioning they were going to sleep not to stay up too late.

Hell , it was fun travelling on the train.

I wished I could see what diesel loco was pulling the train. They held a strange fascination for me, wondered if it was DE 4 English Brush type or the new American DE 6 's. They were painted Green with a yellow and red stripe. I still remember the old Garret class Steam locomotives , when a fireman on the railways was really a fireman !

Sorry to get off on a tangent, but anyhow, it was pitch dark so no such luck as to see the Diesel. Inyazura was the next stop. We had lunch there once at the hotel.

Rusape was next, which had a great hotel where you could get meat pies 'out of this world'. Just for an outing we would drive from Umtali to Rusape to get a meat pie. Once, while at the hotel in Rusape, this African chap who had fashioned himself a guitar out of an old Castrol gallon oil tin, was standing singing his version of Cliff Richard's "Bachelor Boy". My Dad liked it so much he gave him a shilling!

Well that was enough, it was time to turn in , as I couldn't stay awake anymore, so I would have to miss the fun of Headlands, Macheke and Marandellas. Soon it was morning and we were pulling into Salisbury station and I was thinking food: "Railway Chips" and a "Sparletta Cherry Plum". You couldn't get them in Umtali , Cherry Plum that is.

"Way too early in the morning", declared my Mom.

We were met by some dear mates of ours. Always good to see old mates! My eyes were scanning the busy streets of Salisbury as our friend manoeuvred his grey and white Vanguard through the bustle.

We enjoyed a breakfast of oats , marmalade toast and tea. I make mention of all of this purely for the nostalgia of the train trip from Umtali to Salisbury !

Later in the day the nephew of our friends arrived. He was my mate. We were about the same age and we had known one another since we were lighties.

"Let's joll to the showgrounds, there are all kinds of Chickies at the stables riding in some gymkana!" He said, so off we go.

Ah yes, lots of fine young Rhodesian Ladies all dressed in their riding pants and black caps. Some grinned at us, others scowled !

If it wasn't for the few grins, hell I would have left, because horses despise me and the feeling is mutual and I probably would never have the this story to tell you.

While we were wandering around, one of my mate's friends came up stating that 'Sea Blue Pools' had a Stand open in the Showgrounds and they were giving away free beer!

What Rhodesian teenager in his right mind is going to refuse free beer?

Off we amble to the Sea Blue stand and none other than Mr. Wrex Tarr is sitting at a table under a tent /canopy discussing the purchase of a pool with a prospective customer.

Well we 'sort of' thought of leaving but we had walked all this way so here now are two acne faced teenagers walking past Wrex trying to act very interested in the pool with comments like,

"Ja, what a lekker pool " and "Ja , you could dive bomb off the diving board!"

Wrex sort of acknowledged us, looking extremely cool in his mirrored sunglasses and white Safari Suit.

We marched over to the refreshment kiosk and told the picanin behind the counter we wanted two Shumbas which he gave us. It was hot and we were thirsty so I reached in my pocket and I can't remember if it was a two bob piece or a shilling but I gave it to the picanin. He was not much older than us. He was quite delighted, probably he had a Matemba (Dry Fish) on his mind. He promptly handed us another beer which we drank with much gusto and left the Sea Blue stand.

We went back to the stables to "observe " the gymkhana riders. As things began to dwindle at the stables, we decided we would pay the Sea Blue Pools stand one more visit. This time the "Ever So Cool" Wrex Tarr was not attending to a customer but looked on with interest at us two young punks wandering in.

Of course we made a few more complimentary comments about Wrex's pool like "Jussus , Chicks would love you if you had a lekker pool in your back yard like this!"

and

"Hell , I'm going to 'chune' my Pop to buy one!"

Apparently this didn't impress Wrex.

Why I'll never know!

I mean they were legitimate remarks!

Like a cat waiting to corner a mouse, Wrex let us head over to the refreshment kiosk. There again was our ever grateful shamwari , who had received a nice tip earlier, being a good host he smiled at us and opened two Castles this time.

"Baas, lo Shumba, henna pellileh!" (sp) (The Lion is finished hence the Castle).

"Azikoo ndaba, Mfane, lo Castle henna moshe futi!" we told him.(Doesn't, matter Son , Castle is good too).

About the time we took our first swig, the kiosk door opens. It's Wrex , trying to sound totally annoyed he says:

"What are you boys doing?"

"Where do you come from?"

"We were checking out the chicks at the stables!"

By now Wrex is fighting back a grin in an attempt to still look hostile.

"Weren't you boys here earlier?"

"Er yes Sir, but it got hot and ..."

By now Wrex is about to crack up but looks at the picanin.

"Aikona neeka lo Baas futi chwala!" (Don't give them any more beer).

"Ja Baas," replied our shamwari, "But henna moshe sterek, henna neekele mina lo mali".(Yes Boss, but they are very nice, they gave me money).

294

"Aziku N'daba, Aikona neeka futi!" (Doesn't matter don't give any more).
Almost in a full smile, Wrex said.
"You boys finish your beer and don't come back!"
Being the idiot I am, I offered to pay, with what I don't know because the picanin was now the proud owner of what change had been in my pocket.
Wrex very kindly said, "That's all right , just don't come back."
I won't bore you with the discussion that followed between my mate and I as we left the Showgrounds, with much consternation, lest somehow our parents found out about this escapade, not to mention the beer.
I will say, years later, I met Wrex and his wife Merry at a Rhodesian reunion in the States and relayed this same tale to him. He roared with laughter and said he remembered the picanin. Apparently he was extremely liberal with Wrex's beers at these pool shows especially so to folk who gave him a "bonsella".
I told Wrex I thought about buying him a beer but since he wouldn't let the picanin give me another I couldn't!
"Forget it!"
Wrex again roared with laughter.
Rest in peace Wrex, thanks for your humour, good nature , making us laugh , for the beer and being a great Rhodesian !
I owe you.
Cheers, Paul Mroz.

In Memory of Wrex Tarr from Pete in Oz

St Peter looked down with a deep, worried frown
As he heard a roar from the tent
Towards the gates climbed two reprobates
Singing "The Terrorist's Lament".

With noisy gusto, came the cheers from below
As the Colonel and Wrex both ascended
Each pausing to toast the heavenly host
As their time down on Earth was now ended.

With a fine single malt from the Colonel's deep vault
Eternally cooled with His ice,
Their glasses stayed full, despite many pulls,
And they knew they had reached Paradise!

'Local Names for Hit Songs from the seventies' by Chris

Dancing Queen	**Lo Mkulu Medem ga lo Eenglish ena enza lo waltz**
Gimme! Gimme! Gimme!	**'Nika mena' tree time**
Money, Money, Money	**Mari mari mari**
Daddy Cool	**Baba Makasa**
Sunny	**Langa maningi**
Le Freak	**Lo Nkosikas**
Don't Go Breaking My Heart	**Aikona bulala lo mutima gamina**
I Will Survive	**Mena aikona efele**
Don't Leave Me This Way	**Aikona yega mena funika lo**
Popcorn	**Ena lo Mielies ena enza "dammit" funika lo bumburu**
Don't Stop 'til You Get Enough	**Aikona shalla lapa 'one place', indaba wena aikona bamba futi**
We Are Family	**Zonke ena broer gamina**
Blame It On The Boogie	**Ena aikona meena, ena lo munia wun**
Go West	**Hamba lapa Wankie**
Y.M.C.A	**Ena lo club ga lo Muntu ena enza funika lo umfasi**
You Are The Sunshine Of My Life	**Wena ena lo Langa gamena**
Me And Mrs Jones	**Meena ena futi lo umfasi ga lo Bwana Jonesi**
Always Somewhere	**Zonke Skaat Upi?**
Somebody to Love	**Meena funa lo umfasi ka lo enza lo jigjig**
Don't Stop Me Now	**Aikona imisa mena manje**
Fat Bottomed Girls	**Umfasi ena mafoota mushi sterek**
Bicycle Race	**Lo Magwagwa lo Bisickoro humba checha sterek**
Stairway To Heaven	**Lo Magwagwa ga humba pezulu**
We Are The Champions	**Zonke Tina lo Number wun**
You Ain't Seen Nothing Yet	**Wena Bonili Azeko Manje**
Father and Son	**Mdoda ena futi Mfaan**
Wild World	**Lo Shebeen**
Candle in the Wind	**Lo candela ena aikona vuka indowa ena mweya maningi**
Wonderful Tonight	**Mushi sterek skaat lo langa ena chorna**
I Want to Know What Love Is	**Mena funa asi, ini lo 'enza play'**
Baker Street	**Lo Mugwagwa next door ga lo Union**
Stuck In The Middle With You	**Mena futi wena chornili lapa pagati**
(They Long To Be) Close To You	**Ena funa lo dusi lapa gawena**
Top Of The World	**Pezulu ga lo zonke funika lo World View**

My memories by Rob Lewin

Standing in the doorway and getting that smell of rain just as the "Heavens open"
Seeing the Lyons Maid Ice cream boy waiting for us as we headed out on break time
Going to the "tuck shop" for a peach or fish
Listening to the BSAP band playing
Standing on the street waving my Union Jack flag at the Queen Mom
Listening to Don Burdett's show 'Silver Lining' - and hearing him call out my name and send me good wishes when I was sick
Drinking an ice cold "Sparletta Cherry Plum"
Biting into a Strawberry Mivie - or eating a Choc 99 from Dairy Den
Listening to Martin Locke's Hits of the week - every Saturday
The smells at the Salisbury show and attending the Texan Rock Band competition.
Creating the "Old Imaplians" old boys association for Mt Pleasant School
Playing tenny twist in the backyard with my family
Meeting my wife
Having President and Mrs. Wrathall attend our wedding
Walking the halls of Lady Chancellor waiting for our first son to be born
Listening to my grandpa telling story of the good old days - he arrived in 1910.
My favourite story of him and Sir Roy Welensky playing truant from school and going swimming "bare bummed" in the Makabusi
Hearing the roar when Reg Nield led the Rhodesian Rugby team onto the field for a Currie Cup match
Watching Gillette Double Wicket - and seeing players like Gary Sobers, Mike Proctor, Barry Richards etc
Listening to the clack of the Rhodesian Railways and knowing that each click or clack brought me closer to Llewellyn Barracks
Seeing Victoria Falls for the first time
The smell of Africa
Watching the sun set on my country Rhodesia

When I was in Form 4 at Mount Pleasant and I was introduced to a new student who had just arrived at the school from Falcon. He invited me to his house one Saturday - assuring me his parents were out of town.
He offered me a cigarette!
Wow a chance to smoke without sneaking around!
With cigarette in hand, I began heading towards his front door when the door opened and there stood the Deputy Prime Minister and Mrs. Wrathall.
The cigarette started to burn the inside of my hand. Luckily they were in a hurry to get into the house. I shook hands and got outside quickly. Over the next couple of years, I spent a lot of time at "Northward" and remember on a number of occasions playing

around on the polo field behind the house when the Prime Minister and Mrs. Smith were taking their dog "UDI" for a walk. They would always stop to chat.

Mr. Wrathall went on to become President and my second home became Government house. They attended my wedding and were like parents to my wife and I.

We are still friends with Jonnie today and often reminisce about the "good old days".

Harry Potter

The lady at the book shop in Harare wanted to advertise the launch of the latest Harry Potter book in the Herald.

So she calls up the Herald and says "Can I speak to somebody about putting an advert in the paper about the New Harry Potter book"

Reply ...."Yes I am Harry Potter"

The lady says, "No you don't understand, there is a new book called Harry Potter and I need to put and advert in the paper"

Reply......... "Yes I am Harry Potter"

"YOU ARE NOT HARRY POTTER"

Reply ...." I am Harry Potter"

The women got angry and slams down the phone.

She calls again - this time the same thing, the dude calling himself Harry Potter.

Finally she calls her assistant and asks him to phone and speak to the guy in Shona, which he does.

A couple of minutes later her guy is laughing on the phone - gives the message and hangs up.

"Whats so funny ? " She asks, "What was the man from the Herald saying ?"

"I AM HA REPORTER" (add accent)

"Brightlights" by Ian Watson

I was sent out to help guard a farmer's home which was situated near Espungaberra in Mozambique. It was part of the "Bright Lights" programme in which men from the BSAP were deployed to give support to people in outlying districts in an effort to reduce farm attacks.

The farmer and his wife were French, and they had started their farming life in Algeria and lost everything when the French pulled out. They then went to the Belgian Congo, where later the same thing happened when the Belgians pulled out of there. They arrived in Rhodesia thinking that for this third time they would be lucky and be able to spend the final part of their lives farming in peace.

With the war heating up it seemed as though history was repeating itself.

All went reasonably well with my guard duty until the farmer decided to show me around the farm. He led the way down to some deserted buildings that used to be a part of the customs and immigration facilities in this isolated region. I gathered that this was where border officials used to be sent, when they had displeased their superiors in Salisbury!

He pushed his way into the building and started looking around.

I passed him with my FN at the ready, just in case.

The place had been trashed inside with rubbish lying around on the floors.

I entered one of the bedrooms and edged one of the cupboard doors open with my rifle barrel. Inside I saw a web of electrical wires leading up into the roof. As I realised that the place was booby-trapped, I started to shout to the farmer to not touch anything.

It was too late.

He opened a door somewhere and five claymores went off simultaneously.

One was in the top of the cupboard that I had just opened and the blast went over my head and reflected off the wall behind me and hit me in the back. The combination of the blasts blew the roof off the building.

I picked myself up out of the wreckage, retrieved my rifle and did a search for the farmer. I could not see him anywhere. I was dazed and deaf so I zigzagged my way back to the farmhouse. The farmer's wife was running down towards me, as she had heard the blast.

It was she who found the remains of her husband in the blasted building.

I radioed for backup, which is a little awkward when you can't hear anything.

Support arrived, but there was not a lot anyone could do, except take me off for treatment.

This was just one of the incidents of the war, but the poignant part was that the explosives in the building had been laid by one of my mates that I used to sail with whenever I was off duty, Brian Pearce-Flemming of the RLI Engineers.

Maybe we should have chatted a little bit more about our respective rôles in the war!   Perhaps the "lights" would not have been so instant, loud and "bright"!

"Amazing Grace" Chapter 2 by Basil O'Connell-Jones

I was smoking grass when the hooter blew. First I swore, then I shoved the joint in my pocket with an instinctive movement, like pulling on my pants in the middle of the night. I jerked the tent flap open, and ran out into the blinding African sun.

It had started like any regular day, which seems strange now. Something should have been different, something in the air, in the way I felt when I woke up. Surely a man should feel something unusual on the day he is about to die.

I woke up hot and sweaty, like every other day, and slipped my purple beads over my head. I adjusted the beads around my dog tags, and then kicked Guy, who slept on the floor next to me. It seemed like another ordinary day in bush camp.

After breakfast and morning drills, I wandered over to a tent on the edge of the camp where my buddy, Glenn, was waiting with the first smoke of the day.

Glenn and I were part of the Rhodesian Light Infantry, an elite military force specially trained to fight in a war which had been going on secretly and silently since we were children. Rhodesia, a country the size of Texas, is located on the south-eastern portion of the African continent. The land varies from lush mountain jungles to hot desert plateaus and boasts some of the best wild animal habitat in the world. Political control of the country has changed hands every hundred years or so, the most recent trade having been a declaration of independence from Britain when I was ten years old, which didn't affect me much. Neither did the rumours of enemy soldiers sneaking across the border from neighbouring countries to infiltrate remote villages or take over out-lying farms.

But eventually, the war became hard to ignore. Missionaries were gunned down in their stations. School children were abducted. And the spirit-mediums of tribal religions began working together with the enemy.

By the time I joined the RLI, the inhumane acts of enemy soldiers had made their earlier atrocities of murdering missionaries and stealing of children seem mild. But I wasn't fighting for any humanitarian reasons or political causes. I joined the army because I was looking for a cause to throw myself into. Smuggling drugs and avoiding cops had lost some of its attraction, and I was looking for anything that offered excitement. Killing the men who were performing such atrocities sounded like justice to me. Hunting them down, chasing them through the bush, playing a dangerous game of hide-and-seek with men's lives at stake seemed like a new thrill.

But I hadn't counted on sitting on a canvas stool for hours at a time, playing cards and talking rubbish. I hadn't anticipated the spastic bulging of my leg muscles while I sat there. Always tense, always ready, always listening for the sound of the hooter screaming us into action.

The hooter was a square, grey loud speaker mounted on a tree trunk in the centre of camp. And it controlled our lives. We listened for it in our sleep and watched it when we were awake. As if we might be able to see the sound before we heard it and therefore gain a split second of time for the chase.

When it blew that February morning in 1977, I sprinted across the camp to the air strip and grabbed my kit from its place beside the chopper without breaking stride. The three other guys assigned to my unit followed in a matter of seconds.

Four choppers sat on the airstrip, always fuelled and ready to fly. The whole thing was designed to get twelve fully-trained Commandos in the air ready for a contact within seconds. It was possible to go from slamming a volleyball across a net to finding ourselves involved in a contact in less time than it takes to smoke a cigarette.

Today, my unit of four guys was first wave. The first to be called out after an enemy sighting. As the chopper pulled away from the camp, I looked around at the other guys who were checking equipment or staring out at the dense foliage below us. I knew them fairly well, but they weren't part of the crowd I ran with.

Guy and I shared a tent and occasional parcels from home, but we didn't share much social life. Our unit leader, Trevor, had been my sergeant back in training troop. I had hated him during training. I thought he had the crazy idea that with enough physical and mental abuse, he could make a crack commando out of a dope headed hippie. I eventually realized that he was a professional soldier. He knew that a dope head wouldn't make it in war. He knew I would have to change. I didn't appreciate his torture training until the first time I chased an enemy unit through the mountains for three hours and managed to stay alive.

The thought of staying alive was on everyone's mind as we loaded into our chopper. No one said it out loud, of course, and we would all forget it as soon as the contact was finished. But in those long moments before the action started, the fear of death sat beside each one of us like an unwelcome guest.

The first phase of our flight was short, only about fifteen minutes, and during that time I thought of boarding school for some reason. I wondered if my mother would be pleased if she could see me today. She had so badly wanted me to make something of myself. That's why she packed me off to Eagle College Boarding School when I was twelve years old. At Eagle young men were taught to play sports, eat cucumber sandwiches, and speak the Queen's English.

I hadn't done so well.

Our chopper landed in dense foliage shaking me back from boarding school to bush war, and I jumped down to get a briefing on today's contact. But my mind continued to wander back to Eagle College, because the briefing officer that day was the older brother of my worst enemy at school. Just listening to his voice brought back memories of Alfred.

Alfred was big, as tall as my dad. I'm sure because I can remember staring both of them directly in the chest during their most intimidating tirades. Alfred had a neck so thick his head appeared to sit directly on his shoulders, and he was heavy. He used to sit on my chest, smile his crooked smile, and peck my breast bone with his index finger until I was red and bruised. It was some kind of Chinese torture game or something and he called it "pecking the chicken." It could drive a guy Insane.

Alfred was my prefect at boarding school, the guy in charge of my dormitory. He demonstrated that authority in various ways. Like slamming a guy into his school trunk then shoving it under a scalding shower for fifteen minutes. He took an opposite approach with me. He forced me to take icy showers during the cold weather terms when we were allowed our only hot water for the year. I think it was when I stood shivering in the shower one day, watching steam rise from the other stalls, that I realized how much I hated him.

But I'd never seen Alfred since he left school, and it wasn't something to bring up during jungle war manoeuvres. The briefing officer interrupted my memories and I realized that I wasn't twelve years old anymore, playing school boy games. I was a twenty-two year old soldier, trained to kill, and I'd do well to listen to my orders for the day.

"We've got eighty targets sighted in the area," he said. "One Commando will be parachuting in to surround the perimeter and prevent escapes. Two Commando will be going in as fire force."

In other words, twenty-four of our best against eighty of theirs.

Then he looked at the four soldiers in my unit, "You guys are Stop One. You will make first contact."

He paused for a minute and stuck out his jaw.

Then he finished the briefing with a quiet sentence, "Eliminate them."

We reboarded the chopper and settled in for the ninety minute flight. While we flew, I thought about the contact we had made last Sunday.

The Selous Scouts travelled through the country disguised as the enemy. These guys looked, talked, and acted like the enemy. And they had guts. They carried Russian AK automatic rifles captured during contacts and played a dangerous game of bluff with men who were trained to torture you before they killed you.

The scouts could set up camp on a mountain top and watch for activity in the villages below. If they caught a glimpse of soldiers walking into a village, they would wait a few hours and then approach the same village. Then they pretended to be part of the original group who had simply fallen behind.

"Which way did our brothers go?" they would ask the head man.

The villagers, who were regularly killed and maimed for withholding information, would point the scouts in the right direction. Sometimes into the very heart of a camp. Then the scouts would sit around listening to the leaders plan the next day's activities. They took detailed mental notes as the enemy soldiers discussed various plans and strategies.

Security Forces weren't allowed into an area the scouts were working because we wouldn't be able to tell them apart from the enemy. But once information was gathered, the scouts would wander out of camp, run back to base, and radio a Commando Unit. Then the hooter would blow.

Once we were dropped into the area, a helicopter would direct us by radio to the place the enemy had last been seen. Sometimes the soldiers would get wise and take off. Then we would follow them at a dead run, until their tracks either disappeared or crossed the border into Mozambique or Zambia. Or, until we ran into an ambush like we did last Sunday.

During that contact, we were splattered with enemy fire only minutes after we began our sweep. I ran toward the sound of the shooting and smashed through the brush. Several soldiers were firing at our helicopter, and I raked my gun in a wide arc, blasting them from behind.

Things go crazy once the shooting starts. I had been in this army for two years and had encountered the enemy before. The steps were always the same up to this point. The hooter, the briefing, the formation up the mountain. But once the shooting started, it was always a new experience. You couldn't rely on what had happened last week, or yesterday. You had to react with the instincts you had been trained to follow.

I fired at the nearest guy and saw him spin from the impact and then drop on his back. In those first few seconds men died and bushes exploded all around me. It didn't seem possible to stand in the midst of such insanity and escape unscathed. Surely we would all be destroyed. Suddenly my mouth went dry and I got scared. I mean really scared. The kind of scared that caused something buried deep inside of me to rise up. Almost as an instinct, I cried out to God for help.

Which shocked me as much as it must have shocked God. When I was a boy at Eagle College, I had been forced to attend chapel services every day. In chapel we were expected to kneel, stand, sing, shut-up, and get out. God soon joined my long list of mandatory unpleasantries which must be endured in order to succeed at Eagle and satisfy my parents.

But, secretly, I continued to hope that God might prove to be something more than that. I prayed some. Mostly for rugby victories or history exams. But sometimes I prayed for something I didn't even understand, some tangible sign that God was real. That He wasn't a cruel Headmaster who carried a dusty book around with my every move recorded.

At boarding school, confirmation classes were optional. But my friends and I decided to attend when we heard about the gulp of wine everyone swallowed during the final ceremony. That gulp of wine became my goal Until the classes began to require more from me than I was willing to give. Then I discovered there were easier ways to get a drink of wine.

After that it wasn't long before the prayers stopped and the curses began. I hadn't thought much about it until the shooting started ten years later.

Now I was pinned down, flat on the ground with automatic rifle fire blasting the dirt all around me. I tried to crawl backward toward the cover of the bush. But, with incredible horror, I saw our own chopper loaded with a 20mm cannon coming straight for me. I was sure the pilot had mistaken me for the enemy.

The gun fired before I could react, hitting a boulder ten feet ahead of me. Dirt, rock, and pieces of human flesh splattered the ground, killing the guy who had been waiting for me behind the boulder. The explosion gave me a split second to move for cover and I retreated twenty metres without coming more than a centimetre off the ground. Sort of like a mad snake going full throttle in reverse.

We regrouped for a few seconds, checked our weapons, and then began crawling forward. The air strike had sent one enemy soldier running across a near-by grain field. I lifted my gun, and shot him in the head. Another enemy soldier raised his rifle in what I thought later might have been a gesture of surrender, but at the time it was just a threat. I emptied an entire magazine into him and watched him bounce through the bush.

One of the guys in my unit shouted at me suddenly that his rifle had jammed, and he was taking fire from someone behind a tree. Two of us swung around at the same time and fired half a belt of rounds into the guy. Then we dropped back to our bellies and began crawling forward, past the dead soldier. We were within easy reach of him, but ignored his weapon and gear, knowing we could come back for them when the contact was finished and the looting began.

In a matter of minutes the shooting stopped. We stood up in the silence and surveyed the damage. Death everywhere. Blood, flesh, and mangled branches lay tangled together in the dust. Our sergeant just nodded once, picked up his gear, and said, "Well done."

Then my ego trip started. I'd done some big things in my life but this was the top. 1 had contacted the enemy, and I had destroyed him. In my exhilaration, I totally forgot about that moment when my mouth had gone dry and I had resorted to the prayers of my childhood. Instead, I joined my friends in looting the dead bodies and then stuffing them into canvas bags for the return trip.

I took a watch from the first guy I had killed, along with a small amount of grass which I would smoke later, and a water bottle that appealed to me for some reason. Then we came across the enemy soldier who had been lying on his back with his eyes wide open when we crawled past. I reached down to retrieve his weapon and he flinched. The guy was alive, not even wounded, just scared stiff. I pulled him to his feet and began punching and kicking him. I don't know if my anger was directed at him for being alive, or at myself for being such a lousy shot. I was just mad, and I had to vent it.

On the flight back to Grand Reef Air Strip that day, we flew in single file victory formation making one high sweep above our camp, signalling a good contact to the guys below. Then one by one we dropped straight down toward the ground, pulling up at the last second to land in perfect formation. We laughed and shouted and sang and congratulated ourselves on living up to the lofty name our Commando Units had been given.

We were the Fire Force of the Rhodesian Light Infantry.

And we were The Incredibles!

Advertisement on the back of the KK Dictionary, 1953

P.O. BOKISI 1504.
TEREFONE 23007.
TEREGRAMS: "CAWDIRR"
169 SALISBURY STREET
SALISBURY

Zonke Shamwari gatina lapa Southern Rhodesia

Mena bala, lo brief lapa gawena indaba zonke tina maboy lapa 'Whitehead and Jack' tina funa wena, izwa lo indaba gatina. Tina funa wena na lo umfasi gawena na lo mombie gawena yena bona lo mugodi ga lo manzi ga lo mushi sterek.

Tinasi jabula sterek skat wena bona manzi maningi indaba wena asi kurisi mombie maningi ga lo Nyama na lo skoff na lo gwaai bitchana futi.

Zonke lo yena asi enza wena sterek. Futi wena asi jabula too much. Skat wena jabula na tina futi tina asi jabula. Skat tina jabula tina asi sebenza maningi lapa lo Boss gatina na yena, yena sabenza maningi lapa gawena. Skat yena ena sebenza maningi lapa gawena, wena asi bona maningi na lo magodi yena hamba pansi faniki lo "magic".

Mushi zonke tina enza heppy maningi na lo manzi na lo skoff maningi.

Goodiby,

Mena boy gawena,

Boss

 Signed by R K. Whitehead

For Jim Fish

Free Translation : See over leaf

305

Whitehead and Jack KK advertisement (the only KK one I know)
Translation.

To all my Friends in Southern Rhodesia,

I am communicating with you in order to convey to you the untold advantages that you may realise should you avail yourself of the professional services of our company, Whitehead and Jack.

We wish to draw your attention, and also that of your wives and also your cattle, to the benefits a borehole installed by us that they may all enjoy the wonders of a plentiful water supply.

We know that you will be ecstatic when see the abundant water because you will be able to raise many beef cattle for food and also you will be able to increase, somewhat, your tobacco production.

All these things we know will benefit you enormously. We know that you will rejoice too much.

When you rejoice, so we also will rejoice!

When we rejoice at the blessings of life, why, that makes us even more dedicated to bring to your Boss the untold benefits of our professional labour, and you will see numerous boreholes sinking into your properties as though inspired by Magic.

That means that all of us will be gloriously happy because of the copious water and bountiful food.

Salutations.

I remain, Sir, your obedient servant,

Jim Fish.

(Who says KK was only for use on the mines! Ed.)

Caruso by Richard Randall

There's something unnerving, even shocking, about seeing a grown man cry; it's somehow not natural and certainly runs counter to Anglo-Saxon social conventions. I therefore felt most uncomfortable seeing Big Jim's tears stream down his handsome English face. Of all people in Nuanetsi district the last person I expected to see overcome by events was James Henderson; yet here he was, seated in my office in Rhodesia's Lowveld during official government hours one December day in 1976 recounting his recent misfortune. I had called the police Station Commander to join me to listen to his story.

The Lowveld of south-eastern Zimbabwe is a vast, flat, wooded savanna, torrid in the summer, wonderfully mild in the winter. Thirty years ago, in Henderson's time, the country was called Rhodesia and in those days of European rule the endless mopane forests of the Lowveld, encompassed some of the world's greatest cattle and big-game ranches. A huge swathe of this area was administered from the government station at Nuanetsi where the District Commissioner, the Police, the Agricultural Officer and one or two other government officials were based.

The ranchers, mostly rugged individualists with English or Afrikaans names, passionate about rugby, hunting, fishing, would come to the government station on Friday and Saturday nights and consume great quantities of Castle and Lion lager at the Sable Arms, the only pub in the area. It was at this pub that I first met Henderson in 1975, when I took up my new posting as District Commissioner of Nuanetsi. That year the guerrilla war in Rhodesia was in full swing. The Portuguese, whose troops in neighbouring Mozambique had for many years acted as a buffer against guerrilla incursions on Rhodesia's eastern front, abandoned their colony in 1974, with the inevitable consequence that guerrillas poured into eastern Rhodesia. These joined other armed insurgents based in Rhodesia resulting in a dramatic increase in ambushes on civilian and military vehicle convoys, landmine explosions, attacks on Government and civilian targets and atrocities perpetrated on Black African villagers deemed to be pro-government.

The insurgency put a lot of strain on the organs of government and on the rural farming and ranching community. Some landowners retreated to the towns for security, but the majority stubbornly refused to be intimidated into abandoning their properties and braved it out in remote isolation. Amongst the ranchers of Nuanetsi Henderson was easily the best shot and the most popular man in the district. At six foot two, powerfully built, looking younger than his 43 years and with a healthy ruddy complexion, sandy-coloured hair and piercing blue eyes he was the beau ideal of an Anglo-Rhodesian. He had been to Winchester as a boy and his subtle public school accent distinguished him from the less polished Rhodesian and Afrikaans intonations predominant amongst the Europeans (Whites referred to themselves as "Europeans" in those days, even though the majority had never lived in Europe). He had the easy grace of a gentleman and was proficient in several sports. He possessed a great collection of classical music records and could often be found on a chaise-longue on his verandah listening to opera at sunset, whisky in hand, sometimes accompanying a recording with his clear, baritone voice.

In a lesser character his musical taste would have been deemed by many Rhodesians an affectation, even effete. Just how much his music meant to Henderson only became apparent to me as his story unfolded in my office that December day.

The frequent week-end shoots and barbecues at Henderson's ranch, attended by half a dozen ranchers and their families, were the main social events of the district. The beer flowed copiously and huge quantities of steaks and boerwors were consumed. Guests would arrive around 10 a.m. and, for security reasons, those who did not take up the standing invitation to overnight there, would leave an hour or so before dark. Only one family was ambushed driving home from Henderson's after a guineafowl shoot. One of the children was shot through the stomach while his father drove through a hail of small-arms fire, continuing non-stop to the hospital at Fort Victoria. The child eventually made a full recovery. This incident didn't deter us from continuing to enjoy Henderson's excellent hospitality, and, in defiance of such cowardly attacks, a bigger crowd than ever gathered at his ranch the following Saturday for polo-cross, tennis and a barbecue.

The European community, feeling besieged but confident it would prevail in the end, took to carrying firearms everywhere it went. We slept with loaded automatic weapons at our bedside and were in constant radio communications with each other so that we could respond to reports of guerrilla attacks, though the distance between one farmstead and another was so great that by the time anyone arrived at an attack site the guerrillas had usually long gone. The security situation in the country made life more intense for us. Threatened communities throughout the country became more close-knit and we found increased enjoyment in life's simple pleasures – sundowners, various kinds of social gatherings, sport, even shopping trips. We took pains to maintain a semblance of the old Rhodesian, pre-insurgency, way of life, but the pile of automatic rifles stacked every night at the entrance of the Sable Arms and in a corner of Jim Henderson's verandah during the week-end gatherings bore testimony to radically changed times, as did the daily radio security "sitreps". (Situation reports – bulletins about the current security situation.)

Big Jim, as he was often called, was always ready to respond to alarm calls and often rushed out alone to render assistance to a rancher under attack. He was fired on several times, though never wounded, and was the toast of the district after he shot two guerrillas who were firing on a neighbour's farmstead from the property's perimeter fence. Responding to a radio distress call, he had approached the ranch quietly with his Landrover, headlights switched off, and, undetected, crept up to within 50 yards of the gang of ten or so and opened up on them with his army-issued .762 F.N. Attacks almost invariably took place at dusk or shortly after dark, giving the guerrillas plenty of time to get away before light. In general, a rancher facing enemy fire - usually from AK 47s - from the outside of a strong security fence placed well away from the main house had to fend for himself and his family, and most ranchers being excellent shots and not easily intimidated warded off attacks successfully with accurate automatic bursts. Occasionally the guerrillas attacked with mortars, but were usually way off target. In this respect their Chinese and Russian communist instructors in camps in China, Russia, Tanzania and Zambia, clearly failed them.

I can't remember just what it was that prompted Henderson to send his wife (a third generation Rhodesian farmer's daughter) and seven year old son to stay with his brother-in-law in Bulawayo – it might have been the military intelligence that indicated a large influx of guerrillas from the east and the north into Nuanetsi district, or one particularly prolonged assault on a neighbour's home, or perhaps the increased incidences of atrocities in the district's Tribal Trust Lands. A month later, and after what appeared to be a lull in guerrilla activity, Henderson decided to visit his family in Bulawayo, leaving the ranch in the hands of his young bachelor manager, Mike Happelt.

It was the second Sunday in December, 1976, and Happelt had gone fishing for the day at the far end of the ranch where there was a dam well stocked with bass. (I often fished there myself and once landed a 4.2 kg largemouth bass, the second heaviest recorded in the Lowveld. Henderson himself, of course, held the record, a 4.9 kg monster that was mounted and placed above the fireplace of the Sable Arms where beady-eyed and with cavernous gape, it triumphed, defiant and unequalled, a perpetual challenge to our angling prowess).

Towards sunset, Happelt packed up his tackle and was about to make for the ranch when he saw black smoke rising, far in the distance. The smoke came from the direction of the farmstead. It was December, the green season, and not a time for bush fires which, furthermore, typically gave off a light grey smoke. With a sinking feeling Happelt sped to the farmstead. He unlocked the entrance gate and proceeded, fearing the worst. A scene of devastation greeted the manager's eyes as he sped down the long, Jacaranda-lined driveway to the house: through the billowing smoke he could see that the thatched roof had been entirely consumed by fire the flames of which could still be seen flickering within the interior of the spacious building. He stopped well short of the house, took his F.N. rifle and ran around the house to observe the damage, keeping a sharp lookout for guerrillas which he knew had caused the inferno. A whimper drew his attention to a pile of fencing material under which lay Henderson's black Labrador, wounded in the leg. A couple of minutes later he found the German Shepherd dead near the driveway; no doubt it had died protecting the property.

The perpetrators of this outrage had gone. Happelt walked around the perimeter fence and saw where the Guerrillas had cut their way in. Their tracks, leading in and out again, revealed there must have been half-a-dozen of them. He went back to the house, kicked open the smouldering front door and saw that the building was well and truly gutted. A tractor, the Lister generator and Henderson's beautifully restored blue 1934 MG NA Magnette classic sports car were peppered with bullet holes. Alert and tense Happelt drove to the staff compound half a kilometre away. There was no-one there. He shouted and sounded the car's hooter. Eventually his boss's cook, a gardener and a few of the ranch hands emerged from the bush. Their tale was simple: the guerrillas had arrived in the compound shortly after Happelt had gone fishing - contrary to their usual modus operandi when they attacked around nightfall - and had told the staff to remain in the compound, warning them that they would be shot if they interfered with the guerrillas in any way or made a noise. The guerrillas ascertained from the cook that there were no Varungu (Whites) around and then made for the farmstead. From where they were cowering the staff heard shots, then the crackling of flames and then saw the billowing smoke, but, understandably, were too terrified to investigate the scene at the farmstead.

Happelt rushed to the government station, less than an hour's drive away, arriving well after dark, and reported the incident to both the Station Commander and to me in our homes as we had already left the Sable Arms. He used my telephone to inform his boss of the arson.

At first light the next day Henderson drove furiously to his ranch, arriving there around lunch time. It was towards office closing time (16h30) the same day when Henderson admitted himself unannounced into my office. I was startled by his appearance. He was a changed man: dishevelled, crestfallen, with puffy eyes. He collapsed into a chair facing my desk and held his head in his hands. The Station Commander, whom I had telephoned immediately Henderson entered my office, arrived a few minutes later and stood by my desk. The police officer and I started to commiserate with Henderson, telling him how shocked and appalled we were about the arson, but he didn't seem to be listening to us. Naturally, to lose a house in such a dramatic fashion would be a blow to any man, but, after all, no-one had been killed or injured in the incident, and his cattle had not been touched, so we were a little surprised at the intensity of Henderson's grief. Even greater was our astonishment when we discovered what had most affected him. (We had presumed it was the loss of the house itself, the damage to his M.G. sports car, or even the killing of his dog).

"The bastards", he blurted out. "All my Caruso record collection, arias and complete operas recorded between 1911 and 1921 – all gone, not one left. Irreplaceable. All 78s, collectors' items. I found them in the living room, still in their record racks; still shaped like discs, but just bloody ashes. Took me over twenty years to collect them. You can't get 78 RPMs any more. Irreplaceable. The greatest tenor, the greatest voice of all time. Forget Pavarotti and Domingo: Caruso is the best ever". Henderson, the larger-than-life bold man of action, seemed crushed; his voice choked and tears trickled down his well-tanned face. Before the Station Commander and I could figure out something to say to comfort him, he got up, stumbled to the door and let himself out.

Henderson never came back to the station and left the district a week later having instructed his attorney to sell the ranch. We never heard from the rancher again. Was it the loss of his precious record collection that goaded him to leave? I'm convinced it was. A couple of months later Happelt, who stayed on to work for the new ranch owners, told us that his former boss had gone back with his family to England.

We missed the live-wire presence of Henderson in the district - especially the week-ends at his ranch - and somehow the atmosphere at the Sable Arms was never quite the same. But the bass above the fireplace, looking down imperiously on the dwindling and brave band of Rhodesians was a perpetual reminder of the unfathomableness of human nature … and of the enduring influence of Enrico Caruso, the great Neapolitan tenor.

Rhodesian Timeline by Ed Goldberg
with assistance from Hugh Bomford and Richard Allport

1817	Mzilikazi, Shaka's greatest general, has to flee for his life from the wrath of Shaka. He gathers a powerful army and treks northward, eventually settling in Matabeleland, near Bulawayo. He founds the Matabele nation and becomes their king.
09 Feb 1853	Leander Starr Jameson born at Edinburgh
15 Feb 1853	Alfred Beit born at Hamburg
05 Jul 1853	Cecil John Rhodes is born in vicarage at Bishop's Stortford
1855	Dr. David Livingstone discovers the Victoria Falls
1859	Inyati Mission Station founded by Dr. Robert Moffat. This was the first permanent settlement by Europeans in Rhodesia
1868	Adam Renders discovers the Zimbabwe Ruins
1868	Death of Mzilikazi
1870	Lobengula, son of Mzilikazi, installed as king of the Matabele
1870	Rhodes emigrates to Natal on account of his health
29 Aug 1871	Lobengula signs Baines Concession
1872	Rhodes follows his brother Herbert to the new diamond diggings at Kimberley
1880	Rhodes founds the De Beers Diamond Mining Company and enters the Cape House of Assembly
14 Mar 1885	Bechuanaland Protectorate declared
30 Jul 1887	Lobengula signs treaty with Transvaal's P. Grobler
11 Feb 1888	Lobengula signs Moffat Treaty
30 Oct 1888	Lobengula signs Rudd Concession giving Rhodes the mineral rights of the territory
29 Oct 1889	British South Africa Company incorporated by Royal Charter
1890	Rhodes becomes Prime Minister of the Cape Colony at the age of 37
06 May 1890	The Pioneer Column leaves Kimberley for Macloutsie
28 Jun 1890	British South Africa Company's Pioneer Column enters Rhodesia
01 Jul 1890	180 Pioneers, 500 Police and 117 wagons reach Tuli

13 Aug 1890	The long and difficult ascent of Providential Pass begins, and at noon next day the first wagon emerges on to the plateau. The Pioneers build a fort some distance from the Pass and name it Fort Victoria
12 Sep 1890	The Column reaches the foot of Harari Hill, now Salisbury Kopje
13 Sep 1890	Hoisting of the flag and the Pioneer Column founds Fort Salisbury
01 Oct 1890	The Pioneer Corps is disbanded
15 Feb 1891	Temporary frontier with Portuguese territory established in Manicaland
08 May 1891	British Order-in-Council declares protectorates over Bechuanaland, Matabeleland and Mashonaland
12 Jun 1891	Anglo-Portuguese agreement and boundary convention signed
17 Nov 1891	Lobengula signs Lippert Concession
17 Feb 1892	Telegraph to Fort Salisbury completed
05 May 1892	Moodie's Trek sets out for Rhodesia
10 Oct 1892	Dominican Sisters open the first school for European children
1893	Jesuit Fathers open a school in Bulawayo, later transferred to Salisbury as St. George's College
1893	Moodie's Trek reaches Chipinga
18 Jul 1893	Ndebele raid Shona near Fort Victoria
03 Oct 1893	War on Matabele authorized
24 Oct 1893	Battle of Shangani - Matabele forces of 5 000 engaged and routed
01 Nov 1893	Battle of Bembezi - 7 000 Matabele defeated
03 Nov 1893	Bulawayo destroyed by fire on order of Lobengula
04 Nov 1893	British occupy Bulawayo - Union Flag and BSAC flag hoisted in Bulawayo for the first time
04 Dec 1893	Major Allan Wilson and his patrol of 33 men annihilated near Shangani River, 100 miles north of Bulawayo
1894	The death of Lobengula is presumed
03 May 1895	Territory proclaimed Rhodesia
29 Dec 1895	Jameson Raid leaves Mafeking

02 Jan 1896	Dr. Jameson surrenders near Krugersdorp in the Transvaal
02 Jan 1896	Rhodes resigns from all public offices
20 Mar 1896	Ndebele Revolt begins and 141 settlers are murdered
02 Apr 1896	The Rt. Hon. Earl Grey succeeds Dr. Jameson as Administrator of Rhodesia
14 Jun 1896	Shona Revolt begins and 103 settlers are murdered
21 Aug 1896	First of Rhodes' five Indabas with southern Ndebele rebels at the Matopos
13 Oct 1896	Submission of Matabele chiefs
1897	Municipalities of Salisbury and Bulawayo created
27 Oct 1897	Shona Revolt pronounced ended
04 Nov 1897	Railway from the south reaches Bulawayo
04 Feb 1898	Railway from Beira reached Umtali
15 May 1899	First session of Legislative Council
22 May 1899	Beira railroad reaches Salisbury
11 Oct 1899	Outbreak of Boer War - Rhodes is besieged in Kimberley
Feb 1900	Relief of Kimberley
Dec 1901	W. H. Milton is appointed Administrator of Southern Rhodesia
26 Mar 1902	Death of Cecil John Rhodes at Muizenberg
10 Apr 1902	Rhodes is buried at World's View in the Matopos
31 May 1902	End of the Boer War
06 Oct 1902	Bulawayo-Salisbury Railway is completed
19 Jun 1904	The railway to the Victoria Falls is completed
12 Sep 1904	Victoria Falls Bridge is opened
16 Jul 1906	Death of Alfred Beit
03 Jan 1913	Death of the Duke of Abercorn, President of the British South Africa Company, Sir Starr Jameson succeeds him
04 Aug 1914	Outbreak of World War I
01 Nov 1914	Mr. (later Sir) Drummond Chaplin appointed Administrator of Southern Rhodesia
13 Mar 1915	British South Africa Charter extended 10 years

26 Nov 1917	Death of Sir Starr Jameson
11 Nov 1918	End of World War I
08 Apr 1919	Ian Douglas Smith born in Selukwe, Rhodesia
30 Apr 1920	Elections for last Legislative Council under the British South Africa Company Administration
12 May 1920	Council debate and approve Responsible Government by 12 votes to 5
1921	Deputation to England regarding new constitution
Apr 1922	Delegation to Cape Town to interview South African Government in regard to terms of admission of Rhodesia into the Union of South Africa
27 Oct 1922	Referendum on whether Southern Rhodesia should join the Union or assume Responsible Government. 2,785 majority for Responsible Government
12 Sep 1923	Great Britain annexes Southern Rhodesia as a Crown Colony with J.R. Chancellor as first Governor
01 Oct 1923	Responsible Government established with Coghlan as first premier
1924	First elections to Legislative Assembly
1924	Sir Charles Coghlan becomes first Prime Minister
30 May 1924	New Legislative Assembly opens
02 Sep 1927	H.U. Moffat (a grandson of the famous missionary, Dr. Robert Moffat) succeeds Coghlan as premier after latter's death
14 Jul 1928	New Zealand vs Rhodesia Rugby Score: 44-8
31 Aug 1929	Beit Bridge opened on Limpopo
10 Oct 1930	Promulgation of the Land Apportionment Act
29 Jun 1933	Government buys British South Africa Company's mineral rights for £2 000 000
06 Jul 1933	The Hon. H. U. Moffat resigns Premiership and is succeeded by the Hon. George Mitchell
06 Sep 1933	General Election. The Hon. G. M. Huggins becomes Prime Minister
1934	Split in the Reform Party. A General Election is held and the

	United Party is returned with large majority. Hon. G. M. Huggins, Prime Minister
1935	Birchenough Bridge across the Sabi River is opened
1935	First State Lottery draw is held
1935	Rhodesia House, 429, Strand, London, is opened
1935	Salisbury becomes a city
1935	Trade agreement with South Africa comes into force
1937	Royal Commission under Lord Bledisloe considers question of closer association between the Rhodesias and Nyasaland
21 Mar 1939	Publication of the Bledisloe Report respecting amalgamation of the Rhodesias
14 Apr 1939	Huggins' United Party again carries general election
24 May 1939	Otto Beit Bridge over the Zambezi River at Chirundu is opened
03 Sep 1939	Outbreak of World War II
1940	Army camps were established in Salisbury, Bulawayo and Umtali for initial and advanced training. During the 1939-45 war, Southern Rhodesia contributed, on a pro rata population basis, more fighting men than any other Commonwealth country
24 May 1940	First Empire Training School for the Royal Air Force is opened at Salisbury
1942	Southern Rhodesia Military Forces come under Union of South Africa Command
18 Oct 1944	Establishment of Central African Council
08 May 1945	Surrender of all German Forces in Europe
15 Aug 1945	Japan surrenders. End of World War II
25 Apr 1946	Huggins' United Party wins general election in which Liberal Party shows major gains
07 Apr 1947	Royal visit to Southern Rhodesia. The Royal Family arrive by air in Salisbury and King George VI opens the second session of the Sixth Parliament
30 Apr 1947	Parliament agrees to purchase the Rhodesia Railways for £30 million
15 Sep 1948	Sir Godfrey Huggins' United Party again wins general election, in

which Ian Smith enters Legislative Assembly

Feb 1949	Preliminary conference at the Victoria Falls between representatives of the Southern Rhodesia Government and unofficial representatives of Northern Rhodesia and Nyasaland on the federation of the three territories
27 Jul 1949	New Zealand vs Rhodesia Rugby Score: 8-10
30 Jul 1949	New Zealand vs Rhodesia Rugby Score: 3-3
12 Mar 1951	100 young Rhodesians depart for the Far East to form a squadron of the Malayan Scouts
06 Feb 1952	Death of King George VI
08 Feb 1952	Princess Elizabeth proclaimed Queen
18 Jun 1952	The White Paper on the proposed federation of the Rhodesias and Nyasaland is tabled in the Legislative Assembly
29 Sep 1952	Lake McIlwaine near Salisbury is opened
Jan 1953	The Prime Minister, Sir Godfrey Huggins, attends the final conference on federation in London
09 Apr 1953	European voters ratify federation in general referendum. 25,560 voted for, and 14,729 voted against
03 Jul 1953	Queen Elizabeth the Queen Mother opened the Central African Rhodes Centenary Exhibition at Bulawayo
07 Sep 1953	Sir Godfrey Huggins resigns his Premiership and is succeeded by Mr. R. S. Garfield Todd
15 Dec 1953	General Election for the First Federal Assembly was won by the Federal Party with Sir Godfrey Huggins as Prime Minister
27 Jan 1954	The General Election for Southern Rhodesia's eighth Parliament is won by the United Rhodesia Party. R. S. Garfield Todd, Prime Minister
03 Feb 1954	First session of the first Parliament of the Federation opened
01 Apr 1954	Sir Gilbert Rennie, formerly Governor of Northern Rhodesia, becomes the first Federal High Commissioner in the United Kingdom
01 Mar 1955	The Federal Government announces its decision to proceed with the construction of the Kariba hydro-electric power project, and in August the river diversion works are started

01 Aug 1955	The new railway line to Lourenco Marques, through the Lowveld, s opened
03 Mar 1956	Mr. Winston Field is elected leader of a new political party, the Dominion Party, at a meeting in Salisbury
01 Jun 1956	The first day of official civil operations at Salisbury's new international airport
31 Oct 1956	Roy Welensky succeeds Huggins (now Lord Malvern) as federal prime minister
06 Jun 1957	Mr. Winston Field wins the Mrewa by-election and becomes Leader of the Opposition in the Federal Parliament
12 Sep 1957	Founding of African National Congress
1958	Dr. Hastings Banda returns to Nyasaland after an absence of 40 years and assumes leadership of African National Congress party
18 Feb 1958	Edgar Whitehead replaces Todd as Southern Rhodesian prime minister after cabinet revolt. Sir Edgar forms Cabinet and stands for Parliament in by-election at Hillside (Bulawayo) but is defeated by Dominion Party opponent
05 Jun 1958	Rhodesia Party merges with Federal Party to form United Federal Party . Whitehead retained as prime minister after UFP barely carries general election (17 seats to 13 for the Dominion Party)
1959	Troops and police from Southern Rhodesia sent to assist local security forces. Dr. Banda and principal lieutenants arrested and sent to Southern Rhodesia for detention
1959	Widespread riots and disturbances break out in Northern Rhodesia and Nyasaland, being particularly serious in Nyasaland where plot to murder Governor and top officials is revealed
25 Feb 1959	Security Branch in Southern Rhodesia arrests African Congress leaders and nips planned rising in bud. In Northern Rhodesia the Governor, Sir Arthur Benson, bans the A.N.C.
26 Feb 1959	State of Emergency declared in Southern Rhodesia
1960	Monckton Commission appointed to consider future of the Federation, and visits all three territories. It is boycotted by the African nationalists in the two northern territories. The Commission recommends that individual territories be given the right of secession
01 Jan 1960	Formation of National Democratic Party

17 May 1960	Kariba Dam formally opened by Queen Elizabeth the Queen Mother
29 Jun 1960	New Zealand vs A Rhodesian XV Rugby Score: 13-9
02 Jul 1960	New Zealand vs Rhodesia Rugby Score: 29-14
19 Jul 1960	Arrest of National Democratic Party leaders leads to bloody rioting
Dec 1960	Federal Review Conference assembles at Lancaster House, London, under chairmanship of British Prime Minister, Mr. Harold McMillan. African nationalist leaders of three territories walk out on opening day. Conference adjourns for Christmas break and is not resumed
1961	New Constitution granted to Northern Rhodesia which aggravates relations between Federal and British Governments
Feb 1961	Conference to review Southern Rhodesia's Constitution opens in Salisbury with British Commonwealth Secretary, Mr. Duncan Sandys, as chairman. Conference agrees on removal of reservations in return for Declaration of Rights and appointment of Constitutional Council. Parliament to be enlarged from 30 to 65 members and Africans to be given representation through "B" Roll. African Nationalist militants start civil disturbances
26 Jul 1961	New constitutional proposals approved in referendum by 41,940 votes to 21,836
18 Sep 1961	Dag Hammarskjold, Secretary-General of the UN, was killed in a suspicious plane crash in Northern Rhodesia. He was flying to negotiate a cease-fire in the Congo. Hammarskjold was the son of a former Swedish prime minister. In 1953, he was elected to the top UN post and in 1957 was reelected. During his second term, he initiated and directed the United Nation's vigorous role in the Belgian Congo.
09 Dec 1961	National Democratic Party banned
18 Dec 1961	Zimbabwe African People's Union founded
1962	New Constitutions granted to Northern Rhodesia and Nyasaland which ensure the return of African nationalist governments
16 Mar 1962	British Government creates new office of Central African Affairs, headed by Mr. R. A. Butler, Home Secretary, to look after Federation and constituent territories

16 Mar 1962	Sir Roy Welensky resigns to hold General Election to obtain new mandate on future of Federation. Official opposition, Rhodesian Front (formerly Dominion Party), decides not to contest election
27 Apr 1962	General Election results in U.F.P. controlling 54 out of 59 seats in Federal Assembly
May 1962	Mr. R. A. Butler visits Federation and indicates that Nyasaland will be allowed to secede
Jun 1962	Team of advisors to investigate consequences of Federal break-up
20 Sep 1962	Zimbabwe African People's Union banned
Nov 1962	New Nyasaland constitutional talks held in London. Territory to be granted self-government without delay
Dec 1962	Officially announced that Nyasaland will be allowed to secede. British decision is bitterly attacked by Sir Roy Welensky, who charges Britain with "bad faith"
14 Dec 1962	Rhodesian Front wins Southern Rhodesian election, Winston Field becomes prime minister. Rhodesian Front gains 35 seats to U.F.P.'s 29, and Central Africa Party (left wing) eliminated
Mar 1963	Federal, Northern Rhodesian and Southern Rhodesian Governments invited to London to prepare agenda for conference on future of federation
26 Mar 1963	Kaunda demands that Northern Rhodesia be given right to secede
29 Mar 1963	British Government announces that any territory will have right to secede
Jun 1963	Federal break-up conference held at Victoria Falls with all governments represented
08 Aug 1963	Zimbabwe African National Union founded, Communist-trained saboteurs are arrested
10 Aug 1963	People's Caretaker Council formed as ZAPU front
27 Sep 1963	Order-in-Council signed by Queen detailing functions to be handed back to territorial governments
10 Dec 1963	Federal Parliament meets and is prorogued for last time by Acting Governor-General, Sir Humphrey Gibbs
12 Dec 1963	British Order-in-Council published detailing arrangements for liquidating thc Federation
31 Dec 1963	Federation of Rhodesia and Nyasaland officially dissolved

01 Jan 1964	Mr. Evan Campbell, C.B.E., appointed Rhodesian High Commissioner in London
01 Jan 1964	Southern Rhodesian Government launches drive to stamp out intimidation in African townships
13 Apr 1964	Ian Smith (Minister of the Treasury) displaces Winston Field a prime minister
16 Apr 1964	Government detains Joshua Nkomo
May 1964	Dr. W. Alexander, Speaker of the Legislature Assembly dies. He is succeeded in July by Mr. A. R. W. Stumbles, M.P. for Avondale
22 Jul 1964	Kenneth Kaunda is the first premier of Northern Rhodesia
26 Aug 1964	Government bans ZANU, PCC, and African Daily News and declares Highfield an emergency area. Sithole and Mugabe detained
Oct 1964	By-elections held in Arundel and Avondale constituencies. Sir Roy Welensky, Rhodesia Party leader, is defeated at Arundel by Deputy Prime Minister, Mr. C. W. Dupont, and Rhodesian Front candidate wins Avondale. Both are Front gains from Rhodesia Party
Oct 1964	Rhodesian Chiefs hold indaba at Domboshawa, near Salisbury, and vote unanimously in favour of independence. Indaba is boycotted by British Government
Oct 1964	Southern Rhodesia to be henceforth known as "Rhodesia"
24 Oct 1964	Northern Rhodesia becomes independent as Zambia
05 Nov 1964	Public referendum by European voters endorses independence. Votes in favour 58,176, votes against 6,101. Overall percentage poll, 61,6 per cent, of which 89,1 per cent, votes "yes"
Dec 1964	Sir Roy Welensky announces his retirement from Rhodesian politics and resigns as leader of the Rhodesia Party
Feb 1965	British Secretary for Commonwealth Relations, Mr. A. G. Bottomley, and the Lord Chancellor, Lord Gardiner, visit Rhodesia to discuss independence issue with all sections of the population. Mr. Bottomley stresses that while the British Government favoured a peaceful
Apr 1965	Prime Minister announces General Election with a view to securing a two-thirds majority in Parliament. On Nomination Day

	22 Rhodesian Front members are returned unopposed
07 May 1965	Country goes to the polls. Result is a clean sweep of all the 28 "A" Roll seats contested in favour of the Rhodesian Front. Rhodesia Party secures majority of "B" Roll seats. An African member, Mr. Gondo, is appointed Leader of the Opposition
31 May 1965	United Peoples Party founded
Jun 1965	Rhodesia Party is dissolved
09 Jun 1965	Official opening of the First Session of the 11th Parliament of Rhodesia. In the Speech from the Throne, the Governor, Sir Humphrey Gibbs, said that the Government's return to power at the General Election with a greatly increased majority was a mandate for it to lead Rhodesia to full independence. Referring to the economy, the Governor said that it was poised for an even higher rate of growth than that achieved in 1964
16 Jun 1965	Mr. Campbell, C.B.E., relinquishes his appointment as Rhodesian High Commissioner in London, and is succeeded by Brigadier A. Skeen, O.B.E.
21 Jul 1965	Mr. Gledwyn Hughes, Minister of State for Commonwealth Affairs, arrived in Rhodesia to have personal talks with Mr. Smith concerning negotiations on Independence
27 Jul 1965	Mr. Gledwyn Hughes leaves to report progress to Mr. Bottomley with specific proposals on the Independence issue from Mr. Smith
08 Oct 1965	London talks break down. Independence based on 1961 Constitution not acceptable to Britain
17 Oct 1965	The Prime Minister, Mr. Smith, returns from London. Mr. Wilson proposed a Commonwealth Prime Minister's mission to be sent to Rhodesia in a bid to solve Rhodesian independence crisis
20 Oct 1965	Mr. Smith proposes Independence on 1961 Constitution and offers treaty to guarantee undertaking not to vary it after Independence
26 Oct 1965	Harold Wilson and Mr. Bottomley visits Salisbury to discuss independence
30 Oct 1965	Royal Commission proposed to find a solution to Rhodesian problem to consist of Chief Justice of Rhodesia as Chairman and two other persons, one appointed by Rhodesian Government and one by British Government. Mr. Wilson leaves

11 Nov 1965	Press censorship imposed
11 Nov 1965	Unilateral Declaration of Independence issued under 1965 Constitution. This new Constitution being based on the 1961 Constitution, amended as necessary to suit a fully independent Sovereign State
16 Nov 1965	British Government passes Southern Rhodesian Enabling Act permitting Orders in Council to make provision to amend, revoke or add to any of the provisions of the 1961 Constitution and also to apply sanctions against Rhodesia
17 Nov 1965	Mr. C. W. Dupont appointed as Acting Officer Administering the Government
25 Nov 1965	British Parliament approves sanctions imposed by Orders in Council on 16th November
03 Dec 1965	British Government suspends Governor and Directors of Reserve Bank of Rhodesia and seized Rhodesian reserves in Great Britain.
16 Dec 1965	Wilson appeals to U.N.O. for support to end "rebellion" in Rhodesia. He rules out use of force and accepts responsibility for dealing with the matter
17 Dec 1965	Wilson, having received U.N.O. support, declares oil embargo against Rhodesia and starts oil airlift to Zambia. Rhodesia bans oil exports to Zambia
28 Dec 1965	Petrol rationing introduced in Rhodesia
02 Jan 1966	The Prime Minister, Mr. Smith, offers to restore flow of petrol and oil to Zambia quite unconditionally, subject to acceptable arrangements for payment
14 Jan 1966	Lagos Commonwealth Prime Minister's Conference. Wilson accepts that use of force cannot be precluded
31 Jan 1966	Wilson imposes total embargo on all trade with Rhodesia
18 Feb 1966	His Excellency the Officer Administering the Government, Mr. Clifford Dupont, assents to the Constitution (Ratification) Bill which had previously been passed by Parliament by more than a two-thirds majority. The 1965 Constitution therefore becomes Law
10 Apr 1966	Security Council agrees that Britain should use force to prevent oil flowing to Rhodesia via Beira
27 Apr 1966	British Prime Minister announces informal talks at official level

with Rhodesia

28 Apr 1966	ZANLA combatants engage Rhodesian Security Forces at battle of Sinoia
16 May 1966	European farmer and wife murdered by terrorists
19 Sep 1966	Royal Air Force units withdrawn from Zambia. Oil airlift ended
02 Dec 1966	Harold Wilson and Ian Smith meet off Gibraltar on board H.M.S. Tiger in "Tiger Talks"
05 Dec 1966	Rhodesian Government accept Wilson's proposals as a basis for a new Constitution, but reject those concerning the return to so-called legality by handing over powers to the Governor, and renouncing its Independence
16 Dec 1966	On the illegal application of the British Government, the United Nations unlawfully vote for Selected Mandatory Sanctions, including oil, against Rhodesia
20 Dec 1966	The British Prime Minister states in their House of Commons that Rhodesia will not be granted Independence before African Majority rule
22 Dec 1966	Rhodesia leaves the Commonwealth
09 Mar 1967	Five-man Constitutional Commission headed by Mr. W. R. Whaley sworn in by the Officer Administering the Government
14 Jun 1967	British Prime Minister sends Lord Alport, ex-British High Commissioner to the defunct Federation, to Rhodesia to see if the 18-month deadlock can be broken
26 Jul 1967	Mr. Wilson announces a new initiative on Rhodesia, which amounted to discovering whether the Tiger constitutional proposals should be re-negotiated through Sir Humphrey Gibbs, by correspondence
09 Nov 1967	Mr. Thompson and Rhodesian Prime Minister have four-hour secret personal discussions
24 Feb 1968	Sir Alec Douglas-Home visits Rhodesia
03 Mar 1968	Rhodesia's' Appeal Court dismissed the appeal of three Africans convicted of brutal murder, as it had been decided that the Rhodesian Government was the de facto Government, and there was no right of Appeal to the Privy Council, under the 1965 Constitution. The Queen reprieves the three Africans under sentence of death that night, and commutes death sentences to one

of life imprisonment

04 Mar 1968	Mr. Justice Fieldsend resigns as a Judge of the High Court in protest against recent happenings
05 Mar 1968	Application to the Appellate Division of the High Court following the Queen's reprieve. Application dismissed
06 Mar 1968	Three African murderers hanged in accordance with the Law. Rhodesian Government issues statement on the execution
31 Mar 1968	Francistown Radio closed
06 Apr 1968	Censorship in Rhodesia lifted
10 Apr 1968	Whaley Commission Report published
11 Apr 1968	Mr. J. M. Greenfield appointed Judge of the High Court in terms of the 1965 Constitution
09 May 1968	Sir Frederick Crawford, Resident Director of Anglo-American Corporation, has his passport impounded by British Government on a visit to London
29 May 1968	United Nations votes comprehensive mandatory sanctions
18 Jun 1968	House of Lords defeats sanctions order passed by House of Commons
04 Jul 1968	Mr. W. J. Harper, Minister of Internal Affairs, resigns his post at the request of the Prime Minister
09 Aug 1968	High Court refuses to accept order from Judicial Committee of the Privy Council
13 Aug 1968	Mr. Justice Dendy Young resigns as a Judge of the High Court
28 Aug 1968	Abel Muzorewa made UMC Bishop of Rhodesia
13 Sep 1968	The Appellate Division of the High Court of Rhodesia ruled that the Government was now in its opinion the de jure Government
30 Sep 1968	Bechuanaland becomes independent as Republic of Botswana
10 Oct 1968	Talks between Mr. Smith, Prime Minister of Rhodesia, and Mr. Wilson, Prime Minister of Great Britain, aboard H.M.S. Fearless
04 Nov 1968	Talks begin in Salisbury between Mr. Thompson and Mr. Smith
11 Nov 1968	New (green and white) flag raised in Rhodesia
18 Nov 1968	Mr. Thompson's mission ends in failure. Rhodesia's rejection of the proposals based on Fearless talks announced

Jan 1969	Rhodesia attacked at Commonwealth Conference in London
12 Jan 1969	Four hundred demonstrators attack Rhodesia House and South Africa House
13 Feb 1969	The Rev. Ndabaningi Sithole, leader of the banned Zimbabwe African National Union, is sentenced to six years' imprisonment in Salisbury for plotting to assassinate Mr. Ian Smith and two members of the Rhodesian Cabinet
16 Mar 1969	Mr. Winston Field, C.M.G., M.B.E., the first Rhodesian Front Party Prime Minister, dies in Salisbury
19 May 1969	Mr. Ian Smith said that the "intractable British attitude" had ended hopes of a negotiated settlement of the independence dispute. He announces that proposals for a new constitution were to be published in a White Paper on 20th May, which would be voted on at a referendum on 20th June. The referendum would also decide whether Rhodesia should assume Republican status
20 Jun 1969	European electorate votes in favour of a Republic in referendum. Eighty-one per cent, of the votes cast were in favour of becoming a Republic and 72,5 per cent were in favour of adopting the Constitutional proposals put forward by the Rhodesian Government
24 Jun 1969	Mr. Clifford Dupont, the Officer Administering the Government, opens the last session of the Rhodesian Parliament
24 Jun 1969	Sir Humphrey Gibbs resigns as governor
09 Jul 1969	Sir Humphrey Gibbs is appointed a member of the Privy Council and promoted to Knight Grand Cross of the Victorian Order
14 Jul 1969	Rhodesia House in London, and the British Residual Mission in Salisbury, both close
17 Nov 1969	The Constitutional Bill is passed by the Rhodesian Parliament
29 Nov 1969	New constitution becomes law. Mr. Clifford Dupont, Officer Administering the Government, signs the new constitution
19 Dec 1969	The University College of Rhodesia decides that it will award its own degrees and not those of the University of London
17 Feb 1970	Decimal currency is introduced into Rhodesia
02 Mar 1970	New Constitution comes into effect (including Land Tenure Act)
02 Mar 1970	Rhodesia declared a republic. Parliament is dissolved

17 Mar 1970	Great Britain and the United States of America both use their United Nations veto to avoid complete sanctions against Rhodesia being made mandatory
17 Mar 1970	United States Consulate closes down
10 Apr 1970	Rhodesian Front sweeps European seats in general election
16 Apr 1970	Clifford Dupont sworn in as first President
28 May 1970	First Senators sworn in
28 May 1970	Rhodesia's first Republican Parliament is opened by the President
21 Jul 1970	New Zealand vs Rhodesia Rugby Score; 27-14
08 May 1971	Death of Lord Malvern (G. Huggins)
14 May 1971	Petrol rationing, in force since 1965, ends
30 Jun 1971	Britain's special envoy, Lord Goodman, arrives for talks with Rhodesian officials
07 Jul 1971	Johannesburg Consolidated Investment Co. Ltd. announces that at least $20,000,000 will be invested in a nickel copper mine, concentrator and smelter in the Shangani area
15 Nov 1971	Sir Alec Douglas-Home arrives in Salisbury to discuss settlement proposals
17 Nov 1971	U.S. President Richard Nixon signs bill containing "Byrd Amendment"
24 Nov 1971	Ian Smith and Sir Alec Douglas Home sign Anglo-Rhodesian Settlement Proposals
16 Dec 1971	African National Council formed
11 Jan 1972	Pearce Commission under Lord Pearce arrives in Rhodesia to carry out a test of acceptability in terms of the settlement proposals
13 Jan 1972	Commissioners of the Pearce Commission commence their enquiries in the seven provinces
18 Jan 1972	Garfield Todd and his daughter Judith are arrested
19 Jan 1972	Violence erupts in the African township of Harare in Salisbury and in Gwelo and Umtali African townships
11 Mar 1972	The whole Pearce Commission leaves Rhodesia
23 May 1972	Pearce Commission's Report published in London. The Prime

Minister broadcasts to the nation on the report of the Pearce Commission, who found that the proposals were not acceptable to the people of Rhodesia as a whole

31 May 1972	The U.S. Senate votes against reimposing an embargo on Rhodesian chrome
06 Jun 1972	An underground explosion and cave-in at Wankie Colliery's No. 2 shaft claims 427 victims
22 Aug 1972	The Rhodesian team is barred from participating in the Munich Olympics
31 Oct 1972	The Rhodesia Party is formally launched
21 Dec 1972	Altena Farm in the Centenary area, attacked by ZANLA terrorists wounding an 8-year-old girl, marking beginning of new stage of large scale terrorist war in north-east
09 Jan 1973	Rhodesia closes border with Zambia , pending the assurance that Zambia will not harbour terrorists
01 Feb 1973	Zambia closes its border with Rhodesia
04 Feb 1973	As a result of messages received, Rhodesia opens its border with Zambia, though Zambia's side remains closed
09 Feb 1973	A Rhodesian angler is killed on the Zambezi by machine-gun fire from the Zambian Army
14 Apr 1973	Air Rhodesia acquires three Boeing 707 jet aircraft from an undisclosed source
15 May 1973	Zambian troops open fire on a group of tourists at Victoria Falls from across the gorge, killing two Canadian girls and wounding an American man
22 May 1973	Britain and the U.S.A. veto a United Nations Security Council resolution to extend sanctions against Rhodesia
17 Jun 1973	Five R.C. Bishops stated in a resolution that they would not comply with some of the provisions of the amendment to the Land Tenure Act and the African Affairs Act
23 Jun 1973	Members of the British Foreign Office visit Rhodesia and have talks with Rhodesian officials and Bishop Muzorewa, in order to report back to the British Foreign Secretary
05 Jul 1973	A heavily armed gang of terrorists abducted 295 African pupils and staff members of St. Alberts Mission in the north-eastern

border area. All but eight of those abducted were very shortly rescued

03 Aug 1973	About 150 African students demonstrated against low wages paid to African workers at the University of Rhodesia
07 Aug 1973	On a recommendation by a disciplinary committee that six students should be expelled, and eight suspended for their activities, rioting African students stoned buildings on the campus. The Principal called for police protection, and as a result 155 students were arrested
01 Feb 1974	Petrol rationing comes into force
17 Apr 1974	Government offers cash awards for information leading to the death or capture of terrorists
25 Apr 1974	Portuguese government falls in coup d'etat; new government pledges independence for African colonies
19 Jun 1974	New York Office of Air Rhodesia closed, U.S. Treasury order issued under sanctions regulations making it impossible to continue operations
31 Jul 1974	The Rhodesian Front win all 50 European seats in the General Election
27 Aug 1974	The Rhodesian National Anthem played for the first time at the opening of Parliament
15 Sep 1974	Direct railway link to South Africa opened through Beit Bridge
18 Sep 1974	The Rutenga-Beit Bridge rail link is completed and officially opened by the Prime Minister
02 Oct 1974	Z.A.N.U. offices in Lusaka blown up by a bomb and destroyed
16 Oct 1974	Bishop Muzorewa stated in a circular that he had been cheated into signing the undertaking he signed on 17th August
08 Nov 1974	The Sanctions Order against Rhodesia, signed by the British Government for the tenth time
11 Nov 1974	The Prime Minister in a broadcast to the Nation stated that as a result of recent developments in other countries there was a possibility of a settlement
11 Nov 1974	Two ministers in Government, Mr. Howman and Mr. Lance Smith retired
14 Nov 1974	The weekly Roman Catholic publication Moto permanently

banned

06 Dec 1974	Cabora Bassa gates fixed and lake begins to fill
08 Dec 1974	Leaders of ZANU, ZAPU, and FROLIZI announce acceptance of ANC as "umbrella" organization with Muzorewa as head
11 Dec 1974	Ian Smith announces agreement with nationalists for cease-fire, release of political prisoners, and plan for new constitutional conference
12 Dec 1974	The South African Prime Minister stated the S.A. Police will be withdrawn from Rhodesia once it is clear that terrorism has ended
25 Dec 1974	The British Foreign Secretary stated he will meet Rhodesian African leaders in Lusaka, during his African tour next month
1975	Marxist-oriented FRELIMO assumed power in Mozambique and its independence made it easier for the guerrillas to attack Rhodesia
10 Jan 1975	Release of detainees halted as terrorist incursions increase
06 Feb 1975	McIntosh, the sanctions spy serving a 14-year sentence, escaped from jail
06 Feb 1975	Rhodesian Prime Minister and leaders of the A.N.C. meet for two hours
25 Feb 1975	Portuguese Frontier Police handed McIntosh back to Rhodesian Police
05 Mar 1975	Rev. Ndabaningi Sithole detained on the grounds of plotting to assassinate certain opponents
15 Mar 1975	Rhodesian Prime Minister and senior Ministers go to South Africa for talks
18 Mar 1975	Rhodesia's Diplomatic Mission in Lisbon told to leave by 30th April
19 Mar 1975	Herbert Chitepo and his bodyguard killed by a land-mine in Lusaka
03 Apr 1975	Special Court reviewing Sithole's detention found it was fully warranted
06 Apr 1975	Acting on the request of Bishop Muzorewa and supported by the S.A. Government and other African Heads of State, Sithole was released from detention in order to attend the O.A.U. meeting in Tanzania

27 May 1975	Rhodesian Prime Minister issued an ultimatum to the A.N.C.- get to the Conference table or Government will turn to other groups
02 Jun 1975	Thirteen people killed and 28 injured when police opened fire on a crowd of 5,000 Africans in Highfields who were rival nationalist factions
05 Jun 1975	Number of arrests made on allegations of recruiting for terrorist training
07 Jun 1975	Bishop Muzorewa returns to Salisbury
15 Jun 1975	Meeting between Prime Minister and A.N.C. ended in deadlock over venue for a Constitutional Conference
25 Jun 1975	Minister for Information and five other Rhodesian M.P.s visited President Kaunda in Lusaka over the weekend
25 Jun 1975	Mozambique becomes independent with Samora Machel as President
25 Jun 1975	Opening of Parliament
29 Jun 1975	The Prime Minister and Mr. Ennals had a 90-minute talk together on the settlement issue
08 Jul 1975	Rhodesian government announces set-up of anti-terrorist campaign after failure of cease-fire
09 Jul 1975	Government sets up a Commission to investigate racial discrimination
25 Jul 1975	Curfew put on 500-km strip down the Eastern border
06 Aug 1975	Curfew imposed along the Botswana border
13 Aug 1975	Government confirmed that a Constitutional Conference would be held in South African Railway's coaches on the Victoria Falls Bridge. Conference will be subject to an agreement made in Pretoria between the Rhodesian Government and the A.N.C. representative, and subscribed to by other heads of State
25 Aug 1975	Conference opened at the Victoria Falls Bridge, attended by President Kaunda and Mr. Vorster
28 Aug 1975	Government is to introduce a national registration for all residents irrespective of race
03 Sep 1975	Rev. Ndabaningi Sithole announced an external wing of the A.N.C. to be formed called the Zimbabwe Liberation Council (Z.L.C.)

04 Sep 1975	Split appears in the A.N.C. between members of the former Z.A.N.U. and Z.A.P.U.
10 Dec 1975	J.J. Wrathall succeeds Dupont as president
15 Dec 1975	Ian Smith and Joshua Nkomo begin weekly talks in Salisbury
03 Mar 1976	Mozambique closes its borders to Rhodesia
19 Mar 1976	Smith-Nkomo talks break down
26 Apr 1976	Government publishes regulations increasing censorship
27 Apr 1976	Ian Smith announces addition of government chiefs to his cabinet
09 Aug 1976	Raid on Nyadzonya terrorist base by Rhodesian forces in Frelimo disguise. Over 1200 ZANLA killed
19 Sep 1976	Ian Smith and U.S. Secretary of State Henry Kissinger meet in Pretoria
24 Sep 1976	Ian Smith announces willingness to bring about African majority rule within two years
09 Oct 1976	Joshua Nkomo and Robert Mugabe (ZANU and ZAPU) announce formation of Patriotic Front. The military forces of the two also combined to form ZIPA
14 Oct 1976	All-Party Geneva Conference on Rhodesia held. This was a mediation effort involving US secretary of state Henry Kissinger and John Vorster. Kissinger practiced "'lying to both sides'" and failed. A commitment from Smith to majority rule was obtained
09 Dec 1976	Geneva Conference adjourns for holidays, never to reopen
29 Dec 1976	Government chiefs found Zimbabwe United People's Organization
1977	197 Rhodesians were killed in action and close to 11,000 emigrated
18 Mar 1977	U.S. President Jimmy Carter signs repeal of "Byrd Agreement"
Apr 1977	The Anglo-American mediation effort carried out by Britain's foreign secretary David Owen and US secretary of state Cyrus Vance failed
01 Apr 1977	Amendments to Land Tenure Act lift some colour bar laws
13 Apr 1977	British Foreign Secretary David Owen presents Anglo-American constitutional proposals to Ian Smith in Cape Town
16 Apr 1977	David Owen consults with Ian Smith in Salisbury, becoming first

British cabinet-level official to visit Rhodesia in six years

18 Apr 1977	Emergency Rhodesian Front convention endorses principle of eventual majority rule
29 Apr 1977	Ian Smith expels hard-line opponents from the Rhodesian Front
16 May 1977	President Kaunda announces that Zambia is "in a state of war" with Rhodesia
27 May 1977	UN Security Council tightens mandatory sanctions
04 Jul 1977	Rhodesian Action Party formed
05 Jul 1977	General meeting of OAU endorses Patriotic Front as sole representative of people of Zimbabwe
31 Aug 1977	Rhodesian Front sweeps European seats in general election
01 Sep 1977	British Foreign Secretary Owen and U.S. Secretary of State Cyrus Vance announce proposals acknowledging that the Patriotic Front must play a leadership role in any future government, and that armed forces of an in dependant Zimbabwe should be based upon ZANLA and ZIPRA forces
24 Sep 1977	Frontline President's group endorses Anglo-American plan
28 Sep 1977	Britain presents Anglo-American proposals to UN Security Council
23 Nov 1977	Rhodesian Security Forces mount major raids into Mozambique. Massive air and ground strike on Chimoio and Tembue terrorist bases. Over 2,000 ZANLA killed for 1 Rhodesian killed and 8 wounded
24 Nov 1977	Ian Smith announces conditional acceptance of "one man, one vote" principle
02 Dec 1977	Ian Smith opens new round of internal negotiations with Abel Muzorewa, Ndabaningi Sithole and Jeremiah Chirau
07 Dec 1977	Zambia announces withdrawal of support for Anglo-American plan
06 Feb 1978	Abel Muzorewa, Ndabaningi Sithole and Jeremiah Chirau reject Anglo-American plan
03 Mar 1978	Ian Smith, Abel Muzorewa, Ndabaningi Sithole and Jeremiah Chirau sign internal settlement agreement; agreement is immediately denounced by leaders of both the Patriotic Front and the Frontline States. Black majority rule (one person, one vote)

was granted but interests of the whites were protected

21 Mar 1978	Rhodesia officially governed by an Executive Council, with Ian Smith, Abel Muzorewa, Ndabaningi Sithole and Jeremiah Chirau alternating chairmanship.
Jul 1978	At Khartoum, OAU Council of Ministers denounced the internal settlement and praised the Patriotic Front
03 Sep 1978	ZIPRA terrorists shoot down a civilian commuter Air Rhodesia plane (the Hunyani) near Kariba with a SAM-7 missile. Eighteen of the 56 passengers and crew survived the resulting crash, but 10 of them were almost immediately callously murdered by ZAPU terrorists
09 Sep 1978	Memorial service held by the Very Rev. John da Costa, Anglican Dean of Salisbury in the Anglican Cathedral of St. Mary and All Saints. His sermon titled, "The Silence is Deafening", accused the world of ignoring atrocities against Rhodesian civilians
19 Oct 1978	The legendary "Green Leader" raid on terrorist camps in Zambia, while the Rhodesian Air Force completely controlled Zambian air space. The series of raids carried out resulted in 1,600 ZIPRA dead for the loss of one Rhodesian soldier
20 Dec 1978	The war was into its thirteenth year. In 1978, 13,000 whites had emigrated and 2,450 guerrillas, 282 Rhodesian troops, 3,406 black civilians, and 173 white non-combatants lost their lives. The civil war cost Rhodesia one million dollars each day and whites emigrated at a rate of 1,000 per month
02 Jan 1979	Government announces plan for new constitution to implement conditions agreed to in Internal Settlement
30 Jan 1979	European electorate approves referendum on new constitution
12 Feb 1979	ZIPRA terrorists shoot down a second Air Rhodesia civilian commuter plane (the Umniati) killing all 59 people on board outright
21 Feb 1979	UN Human Rights Commission rejects the Internal settlement
28 Feb 1979	Ian Smith dissolves Rhodesian Parliament, officially ending 88 years of white rule
14 Apr 1979	SAS raid on Nkomo's headquarters in Lusaka
17 Apr 1979	First general elections in which Africans vote for government officials are held, and 64 percent of African electorate cast votes;

Rhodesian Front wins all 28 seats reserved for Europeans, while UANC under Abel Muzorewa wins 51 of 72 seats elected by African voters: Sithole and Chirau refuse to recognize results as official

01 May 1979	Smith hands the office of prime minister to Muzorewa but the whites retain the key points in the civil service, government and in the army. International diplomatic recognition of Zimbabwe-Rhodesia, as it was now called, did not take place
03 May 1979	Conservatives win the elections in Great Britain. Margaret Thatcher wants to be rid of the Rhodesian problem. The Conservative Manifestation had said that if Rhodesia met certain principles then it would be recognized by Britain
20 May 1979	Zimbabwe Rhodesia declared an independent republic
25 May 1979	OAU announces its opposition to Muzorewa's government and lifting of sanctions
28 May 1979	Abel Muzorewa sworn in as first African prime minister
01 Jul 1979	At Canberra, the Australian Prime Minister, Malcolm Fraser, startles Thatcher by announcing that Australia was against any leniency towards Smith and Muzorewa and that they are in agreement with the Front-line states
01 Aug 1979	Commonwealth Conference in Lusaka opens. A compromise plan is agreed. Britain receives a mandate to mediate
14 Aug 1979	Britain extends invitations to Muzorewa government and the Patriotic Front
01 Sep 1979	The Rhodesian Green and White flag lowered for the last time, to be replaced by a new Zimbabwe-Rhodesia flag the next day
05 Sep 1979	Operation Uric starts, external raids on ZANLA and Frelimo bases in Mozambique
07 Sep 1979	At Non-aligned Movement summit meeting in Cuba, Patriotic Front members are coerced into going to London. Patriotic Front say that they will only negotiate with the British
10 Sep 1979	Britain convenes Lancaster House Conference under chairmanship of British Foreign Secretary Lord Carrington; government of Zimbabwe Rhodesia delegation led by Muzorewa and Ian Smith, and Patriotic Front delegation led by Mugabe and Nkomo. Carrington's agenda constituted first agreeing on a constitution, followed by transitional arrangements and new

elections, and finally the cease-fire plan

10 Sep 1979	Lord Carrington delivered his opening address and presented his outline of the constitution as the basis for negotiations and maintained that constitutional issue must be solved first. Patriotic Front put forward its own agenda
12 Sep 1979	Smith caused the first split in the Rhodesian side by supporting the Patriotic Front agenda (he wanted to see the entire deal)
14 Sep 1979	Patriotic Front presented its constitutional proposals; Carrington said that only British proposals could be negotiated
18 Sep 1979	Carrington decided to hold bilateral meetings (and the practice of first negotiating with Rhodesian commenced)
19 Sep 1979	Ian Smith argued that white safeguards must not be diluted. Carrington presented the Salisbury delegation with numbers (twenty out of 100 seats would be reserved for the whites and seventy votes would be necessary to amend the constitution). The Salisbury delegation accepted the offer
02 Oct 1979	The negotiations between the British and the Patriotic Front became heated. Mugabe and Nkomo gave their first joint press conference and accused the British of complicity with Rhodesia
03 Oct 1979	Carrington delivered his first deadline: He wanted an answer by the eight. Muzorewa accepted but the Patriotic Front refused and offered to move on to the next item. Carrington rejected the offer and extended the deadline
11 Oct 1979	Carrington decided to seek support from the presidents of the Front-line states and the Commonwealth
15 Oct 1979	So as to break the deadlock, Carrington used, for the first time, a 'second-class solution' tool. This tool would have meant recognizing Rhodesia. To make the threat more credible, he suspended the Patriotic Front from the negotiations. This resulted in the secretary-general of the Commonwealth, Shridath Ramphal, scolding Carrington. Britain became more accommodating
15 Oct 1979	The United States offered economic support to Zimbabwe which was of crucial importance (i.e., compensation for land)
16 Oct 1979	Patriotic Front started to back down and said that they would join the negotiations as soon as the issue of compensation for land was solved
18 Oct 1979	Patriotic Front announced that "there will not be need to revert to

the discussion on the constitution" provided that they were satisfied with the transitional arrangements

22 Oct 1979	Carrington presented the British proposals on the transition period: It was to last for two months and a British governor was to direct the country, through the existing bureaucracy and the security forces, as well as supervise the elections. The plan was equally unwelcome to all sides
26 Oct 1979	Patriotic Front denounced Carrington's "dictatorial attitude;" they were particularly angry at the fact that the British were going to be using the Rhodesian bureaucracy and security forces which they believed would not be impartial. They wanted UN and Patriotic Front forces to be used
28 Oct 1979	Prime Minister Muzorewa agreed to step down after a night of prayer
01 Nov 1979	Patriotic Front threatened to leave the negotiations but, without support from the Front-line states, they did not seem credible
02 Nov 1979	Britain wanted an answer by the fifth. The date was important because that week the British Parliament would debate the continuation of sanctions imposed on Rhodesia
05 Nov 1979	Muzorewa said that they had accepted the British proposals. Patriotic Front was not forthcoming
07 Nov 1979	Britain introduced into its Parliament a bill that would have started the motion of bringing Rhodesia back under British authority; the Patriotic Front was furious. Carrington placed a deadline for the next day
08 Nov 1979	Carrington rebuked the Patriotic Front for not providing an answer. The Patriotic Front said it was a misunderstanding and that they had met President Kaunda of Zambia who had flown to London to help break the deadlock. Ian Smith accepted 'defeat' and said "'the time has come to tell our people back home that to continue the fight would now be sterile, even counter-productive.'"
10 Nov 1979	Britain agreed to set up a Commonwealth force and gave more time and increased the transition time by a couple of weeks
13 Nov 1979	Carrington offered the Patriotic Front a face-saver by recognizing the equality of the forces in the conflict
14 Nov 1979	Carrington and Mugabe discussed areas of agreement and

disagreement

15 Nov 1979	Patriotic Front accepted the transition plan
16 Nov 1979	Britain presented its cease-fire plan which called for the cessation of movement of troops (bases for the Rhodesian troops; assembly points for the guerrillas), and coming under the command of the British governor
16 Nov 1979	Zambia's few remaining links to the outside world were bombed by Rhodesian troops but President Kaunda did not retaliate
19 Nov 1979	The Patriotic Front counter-proposals demanded a substantial Commonwealth presence and the disbandment of certain Rhodesian units
22 Nov 1979	Britain presented ultimatums (demanding a reply by November 26th) which resulted in Mugabe remarking that Lord Carrington "could 'go to hell.'"
25 Nov 1979	Following a meeting with the Front-line Presidents at Dar es Salaam, Nkomo and Mugabe declared that they had their backing but in private, the Presidents urged greater accommodation
26 Nov 1979	Muzorewa's delegation embraced the British proposals but the Patriotic Front took their time
06 Dec 1979	Patriotic Front gave partial acceptance but demanded more time and more assembly points
07 Dec 1979	Queen Elizabeth appoints Lord Soames as governor and the Zimbabwe bill on the granting of a status of republic was published angering the Patriotic Front in the process
11 Dec 1979	The Rhodesian Parliament dissolved itself
12 Dec 1979	1979 Zimbabwe Rhodesia House of Assembly votes to return country to colonial status; later that day Lord Soames arrives in Salisbury to take office, officially marking end of UDI
13 Dec 1979	Sanctions on Rhodesia were lifted (and further angered the Patriotic Front who believed that the British were acting rashly)
14 Dec 1979	Carrington demanded firm reply which caused the Patriotic Front to express their hostility: "Thatcher can jump in the Thames;" "The answer, Lord Carrington, is No . . . No . . . No . . .;" and "Carrington can go to hell". President Machel stepped in and supposedly had a message delivered to Mugabe to accept or "he would be welcomed back to Mozambique and given a beach villa

where he could write his memoirs."

17 Dec 1979	The Patriotic Front signed the cease-fire agreement
21 Dec 1979	The final agreement was signed by all parties on the 102nd day of the conference
29 Dec 1979	Cease-fire takes effect, ZANLA and ZIPRA terrorists begin to gather at 16 assembly points throughout rural areas; Rhodesian security forces assemble at their bases
01 Jan 1980	Seven guerrillas were killed in a clash with Zimbabwe-Rhodesian forces 60 miles north of Salisbury
04 Jan 1980	By the deadline, 18,500 Patriot Front guerrillas had reported to assembly points around Zimbabwe-Rhodesia
09 Jan 1980	First direct links with outside world were re-established with the arrival of a passenger airline flight from Lusaka, Zambia
13 Jan 1980	Joshua Nkomo returns to Zimbabwe-Rhodesia after three years of exile. 100,000 greeted him
14 Jan 1980	Ten black parties registered for the elections. Nkomo registered ZAPU under the name of Patriotic Front
18 Jan 1980	The state of emergency was extended until July
21 Jan 1980	First group of refugees (1,000) returned from Botswana
22 Jan 1980	Lord Soames, British governor, accused Mugabe's ZANU and outgoing Prime Minister Muzorewa's irregular troops of truce violations
26 Jan 1980	The withdrawal of 26 South African contingents guarding links from South Africa to Zimbabwe-Rhodesia was announced
27 Jan 1980	Robert Mugabe returns after more than four years in exile, more than 200,000 greeted him
02 Feb 1980	UNSC adopted a resolution calling upon Great Britain to insure fair elections for a black majority government took place
10 Feb 1980	Mugabe escaped assassination as a bomb blew off behind his car amid growing political violence
14 Feb 1980	Whites voted. Ian Smith's Rhodesian Front won all 20 seats reserved for the whites
25 Feb 1980	The process of readmitting refugees was halted until after the election. A symbolic step toward creating an integrated force took place when a contingent of ZAPU's guerrillas started manoeuvres

with the regular army

27 Feb 1980	General elections in which 94 percent of the African electorate casts votes; ZANU wins overwhelming victory with 63 percent of the African vote and 57 of 80 parliamentary seats; ZAPU receives 24 percent of the vote and wins 20 seats
02 Mar 1980	A Commonwealth observation team concluded that the election had been free and fair. Other observers pointed to wide-scale intimidation by Mugabe's ZANU
03 Mar 1980	Lord Soames and Zimbabwe-Rhodesian officials went on television to urge the population to remain calm after it was clear that Mugabe would win. Soames had by this time sorted out his differences with Mugabe and allowed his intimidation of voters to go unchallenged. The withdrawal of Commonwealth peacekeeping forces began
04 Mar 1980	Robert Mugabe's ZANU won the elections for a new black government in Zimbabwe-Rhodesia. ZANU obtained 62.9% of the popular vote which meant 57 of the 80 seats reserved for blacks in the 100-member parliament; Nkomo received 24.1% (20 seats); and Muzorewa got 8.2% (3 seats). In Mugabe's public announcements, he appeared moderate
05 Mar 1980	Mugabe agrees to form a coalition government, but appoints only four ZAPU party members, including Joshua Nkomo as minister of home affairs, to ministerial posts
05 Mar 1980	ZANU guerrillas started training with the regular army
11 Mar 1980	Prime Minister-elect Mugabe presented a list of his Cabinet appointments to Lord Soames. Two whites were given portfolios. Mugabe kept for himself the post of defence minister; Nkomo was given the post of home affairs (i.e., control of the police). There was one woman in the Cabinet
13 Mar 1980	Mugabe promised changes to enable more blacks to enter the civil service. Nkomo would also oversee immigration. The government announced that it would respect all old debts, as long as they were not for arms purchases
15 Apr 1980	Britain proclaimed that it would give Zimbabwe $165 million between 1981-83 partly to train black civil servants and the Zimbabwean army
15 Apr 1980	Lt. Gen. Walls was appointed to head the new Zimbabwean army

17 Apr 1980	The US was the first country to open an embassy
17 Apr 1980	Zimbabwe-Rhodesia officially became the independent nation of Zimbabwe
18 Apr 1980	Republic of Zimbabwe declared
19 Apr 1980	The 21 ministers were sworn in
20 Apr 1980	The government's first official action was issuing the budget which gave priority to helping poor blacks
30 May 1980	Prime Minister Mugabe asked for more British military training personnel to help integrate the armies into the new national army. Mozambique and Zimbabwe "exchanged pledges of assistance in security matters"
27 Jun 1980	Zimbabwe closed South Africa's diplomatic mission in Salisbury
17 Jul 1980	Lt. Gen. Peter Walls, the white chief of Zimbabwe's joint Military High Command, announced that he intended to leave his post as of July 29 because "'it's the overcoming of the problems which has made me feel that it is okay for me to retire now.'"
23 Jul 1980	The Parliament renewed for six months the state of emergency first introduced by the white Rhodesian government in 1964
25 Aug 1980	Zimbabwe became the 153rd member of the UN
27 Aug 1980	In New York City, Prime Minister Mugabe praised President Carter for his role in settling the civil war
31 Aug 1980	Ian Smith urged the whites to remain and made favourable comments about the majority-rule government
30 Sep 1980	Emigration had risen in August to its highest level since 1978
10 Nov 1980	Near Bulawayo, the country's second largest city, where more than 3,000 former guerrilla soldiers from both factions had been resettled, at least 43 persons were killed and 300 injured in the most violent fighting between the rival guerrilla factions since independence
13 Oct 2002	Sir Garfield Todd (93) prime minister 1953-1958 died after suffering a stroke

RELUCTANT ASSASSIN 1

BY

CHRIS HIGGINSON

The victims of past become killers of now
Their sons and their daughters make sabre from plough
They return to wreak vengeance with bombs suicide
Back to kill those who on them violence plied

ISBN 1-4196-1975-6

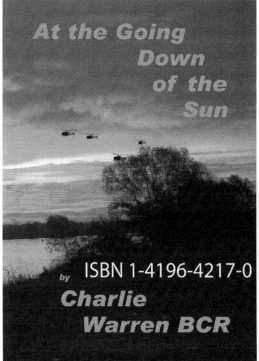

At the Going
Down
of the
Sun

by ISBN 1-4196-4217-0
Charlie
Warren BCR

1st Provocative Verse
by
Chris Higginson

Poetry to pass the time each and every day
Words set down to make a rhyme with not a lot to say
Nothing will be changed by these verses in this book
Except to tempt you, or to tease, to have a little look.

ISBN 1-4196-1765-6

Steve Bailey's Internet logo
http://www.pbase.com/mashona/my_africa_2

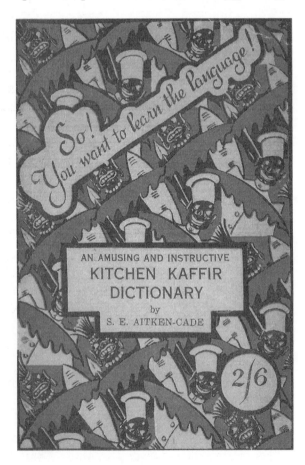

A brief look into the future ....:

Harare Herald:
Zimbabwe's prisoners face acute food shortages, reported a parliamentary committee on Friday. The report found that malnutrition and disease were widespread in Zimbabwe's overcrowded jails.
Prison authorities have insufficient funds to buy food.

The Minister of 'Economical Affairs', Mr. Swindle Embezzlemunt, met today with the Head of the Prisons Services, Mr Escarpmunt, who has returned from leave in the Eastern Highlands.

There were many points raised at the meeting, which were taken down by the Secretary of Home Affairs, Miss Biggamunt. She was able to cope with them all.

The Minister was proud to announce that Zimbabwe had the highest inflation in the world.

"This means," he continued, "that we are giving the people ever more cash in their pockets. We have exceeded our promise of making ordinary citizens into Millionaires."

On the question of food for prisoners in Jail Mr Ailmunt, the Prisons Medical Officer, said, "The Medicamunts I need with the Treatmunts are missing and that the malnutrition in the Prisons is serious, according to the Officer in Charge of Catering, Mr Undernourishmunt."

The Chief Warden, Mr Speedy Advancemunt, went so far as to say,

"The Chief Executioner, Mr Vertebral Rearrangemunt has been laid off because so few prisoners are surviving the wait after the Judgemunt for the Final Punishmunt.

Mr Rearrangemunt says that the Chief torturer Mr Disfiguremunt is taking away his business."

"The Prison Chaplain, Reverent Judas Betraymunt," he continued, "is also seeking an alternative posting from the Department of Employmunt, because he has too many Bereavemunts asking for the Final Testamunt!"

The Chief Accountants to the Offices of Procuremunts and Establishmunts, Mr Bamboozlemunt and Mr Figamunt were also unable to explain the reasons for the Discontentmunt.

The Minister of Transport, Mr Instant Derailmunt was also not able to shed any light on the matter of non delivery of goods to the jail.

"It really is a puzzlemunt. We are very confused! Shipmunts have failed us. They claimed the paymunts hadn't!" he said. "Perhaps we should find a Settlemunt or consult with the Party Astrologer Miss Aligned Firmamunt."

The Party Officials were amazedmunts at this suggestion.

This would Excitemunts of the Establishmunt. It was 'They' who decided what was permitted via the Weakly Announcemunt.

The Managemunts would not agree either! It was they who laid the Rules for Engagemunts.

The Improvemunts then went to the Arguemunt to ask the Involvemunts what was required to reach Contentmunt. The Acknowledgemunt said he would get back to them after he had consulted the Requiremunts.

All these Officials and Committees were finally sent to Banishmunt who has allocated them new quarters in Birmingham.

"They are to be known as Apartmunts!" he said.

All because the Investmunt hadn't.

In an attempt to rescue his failing programme of land redistribution, Zimbabwe's President Robert Mugabe is trying to involve the army in a "command agriculture" programme. "Instructions have already been passed onto battalion commanders," a Zimbabwean army major told the BBC.

" AAAAA -TEN - SHUN" shouts the Comrade Major.

There be a shuffle of Fordson Tractor tyre treads.

"Slo-ope Arms!"

"Aaah!.....   No Sah" say Fineas…. Comrade Corporal second klass.

"Waatee… You disobey Order from ME!"

"Yes Sah…. Ah mean No Sah!... Butee…. Lo Plesident, he say we not allowed to say "Slope" Arms, Sah……. He say 'Slope' is name for 'White running   dogs" ……. Sah?...."   , says Fineas hopefully.

"Aaah! Another wun broody Plesident Order!" the Major mutters to himself.

"RI-Ight! Put de Arms on Shoulder!"

Blank black faces stare back.

Eyes roll.

Bottom lips gape open.

A couple of fingers edge their way upwards and enter nostrils…. to the hilt.

Brains are scratched.

There is a quiet hum, while this new order is pondered………..

"Butee Major Sah…….. Our arms are already on de shoulders, Sah…! Both sides!"

The Major sighs.

It was not like this in the old days.

Those days before the amalgamation with the Rhodesian Security Forces.

It was much simpler then.

So they said……

"Right….. PI-ICK up your Budzas!"

"Sah…. We got no picks Sah!"

The Comrade Major eyes his troops.

They stand in a ragged line with tattered uniforms, carefully torn so that they resemble farm workers' clothes.

Some have hats and most of them have tyre-tread boots.

Comrade Corporal Fineas has already lost one of his special-issue Bata tackies. Each member of the company has been issued with a farm implement so that he can be taught the rudiments of agriculture.

The parade square where they are assembled has several large cracks zig zagging across the surface, from which sad drought-stricken tufts of grass cling to life.

A vulture, perched on top of the flagpole, which is missing both halyard and flag, gazes at the men assembled below it with a professional interest.

There are only seven of them.

The rest of the company has been variously distributed to the cemetery, the queue for the "Aids Ward" at the sanatorium or to attend the ritual family Christmas funerals.

A lone lean Ox stands at the edge of the parade square chewing the cud.

He is the 'Tlactor' replacement. His team mate was last week's rations.

The plough is broken.

The Major contemplates his situation.

There are no military orders that he can think of that pertain to agriculture. He has not had the benefit of a Sandhurst training, where he might have picked up a modicum of Latin, and thereby have learned how the Romans "laid waste the fields of Gaul".

The only fields he knows about are 'Mine Fields', and he doesn't have any of those.

Only Generals and above were issued with those.

He wonders why they are called 'mine', when actually they are 'theirs'.

He removes his straw hat and scratches his eighteen year old head.

As a war veteran, from the war that ended twenty five years ago, he should have been given at least a farm, if not several fields.

He wonders what a field really is.

"Oh, all right then", he mutters. "Follow me!"

He turns and walks towards the gates of the army barracks which give access to the main airport road. The remnants of the Company shamble after him carrying their farm implements in various different positions. The Ox watches their departure with a rheumy eye and then wanders to stand in the shade of a leafless acacia.

There is no transport for the "Engineers Agricultural Division" as all the trucks have been stolen.

The six 'budzamen' take up a defensive position in the ditch at the side of the road, facing each other and sharing their last cigarette, which has been created from various ingredients, as tobacco is in short supply. They stare at their budzas and wonder what they are for.

The Comrade Major stands with thumb at the ready, to flag down a passing motorist.

There are no motorists.

There are no cars.

There is no petrol.

It's got to be the White Man's fault.

The New Land Owners of Zimbabwe........

Gideon Murrunga leans back on his seat with his hands on his knees and surveys the view.

"How satisfying it is to be a land owner." He thinks to himself.

"Well, perhaps not exactly a land *owner*, but it is the next best thing........ the *occupier* of a farm given by the Government."

This has to be better than in the 'old days'.

He remembers having to learn about those 'old days' when he was at school. The scholars were supposed to learn reading, but he never bothered.

In those days King Lobengula owned all the land and gave parts of it to his close family, but all the cattle were still really his poperty.

Then they were taught how the King signed away all the rights to land to some foreigner. That shows you the dangers of reading and writing!

Well....... that was in the 'old days'.

"But now we have got it back", he smirks to himself, with satisfaction.

In fact, for Gideon, it is better than before, because now he has total control of the land that stretches away in front of the house. He looks at it with the pride of a proprietor.

Slightly to his right, in what used to be the 'garden', stretches an expanse of green water with lumps of floating algae.

Tadpoles gasp for air at the surface as they 'nose' their way past the remains of a decaying Puffadder. Their legs will soon be sufficiently developed to enable them to climb on top of the floating debris, but it is unlikely even then, that they will be able to escape the confines of what was, once upon a time, a swimming pool.

The tiled edges of the pool loom two feet above the surface of the water, as there has been no rain for months.

Gideon does not seem to notice the pool.

It is of no interest to him.

He heard about how the previous owners of the farm used to swim in it.

Who ever heard of such a silly idea!

His herd of cattle…….. that is what it is all about!

He looks at the six animals grouped in the shade of a Flamboyant tree.

Their hip bones are prominent as their lacklustre hides stretch across their well defined racks of ribs.

Even to Gideon's untrained eye, the animals are not looking very well.

That herdsman….. What was his name…….. Jacob?......... The one that worked for the white farmer before him…..

What did he say?

Something about 'dipping' the cattle every week because of ticks?

Well Jacob obviously did not know much about that 'mutti' that the white man used to put in the dip.

How much it *cost!*

As much, at least, as a crate of beer!

Stupid!

And where did this Jacob think the water to fill the 'dip' was going to come from?

Didn't he know that the borehole pump was broken?

Gideon shakes his head at the stupid complications with which all these people confuse themselves.

If the cattle are no good, then they will die.

That is the way it should be.

Most of them had.

Funny how the farm workers, that used to work for the white farmer, would not take the meat from the carcasses of the dead cattle.

"Well, that is their problem, not mine!" thinks Gideon.

He wonders when he should get around to chasing them off the farm completely.

They really are a nuisance.

At least they had stopped coming and asking him for work and food to eat.

"Their problems are not my problems," he thinks.

They should not have worked for the white farmer in the first place, and they certainly should not have resisted his "Land Re-Patriation Committee", when he first came to the farm.

It was right that some of them had to die and have their huts burned down, in order to learn the way the new system worked.

Acquiring Land does seem to have its problems, but nothing that can not be sorted out with a little violence!

Mind you, getting the farmer off the land in less than twenty four hours……. That was a good move!

Gideon had helped 'displace' a number of white farmers, before the Government gave him his very own farm.

They used to always make the same mistake in the past, by giving the farmer time to pack all his possessions and take them away.

This new system is much better!

No warning!

Just arrive at the farm and threaten everybody.

Why here on this farm, the farmer was chased off so quickly that he did not even have time to take his car!

"I really must learn to drive it sometime", thinks Gideon, "when I find out where to put the petrol".

He had tried sitting in the car a few times.

At first, the lights used to come on inside the car when he opened the door and the radio made a hissing noise but recently that had stopped happening.

Gideon wonders at the temporary nature of White-mans' inventions.

Nothing they have seems to last and everything they make seems to break, or has bits of itself that fall off and get lost.

Like the lawnmower.

What sort of useless contraption is that!

Firstly it doesn't start, and even if it did, all it does is cut grass!

Grass is for cattle to eat, and anyway, that useless grass around the house was all too short. Not that it matters now, because it has all turned brown and died. Gideon looks at the ground where the last vestiges of lawn are being carried away by termites.

A couple of empty chongololos show where the black ants have already forayed.

Good riddance!

Bare earth is much better than all this vegetation around the house. All those bushes and hedges! They are only places where snakes and chameleons lurk. Well, most of them are gone now. Their branches made good kindling for starting the cooking fire.

Firewood!

"There is a success story," thinks Gideon.

He looks over to his left where there citrus orchard once stood.

Stupid fruit trees!

All they did was make rotten fruit!

Elijah, who said he was the white farmer's 'garden boy', had said that the fruit trees must be sprayed with "insect spray".

What nonsense!

They have got lots of insects already!

It did not take long to get rid of Elijah...... useless white man's lackey!

The fruit trees made good firewood.

Pity they are all gone now, but there are still those useless trees that produce all those flowers around the house.

They will burn well when the time comes.

Their branches are no good for building huts because they are all crooked, but for use as firewood......... great!

Gideon sighs happily.

There is enough firewood there for at least a year, if he can keep those thieving labourers away from it.

Maybe he should get some dogs for protection.

Pity he had to kill the previous farmer's dogs. They would have been quite useful, except they kept barking at the wrong people.

The other problem with dogs is that you have to feed them from time to time.

Normally they should feed themselves by hunting, but there is nothing left to hunt. All the rabbits and buck on the farm have already been trapped by the ex-labourers. The chickens that the white man left only lasted about a week, before they were all finished, along with the sheep.

The Farm Store was better.

That had made a profit.

Gideon had sold everything..... all the contents, and then the door, the windows and the roof!

Pity that there was only one store.

Mind you, there are still plenty of stores left in town that need a change of ownership.

Ah, what a happy future.....

Unlimited resources..........

Gideon stands up from the rock he has been sitting on and stretches his arms wide.

Behind him stands the remains of the farmhouse.

The blackened roof trusses have lost that stark look that they had after the fire. Now they have a softer appearance as the glow of the setting sun gently highlights the stains on the walls from the soot above each of the broken windows. The gutters have become half detached and hang at drunken angles. It doesn't matter because there is no roof for them to drain and there is no sign of the end of the drought.

Gideon wanders around the house to what was once the stable block, where he now lives.

The bleached bones of the previous occupants of the stables still lie under the tree with their halters on. The maggots have long since cleaned away the last hide and gristle, and the smell is almost unnoticeable.

Gideon's wife is pounding on some grains of maize with a wooden pole in an old hollow tree trunk.

That is good.

That is the traditional way.

The way of the people.

On the ground lies an empty sack with "**First Grade Maize Seed**" printed on it in large letters.

Underneath is written in smaller print: "**Gift from the United States**".

And under that in still smaller print: "**This seed has been treated with insecticide, and is not fit for human consumption**".

They will eat well tonight.

Oh…………. Who says you need an education to enjoy
                        the pleasures of being a Land Owner.

****

Thank you for staying with us all the way through to this point.

This book of memories is far from complete, so if you would like to contribute your version of events, or remember some person or place that is important to you, please consider forwarding your recollections to
                    rhodesianmemories@gmail.com
in order to share them with others in the sequel to this book which will be called Rhodesian Memories 2.

Cheers Chinas, we'll check you out next time around!